California Standoff
Miners, Indians and Farmers at War
1850–1865

MICHELE SHOVER

STANSBURY
PUBLISHING
Chico, Ca.

California Standoff
Miners, Indians and Farmers at War
1850–1865

Copyright © 2017 by Michele Shover
First Printing

ISBN 978-1-935807-15-5 hardcover
ISBN 978-1-935807-16-2 paperback
ISBN 978-1-935807-17-9 ePub

Stansbury Publishing
An imprint of Heidelberg Graphics
Chico, CA 95928-9410

All rights reserved including the rights
to translate or reproduce this work
or parts thereof in any form or any media. Published 2017.

Library of Congress Cataloging-in-Publication Data
Names: Shover, Michele, author.
Title: California standoff : miners, Indians and farmers at war, 1850-1865 / Michele Shover.
Description: Chico, California : Stansbury Publishing, [2017] | Includes bibliographical references and index.
Identifiers: LCCN 2015047466 (print) | LCCN 2015046975 (ebook) | ISBN 9781935807155 (hardcover : alk. paper) | ISBN 9781935807162 (pbk. : alk. paper) | ISBN 9781935807179 (epub)
Subjects: LCSH: Indians of North America--California--Wars--1815-1875. | Maidu Indians--Wars. | Mill Creek Indians--Wars. | Indians of North America--California--Butte County--History. | Bidwell, John, 1819-1900--Relations with Indians. | Frontier and pioneer life--California--Butte County. | Butte County (Calif.)--History--19th century.
Classification: LCC E78.C15 S564 2017 (ebook) | LCC E78.C15 (print) | DDC 979.4/3204--dc23
LC record available at https://lccn.loc.gov/2015047466

In memory of

Special Indian Subagent James Franklin Eddy,

whose singular commitment to the

removal Indians in 1863

distinguished his service

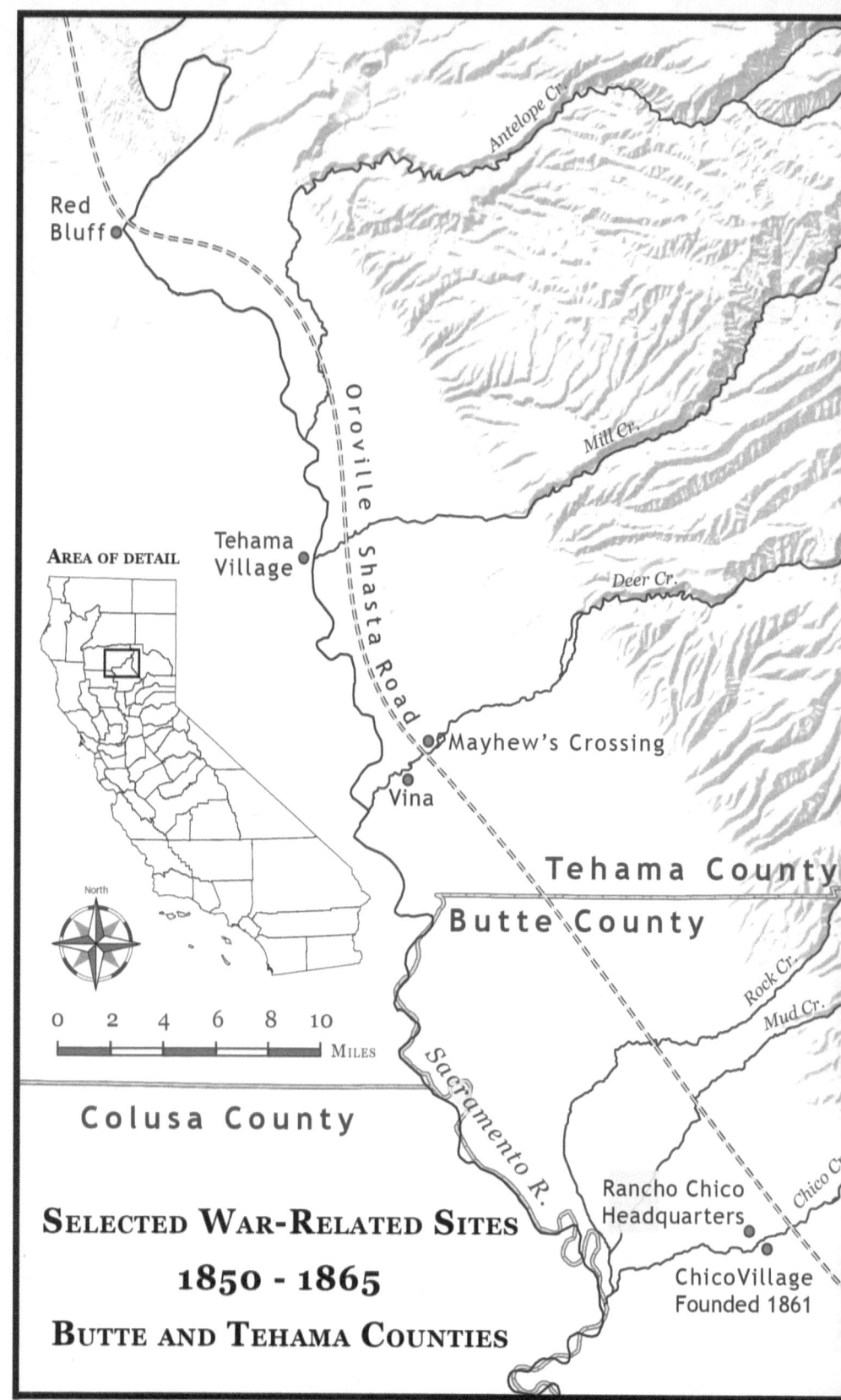

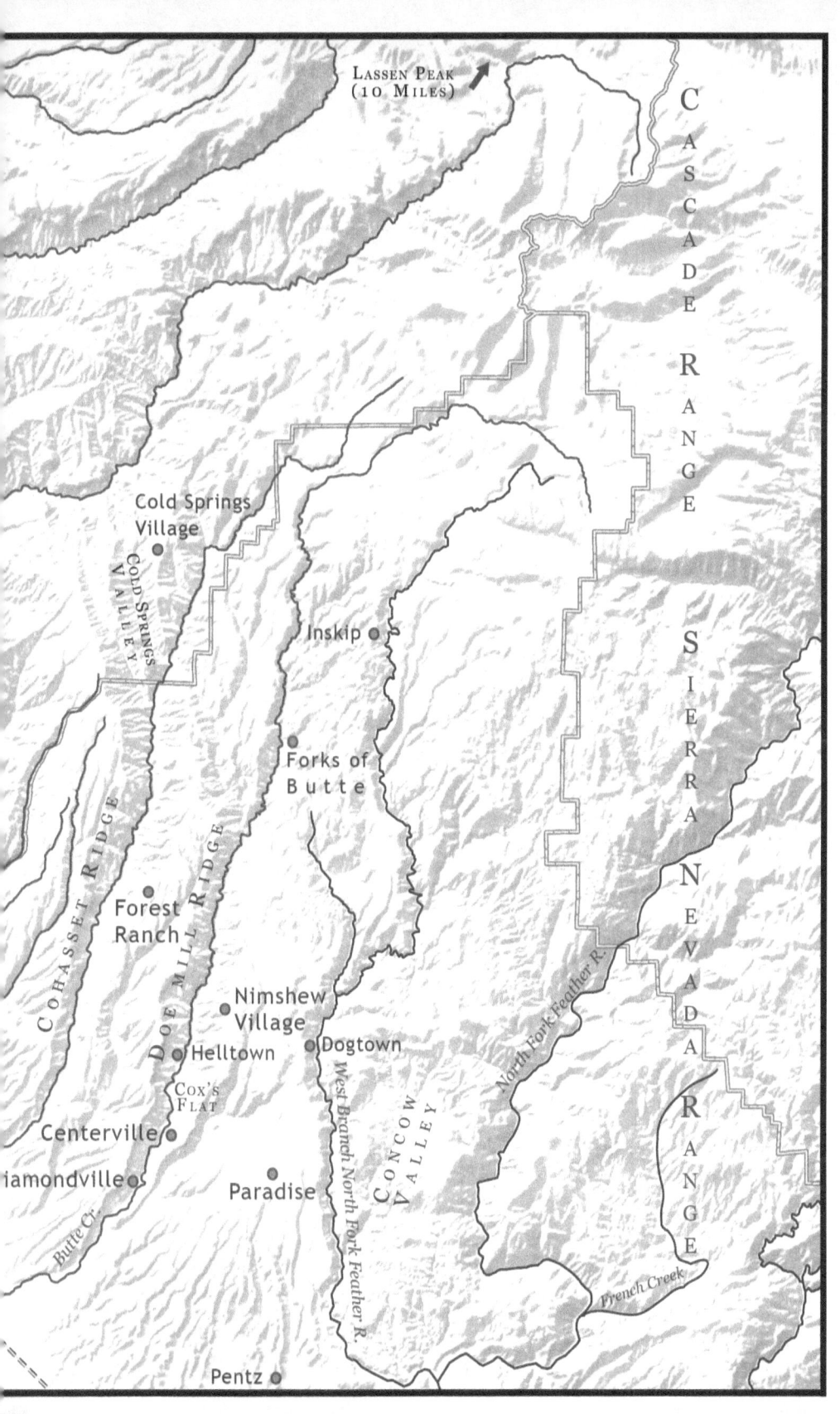

Contents

Illustration Credits ix
Preface xi
Introduction to the People and Places
    The Mountain Maidu and the Valley Maidu xv
    The Settlers and John Bidwell..xxx
1 "Big Times" at Bidwell's Rancho:
    The Indian Treaties of 1851 1
2 Defeat of the Treaty...31
3 Bidwell: Under Siege and in Pursuit 49
4 The Butte Creeks Become Mill Creeks.............................73
5 Settlers Avenge the New Mill Creeks 83
6 Kibbe's 1859 Pit River Expedition 121
7 Child Killings in Civil War Politics 135
8 Harassing Rebs, the Indian Soldiers' Pastime 159
9 The Military Response to New Child Killings 173
10 John Bidwell Outfoxes Soldiers, Bureaucrats and
    Settlers 205
11 The Death Trail 217
12 Retribution on Mill Creek 253
    Bibliography..273
    Acknowledgments..299
    Appendix A 1851 Treaty...303
    Appendix B John Bidwell to Joseph McCorkle 307
    Appendix C Confusion in Accounts................................311
    Appendix D The Kroeber Version...................................313
    Appendix E "Dan's Place" 319
    Abbreviations...345
    Endnotes 347
    Index..401

Illustration Credits

Cover painting, "Chico Creek Canyon" by Lenn Goldmann.
Map. Selected War-related Sites, Butte and Tehama counties, 1850–1865. Prepared by Steve Stewart.
John Bidwell. 1850. California Room, California State Library.
Map. Proposed Maidu reservation boundaries. *California Territorial Quarterly*.
Headmen at treaty meeting. George Eastman House, International Museum of Photography and Film.
Emma Cooper. Dorothy Hill Collection, Special Collections, Meriam Library, California State University, Chico.
Garner ranch wheat threshing ring. David and Vicki Garner.
U.S. Senator William Gwin. National Archives.
Iron Canyon along upper Chico Creek. Special Collections, Meriam Library, California State University, Chico.
Rancho Chico headquarters. Special Collections, Meriam Library, California State University, Chico.
Mechoopda sweathouse. Zella Bleyhl and Special Collections, Meriam Library, California State University, Chico.
Harmon Good. Larry V. Richardson Collection, Special Collections, Meriam Library, California State University, Chico.
Robert Anderson. Frank Farmer and Special Collections, Meriam Library, California State University, Chico.
Gold miner Irvin Smith. Larry V. Richardson Collection, Special Collections, Meriam Library, California State University, Chico.
Butte Creek. Bidwell Mansion State Park and Special Collections, Meriam Library, California State University, Chico.
Mountain Maidu woman. Author's print of photograph by E. P. Curtis.
Map. Chico Village layout, 1862. The Official Map of Butte

County of 1862. Copy by M. C. Polk, Buswell & Co., San Francisco.

James Keefer. Kathleen Gabriel and Special Collections, Meriam Library, California State University, Chico.

Rancho Chico cattle gate. Special Collections, Meriam Library, California State University, Chico.

Sandy Young, Jay Salisbury, Harmon Good and Indian Ned. Larry V. Richardson Collection, Special Collections, Meriam Library, California State University, Chico.

The Humboldt Road. John Nopel Collection on loan to Special Collections, Meriam Library, California State University, Chico.

Shave Head. Dorothy Hill Collection, Special Collections, Meriam Library, California State University, Chico.

Michael Wells' Concow hotel. Pioneer Museum of Oroville, CA to Special Collections, California State University, Chico.

Bidwell's farmhouse [long misidentified as "Bidwell's Mill"]. Special Collections, Meriam Library, California State University, Chico.

Brig. General George Wright. National Archives.

Capt. Augustus Starr. Donald Treco and Company F, Sacramento Rangers [re-enactors].

James Short. www.mrlincolnsfriends.com. This website has became unavailable.

Bill Preacher. Dorothy Hill Collection, Special Collections, Meriam Library, California State University, Chico.

Bud Bain. Dorothy Hill Collection, Special Collections, Meriam Library, California State University, Chico.

Preface

This account has been underway, to one extent or another, since 1990. At the time, I did not intend to start on a new project because, after fifteen years of research on nineteenth-century Chico, how much more could I learn about a remote town that peaked then at about four thousand residents? Well-known anecdotes about tragic events in Butte County Indian-settler conflicts of the 1850s and 1860s seemed to cover the topic.

However, as I scanned Dorothy Hill's *The Indians of Chico Rancheria*, my attention froze at a section on the treaty meeting John Bidwell hosted at his ranch in 1851.[1] While I was familiar with Bidwell's papers in Meriam Library's Special Collections at California State University, Chico and at the State Library in Sacramento, I recalled no mention of such a meeting. Incomplete accounts are a common problem in local history. For example, Butte County's violent clashes between settlers and Indians were treated as random "one-off" events—intermittent atrocities sprinkled among accounts of Victorian-era "happy talk." Even observations by locally powerful individuals such as Bidwell suggested the effects of such events were peripheral distractions, not core experiences.

For example, after a stay at Bidwell's Rancho Chico, naturalist C. C. Parry concluded in his 1888 article, "Whatever may be the outgrowth of Rancho Chico in the distant future, no taint of injustice or wrong can ever attach to this fair heritage; possible mistakes or shortcomings will pass into oblivion, while the good and true will maintain a perennial freshness."[2] While Parry captured the positive essence of Bidwell's creation, his passing mention of "mistakes and shortcomings" hinted at problems central to the present account.

Throughout the course of the Indian-settler war in northern

Butte County, principled actions, frailties and courage surfaced in people of all stations, races and cultures. As the area's leading figure and a man with a moral compass, Bidwell made many conscious efforts to do the right thing. However, circumstances placed him in positions where, at times, he could only defend his own interests (and those of his dependents) at a cost to others, settler or Indian. The figure of Bidwell brings to mind I. F. Stone's comment, when asked why he admired slave owner Thomas Jefferson: "Because history is a tragedy, not a melodrama."[3] Bidwell and fellow settlers addressed interconnected, many-layered problems to which they brought an uneven mixture of resources and aptitudes. Indians, who brought personal, cultural and geographic assets to their struggle with settlers, confronted the more profound challenge, their survival as a people.

When I pondered whether to take up work on the 1850s period, I asked professor of history Lisa Emmerich, an Indian specialist, where I might start research on California tribes. She immediately mentioned Albert Hurtado's *Indian Survival on the California Frontier*.[4] Her contribution was a perfect choice. Hurtado, like Hill, noted the treaty meeting at Rancho Chico, but he also addressed the work by Bidwell and other farmers to defeat the treaty. This made me curious: Why would Bidwell advance the treaty meeting at his ranch and then throw himself into its defeat? All of my work on previous subjects stemmed from that question: Why? Of course, Hurtado's scholarly footnotes led me to archives where an abundance of primary sources waited.

While this account profits from the contributions of historians and relies on the work of anthropologists, my academic discipline shaped its focus and analysis. Years ago, I opted for political science because political theory, my principal field, considers normative questions at the core of public life. This focus takes into account historical political institutions, political actors' objectives, the influences that shaped them, their ideas' implications and the like. In all of this, the back story in political practice is an essential component. Drawing on this approach, my analysis of the data complements the work of historians, archivists and anthropologists.

The approach here, as in my courses, reflects my respect for historians such as Vernon Parrington and Amanda Foreman.

Parrington created an intellectual tapestry of American colonial political thought. Foreman's nineteenth-century histories produce "history in the round," by which she means her narrative follows an idea through its course, on multiple levels. While Bidwell was not a George Washington and Indian subagent James Eddy was not a Thomas Jefferson, the more I learned about both men's ranges of experience—as well as those of townspeople, rural residents, the Maidu and other tribes—the more I respected their overlapping roles. My object was not to focus on Bidwell because I long considered too little attention had gone to other dimensions of area history. While I have kept to that purpose, in the larger picture I have found his importance inescapable. Even the experiences of other figures illuminate him. David McCullough was right when he said, "It's the secondary characters that can tell you about the main character."[5]

In the focus here, on the eastern Sacramento Valley and the Sierra Nevada which rise from its floor, the purpose has not been to scatter a catalogue of grievances across a battle chronology. While some of that is appropriate, the purpose of this account is to explain the roots and consequences of settlers' and Indians' actions. It became obvious to me early on in this project that, even as Indians and settlers differed from one another, and, it is important to note, differed *among themselves*, they were also similar to one another in their approaches to the conflict. In each camp, the "plain people" on both sides had no effective outside champion to defend them and advance their claims. Therefore, each people relied on a few willing men from among themselves to make their fight. Settler fighters and Indian resisters employed horrific methods to avenge grievances and terrify opponents into submission or flight. Despite such brutality, inflicted on guilty and innocent alike, each people considered these men their only protectors and their last hope to prevail.

In the canyons, mountains and foothills, impoverished Indians and hard-strapped settlers reared children to adulthood, all the while at mortal risk. Their vulnerability to extreme measures sharpened their divisions and enfeebled both peoples until their lengthy gridlock collapsed and the Indians' last haven fell to settlers in the mid-1860s. Along the way, I have answered most of my "whys." Others will bring to this subject their own curiosity, judgment and assumptions. They will find what I found—a compelling journey.

Introduction to the People and Places
The Mountain Maidu and the Valley Maidu

From the early 1850s through the mid-1860s, Indians and settlers alike were perpetrators and victims in the contest to seize, hold or recover the Maidu tribe's territory in California's Sacramento Valley and Sierra Nevada. Countless anecdotal accounts have described events in that war, but this is the first comprehensive, chronological reconstruction of the conflicts as they interconnected and evolved across a two-county front. While analysis centers on conflicts between Butte County settlers and branches of the Maidu tribe there, attention shifts to Tehama County, where Mountain Maidu, collaborating with the Yana Yahi tribe, began launching raids out of Deer Creek and Mill Creek canyons in the late 1850s. Chapters on the 1860s chronicle the return of the Mountain Maidu's focus to Butte County where they resumed raids after miners lynched five Maidu Kimshews.

Information about the Maidu derives from reports by major anthropologists, newspaper accounts, memoirs and primary documents in government, university and private archives. Interviews with Indian descendants over several generations and secondary sources have made it possible to provide a fresh perspective on the Maidu's offensive and defensive roles.

This Introduction, which examines the makeup, strategies and tactics of settler pursuit parties and cross-tribal Mountain Indian resisters, does not review the Maidu's broader culture or history, but instead identifies factors related to how tribesmen handled conflict. Settler culture and history receive close attention in the narrative.

In response to the threats that settlers—miners and farmers—presented to the Maidu, about two hundred resisters, the Butte Creeks, attempted, over the course of fifteen years, to recapture their lands and avenge other wrongs their people incurred from the invasion of gold miners, farmers and other speculators. In the late 1850s, by joining forces with Yahi fighters, the Butte Creeks were able to sustain the enduring standoff with settlers. Each side managed to deny the other security and control over territory Indians had competed with one another to seize or hold for centuries. Butte and Tehama County settlers were no less determined to keep the lands they had taken over as squatters or purchased—according to the American government. They believed possession, legal or otherwise, entitled them to ownership of ancestral Indian lands and state or federal protection for both their lives and property.

In reconstructing the conflict, a key question here is, why did victory elude both sides for so long? While the Indians feared settlers' powerful weapons, settlers were terrified of Indians' stone clubs and their expert marksmanship with arrows. Like other Mountain Indians, the Maidu's Yahi neighbors lodged in rugged and almost impenetrable terrain and were such masters of covert surveillance that settlers aware of their presence could rarely see them, much less confront them. Tehama County farmers only became a real threat to resisters of both tribes after a few trained themselves in Mountain Indian war tactics and the nuances of Yahi territory. The harsh tactics used by aggressors on both sides were not products of pathological drives or moral corruption, but were anchored in perceptions of necessity in support of "Right"—as each people understood it.[6] Each fielded fierce adversaries who showed little concern for casualties among the other's innocents.

For example, actions by Indians and settlers were consistent with each culture's customary ideas about land occupation. Ancient traditions obliged Maidu to protect their own subgroups'—or tribelets'—territory against others.[7] Settlers acquired California land for sustenance and, over time, for profit. However, miners and farmers were often at odds, competing for control over the new county board of supervisors, which they expected to favor the development of one at the expense of the other. As Chapter Five explains, in 1859, miners aligned with Butte Creeks against Tehama County farmers. Similarly, ongoing rivalries among the various Maidu tribelets undermined any chance

People and Places

they might have had to unify against the settlers.

Because, for many years, Indians could not tell one White from another and Whites could not distinguish any Indian from the next, each pursued justice by proxy; that is, by taking the life or property of anyone from the other race who came into view. For Indians, it was more important to find justice in an equivalent killing than to be picky about the target's identity. For both sides, victory was capricious, lighting on the side best able to impose its will at the moment. A "win" one day simply meant to survive to another when the contest might play out all over again.[8] Neither side could drive off the other.

Northwestern Maidu were then, as now, the principal tribe of Butte County, where they had lived virtually untouched by Spanish or Mexican influence. Anthropologists have disagreed about boundaries of the sprawling tribe's remote territory. Francis Riddell abandoned the idea of a single, fragmented tribe and introduced the notion of two tribes: (1) the Concow, or Konkow, at higher altitudes in the direction of Plumas County, well distant from (2) the Maidu, their Sacramento Valley counterparts.[9]

For practical reasons, the usage here will treat the Maidu as a single tribe divided into two branches. This reflects the practice in the 1850s and 1860s when all Maidu referred to themselves at large as (1) Mountain Indians, the canyon or mountain tribelets of the Sierra Nevada, or as (2) Valley Indians, the Sacramento Valley tribelets. Butte County settlers adopted their terminology.[10]

Consistent with the usage in mid-nineteenth-century to mid-twentieth-century government reports, correspondence and newspapers, Butte County's tribe is called the Maidu. Among tribes in the Sierra, it was distinctive for its division into Mountain Maidu and Valley Maidu.

Within each branch, tribal members' primary sense of identity stemmed from their local tribelet. Each tribelet lived in family-centered villages, or rancherias, with as few as thirty or as many as one hundred residents. Many present-day Maidu descendants prefer their historic tribelet identities, such as Berry Creek, Concow or Mechoopda. Tribelet names remained so important that in the late twentieth century, those that survived won legal standing as discrete tribes. In the present look at their shared past, when their territorial divisions influenced the course of the war with the settlers, a distinguishing characteristic of the Maidu was the intense traditional rivalry between and within Mountain Maidu and Valley Maidu.

According to the approach adopted here, in the 1850s and 1860s, the Concows, for example, were one principal Mountain Maidu tribelet among others, including the Nimshews, Kimshews, Sulemshews and Picas. By contrast, Mechoopdas represent a principal Valley Maidu tribelet. The tribelets commonly "named" themselves and others by where they lived; that is, by a particular creek or some other identifiable place they held by right or could defend. Annie Kennedy Bidwell said of the tribelets' villages, "All ... I have seen have been located on the borders of streams and on high land where floods could not overtake them."[11]

Two factors contributed to the divides among the Maidu tribelets. First, the rugged geography of the expansive Maidu territory which separated most Maidu tribelets from one another. Second, according to Butte County rancher John Bidwell and explorer Jedidiah Smith, the Maidu's Penutian-based language produced four major dialects with countless variations in vocabulary, syntax and grammar. Across the mountainous locations, tribelets fifty or more miles apart struggled to communicate with one another. Two chapters consider the complications this presented.[12]

In 1860, rancher John Bidwell made a partial count of 1,750 Maidu between the Sacramento River and the small hamlet of Honcut on the Feather River. This calculation evidently did not include the Concows, a Mountain tribelet, because it alone had roughly a thousand inhabitants in rancherias centered on Yankee Hill. Bidwell's estimate was made after losses from settler-caused diseases such as malaria and sexually transmitted diseases or alcohol-related causes had decimated the Indians. By the time of the Gold Rush, the Maidu had experienced the loss of 58 percent of their population to an 1833 smallpox epidemic.[13] Counts by Sherburne Cook, a physiologist who immersed himself in California Indian studies, did not include deaths from traditional tribelet clashes.

The numbers of Mountain and Valley Maidu deaths from diseases dwarf the number of war-related post-Gold Rush deaths that are the subject here. Nonetheless, the small size of the general population makes the couple of hundred Mountain Maidu resisters, whom Valley Maidu called "Butte Creeks," a significant proportion of the populace of young males. It also points up the importance to tribelets of any men lost in tribal or settler conflicts.

A positive counterpart to intra-tribal conflict was the tradition of periodic "big times." These gatherings facilitated matchmaking and fostered cross-tribelet alliances, albeit temporary and easily severed ones. Trade featured valley tobacco, medicinal herbs, mushrooms, mistletoe, nutmeg, spiceberries, nuts and furs. Also important in exchanges were artisans' wares, such as finely woven baskets and bows and arrows. The master of a particular craft at one time might be a Valley Maidu; in another, the work of a Mountain man or woman was in demand.[14] The intermarriages that came from "big times" created a constructive counterpoint to the rivalries, but they did not overcome long-lasting memories of offenses. Once tribelets approved a "big time," elders negotiated terms for their members' safe passage across boundaries. Absent agreements, travelers risked capture, death or enslavement. Similar negotiations laid the groundwork for occasional collaborations in the late 1850s between some Valley Maidu men in Mountain Maidu raids against settlers. In 1861, in the mountains northeast of Red Bluff, Pit River Indians joined forces with their mortal enemies, the Paiute, to attack a cattle drive.[15] Instances of cross-tribelet and cross-tribal cooperation became less rare over the course of the settler conflicts.

Leaders of the Maidu had no overarching authority. These tribelet headmen and leading elders were respected for their skills in battle and leadership in mediations with adversaries. Instances of theft were an example of this. Although the Valley Maidu disapproved of theft within their own tribelets, they overlooked instances when their members stole from other tribelets. On the other hand, when an incident became a serious issue, negotiations could produce peaceful resolutions. Federal Indian agents spoke with respect for Maidu and other Northern California Indians as negotiators.[16]

While the Maidu recognized distinctive characteristics among the tribelets, most settlers made no effort to understand tribelet

Standoff

variations. This made it a constant challenge for white pursuers and journalists to identify individual tribelets or their members and their rancherias' locations. This may be why editors, at their desks, regularly blamed just a few well-known tribelets for offenses against settlers. Apart from Riddell's attempt to map rancheria sites, the anthropological and historical data are replete with incomplete descriptions. Therefore, while an effort was made here to attribute actions to the correct tribelets, readers will encounter "best guesses" about which was responsible for particular events. For example, the most often blamed tribelets were the Concow, Pica, Nimshew and Kimshew. (Reports sometimes confused Kimshew with Nimshew and, at times, Kimshew, Tigu and Pica each were called "Tigers.") While specific tribelet information is provided, in some cases it seemed best to generalize within the more inclusive and distinctive Mountain or Valley Maidu branches.

There was a small, third Maidu branch, the Foothill Maidu. When immigrants drove them off to create farms, some became members of Valley tribelets; others receded into the canyons and mountains, where the Mountain tribelets accepted them, perhaps in appreciation for use of winter havens in the Foothill Maidu's former territory. This might also explain why Foothill and Mountain Maidu nursed similar resentments against Valley Maidu tribelets that kept both out of their territories. For this reason and for simplicity, the Foothill Indians are treated here as Mountain Maidu. Yuba County's Southern Maidu, a fourth branch, were removed to the Nome Lackee Reservation in the early 1850s.[17]

When the Maidu and their Tehama County neighbors, the Wintu, invaded the Sacramento Valley around 500 A.D., they drove the resident Yahi east into the foothills overlooking the expanse of fertile, well-watered lands they had lost. About 1500 A.D., the Wintu and Maidu seized those foothills as well, pushing the Yahi farther east into the deep, precipitous and forbidding Mill Creek and Deer Creek canyons. While conditions there were harsh, the Yahi also discovered some advantages: the topography was so difficult that no other Indians coveted it. Later, miners stayed away because the two creeks had no gold and the land was too barren to attract farmers. Finally, from their

People and Places

perches on the steep canyon walls, Yahi could easily monitor intruders. Author Steve Schoonover postulates that in the nineteen century the several hundred Yahi lived most of the year in mountain meadow villages near Lassen Peak, but waited out brutal winters below there in Mill Creek and Deer Creek canyons. About five miles in from the two canyons' ingresses, the Yahi created villages of creek-side huts or camped in caves that dotted the towering canyon walls.[18]

Sacramento Valley Wintu, were historically raided by Yahi warriors they called "Mill Creeks." Therefore, when, beginning in the 1840s, they raided Tehama County farms out of Mill Creek and Deer Creek canyons, farmers also called them Mill Creeks. However, as discussed in Chapters Four and Five, Mountain Maidu became the principal raiders from those canyons in the late 1850s and much of the 1860s. By the end of the 1850s, Mill Creek raiding parties were comprised of Butte Creeks, who were Mountain Maidu fighters, as well as varying mixtures of Yahi and renegade drifters from temporary camps around Lassen Peak. Mid-twentieth-century accounts of those events therefore erred in naming Mill Creeks as solely warriors from the Yahi tribe.

There is no accurate count of settler or Indian deaths over the course of the conflicts.[19] When Indians killed miners along the county's remote streams, their corpses were not always found; if found, some had no identification. An early 1850s incident is a good example. Foothill farm girl Jessie Smith was at home with her sister when Mountain Maidu broke in and kidnapped them. Although her sister managed to escape, Jessie's remains were not discovered until 1907, when utility workers found them in a deep "miner's hole" north of Oroville.[20]

Although the number of Indians killed by settlers was far less than the number who fell to settler-borne diseases, Indians killed in conflict were more numerous by multiples than the number of settlers who perished. This finds support in Indian sources, as well as in accounts by ranchers Bidwell, James Keefer and Robert Anderson. Indian retaliation against even one settler could result in the retaliatory killings of many Indians, including women and children, who had no identifiable link to the precipitating crime. In addition, some settler pursuit parties exaggerated the number of casualties in their assaults. Settlers and Indians spoke of Indians they knew or observed who had been seriously disabled by injuries in clashes, so the subsequent deaths of many wounded probably raised the Indians' real death rate closer to the high numbers pursuers claimed.[21] Although Bidwell was troubled by the disparity between numbers of Indians and settlers killed, in rural areas where settlers were vulnerable to Indians' raids, residents rarely, if ever, condemned the brutality of pursuit parties.

This account does not presume to analyze how these events fitted into the Maidu's understanding of the world. Characteristic of their culture was the animistic, shaman-based belief system which appears in their mythology. Nevertheless, the research presented here supports the finding that, whatever thought patterns and belief systems shaped Indian motives and actions in this place and period, they can also be understood in rational and Western terms.

Like settlers, Indians identified with place, had a sense of what was in their interest, recognized the implications of concentrated power, knew how to negotiate to their advantage and related justice to fairness. Also, Indians, like settlers, were made up of various types of individuals. In this account, while most acceded to or hid from the invaders, some became resisters ready to die to repel the offenders.

Mountain Maidu

Mountain Maidu were a physically fit and assertive people whose many tribelets spread throughout northeastern Butte County. Those displaced by gold mining were clustered along branches of the Feather River, as well as along upper Butte, Rock, Mud, Chico and other creeks. Butte Creek was chief among those drainages. In 1849, the U.S. Army's Lt. George Derby described it as equal to the Yuba branch of the Feather River in the amount of water flowing to the Sacramento River.[22]

Mountain Maidu were distinctive for their violent tactics in clashes among their rival tribelets. Because their food sources were limited and unevenly distributed, they could not observe strict boundaries and had to hunt and fish across tribelet territories. They became highly skilled at making surreptitious entries to spy on or raid one another, the Valley Maidu, Yahi or neighboring Paiute. Their fighters' responsibility was to defend their tribelet and territory against invaders, secure access to the Sacramento River, redress a grievance against another tribelet or steal something their tribelet needed—food, acorn baskets, a woman or an arrow stash. According to Roland Dixon, Mountain Maidu "always competed among neighbors over scarce resources."[23] This meant, by contrast to Valley Maidu (considered below), their tribelets would "form fleeting coalitions and enter into periodic hostilities among themselves." So entrenched was this aggressive behavior that while, until about 1851, Mountain Maidu primarily engaged in tribelet rivalries among themselves, they also carried out opportunistic attacks on lone miners.[24]

As yet, miners seemed more an annoyance than a threat. Mountain Maidu initially acquiesced to the intrusion, accommodating themselves as best they could to life among the "the new people."[25] For example, in 1850, Kimball Webster, a miner at Bidwell's Bar, saw a Mountain Maidu war party approach in full regalia, but the men paid him no mind as they walked past in single file. Word later reached him the warriors had "slaughtered" all of another tribelet's men and had taken the women and children back to their own village.[26] In another example, miner Edward McIlhany was in the Sierra Nevada in 1850 when "about 100 Indians ... surrounded me. My mule was very much frightened. They were all painted, had their war materials, going to the valley to fight the Indians .... [One of them] pointed his bow and arrow right at my breast. In an instant I opened the bosom of my flannel shirt. He drew the string tight and then let it go, holding to the arrow and muttered, "Much brave Americano."[27] Words from a Maidu lyric capture their confusion: "Who are these strange people?/What is happening anyway?"[28]

A trace of this acceptance surfaced as late as 1857, when the camp commander of the Nome Lackee Reservation, west of Red Bluff, which held a mix of Mountain and Southern Maidu (there since the early 1850s), declared they were still "perfectly quiet" and "in no danger of ... organizing against Whites." He explained, however, "their different languages and petty jealousies ensure [that they are] more apt to attack each other than Whites...."[29]

Standoff

By 1851, however, Mountain Maidu, dodging gold miners at every turn, registered the magnitude of miners' and farmers' threat to their resources, lives and culture. Tribal resisters, driven by vengeance, "a kind of religious sentiment" terrifying to even their own peaceful tribelet members and to Valley Indians, now extended their responsibilities to include driving out miners and valley farmers.[30] Cook noted, "Moreover, not only did some [interior California] Indians stand their ground over … large territory, but they actually, and with some success, took the offensive."[31]

Between 1852 and 1856, a Mountain Maidu campaign targeted Bidwell and his Mechoopda workforce. Their anger originated with his use of Valley Maidu to mine for gold in Mountain Maidu territories, violating intra-tribal boundary restrictions. Mountain Maidu not only targeted Mechoopdas in the gold camps, they extended their retaliations to the Mechoopdas on Bidwell's ranch. This indicates the Mountain Maidu also were punishing the Valley tribelet for collaborating with their new enemy, John Bidwell.[32]

At the onset of the Indian-settler conflict, miners and farmers had the apparent advantage of rifles and, at times, the military. In contrast, Mountain Maidu resisters were armed with primitive weapons and only sometimes attracted allies from other tribelets. But the Indians soon realized that, once they established impregnable hideouts out of the settlers' reach and acquired rifles, they could maximize settlers' terror by their mastery of "guerilla tactics," to borrow Cook's description.

The Mountain Maidu's tactics compensated for their limited numbers. Diaries and memoirs spoke of flight by frightened miners and farmers escaping their raids. Like Hat Creeks, the Yahi and Pit Rivers just north, Mountain Maidu tradition allowed the killing of male prisoners whose scalps they carried away on poles. As evidence of scalping, in an Indian cave where tools and animal skins were strewn near a pile of settler clothing, Isaac Speegle found "a human scalp with the hair long and black and the skin dried and shriveled."[33] Indian women and children, who had value as slaves, often were spared such fates and tribal stories recounted the accounts of some who escaped.

From time-to-time settlers declared Indians were cowards

because the resisters would not fight face-to-face, according to "civilized" protocols. Such allegations were unconvincing even then. In Butte Creeks' and Mill Creeks' lightening strikes, soldiers recognized a "tactical sagacity they could not construe as cowardice."[34] Unlike the Comanche of the Great Plains, whose large population included thousands of warriors who were masters of war ponies, Mountain Maidu could only rely on their extraordinary physical dexterity, keen tactical intelligence and courage. They rapidly clambered up and down steep canyon walls and navigated impenetrable brush tough as iron, executing every raid on foot.[35] Relying on tactics perfected against rival tribelets over centuries, parties of a couple of dozen, or even only a few men, made swift dawn raids with little risk to themselves, because most sleepy victims' disorientation made them practically defenseless. Confusion at multiple assailants' quick actions in a blur of motions intensified victims' terror, muddled their mental clarity and heightened their sense of isolation from rescue.

Miners feared the fate of C. H. Person. In June 1854, near Oroville, in the vicinity of the Mountain House hotel, a passerby discovered his body, pierced by ten arrows and bullets, near the remains of his young Indian helper. While Indians sometimes tortured settlers, recorded anecdotes suggest they did so less often and usually with less extended and extreme methods than they used against one another. Torture required a block of time in a setting safe from interference by rescuers. Indian raiders, who placed a premium on quick departures, apparently found it dangerous to waste precious time spiriting away adults when neighbors might see evidence of their attack in smoke from a burning field or cabin and set off in pursuit. However, kidnapping of children, Indian and settler alike, of all ages, sometimes occurred and allowed the use of later torture and enslavement.

While settlers condemned such methods as barbaric, their own Western culture was replete with extreme violence. Only a few generations earlier, rulers of their European ancestors would draw and quarter, burn at the stake and disembowel those who crossed religious or political lines. Like the Maidu, New England colonists displayed the heads of violators on pikes. At the time of the conflicts set out here, Confederate "bushwhackers" were sweeping through Missouri farm country, beheading, disemboweling and scalping suspected Union supporters who reciprocated in kind.[36]

The challenge Mountain Maidu presented to the immigrant settlement was the principal concern of federal treaty commissioner Oliver Wozencraft, who led a treaty meeting at Bidwell's ranch in 1851. Wozencraft described the Mountain Maidu as handsome and formidable people who hunted deer and other game in their rugged territory, which demanded they be expert swimmers, climbers, and runners. Maidu skill in the use of their weapons was common knowledge.[37] In 1856, at Oroville, the Butte County seat, settlers watched as Indian children with bows and arrows repeatedly shot a small coin off a distant stick. Settlers who dismissed bows and arrows as archaic and feeble did not live in range of them. For example, in 1850, Indian agent George Barbour witnessed an arrow that flew thirty feet, then penetrated a tree a foot deep. Another observer reported an arrow that flew about a quarter mile before entering a green tree a quarter inch. With fires a natural summer phenomenon throughout the area, it was common practice for Maidu to ignite heavy underbrush to expose their enemies' approach, reduce the threat of large, destructive fires, ease foot travel or nourish plants they relied on for food, medicine, birth control and sexual performance. They were so expert at setting fires, they could even guide them around prized mushroom beds. They also used fire to raze rivals' rancherias, miners' campsites and settlers' cabins. In their conflicts with other Indians, Mountain Maidu sometimes burned enemy captives at the stake. They also used rocks to bludgeon enemies. And, by the late 1850s, settlers in pursuit parties were anxious about their growing proficiency with rifles.[38]

Valley Maidu

In the 1840s, the campfires of Valley Maidu rancherias were "strung like beads on a chain" along the banks of the bountiful Sacramento River and its feeder creeks.[39] Indian subagent Adam Johnston observed about the Valley Maidu, "Of all Indians west of the Sierra Nevada, they are the least war like or savage of any Indians on the face of the globe."[40]

Observers were impressed by Valley Maidu's dramatic

ceremonies, featuring elaborate costumes decorated with feathers and shells from coastal Indian traders. Apart from minor clashes among their individual members and with other tribelets, the numerous Valley communities were largely compatible. The Valley Maidu tribelets, whose similar dialects facilitated communication among themselves, dealt with infractions in the same way they organized multi-tribelet ceremonies: they mediated their differences.

The Valley Maidu benefited from the moderate valley climate and rich soils on which oak groves produced ample crops of acorns, the staple of their diet. They supplemented this with grasses, roots, manzanita and elder berries, blackberries, rabbits, grasshoppers and river salmon. During winter downpours they filled baskets with ground squirrels driven from their burrows. Such ample resources enticed hungry, cold Mountain Maidu to negotiate passage or covertly cross the Valley tribelets' borders for game, acorns and fish.[41]

For hundreds of years or more and through the Gold Rush, Valley Maidu tribelets retained "a definite idea of their right to the soil."[42] They did not believe they owned land, but considered themselves the only rightful guardians of their territories. Tribelets moved their rancherias or villages within those territories to take advantage of seasonal benefits, to be secure from the dangers of floods or to escape evil spirits arising from troubling incidents. Valley Maidu tribelets were so territorial that parents taught their children never to cross boundary markers—this rock, that slough, the cottonwood tree over there. A hunter who shot game in his tribelet's territory was at risk if his injured quarry staggered across another tribelet's boundary and he attempted to go after it.

According to Cook, Valley Maidu demonstrated subtlety in their relations with settlers. Farmers were impressed by their truthfulness and the skills they developed as farmhands. Because Indians sometimes appeared evasive or devious, farmers complained they were disloyal. Although loyalty was a central concept to Maidu within their tribelets, they did not extend such allegiance to settlers. John Bidwell recognized a few of his own Maidu ranch hands' secret complicity with Mountain Maidu in attempts against his property and himself. This would change when virtually all the Mechoopdas realized their dependence on Bidwell's protection from Mountain Maidu raiders.[43] While it has often been stated that he was protecting them from settler threats, research found no examples of such a danger before very real threats in 1862 and 1863. In the latter case, he refused to allow ranch Indians to escape an explicit threat to kill them, addressed in Chapters Nine, Ten and Eleven. It cannot be over-emphasized that Valley Maidu "had the liveliest horror" of Butte Creeks, the most common name settlers and Valley Maidu used for all Mountain Maidu warriors before 1860.

In contrast to Indian subagent Adam Johnston's remark about Valley Maidu's peacefulness, according to Sherburne Cook, when negotiations failed, "... arms were resorted to and an elaborate ritual followed, the actual fighting was negligible, with perhaps half a dozen casualties, or even none at all.... Rarely, if ever, was the *casus belli* more than an affair of tribal honor or minor infringements upon some territorial right."[44]

While Cook's comment trivialized formal conflicts between rival tribelets, they actually involved skilled shooters who stood in opposing lines, their bows launching thick waves of often-poisoned arrows.[45] While the Maidu's battles were not on the scale of European wars, even a few casualties exacted a serious price: in a tribelet of fifty persons, the deaths of even two or three men presented a critical loss. This history of intra-tribal rivalry was a major impediment to an all-Maidu strategic unity. It appears Maidu councils, sometime in this period, reached agreement that, although they could stand up one Indian party to another in overt lines of battle as equals in weaponry and skills, to frontally face settlers wielding rifles and pistols would place them at a lethal disadvantage. Such a calculation is consistent with others of importance this account sets out.

Historical and anthropological accounts have not recognized the defensive capability of the Valley Maidu. Instead, the impression is that of a weak and passive people. However, Valley Maidu men must have been skilled at the arts of war and focused on the defense of their people. Otherwise, they could not have held their much envied territory against the aggressive Butte Creeks for centuries. Valley Indian anecdotes indirectly reveal they were tough-minded regarding their security on every level. For example, when elders guarding borders failed to alert their fighters to signs of danger, they were whipped by their juniors. The culture of Valley Indians, like that of other California Indians, included the practice of pruning from their rancherias individuals they considered unlucky, burdensome or weak. According to anthropologists who interviewed the eldest in the early nineteenth century, examples included infirm and old people, female infants or those whose mothers had died, disloyal wives and, because twins were considered "bad omens," one baby of twins or mothers who gave birth to twins. The tribelets' need to limit population was facilitated by the women's use of blue oak mistletoe for sterilization and birth control—all the more important for them because men consumed California nutmeg and spiceberries for sexual endurance.[46]

The modern misunderstanding about the Valley Maidu's defensive strength may have begun with observer Stephen Powers, who spent two years with Valley Indians.[47] He noted they were avid gamblers, sometimes staking family possessions, work tools and women. Sessions lasted into the early morning hours, which would explain why Powers observed the men's proclivity to sleep late and to take regular afternoon naps. (As the principal laborers, adult females did not have that option.[48]) Late-night activities and day-time sleep may have originated from the necessity for warriors to stay awake and alert all night, in anticipation of traditional dawn attacks by rival tribelets or other tribes. While domestic violence was a core part of Indians' and Whites' cultures, the Maidu's harsh practices suggest that Valley Maidu were strong-willed and disciplined people tough enough to repel Mountain Maidu fighters' incursions into their territory.

As Powers noted, while their war tactics were effective, intra-tribal conflicts proved the larger Maidu tribe's ultimate "great and fatal weakness" in their battle against the settlers. One effect of the Maidu tribelets' chronic quarrels among themselves, he emphasized, was their "incapacity to organize over-reaching, powerful, federative governments."[49] Powers seems to have overlooked the Maidu's strategic strengths that prolonged their ability to resist conquest. Distinctive to what follows is the research discovery here of the Mountain Maidu's strategic brilliance. Not only did its resisters continue to draw on traditional tactics and geographic mastery, in 1858, tribal headmen figured out how to restore their flagging manpower, establish a new secure operations base, and target new valley locations for successful raids on settlers. They also made a self-serving truce with some miners to formulate and field their new strategies.

The Settlers

Responsible settlers and government officials periodically acknowledged their forerunners' ultimate responsibility for most of the conflicts with Indians. And, as an observer then familiar with the situation, Powers reminded his readers: "There was never anything perpetrated by California Indians which has not been matched by acts of individual frontiersmen."[50]

The strains among the Maidu tribelets, Valley and Maidu, paralleled divisions between valley farmers and mountain miners. While the latter kept their grip on the county government, businessmen who established large farms they soon called "ranchos" rapidly achieved substantial wealth. They made regular but futile attempts to persuade miner-dominated boards of supervisors to provide greater investments in the northwestern county's roads and bridges. A key disappointment to valley residents was the supervisors' decision to place the only county hospital near Oroville where it was convenient for miners but out of reach for distant farmers. Adding to such regional tensions, each group harbored opposing views with regard to relations with Indians. For example, miners disapproved of farmers who used Indian help to mine for their gold. Farmers, on the other hand, discovered that some miners conspired with Mountain Indians who raided the valley. Chapter Five will address such issues.

American immigrants in California arrived as products of scrappy European cultures in which people were quick to take offense, felt obliged to retaliate and were distrustful of other races. When conflicts soon revealed no public defense in place against Indian raiders, they sought military help. However, as illustrated in this account, the military's response in every case proved worthless. Therefore, settlers turned to private vengeance of a kind already central to Indians' jurisprudence; that is, "an

People and Places

eye for an eye." Because neither Indians nor settlers could count on allies and neither people shared common institutions of justice, both relied on men—warriors and pursuit parties—from their own communities for revenge. The violent acts by both sides only led to more violence. For all the differences between the two warring factions, similarities in their situations and responses are abundant.

In this period, settlers rationalized their resort to vigilante violence because they considered Indian war methods so barbaric that conventional American criminal punishment was inadequate. However, as late as the early twentieth century in the Deep South the violent practices of the Scotch-Irish, who considered the slightest offense to personal honor an affront worthy of a duel to the death, were widely accepted. The nineteenth century was a period of torturous slave owner practices and employers' abuses of free workers. Within European-American male culture, it was common for personal competition to erupt into physical conflict that ranged from wrestling to mob brawls and shoot outs. Advances in weaponry and the ubiquity of rifles and pistols made such confrontations even more deadly. Unlike in most of the country where grievances were resolved in courts, the West resembled a variation on the South. While the criminal justice system there was often fraught with corruption, in northeastern California it was new, fragile and, most important, irrelevant because mountain and canyon terrain provided impenetrable havens for criminally inclined settlers and Mountain Indian raiders.

In addition, settler vigilantism in Tehama and Butte counties was in response to the military's tardy and ineffective responses to crises. For example, the U.S. Army and State Militia units regularly arrived weeks after killings and arsons. When they appeared, all too often they carried orders inappropriate to the situation and their ineffectiveness emboldened Indian antagonists. As readers will observe, although military units camped on Bidwell's ranch between 1863 and 1865 and made occasional "showy" rides throughout the foothills, they provided no protection to rural residents. A surprising twist treated in several chapters is the roles of several military companies sent to Butte County, not to protect farmers at risk, but rather to protect

Standoff

Rancho Chico Indians from angry settlers left to pursue their own private justice against Mountain Indian perpetrators.

While individuals and groups advocated aggression to stave off Indian raiders, Butte County was typical in that its officials and their constituents alike were new to the state, new to the county and new to their jobs and, therefore, reluctant to risk their lives or test their authority in territory still foreign to them. All arrived with assumptions about Indians that sometimes fitted California's native people, but more often did not. County sheriffs operated with the understanding that Indian problems were "not in their job descriptions." Whenever possible, they avoided addressing Indian infractions outside of town settings where there were jails and justices of the peace. They avoided incidents in which miners and farmers instigated crimes against Indians. Examples of these behaviors will appear in the chapters.

John Bidwell: Not Just Any White Man.

While this account is not a biography of John Bidwell, research has demonstrated no single figure was more central in shaping Indian and settler relations in northern Butte County during the period addressed. His commitment to building a major ranch hinged on Mechoopda labor. From 1848 to 1850, Bidwell, with his neighbors William Northgraves and John Potter, relied on one hundred Valley Maidu to mine fortunes in gold at their Butte Creek and Feather River sites in Mountain Maidu territory.

ALTHOUGH MOST AMERICANS WHO ARRIVED in California at the time disdained Indians, Bidwell did not share that attitude. This worked to his advantage because he could not have operated his early ranch without Indian labor. Born in rural New York in 1819, Bidwell's parents were proud but poor. As a young man, he worked at a variety of jobs, finally managing, by his own efforts, to acquire enough education to work as a teacher. However, after moving to Missouri to realize his goal of owning a farm, he lost his property to a squatter. In 1841, he joined what became known as the Bidwell-Bartleson Party, the first emigrant wagon train to reach California. Later, as a key aide to Sacramento settler John Sutter, he learned the business of large-scale agriculture and became familiar with the management of Indian labor. He also became the acquaintance of an international collection of politicians and entrepreneuers as well as other colorful characters across California.

Bidwell came to admire the vast Mexican ranchos. In 1848, he was employed by William Dickey, whose land grant lay along Butte Creek. For two years he and his neighbors relied on one hundred Valley Indians to mine gold for them at their Butte Creek and Feather River sites in Mountain Maidu territory. That labor yielded a fortune for each of the three men. In contrast to their use of a large number of employees to extract gold, lone miners and small parties worked their sites where isolation and exposure made them vulnerable to attacks by hostile Mountain Maidu, called Butte Creeks. While Bidwell supervised the mining camps he struck up a commercial partnership with Sacramento merchant George McKinstry, who regularly sent to his campsites miscellaneous equipment and supplies for their vendors to sell. With the proceeds from his share of the gold and his mercantile earnings, Bidwell bought approximately 21,000 acres of the Rancho Arroyo Chico land grant along Chico Creek (later called Big Chico Creek).[51] In the early 1850s, that property was known as "Bidwell's place" or "Rio Chico."

In Bidwell and his partners' mining camps, the Mechoopda and other Valley Maidu, joined by peaceful Mountain Maidu, extracted gold from frigid creek waters throughout the daylight hours. Following Sutter's practice, Bidwell fed the men boiled wheat which they scooped from a big, common bowl. The best workers' pay was two red handkerchiefs per day; the rest earned one. Like other settlers, he also paid Indians in cigars, scissors, clothing and beads. The Indians considered beads examples of status and sometimes used them as currency. In 1852, when miner Aninais Pond tried to buy a salmon from an Indian man, because Pond had no beads to satisfy the man's demand, he offered gold, silver, a hunting knife or a shirt. The Indian refused them and Pond left hungry.[52] The issue of slavery associated with California Indian farm workers rose during this period. The Bidwell gold camp worked by Indians raised accusations that Bidwell employed slavery practices. Referring to inferences about him by gold miner Michael Nye, Bidwell wrote his partner, "It must be on account of the sway we hold over the Indians, which prevents his [Nye's] success on the river."[53] Bidwell became the county's leading Union advocate in the Civil War, despite his neighbors' recurring charge.

In 1851 neighboring rancher John Potter died in his adobe house, located across Chico Creek from Bidwell's headquarters. Because Mechoopdas had worked for Potter since he built his ranch around 1844, Powers described him as those Indians' first "master." A decade would pass after Potter's death before his heirs would accept Bidwell's offer to buy their land. The Indians continued to occupy campgrounds along Chico Creek and east of the Oroville-Shasta trail. In the meantime, their head man So-wil-le, guided the shift of Potter's Mechoopda workers to Bidwell in exchange for continued residence on their historic lands. Bidwell's understanding with the Mechoopdas did nothing to soften the old tensions between them and Mountain Maidu. While other accounts have inferred that the Mechoopdas made a smooth transition from freedom to dependence on Bidwell, several chapters will demonstrate that was not always the case.[54] In 1852, while Bidwell developed his valley orchard and planted row crops, he also built his herds in the expansive foothills east of the Oroville-Shasta trail. At the point where the trail crossed the heavily used ford over Chico Creek, he erected a frame store and large hotel whose saloon became "must stops" for township residents, freight drivers and other travelers. A common topic of conversation there, as well as in farmhouses and around campfires, was the dangers—and opportunities—Indians presented settlers. While some were sympathetic to individual Indians' plights, their terror of the violent resisters was intense. Although Bidwell stood out for his sense of moral responsibility to protect his Indian workforce from white troublemakers and rival Maidu tribelets, it was common for elements from both peoples to object that his needs conflicted with theirs.

While valley farmers were reliable customers who counted on Bidwell's products, advice, gifts of land or gold and his general leadership, they also resented his success and, in particular, his monopoly of the Mechoopda workforce. Bidwell's prominence and his Indian labor force made him a north county lightning rod. Valley farmers, especially those in foothill locations, pressed him to support private pursuit parties to punish Mountain Maidu who attacked their property or families. During 1862 and 1863 they became convinced that Bidwell had violated their trust and placed their lives at risk when he hesitated to retaliate against Indian raids. Relenting to their pressure, he led at least two Indian pursuit parties and provided goods and cash to other pursuers. His role during that time remained controversial in Chico as late as the 1880s. This explains why Bidwell, in his 1890s unpublished memoir, emphasized his version of his role in the events of that period.

The man Bidwell came to trust on issues related to the 1863 Indian removal to a reservation could not have been more different from him. James Franklin Eddy was an ill-paid public employee whose worldly goods fitted in his carryall. For Eddy to travel any distance he had to rent a horse from Bidwell. Chapters Seven through Nine introduce the roles of Eddy, who, as a special subagent to federal Indian agent George Hanson, became a central figure in events associated with the transfer of Indians from Butte County to the reservation. During those dark months, despite his own fast-advancing tuberculosis, Eddy committed himself to protect innocent Indians subject to death threats from settlers who believed government officials had abandoned them. People who want to get history right will welcome James Eddy to California's cast of worthies. It is regrettable that the identities of the Indians who worked alongside Eddy and his mentor, Dr. Samuel M. Sproul, to keep their people alive are lost to us. However, Indian labor and sacrifices deserve at least this overdue acknowledgment.

IN THE NARRATIVE AHEAD, violence and political conflict are shaped by legal, moral and economic factors. The farmers' objective was to build farms and homesteads like the ones they remembered back home, but their experience with farm labor there did not serve them well in California. While Bidwell established his vast property on deep valley loam, the majority of settlers in the valley foothills lived on small, struggling farms. When those farm owners had to commute for second jobs as freight drivers, timber cutters and gold miners to survive, they left behind young children and women vulnerable to hostile

Standoff

Mountain Maidu attacks. Unchallenged raids meant instability and the prospect of economic failure.

Northern Butte County is a beautiful area to which its residents—native and new—have strong attachments. Generations of local history writers have added to general awareness of its early violent times, whether the Indian land wars or later anti-Chineses campaigns. With respect to the former, historical memory fixed on three Indian raids on settlers by Mountain Indian warriors who, in the later times, came to be mistakenly thought of as exclusively made up of Yahi, known as Mill Creeks. Recognition that aggressive Mountain Maidu participated in Mill Creek bands receded in the twentieth century as researchers confused them with the relatively more pacific Valley Maidu. The work of Theodora Kroeber will be examined in this light.

This book's findings from events in the most remote areas of Butte and Tehama Counties reveal the Indians and settlers as shaped by cultures that prepared them to use violence for protection and to advance needs, such as for territory. Both sides believed they were making the best choices possible under such duress. While the narrative attempts to explain the grounds for setters' and Indians' uses of harsh methods, both sides believed they made the best choices possible under such duress. While the narrative attempts to explain the grounds for settlers' and Indians' uses of harsh methods in actions that modern morality condemns, it also recognizes the claims for "Right" motivated both sides.

According to California historian Robert Chandler, "The Indians treated the settlers just like they treated anyone who encroached on their land over the past centuries. The settlers reacted as they had since the barbarians invaded Roman Empire." [55]

1

"Big Times" at Bidwell's Rancho: The Indian Treaties of 1851

As an old man in the late nineteenth century, pioneer California rancher John Bidwell reminisced with relish, if not full candor, about his long relationship with the Indians who worked his vast property, "Rancho Arroyo Chico." Yet, even though the July 1851 federal Indian treaty negotiation was one of the most dramatic events ever to take place on his ranch, he omitted mention of it from his later speeches and writings.

The treaty events took place in the period when the Department of the Interior's Indian Affairs section, which had taken over jurisdiction from the Army's Indian Bureau, drew on reports from military officers based in Northern California who assessed Indian conditions in the path of Gold Rush immigration. This transfer between the two agencies was not a clean break because the Army retained its responsibilities for Indians' security. The overlap between the jurisdictions of the Interior Department and the Army meant military officers and federal officials would play roles in the treaty meeting and other settler-Indian issues important to Butte County for years to come.[57]

The Proposed Treaties

Federal policy, in place since 1778, recognized Indians' rightful title to their conquered land. In order to legalize the transfer of the tribes' titles to the United States, American law required the government to compensate Indians for their losses. To that end, Congress authorized the government to offer fully funded and staffed tribal reservations in exchange for the Indians' lands. The value of federal reservations was not equivalent to the value of the tribes' losses, of course. However, Adam Johnston, an Army captain in California through the late 1840s and then Indian subagent for the Sacramento and San Joaquin region, recommended that well-run reservations could protect Indians from greedy Americans and foreigners already establishing farms and gold mines on the new state's most productive lands. Officials, who saw no need to preserve Indians' ancient cultures, believed reservations would facilitate their acculturation to American ways. However, the Department of the Interior's plan for reservations depended on securing the Indians' consent through treaty agreements. There were eighteen California treaties, all based on the same model, so they will be referred to here as if they were one treaty.[58]

In order to expedite the treaty process, federal officials transferred California's three Indian agents, whose positions were already in the budget, into three treaty commissioner positions, approved by Congress and President Millard Fillmore on April 29, 1850. Each commissioner was to recommend reservation locations and boundaries in his assigned area for the tribes' approval.

The proposed locations were subject to negotiation with the tribal headmen. The proposal was to establish farms and cattle ranches where federal employees would furnish the Indians basic education, as well as training for agricultural work such as stock raising. They were to operate from the start with government-funded provisions, equipment and livestock. The plan projected future self-support on the reservations, based on the labor of a trained Indian workforce. The treaty terms recognized the Indians' right to remain permanently, if not on their original homelands, then at least in reasonably familiar surroundings.[59] As San Francisco's *Alta California* explained, there seemed no other options: "The reservations must be made where the Indians at present reside ... and that has been the course of the commissioners."[60]

John Bidwell provided the treaty meeting site for the Northwestern Maidu (hereafter, Maidu), made up of Valley and Mountain Maidu, and assisted Indian treaty commissioner Oliver Wozencraft in setting up other meetings. Sources contemporary to these events made it possible to reconstruct the treaty's course here.[61]

Albert Hurtado identified the prospect of reservations as of particular interest to local ranchers. While Bidwell, then 31, hosted the northern Butte County meeting at his ranch, nothing suggests his initial thinking about the prospect of a treaty reservation near his ranch. However, by nature he was an optimist. Chances were this young, serious, accomplished man could shape the treaty's impact to his advantage. A treaty posed both risks and benefits to Bidwell. The federal government intended to pacify California's hostile Indians, such as his Valley Maidu ranch workers' enemies, the Mountain Maidu. Most important to Bidwell, Wozencraft's letters inferred a reservation would not require Bidwell to give up his Indian workforce. Bidwell could also assume his Indian workers, the Mechoopdas, a subgroup or tribelet of the Valley Maidu, would prefer the conditions he offered them and not move to a reservation. According to gold miner Granville Stuart, in 1852, Bidwell provided decently for the Mechoopdas who worked his gold mines. Finally, access to reservation cattle would obviate the Mountain Maidu's need to steal from ranchers' herds.[62]

Bidwell would have been reluctant to oppose federal officials whose future decisions could affect his investments. As their advisor, he could influence the treaty terms to his advantage. California businessmen like him initially expected a reservation system would spread federal funds throughout the state. Although already a merchant in the mining camps, Bidwell had yet to be granted a federal license to trade with the Mountain Indians. It was also likely that reservation security would require a military encampment nearby. This would be an economic stimulus and keep the peace throughout the area as the reservation changeover took place.

On the other hand, Mechoopda workers and their families might consider a reservation an attractive option to Bidwell's ranch. Only a decade ago, they had lived as an independent people. In one instance, when Bidwell intercepted Mechoopda workers walking off his gold mining site, he could not persuade them to return to work. Therefore, if Mechoopdas lived and worked for him in sight of a reservation where other Maidu worked for themselves, would they continue to be contented and reliable? Hurtado noted that men like Bidwell became concerned

John Bidwell, whose development and growth of Rancho Chico was dependent on his extensive use of Indian laborers.

the managers of big reservations in rural counties might undercut the clout of private elites like themselves. Then, too, would cattle from Indian operations drive down cattle prices?[63] Whatever his concerns, Bidwell decided to cooperate.

Lead-up to the Treaty Meeting

When his neighbor, rancher John Potter, died in 1850, Bidwell and the Mechoopdas worked out an agreement by which he allowed them to remain on their ancestral lands if they agreed to work for him. That spring, subagent Johnston sent his report to Washington from "Bidwell's rancho," which area residents and reporters also knew as "Rio Chico." Hannibal Day of the U.S. Army's Second Infantry had accompanied Johnston on a recent tour of northeastern California.

Johnston reviewed the conditions of the Valley Maidu and gathered information about their more elusive fellow tribesmen—the Mountain Maidu—who lived in the foothills and lower Sierra Nevada. While the Valley tribelets were peaceful, tensions were on the rise between the Mountain Maidu and miners east of Bidwell's place. Johnston traced these strains to the attitudes of recent arrivals who, unlike the "Old Californians" from the 1840s, such as Bidwell, regarded all Indians as dangerous enemies. Despite the danger, miners worked along the canyon-lined creek beds that defined Mountain Maidu tribelets' borders throughout those Indians' Sierra Nevada territory. With their food sources now in jeopardy and no place they could staunch the ongoing influx of outsiders, Capt. Johnston expected an increase in violent encounters.[64]

ALTHOUGH BIDWELL WAS IN WASHINGTON, D.C., during Johnston's stay, his ranch supervisor briefed the visitor about clashes among the Mountain and Valley Maidu tribelets. Apart from a scattering of incidents, he reported the Indians' situation, in general, seemed status quo ante: "Warfare between California Indians [rather than with Whites] was more often than not the rule."[65] In an example near Oroville, Valley Maidu battled with the Picas, a Mountain Maidu tribelet, whom a miner described as "very much feared and hated by all their neighbors."[66] The miners' presence as yet still only amounted to a serious annoyance for the Indians. Bidwell's men confirmed to Johnston that, while gold miners in the region never faced war parties mounted on horses, isolated incidents between individual Indians and gold miners produced sporadic deaths on both sides. In 1858, when a lawyer deposed Bidwell as to whether there was any "sanguinary" war between Indians and Whites leading up to, during or after the July 1851 treaty meeting, his response reflected the rarity of such incidents: "Not to my knowledge."[67]

This answer, however, ignored Bidwell's own part in a dramatic clash with Indians. In late 1850, he rode out at the head of a party to retaliate against the Mountain Maidu's Kimshew tribelet which had attacked Valley Maidu workers he and other farmers had lodged in mining camps in Mountain Maidu territory. The next spring, in 1851, a rumor spread that Mountain Maidu stole another settler's cattle between Bidwell's place and Oroville. Even though the cattle had only wandered off to graze and reappeared shortly thereafter, settlers killed over a dozen Indians and burned their rancheria. Wozencraft was troubled when he learned about these hostilities in the Sacramento Valley's adjoining foothills. On May 11, he commented on Indians' territorial issues: "We have an incipient border war, many lives lost, an incalculable amount of property stolen."[68]

In contrast to Wozencraft's concerns about the aggressive

Mountain Maidu, Johnston characterized the Valley Maidu as "the least warlike or savage of any Indians on the face of the globe. ... They are a wild and ignorant people as yet, and though not warlike they will steal and commit murders on individuals but in my opinion it requires but little time to remedy these evils."[69] He believed settlers would not force Valley Maidu such as the Mechoopdas out of the valley to live in the mountain lands of their enemies because Bidwell and other ranchers had a growing dependence on their labor.

However, Johnston did not approve of Valley Indian workers' wages of as little as a shirt for a week's work. While he did not mention Bidwell, he wrote to his superiors in Washington about employers who paid Indians in "clothing, food and beads"—including pants and shirts the Indians readily discarded or only wore for work.[70] Nevertheless, Johnston concluded such pay practices should continue until government agents could adapt Indians to "civilization." Until they valued money, the government should pay Indians in items they considered valuable, such as beads, or useful, such as blankets.

Because Johnston doubted most Mountain Maidu could adapt to working for settlers, he was concerned they would become transients dependent on theft or charity. Wozencraft, Capt. Day and he agreed with treaty commissioner George Barbour's statement that Mountain tribes, including the Maidu, "have been treated in a manner that, were it recorded, would blot the darkest page of history that has yet been penned."[71]

Wozencraft emphasized the importance of "quieting and pacifying the Indians in this country, before they become accustomed to the usages of war, before they learn ... that dangerous experience. ... It is my opinion, if they should gain that knowledge we will have the most formidable of all the aboriginals on this continent to contend with, and a protracted war, terminating only by their extermination and at a fearful cost of life and treasure. They do not lack the nerve and daring of best of the Atlantic Indians, they but lack the experience, and with that, their mountain fastnesses will be impregnable. In fact, they are measurably so now."[72]

On the basis of such concerns, Johnston considered reservations the best solution: "To feed the Indians for a year would be cheaper than to fight them for a week."⁷³ In this, Johnston cited Day, who explained that, while Valley and Mountain Indians, including the Maidu, "are divided into small bands each with

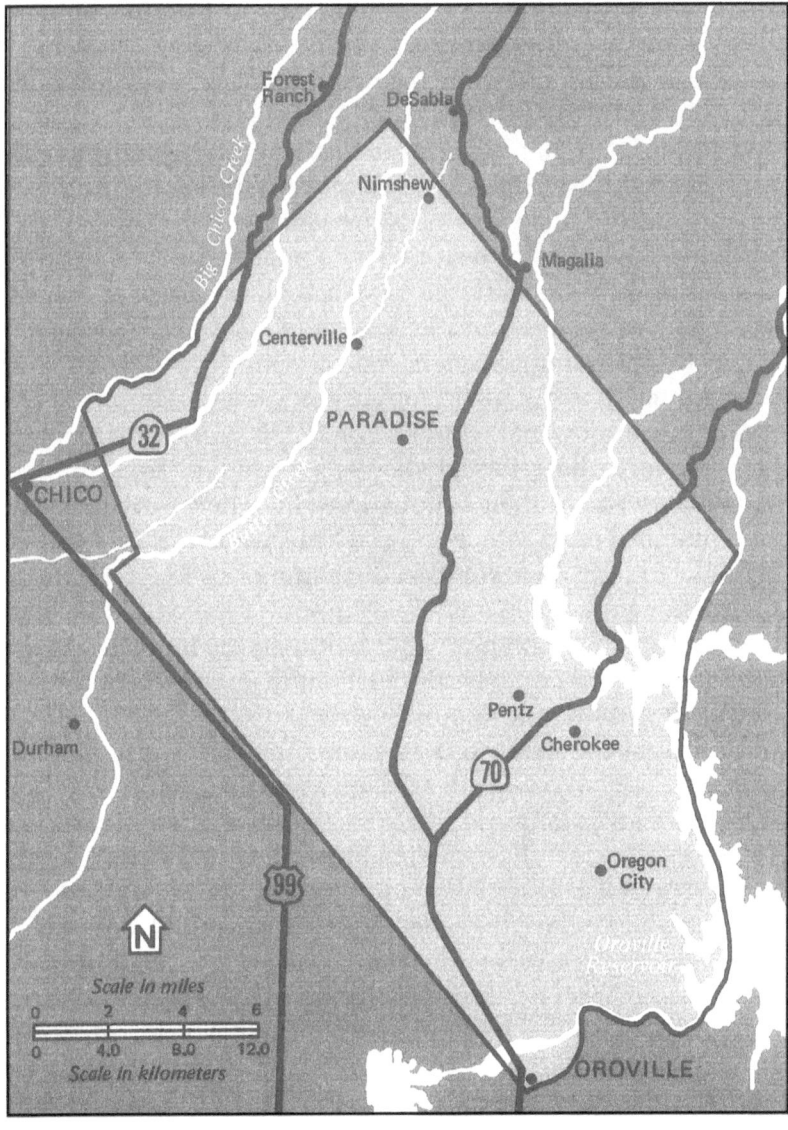

Maidu reservation boundaries approved in the divisive 1851 treaty meeting at Rancho Chico.

individual sub-chiefs," the Mountain Maidu, by contrast, could not survive within their own fixed tribelet boundaries, so they "wander[ed] independent of each other" throughout the regions where gold miners thronged.[74] Traditionally, they had lived on a sparse diet of vegetation supplemented with wild game, which was now disappearing—a casualty of miners' hunting. Similarly, fish were casualties to miners' dams. Johnston concluded, "It becomes a question how are [Mountain Maidu] to be provided for in ... charity, to say nothing of their native right in the soil."[75]

The Mountain Maidu's custom of avenging wrongs by retaliating in kind raised the stakes. Because Whites looked alike to Indians and Indians were indistinguishable from one another to Whites, members from either race sometimes paid a price for others' acts. Johnston advised his Washington superiors the situation between Indians and settlers could go "any which way."[76]

The treaty commissioners' correspondence reveals they were not naïve about settler opposition to reservations or the level of corruption that would come to taint reservation operations. However, even though they soon found the treaty budget inadequate to fund their negotiations, they never expected the government would refuse to fund reservations it had tasked them to promote. Therefore, in the summer of 1851, the treaty commissioners worked on the assumption the federal plan represented a national commitment to compensate Indians for their losses and train them to become self-sufficient workers.[77]

After a tour of the foothills with Alex H. Barber, a Bidwell ranch supervisor, to determine the Maidu reservation's boundary lines, Wozencraft selected a site between twenty and twenty-five miles long and five to six miles wide. To appease the settlers, Wozencraft chose minimally productive land.[78] The proposal described a western boundary that ran northeast from the outskirts of Oroville (two miles above the town of Hamilton on the Feather River). When the line reached Butte Creek, it made a generous jog around the foothill areas of Bidwell's farm. Continuing east along the north bank of Chico Creek, the proposed border rose to a point beyond Magalia, then turned southwest to its starting point. The foothill site included grazing land Indians and miners crossed as they entered and exited the canyons.

Although seven years later Bidwell would disparage

Wozencraft's competence and integrity with accusations that he had chosen poor land for Butte County's proposed Feather River Reservation, in 1851 he likely approved Wozencraft's boundary lines because they eased his concern about the treaty's effects on his ranch operations. The undertone and content of the letters Wozencraft and Bidwell exchanged indicate they enjoyed mutual confidence and an amicable relationship during this period.[79]

Wozencraft understood his job was to meet the basic needs of Indians in a way that accommodated settlers. The vision behind his reservation design was to bring the Maidu down from "their mountain fastnesses" to settle along creeks in the upper foothills at the valley's edge. The miners, as he saw it, would, in turn, fan out and settle into the areas the Indians had left. This would create a "formidable cordon" between the Indians and their old mountain territories, making it difficult for them to move back home. The new arrangements would also make Indian livestock thefts difficult to conceal. At the same time, according to Wozencraft, on the reservations they "can have all the protection which ... should be afforded them, against their prosecutors...."[80]

In his 1858 deposition, Bidwell dismissed as impractical Wozencraft's hope to expand the use of paid Indian labor in the gold mines. Intra-tribal clashes and small miners' resentments about big miners' use of Indian labor in the late 1840s had made such a vision problematic. When Bidwell later stated "I have never sent them," meaning, by context, he never sent Indians to mine, he overlooked his employment of Indians to mine his gold on upper Butte Creek from 1848 to 1850. He also contracted out Indian labor to one or more miners at Shasta as late as 1852.[81]

Bidwell's vision of a grand ranch required local stability. If treaty-based reservations could reduce hostilities and increase Indians' ability to fit within the American economic system, Bidwell must have concluded they would be beneficial. In that light, it appears that, in the summer of 1851, the proposed treaty seemed more an asset than a threat to Bidwell's interests.

Bidwell Advances the Treaty at Rio Chico

During July 1851, more than two hundred Maidu from the Sacramento Valley foothills and higher regions of the Sierra

Nevada, negotiated mountain paths and waded across creeks to reach the Mechoopdas' forest of sycamore, walnut, alder and oak. Promises of food and trade, as well as a firsthand look at Bidwell's ranch, attracted them to his clearing at the ford across Chico Creek where Wozencraft would lay out the treaty terms.[82]

The Indians, many of whom arrived several weeks earlier than expected, set up their camps west across from their historic trail (becoming the Oroville-Shasta Road) and behind Bidwell's new frame hotel and his residence, one of several attached buildings extending back from the road and along the high creekbank. Of particular interest to them must have been the shed that protected his tack and riding horses from theft. Such housing for animals presented a curious contrast to the familiar sight of wild herds that roamed the valley. The Maidu visitors scrutinized the clapboard-sided bunkhouse into which Bidwell had moved "the Indian boys" his men were training to become *vaqueros* (cowboys), shepherds, field workers and gardeners. More familiar were the traditional bark huts of the Mechoopda families east across the creek. As the Indian visitors moved back and forth among their scattered, tree-sheltered encampments, they socialized, courted, gossiped, sized up rivals and stared at something new: long, straight rows of peach trees and grape vines that Bidwell's Mechoopdas and white workers had planted the previous spring.[83]

Smoke from beef roasting on campfires greeted the arriving groups. In his 1858 deposition, Bidwell testified that Wozencraft instructed him to offer the Indians all the beef they wanted, regardless of cost. However, Wozencraft's explicit instructions in an 1851 letter to Bidwell instructed him to distribute only enough beef to "keep the Indians pacified at the least cost to the government" and told him beef allocations "should be governed by necessity."[84]

In the same deposition, Bidwell and fellow ranchers also testified about food supplies in 1851. He stated, "There was no extraordinary scarcity [of food], so as to produce want or suffering among [the Indians]."[85] Contradicting this, in the fall of 1850, Johnston reported to Washington about the Maidu's chronic hunger. And, according to Wozencraft, who wrote from Bidwell's rancho, "Miners have destroyed [Mountain] Indians' fishing grounds, forcing them to move onto higher and higher ground away from acorn grounds."[86] On July 6, 1851, R. Stuart, who worked at Bidwell's Butte Mill, gave fifty-pound bags of flour each to Kimshew, Concow and Pica tribelet leaders to entice their large parties to continue down to the valley meeting where they were assured ample food awaited. Redick McKee, treaty commissioner for the Northwestern tribes of the Coast Range, observed in 1852 that the crop of acorns "was less than ½ or ¾ than in any year since 1849."[87] By then, stands of oak trees had become settler property no longer available to Indians.

Hunger was only one motivation for Mountain Maidu interest in the treaty meeting on their rival Mechoopdas' turf. The event resembled tribal "big times," cross-tribelet gatherings during which rivalries were suspended. "Big times" also provided opportunities for trade with Indian artisans. According to Bidwell, such trading events took place every few years and, when they ended, Mountain and Valley tribelets parted as enemies. In the settlement period, "big times" on his ranch became rare or nonexistent. The treaty meeting provided Mountain Maidu an opportunity to size up changes to the Mechoopda's territory at their leisure. This was an improvement on their usual surreptitious night visits for surveillance or to arrange secret meetings with willing Valley Maidu. While Bidwell thought of the land grant as his property, the tribelets still considered it Maidu territory.[88]

Mountain Maidu were suspicious about the arrangements between the Mechoopdas and Bidwell. However, the Valley tribelet had little choice but to cooperate with him. Surrounded by settlers and Mountain Maidu, as well as hostile Yahi and Paiute tribes to the north and east, they had nowhere they could move to live in safety. While Bidwell's agreement with the Mechoopdas allowed them to remain on their tribal lands, they had to give up their independence, exchanging it for subservience to their new landlord and employer. Using the treaty meeting campsites as their base, Mountain Maidu circulated through Bidwell's ranch, taking his measure, sizing up the Mechoopdas' willingness to cooperate in driving off the rancher. They needed to find some way to restore their former, albeit limited, access to the valley's resources.[89]

Standoff

While the Indians' arrivals intrigued Bidwell's neighbors and passersby, the appearance of Wozencraft's large mounted party riveted Indians and settlers alike. Accompanying the commissioner were the "gentlemanly and efficient" Capt. Edward Fitzgerald and his staff, lieutenants Thomas Wright and George Stoneman.[90] Close behind them, enveloped in a moving wall of dust, were fifty uniformed soldiers guarding heavily laden pack horses. From their travel to other treaty sites, Wozencraft and his men were aware that some Indians were skeptical about military displays of force: they "would run up the sides of mountains and make fun of my soldiers who could not approach them."[91] Nevertheless, when Wozencraft reached Bidwell's rancho, he had reason to be confident of success because he had already sent other signed treaties to headquarters.

When Wozencraft dismounted, he caught sight of hundreds of Indians along the trail. By contrast to some of his other treaty meetings, this one had an impressive turnout. The crowd included Indian headmen and their people from both Valley and Mountain tribelets. The Mountain Maidu tribelets had been difficult to reach and their warriors, the Butte Creeks, were a danger to Whites. In order to impress on his superior the importance of Bidwell's successful turnout, the commissioner reported that Mountain Maidu were "generally at war with one another … they were very distrustful when it is attempted to bring them together."[92]

The treaty commissioner found Bidwell had done more than assemble the tribelets. Because most Indians were unaccustomed to formal presentations his ranch carpenter built a lectern, which became part of the Mechoopdas' oral history, and Bidwell provided two Indian interpreters. One, Rafael, about 12, was the young ward he had removed from a Feather River Mountain Maidu tribelet and trained to serve him. The boy's duties included translation of the many Maidu dialects into English. The second interpreter was Napanni, about 9, a daughter of the new Mechoopda headman, Luc-a-yan, whom a settler woman described as "a man of superior ability, dignity and fine disposition," comparing him to "a bronze statue."[93]

The commissioner was concerned that, because the Mountain Maidu had "no influential chiefs who can control them," their egalitarian culture would undermine a binding commitment.[94] Wozencraft addressed this problem with a plan to foster hierarchical representation. Taking into account the Indians' love of bright buttons and elaborate costumes, the soldiers' pack animals carried a large supply of maroon dress jackets with brass buttons and lace trimmings. Wozencraft intended the jackets for the tribelet headmen as a mark of their leadership. Because the Maidu idea of leadership resembled "first among equals," a modest, fluid distinction between leaders and the rest, his intent was to cultivate ordinary Indians' deference to a few decision makers.[95]

However, the jackets quickly became one of the problems that kept Wozencraft in Chico from about July 20 until August 2. Indian men were not only aware, but were protective of their own status within their tribelets. A natural or acquired ranking

The "military" jacket on the Indian at right back was like one that Oliver Wozencraft distributed to Maidu Indians he thought were headmen. He was likely one of the white men pictured at an unidentified California treaty meeting. In the photo is Indian agent Adam Johnston, who was not at the Rancho Chico meeting but participated in one in San Joaquin Valley in September 1851. [This photo was most likely not taken at Rancho Chico. It had an identification (since disappeared) of "September 1851" and the name "Johnston."]

generally promoted some individuals over others, according to a wide-ranging agreement among tribelet members. Wozencraft was right about the jackets' appeal—each tribesman wanted one. When the soldiers unpacked them and he offered only a few to the headmen, the other Indians started grabbing jackets as the soldiers scrambled to stuff them back into the bags.

Despite the misunderstanding about the jackets, everyone eventually gathered near the lectern where Wozencraft began to explain the treaty terms. As he observed the proceedings, Bidwell noticed the audience becoming increasingly inattentive and restive. He advised Wozencraft to speak "in simple, concise sentences" because the young interpreters were finding it hard to understand the treaty stipulations, let alone quickly translate them into multiple Maidu dialects.[96] While the Indians embraced the treaty's offer of goods such as livestock, tools, food and fabric, they hesitated at the idea of a reservation, even one to protect them from white people. After much discussion, however, most Valley Indians concluded they had no alternative and would have to sign over their lands forever.

Other problems arose. Indians willing to consider a reservation with livestock and provisions did not understand the need to wait for the treaties to be approved in Washington. In their culture, there was no equivalent to such a political process. Then they were told there would be even more delays before they could move onto the reservation. Contributing to their confusion, the Maidu had a different concept of time than Whites: they had no experience with planned stages of projects accomplished over months or years. Therefore, once they heard about the reservation in exchange for the promised goods, they expected Wozencraft to hand them over immediately. Bidwell explained to the commissioner why the Indians were indignant: they believed the soldiers were withholding promised shirts, "linsey" gowns and blankets in the freight packs. (For the list of offered goods, see the treaty terms in Appendix A). Once the Mountain Maidu understood they could not immediately have what they were promised, they abandoned the negotiations and headed home.[97]

Over the meeting's course, according to Wozencraft, he and Bidwell observed rival Valley and Mountain Maidu intermingling and talking in the camps. Each day allowed the Mountain Maidu to identify Valley Maidu cohorts willing to oppose the white "invaders"—the valley farmers. After leaving Rio Chico, Wozencraft immediately wrote his supervisor, "The Valley and Foothill [Mountain] tribes have heretofore ... been inimical to each other ... but of late have been exchanging visits and meeting in council." He and Bidwell suspected them of "confederating against Whites."[98]

Because of the Mountain Maidu's early departure from the meeting, the commissioner, even with Bidwell's help, had no time to overcome their rejection of settler control. He then found the Valley Maidu reluctant, though ultimately willing, to abandon their tribal lands for a reservation on dangerous rivals' territory. Fellow commissioner McKee later commented, "We gave them the land they asked for.... Indians in this portion of California have ... been greatly underrated, both as to shrewdness and enterprise."[99]

This "shrewdness and enterprise" surfaced among the Mechoopdas. The tribelet's oral history spoke of their challenge to Bidwell and Wozencraft.[100] According to their account, the reservation sounded so good to them that they decided to leave Bidwell's ranch and live there. It is unlikely Bidwell would have supported the treaty had he anticipated this. After all, he was protecting them against dangerous Whites and Mountain Maidu alike, was allowing the tribelet to remain on its historic lands, and was providing them with lodging and wages from birth to death.

That a feeling of betrayal and a fear of economic loss were the source of Bidwell's turn against the treaty is inferred in an oral history dictated to Annie K. Bidwell, Bidwell's wife. Later detail came from Emma Cooper, a Bidwell rancheria elder who related it to author Annie H. Currie in 1957.[101] Cooper was born about 1877 to one Valley Maidu parent of the Odawi tribelet and another from the Mountain Maidu's Tigu tribelet. When rivals burned down their hut in the latter's rancheria while they were with the Mechoopdas for a "big time," they joined the Odawi rancheria, which was located at James and Rebecca Keefer's ranch on Rock Creek. According to anthropologist Dorothy Hill, after Keefer disbanded the rancheria, Cooper, a small child, moved

Valley Maidu Emma Cooper moved to the Mechoopda rancheria on Bidwell's ranch after Mountain Maidu destroyed her family's rancheria on the Keefer ranch.

to Bidwell's ranch with other tribelet members.

When Cooper related the Mechoopdas' version of events to Currie, she was about 80. Although she was not present at the treaty meeting, elders from her youth had been present or had heard about it firsthand from others who had attended it. In the early 1940s, it was Cooper, then in her mid-60s, whom Army linguists singled out to teach them her tribe's dialect for the Code Talkers in World War II.[102]

Cooper's memory proved sound in another event. As a later chapter sets out, her version of what elders told their people about Indians hiding by the Sacramento River in 1863 contained nuances different from other Indian oral accounts of that event. Her account not only reflects other oral histories, it fits the written record. Therefore, although Cooper was in her 80s when she recounted Bidwell's crisis during the meeting, her information merits respect. In combination with Bidwell's deposition, it provides clues to the course of the treaty negotiation, why and when Bidwell's doubts about the treaty crystallized, as well as how he and the Mechoopdas reached a separate and private, non-governmental accord they still remember as the

"Bidwell-government treaty."[103]

Here is Cooper's full account of the private agreement between Bidwell and the Mechoopdas from the tribelet's oral history: "Bidwell said 'Come to Rancho Chico. Government will give treaty. Bidwell had as interpreters two children, Rafael and Napanni. Bidwell set a stand in the grove by the creek and made a talk on the treaty. He called the headmen of every tribe one by one, to come up and sign. He said, 'Government will give you land, two horses, cattle, plow, harrow, wagon, money to start with.' Bidwell wanted to keep his Indians, said he would do the same by them that the government was going to do. Grandpa Daniels signed for the Hooker Oak tribe ... and was one they promised to start with. That was the Bidwell-government treaty. Bidwell wanted to keep his Indians, said he would do the same by them what the government was going to do."[104]

While it seems extraordinary that Cooper could render the gist of treaty offerings in such detail, according to Hurtado this was not unusual. The Indians considered the treaty important and impressed on future generations the memory of what it offered by regularly retelling what had been heard, seen and promised at the meetings. In 1874, Joaquin Miller observed during his time in Northern California that those "Indians in the aggregate forget less than other people. They remember the least kindness perfectly well all through life, and a deep wound is difficult to forget."[105]

In addition, Cooper's oral account of the treaty meeting resembled Bidwell's deposition. He stated Wozencraft "promised the Indians that they should have plenty of beef to eat, and that when they removed to the reservation they should have, I think, two hundred head of cattle, and some twenty-five hundred head of mares, I think, to raise stock from, several hundred blankets, shirts, pantaloons, &c."[106] Although the two accounts differ somewhat, they are alike in terms of the core experience and treaty terms. For example, Cooper's version included the lectern and the Indians' agreement with Bidwell. And Bidwell's included information about the red jackets and the translators.

The Mechoopdas, whose work on the ranch must have given them a better grasp of English than other Indians, had listened for so many days during the meeting about advantages the treaty provided that, at some point, it began to sound like a good option for them. But, according to their oral history, they knew Bidwell "wanted to keep" "his Indians." Cooper mentioned how the Indians recalled Bidwell's promise, not once, but twice: "He said he would do the same by them that the government would do."[107]

Bidwell's promise was apparently a tactic to convince the Mechoopdas to stay on his ranch, while showing the treaty commissioner that he supported the removal of Mountain Maidu to the reservation. His promise to provide what the treaty offered not only allayed the Mechoopdas' concerns, but served his own needs because it only required of him what, in effect, he was already furnishing: support and the opportunity of a livelihood. And terms of his 1849 land grant already committed him to provide them with land. Understanding this as a fair and open-ended obligation, he had unsuccessfully urged a similar land provision when he sat on the Indian Affairs Committee during his single term of office in the State Senate. Bidwell's solution to the Mechoopdas' decision to leave the ranch demonstrates his quickness under pressure. In his memoir, this was a personal characteristic he prized: "When I see men in a flurry, I am generally able to be cool."[108] In coming to an agreement with his ranch Indians, Bidwell maintained Wozencraft's respect, quieted his workers and moved the meeting forward. However, his promises to the Mechoopdas would foster expectations he did not intend to meet until sometime in the indefinite future.

Why would the Mechoopdas want to leave the security of Bidwell's ranch to share a reservation with rival Valley tribelets and their mortal enemies, the Mountain Maidu, including men from their tribelet war parties, the Butte Creeks? Such a desire seems more improbable today than it would have then. Modern memory, cultivated and reshaped over the late nineteenth and twentieth centuries, focuses on the fully developed ranch where Bidwell lived with Annie after their marriage in 1868.[109] At that time, the couple did, indeed, provide extensive services to the ranch's Indian workers and families. Therefore, that the Mechoopdas would ever have desired to leave Rancho Chico for a reservation now seems unlikely. Modern awareness of corrupt Indian reservation management highlights the contrast in the

Bidwells' solicitous treatment of their Indian workers. However, although dozens of reservations were in place throughout the East and Midwest in 1851, the Maidu Mechoopdas knew nothing about their shortfalls.

However, a reservation's appeal is not hard to understand from the Mechoopdas' perspective in 1851. When the treaty negotiations took place, it was early in their days as ranch hands for Bidwell, whose support for them was far less generous than later. The traditional kinds of work that once gave the Mechoopdas satisfying lives as a free and independent people within their own borders and culture contrasted to the "alien" work they faced as ranch workers. Stephen Powers spent about two years living among and observing Sacramento Valley tribes. Some consider him the originator of the tribal name "Maidu," the tribe's word for "the people." He noted the Valley tribelets' bountiful habitat, including ample natural resources and a mild climate that accustomed them, over centuries, to a relatively comfortable existence. Most of the men spent their time as lookouts, practicing with their weapons and trapping small game to supplement plant foods gathered by the women. With resources normally ample in the valley, Mechoopdas trapped for deer or antelope, but they had little need to hunt larger game on a regular basis.

While Valley Maidu culture was likely more complex than Powers surmised, what he observed led him to describe Valley Indians as "very indolent": "I lived nearly two years in sufficient proximity to them, and I give it as the result of my extended observations that [in the summer heat] they sleep, day and night, 14 to 16 hours out of the 24. ... During the day they are constantly drowsing. ... Drowse, mope, mope is the order of the day."[110] The "lethargy" of Valley Maidu sometimes stemmed from nightlong gatherings where men danced, gambled and traded stories, probably in part, at least, to stay alert in case of crack-of-dawn raids by Butte Creeks.

When Bidwell started his ranch, which depended on Mechoopda laborers, he discovered their approach to work was problematic. While settlers dismissed Indians as procrastinators and Bidwell, like Powers, described them as indolent, Sherburne Cook explained they traditionally understood work as only necessary to ensure comfort or survival. Indians' sense of time also

Standoff

played a part. In the initial years, they did not feel compelled to complete such tasks well or as soon as possible, but only "good enough" and long enough to satisfy their need for "comfort, pleasure or protection."[111] One of Bidwell's most challenging tasks, therefore, was to teach the Mechoopdas American farm labor practices.

Although in their own culture women's labor allowed the men relative leisure in the abundant valley, as ranch workers Indian men had to work steadily, take few breaks and sometimes sustain hard labor for long hours. Many spent months away from their families mining gold or in mountain camps tending cattle, while those on the ranch learned to plow, plant, weed and harvest. When there were not enough tools, harvest workers used their bare hands.[112] Bidwell's staff trained Mechoopdas as vaqueros to handle his large cattle herds and break wild horses. According to Mechoopda oral history, in the early period, before Bidwell adopted more humane methods, "the Indians were tied

The pounding of horses' hooves as they ran around the inside circle of wheat thrashing rings separated the wheat from the chaff.

on the backs of the horses and the horses were then turned loose. The Indians were kept on the horses until they were broken."[113] However, they also remembered "the general [Bidwell] always cautioned [his supervisors] to never rush the Indians at work."[114]

The Indians who worked with Bidwell's pigs, cows, bulls and horses discovered they could be bitten, thrown, trampled, kicked or gored. Bidwell once described how, during wheat harvests, his superintendent ran dozens of horses in circles over piles of wheat to separate the chaff. When the time came to stop the galloping animals and turn them in the opposite direction, the foreman ordered Indians to run out in front of them.[115] With this new and alien labor, the ranch's Indian workers discovered chronic exhaustion and culture shock.[116]

Traditional tribal life afforded Mechoopda women and girls few opportunities for leisure. Similar to other tribes across the state and continent, while men assisted in berry and nut collections, most food preservation and daily cooking, as well as making clothing, child rearing, basket weaving and the packing and transport of goods from one site to another, fell to females. A grueling sight that caught Powers' attention was the elder women's use of stone pestles to pound acorns in hollowed rock *metatas* "hour after hour" under full summer sun while everyone else napped.[117] In addition to their traditional responsibilities, women's labor on the ranch included digging the ditch from Butte Creek to Bidwell's flour mill, sewing grain sacks, gathering winnowed wheat, and picking fruit and vegetables or other crops.[118]

Although Bidwell treated Indians better than many other ranchers, he adopted some Maidu practices. For a time this included harsh discipline for tribelet elders dependent on the younger generation. According to Bidwell, the old men and women performed the function of "fences" on the open plain: "The way they guarded a field ... was to put an old Indian at each corner ... if it happened to be large.... For large fields an old Indian and his family were expected to keep the cattle away during night and day, storm and sunshine, and if they failed to do so they were severely whipped. They were generally given a quarter of beef a week to eat...."[119] By assigning jobs consistent with the traditional expectation that elders stay useful, Bidwell achieved a modern expectation of economic productivity.

Perhaps the harsh conditions the Mechoopdas encountered as new ranch workers contributed to their conclusion at the treaty meeting that the reservation would be better than working for Bidwell. They had been listening for days as Wozencraft and Bidwell praised the benefits of the reservation.[120] Wozencraft even managed to allay the Valley tribelets' fears of mountain tribesmen with whom they would share the reservation. Its federal government employees—teachers, trainers, supervisors—would provide security and support. And the Maidu's own tribelet mediation skills would help to keep the peace. For example, while Mountain and Valley Maidu kidnapped one another's children and women to use as workers or to produce families, they also generated family connections through negotiated or forced unions. Their intra-tribal "big times" and other gatherings facilitated trade in baskets, arrows and other useful items and they negotiated crossing rights through their territories to reach the Sacramento River or to collect obsidian for carving arrows. They bargained over captives and stipulated conditions for war encounters. In contrast to their customary practice of ending such events as enemies, Wozencraft envisioned the reservation as a place to bring the Maidu branches, with all their disparate tribelets, together, under conditions where their labor could sustain them and they could finally make peace among themselves as well as with the settlers.[121] Also important, he wanted to forestall any use of the reservation to foster a hostile federation of tribelets that would imperil settlers.

Although Bidwell would later mention Wozencraft as the sole treaty advocate, his ranch Indians recalled his own "talk on the treaty" and that he was the one who had requested that each tribelet headman step forward and sign the treaty papers.[122] The Indian elders' notice of Bidwell's prominence at the meeting was probably due to the rancher's concern for how they would perceive him. (In this his model was his old boss, John Sutter, who enjoyed deference and respect for his leadership in Northern California.) This was more important than an issue of personal ego. Bidwell's standing with the Indians and settlers depended, to some degree, on sustaining his image as the most powerful white man in the area. For Indians, or Whites for that matter, to see him defer to Wozencraft at the culminating treaty signing would have diminished his standing. Therefore, under the scrutiny of Indians, Army officers and soldiers, his ranch employees, local farmers and a federal official, it is difficult to imagine the proud Bidwell standing by as an onlooker.[123]

It was also the case that Bidwell's close attention to Wozencraft's needs helped engender the commissioner's good will, which could be materially beneficial to Bidwell as the reservation plans progressed. Its supervisor and the agent to whom he would report could influence or decide issues affecting Indian labor, the granting of trade licenses and lucrative trade contracts with the federal government. And, of course, Bidwell was signatory on the treaty with the Mechoopdas.

The promotional meetings continued until August 2, 1851, when nine valley tribelets signed the treaty: the Mechoopdas on Bidwell's rancho, tribelets from the Hooker Oak area, tribelets near Oroville and the Durham area and one from west of the Sacramento River. While Bidwell and the Mechoopdas signed the same federal treaty as the other Valley tribelets, the Indians believed their private agreement with Bidwell—the Bidwell-government treaty—meant their treaty benefits would come from him, not the federal government. According to the Mechoopdas, "Indians of the other tribes and the army officers were the witnesses" to Bidwell's treaty "promise."[124] Sixty years later, when they had not received the land Bidwell pledged to them "sometime in the future," they held out a wary—or wry—hope: "The future has not come yet and [the Mechoopdas] are still waiting for it."[125]

The Aftermath

While Wozencraft left Rancho Chico gratified by the Valley Indians' support for the treaty, he still needed the Mountain Maidu headmen's signatures. The Concow, Pica, Kimshew and other tribelets had left the treaty meeting after the early misunderstanding over when treaty goods were to be distributed. Concow tribelet leader Kulmeh expressed their skepticism, when he said he "did not believe the words of the white man" and his people would not move from their rancheria to the reservation.[126]

Three days after the treaty meeting at Bidwell's rancho, Wozencraft wrote Indian Commissioner Luke Lea about his treaty concerns: were the treaty to go into effect without the Mountain Maidu's cooperation, they would have no opportunities to benefit from the resources it offered. Their destitution would force them to continue raiding, which jeopardized peaceful Indians, foothill farmers and miners and hampered mountain commerce. The ensuing hostilities would require federal funding for Indian security, food, shelter and settler protection.

While Wozencraft welcomed the Valley Indians' treaty endorsements, they were not his highest priority because they already had lodging, food and work on farms. Even so, he left troubled at the cost to them of this arrangement. He wrote Lea that, while they were "very friendly disposed towards the Whites, [they] have much just cause of complaint as the Whites have taken possession of their homes and they through necessity are reduced to servitude: their labor is required only in the harvesting season, and the balance of the year they may shift for themselves the best way they can...."[127]

Despite his misgivings, Wozencraft welcomed Bidwell's optimism that the Mountain Maidu would eventually agree to the treaty and the rancher's willingness to arrange a second Rio Chico treaty meeting between him and the Mountain Indians. He told Lea, "It is expected that he [Bidwell] will bring in additional tribes from the mountains who are now troublesome."[128]

When the commissioner left for his next treaty negotiation at Pierson B. Reading's Northern Sacramento Valley rancho, Bidwell sent along Rafael to translate. Wozencraft wrote his superiors on September 3 that he "gave a license to trade with the Indians to Mr. Bidwell, who has great influence over the Indians. ... He was very kind and rendered efficient service in forwarding my mission ... he helped a great deal."[129]

In early October, Bidwell, new license in hand, dispatched Nelson Blake, an educated young Easterner, with his carpenter to the mountains to build a general store which included an Indian trading post. Blake soon sent down word that the blanket stock remained unsold, although an Indian customer had assured him that cold weather would bring sales, and that he only had a limited supply left of beads for the Indian customers.[130] In his 1858 deposition, Bidwell acknowledged receipt of the trade license but emphasized he had never used it. He may have meant he did not use it for long because miners told Blake they would not patronize Bidwell's store only when the "lice and other vermin"-ridden Indians were not allowed inside where they might infect the miners. The store closed by mid-November and Blake left to give mining a try at his own "diggings."[131] (Mechoopdas passed down a memory of their "trading store" on Bidwell's ranch. Charles Stilson's 1860s set of diaries described no Indian-related transactions and no Indians as customers in the larger store.[132])

Meanwhile, on August 29, Bidwell, as promised, brought in twelve Mountain Maidu headmen to his ranch for the second treaty meeting.[133] But Wozencraft, still in Shasta County, expected them to wait at Rancho Chico until his return, leaving the rancher to deal with the idle and potentially disruptive visitors. Attempting to keep the peace, Bidwell asked Wozencraft to send him the fancy jackets he later said he disapproved of when the commissioner distributed them to the Indians at the Chico meeting. Wozencraft wrote back that he would send jackets to Rio Chico with Rafael, who had become too sick to translate.

In Bidwell's 1858 deposition he denied he had "brought in" the Mountain Maidu for the second 1851 meeting. All twelve, he said, just "wandered" onto his ranch for the meeting. In 1858 he also disparaged as Wozencraft's foolish whim and a waste of government money the fancy jackets he urged Wozencraft to send him in 1851.

The two men's correspondence reveals that, in 1851, Bidwell was interested in the treaty commissioner's federal contract authority. So were other cattlemen: the cattle supply fell short that year, forcing the government to pay "twice the going rate for beef."[134] Under the treaty terms, Wozencraft was obliged to feed the Maidu until their reservation opened. Bidwell became interested in taking over Samuel Norris's contract with Wozencraft to deliver cattle to the late John Potter's ranch (then in probate). On August 14, Wozencraft paid Norris $8,250 for the first two hundred cattle. This lucrative contract was now open to new bidders to cover the period of time until the reservation opened. Bidwell submitted his bid to Wozencraft, expecting to compete with Norris, whose cattle operation was south of Rio Chico and the Potter place.

On September 3, Wozencraft acknowledged Bidwell's application for the new contract, but, with evident awkwardness, admitted he had already committed it to Norris, who had offered to shift his entire operation east onto the proposed reservation. This, Wozencraft explained, would work best for the Indians. He also informed Bidwell that he could not make it back to Rio Chico to meet with the Mountain Maidu waiting there because he planned to meet with Pit Rivers instead. After that, Wozencraft traveled past Bidwell's rancho to meet with the Colusi Indians. Bidwell dismissed the Mountain Maidu headmen who returned to the Sierra Nevada without agreeing to the treaty. With this, the treaty correspondence on record between Bidwell and Wozencraft ended.[135]

The above narrative illustrates the contributions Bidwell made to two treaty meetings and the organization of a third, which, in the end, never took place. If Bidwell had any apprehensions about the first treaty meeting before it took place, he never said so publicly at the time. However, he had reasons to worry soon after the meeting ended.

By early October, Joseph McCorkle, about to become one of California's two members of the House of Representatives, received a letter from Bidwell protesting the treaty.[136] According to Bidwell's 1858 deposition, in August, a short time after Wozencraft left for the Shasta County treaty meeting, the Mechoopdas began demanding he immediately fulfill the promises he made in their "Bidwell-government treaty." They expected "land, horses, cattle, harrow, wagon, and money to start with."[137] Bidwell's promise of land was particularly troublesome because he had meant to transfer the land to them "someday," that is, in the *future*—a concept of time unfamiliar to the Maidu.

This same problem had arisen at the July meeting when, as earlier mentioned, the Mountain Maidu had expected to take immediate possession of the goods Wozencraft had promised. Now, Bidwell faced the same situation. When he did not deliver the goods the Mechoopdas expected, they turned rebellious, ignored their ranch work and defied his orders, coming and going from the ranch as they pleased.[138] On top of that, the

Mechoopdas had another grievance: they watched as Mountain and other Valley Maidu tribelet members showed up to collect the free beef and flour promised under the federal treaty until the reservation's opening, while they had to work for Bidwell to earn their provisions.[139]

Bidwell's promise to his ranch Indians and his signature on the treaty, in the commissioner's presence, assumed the status of a public contract to which he was beholden. If unhappy Indian workers felt he had defaulted on that promise, they could change their minds at any time and decide to move to the reservation next to his ranch. Neighboring farmers now worried about the likelihood their own Indian workers might demand similar promises.

Mountain Maidu Make Their Move on Bidwell's Rancho

Although Bidwell failed to mention this dilemma in his deposition, the Mechoopdas were not Bidwell's only Indian problem in 1851. After they left the treaty meeting in August, the Mountain Maidu decided they could conduct raids on the ranch and in the surrounding areas with little danger to themselves. For example, in November 1851, Stephen Blake, older brother of Nelson Blake, wrote Bidwell from Yuba County that he was concerned about his brother's safety because of a number of "murders" in Bidwell's "neighborhood."[140] The brief newspaper article Stephen had read paid only passing notice to the killings, identifying no homicide victims. In light of the practices of the press then, this suggests that both victims and culprits were Indians. Blake was relieved to learn Nelson was not a casualty, but his worries returned when he heard Honcut Maidu had attacked Bidwell's ranch about the time Nelson was riding through an area of the valley the Honcut crossed on their return to Honcut Creek, which empties into the Feather River along the Yuba County border. Shortly after this, Blake learned that Honcut Maidu killed four Chinese miners.

Meanwhile, the ranch Mechoopdas' perceived lack of "commitment" must have reminded Bidwell of the similar problem some had presented at his mine. In 1848, he wrote his partner, George McKinstry, "Trouble keeping all as they wander away."[141] In Bidwell's 1858 deposition, he described their conduct after the treaty meeting in the winter of 1851–1852: "I had a number of Indian boys constantly with me that belonged to that village Mikchopdo [Mechoopda]. ... Wozencraft's proceedings rendered these Indians less valuable to me as laborers, and a greater nuisance to the community generally."[142] He was no less direct in his response to a question: "The effect of the treaty, in my opinion was injurious—it was all injurious; the effect was injurious, because it seemed to destroy my authority over the Indians, and no one else had any."[143]

According to historian Hurtado, Bidwell's change of mind was not unusual: "Ranchers like [former] Senator Bidwell used their influence with native people to encourage them to negotiate with the agents, but the nature of the treaties soon gave pause to landholders. ... Had the treaties passed, the reservation would have been federally subsidized livestock ranches with Indian proprietors. Native ranchers might have preferred to work their own herds and fields rather than those of white ranchers."[144]

Wozencraft likely told Bidwell his private "treaty" with the Mechoopdas could raise problems with the federal government. Although signed by both parties before witnesses on Wozencraft's treaty document, their agreement did not legally bind the Mechoopdas to him. While Bidwell promised them the same terms as the federal treaty, his control over them, of course, would not equate with that of federal officials. Even if the U.S. Senate approved the treaty, the Mechoopdas would retain the right to move from Bidwell's ranch to the Feather River Reservation in exchange for having already ceded their lands. A treaty record did not acknowledge the Bidwell-Indian "treaty" or agreement. Also significant in that report, with no comprehensive tribal name (Maidu) yet in place, the name "Mechoopda" was the single term inserted in the document's narrow box to represent *all* the Maidu tribelets under the federal treaty at Rancho Chico.[145] Elder Emma Cooper's oral account of the events suggests the Mechoopdas were unaware that under the treaty, even though they agreed to stay on Bidwell's ranch, they would have retained the option to leave for the reservation at will. Bidwell's determination to keep them on the ranch as his laborers was subject to both practical challenges and arcane legal stipulations.

Work on the reservation could not begin until the lengthy treaty ratification proceedings had been completed throughout California, and the government was obliged to feed the Indians until then. This meant Valley and Mountain Maidu had numerous opportunities to mix when they picked up their allotted goods. Until mid-1852, Mountain Maidu made regular returns to the Sacramento Valley, many crossing Bidwell land to reach the Potter ranch for beef and Bidwell's ranch for flour.[146] That Valley and Mountain Maidu could take advantage of such contact to collaborate against the settlers was not peculiar to California. Texas settlers also observed peaceful and hostile Indians talking with one another when they picked up their federal food allotments. In both states, hatred for the settlers sometimes overcame tribal hostilities, leading to joint raids on farms and ranches.

In October 1851, two weeks after Norris delivered more government cattle under his new contract, Bidwell wrote newly elected Representative McCorkle, soliciting help to defeat ratification of the treaty. He explained he was fed up with the effects of his own private treaty with the Mechoopdas, who were defying his orders and disrespecting his authority. He also objected to Wozencraft's handling of the cattle contract.[147] The treaty commissioner had not left Rancho Chico a month before Bidwell began collaborating with other worried farmers and began pressing for a negative treaty recommendation from the California Legislature, which, they hoped, would lead to its demise in the U.S. Senate. Their campaign to influence state and federal legislators to reject the treaty was underway at the same time commissioners were still negotiating the last of the eighteen treaties and Indians were already moving to the treaty reservations.

2

Defeat of the Treaty

Through the winter of 1851–1852 John Bidwell marshaled all his influence to achieve the treaty's defeat. Two Butte County men were important to him in this. One was Oroville's Charles Lott, who succeeded him in the State Senate on January 16, 1852, and took his place on its influential Indian Affairs Committee. Lott later would vote for the resolution recommending the U.S. Senate not ratify the treaty.[148]

More complicated was the help Bidwell wanted from Joseph "Mac" McCorkle, the newly elected representative who was about to leave for Washington, D.C. Wozencraft had hardly concluded the treaty meeting when Bidwell wrote McCorkle, seeking his help. A Marysville law partner of Stephen Field, who later became a Supreme Court justice, McCorkle had become acquainted with the rancher while a lawyer at Bidwell's Bar. While winding up his affairs in the State Assembly, in preparation for his move to take his seat in the House of Representatives, McCorkle wrote Bidwell on October 4, agreeing to help. However, he also needed to know what alternate policies Bidwell recommended for the "regulation and government" of the Mountain Maidu. Clearly, McCorkle understood the particular dangers they presented to miners. He concluded his letter with an invitation for the rancher to let him "know when I can serve you."[149] Of course, Mac appended a *quid pro quo*: While he was in Washington, would Bidwell board his mare at Rio Chico and breed it with a mule?

While Bidwell was not a politician, he was an active Democrat with a nuanced grasp of the political process. Both he and McCorkle understood there are all kinds of rewards for "service rendered." In this case, services for a constituent of Bidwell's stature might guarantee his backing for McCorkle's future election runs. In 1925, historian W. H. Ellison referred to McCorkle as Bidwell's "man" who "of course, had influence" on the treaty outcome.[150]

Bidwell outlined his objections to the treaty in a December letter to McCorkle. McCorkle was primed to funnel his ideas to the anti-treaty senators to use in the ratification debate. McCorkle, on his own initiative, sent a copy of Bidwell's letter to Commissioner of Indian Affairs Luke Lea, Oliver Wozencraft's superior in the Interior Department. McCorkle represented Bidwell to Lea as "a humane, honest & conscientious man ... who understands the Indians of that Country better than any man in it."[151] He emphasized that Bidwell's letter to him was "intended to be private."[152] While not true, the imprimatur of privacy enhanced the letter's credibility.

In his letter, Bidwell grounded his opposition to the treaty in his expressed desire to protect Indians from heartless, misinformed, blundering bureaucrats. His outpouring has long been thought an example of his humane attitudes and his foresight on Indian issues. However, analysis of the letter's content in the context of the treaty controversy suggests the letter was also a sharp political calculation anchored in Bidwell's financial interests. His phrasing is important not only for what he said, but even more for what he left out.

McCorkle also delivered a copy to Bidwell's preferred recipient, U.S. Senator William Gwin, who was already a treaty opponent on the committee that would recommend on ratification to the Senate. The congressman's personal delivery of the letter to Gwin would assure he would read it and, Bidwell hoped, help Gwin persuade other committee members to endorse the anti-ratification position. Bidwell's appeal to Gwin's committee, through McCorkle, is addressed more fully below. The recommendations Bidwell channeled to the Senate through his response to McCorkle's questions appear, in retrospect, to have been diversions concealing his lack of any real alternative to treaty reservations for the Mountain Maidu.

Slavery Diversion

McCorkle's question about what Bidwell recommended for

the Mountain Maidu had been direct, but Bidwell's response was evasive. Bidwell proposed that "government must let Indians and settlers work out solutions to problems themselves." While this approach seemed sensible, it would only prolong the settler-Indian war underway in the foothills and mountains east of his ranch. Bidwell recognized he could offer no practical alternative to violence in addressing the immediate plight of starving, angry Mountain Maidu, so he filled his letter with ruminations on related issues that might be considered in the future.

Bidwell initially diverted attention from the core problem in the Butte County treaty, the Mountain Maidu: "Where is the line to be drawn between those who are domesticated and the frontier savages? Nowhere—it cannot be found."[153] After that declaration, he shifted his focus to the Valley Indians. The characteristics of the Indians Bidwell described were those of peaceful Valley Indian farm workers and did not apply to the hostile, aggressive Mountain Maidu. Bidwell had established a good reputation for his treatment of the Mechoopdas and his comments reflected a generosity and confidence in the Valley Indians' potential. He made the reasonable argument that those Indians were vulnerable to bureaucratic designs that would transfer them from protective and stable farm homes, under settler patronage, to the uncertainty of life on a reservation.

Ignoring the violence between Butte Creeks and miners or foothill farmers, Bidwell instead predicted the treaty would destroy the working relationship between farmers like himself and Valley Maidu workers: "[Those Indians] look up to the white man with a filial obedience to his commands, and expect from him a kind of parental protection. When he wants them to work he tells them to go into his fields—when they want food they invariably come to him—also clothing and whatever their necessities require. And it would be cruel to force these harmless creatures from the places of their ancient habitations."[154] The moralistic and patronizing tone of this quote is characteristic of Bidwell on the subject of Valley Maidu. He believed his good treatment compensated for his control over them and their land. From his perspective, while he stood to make a lot of money, he also carried great financial risk and was responsible for close to one hundred Indians, as well as a changing array of white workers and customers who also depended on him for their livelihoods and, at times, even their lives.

A Tennessee native who remained a Mississippi plantation owner of slaves, Senator Gwin was already pressing for the extension of slavery to California Indians. The senator likely appreciated Bidwell's carefully worded imagery of domesticated, "contented" Indians and caring, attentive farmers. This wording resembled Southerners' descriptions of their own slaves as contented and in no need of government intervention. Consider Senator John C. Calhoun's defense of slavery in 1837: "I hold that the [relations between Whites and Blacks] in the slaveholding States ... is instead of an evil, a good—a positive good ... Look at the sick and the old and infirm slave, on one hand in the midst of his family ... and under the kind superintending care of his master and mistress...."[155] Yet this argument also reassured Northern and Plains senators reluctant to defeat the treaty. Bidwell was appealing to Gwin's prejudice to lock in his support.

Pro-slavery views were shared by rancher Pierson Reading, a former New Orleans businessman and Bidwell's "personal friend," who, like Bidwell, had worked for John Sutter.[156] According to Reading, "the Indians in California make as obedient and

William Gwin, simultaneously California's U.S. Senator and Mississippi plantation owner, collaborated with John Bidwell and other farmers to defeat the proposed Indian treaty in 1852.

humble servants as the Negroes of the South ... being mild and inoffensive in their manner and easily taught the various duties of the farm. I am confident that by treating them kindly I can easily convert them into useful subjects, and at the same time improve their condition as human beings."[157] Another Sutter veteran, on a visit to Bidwell's ranch, observed "those Indians work like [slaves] for him."[158] Contributing to such a broad-brush characterization was the physical appearance of California's Indians, whom observer William Brewer described as "very dark, black as our darkest mulattoes...."[159] Because of their dark skin, the abuses of some California Indians by Whites resembled those experienced by Blacks in the South.

From Granville Stuart's time mining on the Feather River and Butte Creek, he came to believe that "the Indians belonged to the owners of the grant" and he praised the "owners" for their decency.[160] In 1871, Chico's Dr. Oscar Stansbury, a Mississippi native, would describe Bidwell's relationship to Rancho Chico Indians in terms similar to those of Calhoun: "Bidwell ... cared for them like the better plantation owners cared for the darkies back home."[161]

In fact, throughout the Civil War, as a leading Union Party leader in the north state, Bidwell would oppose slavery. He would hold to that position, despite its cost to his businesses and the harassment it provoked from his neighbors who were natives of slave states.

Land Ownership Diversion

Bidwell's letter proposed the federal government adopt the Mexican provision that required land grant owners to transfer land to Indians residing on their ranches. In acquiring his land grant from Mexico, he had agreed to this and, as a state senator in 1851, had proposed that the incoming state legislature adopt this policy. His "Bidwell-government treaty," which included a promise of land to his ranch Mechoopdas during the treaty negotiations, reflected this same position.

While admirable, in late 1851, land transfers were closed to the Mountain Maidu who lived surrounded by mining camps. They had no generous employers to endow them and Southern Maidu were already headed for an Army reservation. A land promise was only practical for Valley Maidu employed by property owners. In his letter, Bidwell declared his proposal with a flourish, "I for one intend to donate lands for the Indians in this neighborhood." However, such a policy was meaningless absent the support of other farmers. In his letter, having omitted mention of both his own land grant obligation (which few would have known about or remembered) and his recent promise of land to the Mechoopdas at the treaty negotiation, Bidwell's wording inferred his promise was based solely on altruistic generosity.[162] In reality, the State Legislature had already rejected his proposal and Congress, steeped in slavery and free labor issues, was closed to such novel ideas.

Equity Diversion

Bidwell's letter employed yet another high-minded proposal the State Senate had, in fact, already rejected: his call for Indians to have legal standing as Americans. He recommended Indian agents always be present for trials or punishment of native people to protect them from abusive claims or cruelty. Even had such proposals found support at the state level, implementation would have required a long-term, systematic effort by institutions and individuals to convince the Indians to abandon their own cultural ideas regarding justice and rule enforcement in favor of the outsiders' approaches. Such assimilation was unlikely to succeed naturally if left to the Indians, who were satisfied with their own concepts of justice. In fact, during the 1850s, settlers in Northern California already had turned to their own informal, outside-the-law problem-solving strategies because the state's nascent legal system was often nonfunctional or unavailable, particularly in remote areas. And, in any event, when it came to the Mountain Maidu's survival, judicial policy was an irrelevant issue.

Small, Private Reservations Diversion

Unable to create a credible alternative to big government-run reservations, Bidwell's letter made a stab at an alternative: small reservations imbedded in private farms, with the management monitored by government agents. This would keep Indian workers on ranches and resembled the promise he made his Mechoopda workers: that he would give them the same provisions the government had offered if they remained on his ranch. However, he no sooner mentioned this option than he dropped it in favor of his declaration that government should stay out of Indian-settler affairs. Furthermore, with Congress in the grip of politicians with links to the slave states, it is inconceivable that legislators such as Gwin and Calhoun would have countenanced government regulations to protect any farm labor, whether white, black, or Indian.

Bidwell was adamant that government must "let the Indians alone … and they would be sure to cling around and shelter themselves under the protection of him who treats them best."[163] That is, Indians and settlers should be left on their own to work out conflicts. Of course, that was the system in play as the rancher wrote his letter. Its inadequacy to satisfy federal acquisition of Indian lands was the legal reason President Fillmore had tasked the Interior Department to reserve land and services for Indians in the first place.

Abuse of Government Powers Diversion

Bidwell's apprehension about government intrusion was another diversion: he wrote that Valley Indians should not become the subject of arbitrary "rearrangement" by government officials. He argued that "removing the entire Indian population to any one body of the country" would be inhumane, impractical and expensive. A reservation would do just that, removing Indians "who were now semi-civilized, from the locations, which they occupy under the paternal protection of the old residents of the country."[164] Such Indians, who are "residing on private lands, with the consent of the owners, or engaged in cultivating their soil, should not be disturbed in their position...."[165] Again, he was avoiding the core problem: how to compensate and sustain the Mountain Indians.

The calculated quality of Bidwell's letter is nowhere more evident than in his omissions. He made no mention of his recent efforts to advance the treaty. He did not reveal the Mechoopdas' attempt to leave his employ and move to the reservation, nor his problems with them after he persuaded them to stay on the ranch. And he never acknowledged his conflict of interest: his sizeable personal stake in the matter. Should the Mechoopdas move to a reservation, he would lose a great asset—his substantial, cheap, available and usually stable Indian workforce. Bidwell's 1851 letter is a jumble of claims, evasions and tactical feints. As he finished his letter late that evening, he admitted he had "written this very confusedly."[166]

As December ended, everything had gone wrong for Bidwell: Mountain Maidu still had the right to enter his ranch for federal provisions, his Valley Maidu workforce was restless and antagonistic, Samuel Norris was making a lot of money on the beef contract Wozencraft had denied Bidwell, the mountain trading post he built to sell goods to the Indians had already failed. There were no indications of "better times to come."

Finally, because Bidwell was a man of moral principles and held a sincere regard for the plight of Valley Indians, he must have been troubled to find that his efforts to kill the treaty forced him to join forces with precisely those settlers, politicians and government officials who despised all Indians as "savages." Accustomed to a place in the vanguard of Indian policy reform, he had become a key opponent.

The lack of havens for homeless Indians became an ingredient in the next cycle of violence. On April 5, 1852, four months after Bidwell wrote McCorkle, Redick McKee, treaty commissioner for the Coastal Range Indians, made an emergency request to Governor John Bigler for the state militia to protect them from settler attacks. In McKee's words, without a treaty to protect the Indians, the settlers decided "they might just as well take the matter in their hands at once, and rid the country of the whole race!"[167] Bigler not only denied his request, he even refused funds for handbills to discourage settlers from violence.

Although Bidwell opposed federal reservations designed to protect Indians, by inference he was insisting that the government leave ranch Indian workforces subject to the unfettered discretion of big landowners. Another consequence of Bidwell's recommended policy was that no entity would address the grounds for the justifiable anger of the Mountain Maidu and their warriors, the Butte Creeks, and so their peaceful Valley Indian counterparts and settlers would remain at risk. Without treaty reservations, poor Whites would remain antagonistic to Bidwell's Indian-based labor system which so depressed wages they were forced to compete with Indians who were the California equivalent of "slave labor."[168]

Prior to the settlers' arrival, California Indians had lived simply, in independent, self-sustaining communities. Bidwell considered this system dead and unrecoverable. The onslaught of settlers and miners was a *fait accompli*, one that represented unstoppable progress. This diversion from the issue of Mountain Indian survival added bulk to Bidwell's letter, but no weight to his argument.

Instead of Bidwell's obfuscations, he could have opposed the treaty on a number of valid grounds. For example, the corruption that already blighted reservations elsewhere, the potential for Indian abuse by reservation management and the danger to relatively docile Valley Indians were they to live among hostile rival tribelets. But he did not. While those arguments are compelling today and probably troubled a few settlers then, they were not broached in 1851.

State Legislature Rejects the Treaty

In early 1852, Bidwell's and the other farmers' efforts paid off: California's State Senate and Assembly both voted to recommend the U.S. Senate reject the treaty with California's Indian tribes. Their decision vindicated settler claims that the Indians' condition did not warrant federal intervention. The lone minority voter on the State Senate committee was J. J. Warner of San Diego. Reputed to be an Indian expert, he argued that the Indians deserved better. A reservation would "allow them a resting and abiding place on the clay from which they were formed.... Significant portions of land ... should be appropriated for the cultivation and residence of all such Indians as might need a home...."[169] Warner's solution was to support the treaty now and, over time, remedy its inadequacies. In March, the State Legislature forwarded its negative recommendation to Washington, D.C.

Standoff

The tone and substance of the legislative report against the treaty included arguments that employed Bidwell's phrasing in his December letter to McCorkle. It was, and remains, a perennial practice to "re-use" existing language in political documents. According to the State Senate report, the treaty "would withdraw a large body of Indians, who were now semi-civilized from the locations which they occupy under the paternal protection of the old residents of the country." It went on to state that "Indians *look up to the white man with a filial obedience to his commands, and expect from him a kind of parental protection* of the old residents of the country."[170] In another example, just as Bidwell declared to McCorkle that the government should "let the Indians alone," so the state body recommended, "The true policy is ... to *let them alone*" [Bidwell's wording in italics].[171]

BY THE TIME CALIFORNIA'S LEGISLATURE VOTED, Bidwell's letter had reached Senator Gwin. At this time, debates in the House of Representatives were addressing late reimbursements for treaty negotiation expenses. McCorkle implored the House to reimburse all the treaty meetings' creditors, including his constituents, Bidwell and Norris. Although Bidwell had not won the beef contract, he continued to supply bags of flour from his mill to the Mountain Maidu waiting for the reservation to open. Recalling how Bidwell agents' promise of food had attracted hungry Indians to the treaty meetings, McCorkle praised the government's distribution of provisions. He emphasized to his fellow congressmen that "roast beef" was the most "alluring" reward the treaty commissioners could offer to convince the Maidu to endorse the agreement. McCorkle warned that the "root-diggers," a pejorative term for Maidu, would comply with the treaty's peace terms "just as long as your beef holds out."[172] Drawing on his experience in the Feather River mining camps and on his constituents' stories there, McCorkle predicted that, with no food and no treaty, the Mountain Maidu would attack settlers, who would then respond in kind.

U.S. Senate Rejects the Treaty

The U.S. Senate defeated the treaty in executive session on

July 8, 1852. For unknown reasons, all the proceedings' records were sent to storage with orders to be kept secret.

By mid-summer of 1852, word reached California's former treaty commissioners, who had resumed their positions as Indian agents, about the rejection with orders to inform the Indians who expected to move or had already moved. McKee was certain the Indians would not maintain their present calm once they learned there would be no reservations. In a letter to his superior, Commissioner Lea, Wozencraft drew the same conclusion: the treaty's failure "would neither be forgotten nor forgiven by them."[173] When the commissioners began informing the Indians there would be no reservations, McKee conveyed their reactions to Lea: "The Indians cannot understand why the goods and stock we promised them in the treaties have not been delivered. ... The Indians do not understand our distinctions, they look upon a treaty as a bargain between all the Indians on the one side and all the whites on the other...."[174] He continued, "The Law of retaliation is deeply implanted in the Indian nature."[175] And, as expected, the Mountain Indians stepped up their hostility against the settlers on the Eel River and north of Lassen Peak, and in the Sierra Nevada and the Sierra Cascades of northern Butte and eastern Tehama counties.

A Reservation Without a Treaty

Settlers expedited their expulsion of the increasingly impoverished and malnourished Mountain tribes from their homelands. Some died from starvation, others were too weak to work for the settlers and still others committed themselves to vengeance. Even as the warriors' hostilities increased, the dispirited, overwhelmed and underfunded Indian Affairs Department and its Indian agents—the former treaty commissioners—lacked the resources to help the destitute Indians. At Oroville, in 1852, the *Butte Record* reported the "truly deplorable condition of the Indians visible on local streets as they searched for any food to store for the looming winter."[176]

In 1853, a year after Congress rejected the treaty, clashes over resources worsened between Mountain Maidu and settlers. Bidwell's ranch remained a periodic target of Indian raids (discussed in Chapter Three). In 1854, Bidwell raised no objections when the Interior Department and the U.S. Army jointly established the Nome Lackee Reservation (and purchased a nearby farm to supply it), about fifty miles north of Bidwell's place. Its purpose was to incarcerate violent Mountain Indians and also to furnish a safe haven for the peaceful, displaced and impoverished of all the area tribes. Evidently Bidwell concluded this reservation, west of Red Bluff in Wintu territory, was far enough away that it would not appeal to his Mechoopda workers.

Army planners of the "non-treaty" reservation attempted to implement some of the better parts of the defeated treaty by developing a large farm which soldiers protected from angry settlers. Indians learned to farm to feed their families. For several years, conditions at Nome Lackee won enthusiastic reviews in the *Red Bluff Beacon.*

Other Consequences of the Treaty Failure

It was not enough for Bidwell and the other farmers and ranchers to defeat the treaty. They went after Wozencraft, whom they claimed had made Indians restive, by raising their expectations during the treaty negotiations. In 1860, Wozencraft became a target in *Samuel Norris v. U.S.*[177] It concerned the government's decision not to reimburse Norris for livestock he sold Wozencraft for the July 1851 treaty meeting at Bidwell's ranch and for the period afterward when Indians continued to show up for government food, pending the expected reservation's opening. The government alleged Norris had overcharged and that Wozencraft had overpaid, each for his own financial gain. In court depositions, Bidwell and others used the same phrases to denounce Norris, Wozencraft and the treaty. As evidence that the two men had been dishonest, ranchers attested that before and after the treaty meeting, the attending Indians had no immediate need for the beef because their local food supply was at normal levels and a reservation was not necessary because violence between settlers and Indians was not serious enough to warrant such government intervention.

Bidwell was in a difficult position. In order to paint Wozencraft (who went on to pioneer large-scale crop irrigation in southern California) as an incompetent manager ignorant about Indians, he had to admit his own initial support for, and various contributions to, Wozencraft's treaty negotiations. What Bidwell said in his 1859 court deposition in the Norris case contradicted what Wozencraft told him in writing in 1851. For example, as mentioned in Chapter One, Bidwell testified Wozencraft instructed him, in 1851, to feed the Indians all the beef they wanted, at any expense. This testimony contradicted Wozencraft's 1851 letter, in which he instructed Bidwell to provide them only what was necessary and at the least cost.

On another front, in 1853, when the accusations of graft in the treaty beef contracts in Chico and elsewhere became an issue in Washington, the Indian Affairs Office bowed to the attacks and replaced California's Indian Commissioner Lea with Edward Beale, a well-connected naval veteran familiar with the West. The office expected Beale to provide a fresh, disinterested assessment of all the former treaty commissioners' conduct and to re-evaluate whether reservations were necessary and, if not, to propose alternatives.

In his review, Beale asserted that the commissioners had kept poor records and that the federal campaign's total budget of $25,000 for all of California fell short of the funds needed to meet the needs of the numerous tribes across the large state. However, he also concluded the commissioners' accomplishments were worthwhile. Respected "old Californios" had assured him that reservations were essential to the Indians' survival because "if allowed to roam at pleasure their early extinction is inevitable."[178]

This reinforced Lea's position that reservations were essential: "I am slow to believe that the Government, recognizing as it does the possessory right to all the soil inhabited by Indians, would deny them the occupancy of a small portion of the vast country which such extraordinary benefits are in process of receipt."[179] Like Lea, Beale noted that treaty expenditures fell short of the Indians' needs because commissioners, trying to meet their immediate and pressing obligations, had no alternative but to deal with vendors who took advantage of them.

Finally, aware that Indians felt betrayed by news of the treaty's rejection, Beale reported he needed time to prepare them for some alternative to the reservation. "To reject them outright without an effort to retain their confidence and friendship as already secured by inducements of an equally advantageous character would undoubtedly involve the state in a long and bloody war...."[180] While settlers denounced the treaty through the summer of 1852, the Indian agents continued counseling the Indians to trust what they themselves trusted: President Fillmore's intention to honor the government's promises of land and services to the tribes.

The agents' labors as treaty commissioners may have been doomed, but their actions and words on the treaty's behalf had been sincere. They believed, into mid-1852, the government would follow through on its promises to the Indians of land, teachers, trainers, livestock and other essential provisions. They considered reservations far more cost effective than the inevitable wars that were already indicated by clashes between the Indians and settlers and which would certainly escalate without a treaty.

Throughout the 1850s, California farmers remained at odds with Indian agents who sometimes intervened to protect Indian laborers. In 1860, in response to farmers' complaints, the state's U.S. Senator Milton Latham proposed legislation to transfer federal control of Indian affairs to state Indian agents, at ongoing federal expense. Senator Gwin's remarks during the debate on Latham's transfer of power proposal were ironic in light of his role in the treaty's defeat: "[Mountain Indians'] hunting grounds have been destroyed; the rivers ... which supported them ... are now entirely occupied by miners; the whole of the ground ... where they got the acorns they made use of as bread, has been taken up by the miners; and, therefore, they commit depredations. They have nowhere to go ... and around the [post-1853 reservations, including Nome Lackee] white men will settle and they will intrude upon these reservations, and the result ... will be extermination of the Indians sooner or later."[181]

While Bidwell omitted references to the failed treaty in his later speeches and memoirs, he periodically encountered reminders from individuals who recalled it. For example, although he was a Republican, in the 1883 campaign for governor he would back Democrat George Stoneman, the Army lieutenant from the company that accompanied Wozencraft to the 1851 treaty meeting. In addition, there is no little irony in Bidwell's choice of Charles C. Royce as his ranch manager in 1886. A lawyer and Civil War veteran, he had served as chief of the Indian Bureau's land division. In the 1870s, while an employee of the Smithsonian Institution's Bureau of Ethnology, Royce authored an extensive history of federal land treaties from colonial times to the present. This featured a case study of government officials' abuses in their land agreements with the Cherokee Nation. In 1928, Royce's work enabled that tribe to win $14 million in reparations.

Apparently Royce, who had achieved a "high rank as a tireless investigator," recognized the value of the extensive files he found in Bidwell's office and, in the late 1890s or early 1900s, organized them for preservation.[182] Because Royce's report on Indian land cessions reached publication while he was working in Bidwell's office, the rancher certainly read it. It is not possible to know Royce's influence on Bidwell's later talks and written remarks. However, in his later years, Bidwell occasionally expressed regret that the settlers' takeover of Indian land had come at such cost to northern Butte County's Maidu.

DURING THE DEPRESSION OF THE 1890s, when Bidwell was in serious financial straits and advancing in age, he and his wife Annie attempted to deed land to loyal Mechoopda Indians who continued to live on their rancherias and work for them. However, federal Indian authorities would not cooperate with them because the Bidwells' offer of land was only to selected family units. The couple could have chosen to make an all-inclusive land deed to the Mechoopdas and people of other tribes who also worked there as a body, but they elected not to because the conduct of some did not meet their moral standards.

When John died in 1900, Annie, advised by lawyer Frank Lusk, managed their complex estate. She remained devoted to the remaining ranch Indians, but the relationship was not trouble-free. A kind and generous woman, Annie supported social causes such as suffrage and universal education. But she was a rigid Presbyterian and a temperance leader who insisted the ranch Indians meet her personal religious and moral standards, which included banning anyone who used alcohol from the ranch.

An example of the problems that arose from Bidwell's unresolved 1851 promise to deed land to his ranch Indians occurred in 1914, when Mechoopda leader William Conway wrote to the Secretary of the Interior for help. While Conway's letter acknowledged his respect for Mrs. Bidwell, he wrote that the rancheria Indians still had no property and, by inference, no freedom: "As far as Mrs. Annie E. K. Bidwell good friend to the Indians is true: I have nothing to say about Mrs. Annie E. K. Bidwell ... that isn't the question. The question is we have no homes. I will mention why we have no homes. 30th of last December 1913, the Indians gave a social dance: Indians only. Mrs. Bidwell came to the village and told the Indians to get off her Property and said this is my Property. We had no place to go so we remain where we are now. We might get kick off at any time. This is why I ask this government for assistance: where we are now located we have no title."[183]

Conway's complaint must have come to Mrs. Bidwell's attention because, after this, she acted on her and her husband's longstanding promise. However, this time, to avoid the government's stipulations, she deeded to selected Indians small subdivision parcels adjacent to the Mechoopda Cemetery, located on what is now Sacramento Avenue, where she then built them family cottages (the last of which the Indian owners sold in the 1950s).

Legacy of a Failed Treaty

While settlers credited themselves with the treaty's failure, in retrospect, its doom was foreordained. As Robert Chandler pointed out, the early settlers never would have permitted Congress to deed one-seventh of California to its Indians. He added that, had the U.S. Senate approved the proposed treaty, the already established pattern of under- and even unfunded federal budgets for critical projects would have quickly reduced the proposed reservations to the desperate level of their counterparts across the country.[184]

The lack of treaty rights has affected Indians into the current twentieth century. In 1928, about seventy years after the treaty defeat, Robert W. Kenny represented California's tribes in a successful suit against the federal government for reparations for the loss of treaty benefits. However, that was the only compensation ever awarded for the loss of Indian ancestral lands.

When the 1852 records of the Senate Executive Committee's treaty ratification deliberations, which had been filed that same year under an injunction of secrecy, were discovered in 1905, the Senate voted to lift the injunction, allowing Kenny to use the documents to build his case. In the end, he tallied the consequences of the treaty defeat: "The results of the rejection of the treaty left the Indians of California exposed, helpless and largely unprotected against ruthless evictions, unprovoked aggression, bitter persecutions, conscienceless exploitation, dispossessed and, despoiled of their property without recourse, to become homeless wanderers in the lands of their fathers ... in a bitter struggle for existence."[185] Kenny considered this treatment a "shame" and blamed the early ranchers: "California Indians have become homeless vagrants, quickly reduced by eviction, starvation, murder and disease to 17,000 members."[186] Leo Kibby, son of Adj. Gen. Kibbe, who was a key figure dealing with local Indian-settler clashes during 1859, provided a lurid example of the aftereffects: owners of vineyards [Bidwell's excepted] "paid [Indians] in brandy, jailed [them] for drunkenness and bailed [them] out to work off their fine."[187]

In light of the persistent tragedies and injustices that befell the Indians following the treaty rejection, even a weak treaty would have been better than none. California Indians ended up without land, legal standing, rights or entitlements. In other parts of the United States, Indian treaties, all their faults notwithstanding, at least laid the legal groundwork for the state and federal governments' recognition of native tribes as sovereign peoples. Those treaties' value cannot be underestimated because, in the end, they provided Indians a legal basis to demand accountability from local, state and federal governments.[188]

BIDWELL DID NOT FORGET the services of Joseph "Mac" McCorkle. When Mac lost his re-election bid for the congressional seat in 1853 and returned to Butte County, Bidwell sold him and his friend, Dr. John B. Smith, 640 acres a couple of miles north of Rio Chico's headquarters. The price McCorkle and Smith paid was no doubt favorable, but probably somewhat more than the $1 on record.[189]

When word of the treaty's defeat reached California in mid-1852, John Bidwell might have celebrated had he not been busy fending off a Mountain Maidu campaign to destroy his ranch and punish the Mechoopdas for collaborating with him. The next chapter discusses his attempt to address a theft through his private arrest and interrogation of Indian suspects, followed by his and his employees' disastrous pursuit of the thieves' collaborators. These and other complications launched the post-treaty phase of Bidwell's Indian problems.

3

Bidwell: Under Siege and in Pursuit

In 1852, when Butte Creeks, Mountain Maidu warriors, targeted John Bidwell's Mechoopdas, they apparently considered the ranch Indians his collaborators. If so, they were unaware the Mechoopdas had not only rebelled against Bidwell, but that their actions had undermined his operations.

By this time, the Mountain Maidu also realized gold mining operations were to blame for the "dislocations and depletions" of fish, game and edible plants on which they depended.[190] The only Indians capable of driving out the miners were the Butte Creeks; fit and skilled, they knew their territory better than the white newcomers and were able to attract recruits to their ranks.

While Butte Creeks killed the occasional miner, their raids against Bidwell's Mechoopdas became a major commitment. They had gained a close knowledge of the ranch's layout from their sojourn there during the treaty negotiations the previous year. That meeting also enabled them to identify disaffected ranch Indians.

Most settlers believed aggressive pursuit parties would intimidate the Butte Creeks into ending their raids. On the other hand, Bidwell, who had earlier judicial experience with mission Indians, was convinced the American legal system, with its arrests and trials of malefactors, could satisfy the Indians' sense of justice. His neighbors disdained such thinking because they were convinced a pacific approach would only embolden the Indians who would interpret such a nonviolent response as weakness.

Bidwell's Early Experiences with Indians

As one of the first American immigrants to California in 1841, Bidwell encountered Indians on his passage. Unsure of their intentions, he kept his distance and they did the same.[191] Some important exceptions notwithstanding, caution and equanimity characterized his approach to Indians thereafter.

As an employee of John Sutter, Bidwell learned about California agriculture in general and the Valley Indians' value to farmers in particular. Not only did their adaptability to farm labor impress him, he also noted their patience, tolerance of Whites and willingness to work for outsiders at a time when Indians were still the majority population. His open attitude was shared by few settlers.

Bidwell had no tolerance for settlers who abused Valley Indians. One instance that shaped this attitude occurred in 1843 at Sutter's Fort, when word arrived that Indians had killed white men near Red Bluff. However, because Bidwell suspected settlers had provoked the Indians, he declined to join the pursuit party Sutter dispatched. It became characteristic for Bidwell to give the benefit of the doubt to Indians in clashes with settlers. This sometimes erroneous judgment led him into clashes with other settlers through the mid-1860s.[192]

On one of Bidwell's early trips across Mexican California, he and an Indian from Sutter's farm crossed the north-central region searching for stolen horses. Their pursuit took them through the Sacramento Valley's rolling swales to Chico Creek, later the site of Bidwell's ranch.[193] When Bidwell recalled this journey, he inferred his Indian companion worked well with him and was courageous.

In 1841, as the result of a passport dispute with Mexican officials, Bidwell shared a jail cell for a few days with three Indian men at the Mission of San Jose. In 1846, he briefly filled in as a civil magistrate or *alcalde* at the Mission of San Luis Rey where, in one case, he decided in favor of a rancher's Indian victim. When other Indians heard that angry settlers who wanted retribution were looking for him, they hid him. Their action likely influenced his conviction that Indians would accept a fairly administered criminal justice system, which, he believed, could hasten peace between the settlers and Indians.

Bidwell had a good opinion of his Mexican ranch hand Casamiro Fabela, but he did not respect how most Mexican ranch managers treated Indian laborers and, with that in mind, once commented, "I never met an Indian who liked a Mexican."[194] He also considered the Indians' evasiveness or deceit a defensive response to bad management at ranches and missions. However, one of the men he most admired was a Spaniard who was an exceptional manager of the Mission of San Luis Rey.

Padre Peyti: A Model for Bidwell

In his work with Indians, Bidwell took as his model Padre Antonio Peyti, whose treatment of Indian employees contrasted with the labor practices of Sutter and most other ranchers. A community of roughly eight thousand Indians worked the mission's orchards and vineyards. Although Padre Peyti was strict, he was fair and protected the mission Indians from settler abuse.

So apparently contented were the Indians at the mission that they tried to block Padre Peyti's return to Spain. Bidwell believed he could earn such loyalty from his ranch Indians; if he provided for them and was fair, they would neither flee nor cheat. Padre Peyti's example and his own contacts with Indians convinced Bidwell he could provide decent conditions for them and still prosper.[195]

The expansive scale of land grants in Mexican California enlarged Bidwell's vision beyond the small farms he had known in the American East and Midwest. His years with Sutter taught him how to farm a vast tract of land. Despite his reservations about Mexican culture, it influenced the design of his future Rancho Chico. Of particular importance to Bidwell's sense of moral responsibility was Sutter's double rationale: first, that indenture would teach Indians skills and work habits useful in their changing world, and, second, patronage would protect them from rival tribes and unfriendly settlers. And, perhaps even more important, Sutter's operation convinced Bidwell that harsh treatment engendered unreliability and even rebelliousness among Indian workers.[196]

Bidwell was drawn to Padre Peyti's approach because his own upright character was unsuited to any method other than humane relations with Indians. It was helpful on that score that, as a big, confident man, he did not attract challenges to fight. He also conceded, "I was never a good shot...."[197] He did not even hunt game as a sport. On the other hand, when intimidation was in order with other settlers, he found his public stature, combined with his volcanic temper, could produce submission. In later years, when asked about his relations with Butte County Indians, he responded, "Now with the Indians I never had any trouble."[198] This issued from his enduring desire for peace, not from his experiences.

Padre Peyti influenced Bidwell in another respect. The priest had taken into his personal service a young Indian boy whom he reared and educated at the mission. Bidwell declared the Spanish dialect of Peyti's protégé the most perfect he had heard in California. Following the padre's example, as well as the Spanish and Mexican customs of removing Indian children from their families to keep and train as farm workers, Bidwell took Rafael, as earlier stated, a young boy from the Feather River Mountain Maidu tribelet, as his personal servant.[199]

Bidwell's Indian Workforce

No inexpensive labor source other than Indians was available in the valley because most men who streamed into California in the early days came for gold. Referring to the white labor shortage, Bidwell commented, "When I began surveying, not having enough white men, I had to employ Indians."[200] Few white men were willing to accept low wages for the same work. Although transients streamed up and down the Oroville-Shasta trail and hard-pressed squatters lived in the vicinity of Bidwell's ranch, they found it hard to find work that paid a sustainable wage because farmers were determined to maintain the low wages that kept their large scale operations profitable.

The Mechoopdas' acceptance of the private Bidwell-government treaty during the July 1851 meeting created the effect of an alliance between him and them, undermining the traditional balance of power among the Valley and Mountain Maidu tribelets. This became an ingredient in the escalation of Indian-settler hostilities.[201]

Once the Mechoopdas became experienced gold mine workers, Bidwell contracted out their labor to other miners on an "as needed" basis as late as 1852, always stipulating their fair treatment. In one agreement, asserting his "sole control" over the workers, he claimed half the profits but split the cost of the Indians' board with the mine owners.[202] Despite his "fair treatment," Bidwell's own workers were sometimes discontented. For instance, when he noticed five Indian miners had "run away," he caught up with them, but could not convince them to return.[203] An offer of "some presents" persuaded other Feather River Mountain Maidu to replace them.[204]

During the early expansion of Bidwell's ranch, a key project was the training of Mechoopda men as vaqueros. On January 19, 1852, Alex Barber reported from Bidwell's mountain camp on the men's progress: "The boys perform well. In fact Joe is a perfect paragon of a rider. In fact I think he will surpass Ona in a short time. Lafonso is a little timid but is improving fast."[205]

In addition to his other ranch responsibilities, Bidwell oversaw the integration of Indian workers into his gold mining, livestock and crop-raising operations. He also maintained a mercantile trade with Whites and Indians in the valley and the mountains. He was attentive to his clientele's preferences, such as the size of pickaxes, particular spirits and favorite foods. Despite the large amount of liquor he sold to miners and farmers, nothing suggests he sold alcohol to the Maidu. Envisioning their integration into the settler mainstream, Bidwell predicted Indians would eventually want or need the same commodities as settlers, and, indeed, they gradually adopted American fabric, blankets, apparel and foods—much of which they bought from his agents.

Although the high country store he opened in 1851 was short-lived, he sold beads, buttons, mirrors, shiny objects and other similar trinkets directly to Indians at his adobe "trading store" or post on Rancho Chico. Traders bought the same items wholesale from John Bidwell & Co.[206] A Bidwell customer who sold beads to Indians in the mining camps in the late 1850s became upset with Bidwell when Indians stopped buying them on an Indian agent's advice that they were a waste of wages. Bidwell refused the man's demands that he exchange his unsold purchases for credit. But Bidwell suffered a loss too: in 1860, a box containing 6½ pounds of beads still languished on a shelf.[207]

Bidwell's early relations with Indians remained a vivid memory throughout his later life. Having faced one critical situation after another that required him to make quick decisions, in his 1890s memoir he offered examples of incidents with Indians in which his "self possession," as he called it, prevailed. In one instance, he described an encounter with hostile Indians who would have taken his life but for his cool display of a bear claw he carried that aroused their fear of grizzlies.[208] Throughout his life in California, Bidwell's many responsibilities and wide-ranging interests forced him to confront crises that challenged his composure.

Decades later, Bidwell expressed a sense of guilt about his possession of Indian lands. As he explained, "I had for [Indians] a regard, a sympathy—knowing that their lands had always been taken from them without compensation."[209] Others also lived to regret their harm of innocent Indians. Several memoirs of Indian trackers who killed Indians in the 1850s and 1860s expressed remorse, although they recalled they had acted out of necessity. They also acknowledged they had sometimes done so even though they knew Whites' violence against Indians had provoked their revenge.[210]

The demands on Bidwell were so numerous and pressing that Indians' needs competed with other priorities. Between 1850 and 1853 alone, he juggled correspondence, travel, title disputes, visitors, squatter claims, local political clashes, national political contacts, service in the state legislature, job applicants, charitable requests, Indian and white ranch employee assignments, neighbor relations, as well as the demands of row crop, orchard, livestock and merchant businesses he was developing. Each task demanded his time, opinions and decisions and was often complicated by unreliable mail services or long-distance travel (by steamship, horse, mule and on foot that impeded timely communication and delivery of goods. Such persistent distractions might explain, at least in part, Bidwell's lack of animus toward Indians, even those who tried to drive him away—he had neither the time nor inclination to obsess over any issue, including Indians.[211]

Although, from their different perspectives, Indians and settlers often questioned and disagreed with his tactics and motives, from the day he arrived, Bidwell was committed to the area's development into a stable, productive place. As he saw it, all the

Maidu could eventually become an integral part of the emerging American workforce and community. For the most part, he used his influence with public officials in Sacramento and Washington, D.C. to advance that idea.

It is important to keep in mind that Bidwell was only one of many targets of the Mountain Maidu campaign to avenge the incalculable and egregious wrongs settlers committed against them. Diaries from the early 1850s speak of miners and farmers who knew they were constantly watched by hard-pressed Indians waiting for a chance to steal their provisions and clothing or, sometimes, to take their lives. Many settlers gave up altogether and fled to safer areas.

But those who stayed and fought back often exacted a heavy price. In the 1851 clash discussed in Chapter One, after making unwarranted allegations of cattle theft by Mountain Maidu, a foothill rancher and his neighbors hunted down the suspected troublemakers, hanged their Indian leader, killed fifteen other Indians and burned down their rancheria. While Bidwell was never a party to such extreme retaliation, he became a primary target of Indians who singled him out as a leader of the Americans' invasion.[212] They recognized the threat Bidwell posed went deeper than violent clashes: he represented the universal collapse of their entire culture—their lands, customs, values, even their language. The Indians understood John Bidwell was not just any white man.

The Troubles

Forty years later, in the 1890s, early Californians' memoirs finally attracted the attention of historians such as Hubert Howe Bancroft, who hurried to record firsthand accounts of aging settlers. Although Bidwell was an early and influential actor in the "American" period, it seems no historian approached him. So, with his wife Annie's help, he wrote his memoir. After lunch, they would sit on a high bank overlooking Chico Creek, where she asked him questions and he dictated his recollections.[213] Other sources on the same subjects his memoir treats have led to the surmise here that he edited his descriptions of events. He was careful with his words and gave incomplete descriptions of events, perhaps mindful of his wife. Annie Bidwell was so sensitive that even exclamations she heard in a Methodist church service "over-stimulated" her.[214] Bidwell was also respectful of the years Annie devoted to the ranch Indians' welfare, all of which might explain his toning down and omissions of more graphic descriptions about Indian-related incidents.

In response to commentary on this point in Chapter Eleven, historian Robert Chandler suggested Bidwell's approach to what he told Annie resembled how the Maidu elders described the 1863 removal to their children: both worded their stories to match their listeners' sensibilities and expectations. In any case, Bidwell's account and alternate versions inform one another even when they conflict. In his dictation to Annie, although he discounted the severity of Indian resistance, he acknowledged that it took place and provided valuable information regarding clashes between the Indians and him and other settlers.

The Butte Creeks' efforts to recover control of their ancestral lands, whether through negotiations, defense of territory or offensive campaigns to oust settlers, demonstrated they were shrewd and tough adversaries. Settlers then and later were mistaken when they construed the Indians' violent methods as the product of purely instinctual, irrational drives they considered barbarian. To the contrary, the Butte Creeks' campaign to drive out the settlers employed ancient tribal techniques proved effective over centuries to intimidate, punish and prod one another. Their tradition was not to confront their enemies, but to appear with no warning at dawn or dusk, kill or take prisoners and quickly retreat. They did not conduct warfare maneuvers settlers considered legitimate; instead, aside from formalized exceptions, small groups used tribal tactics to apply "private vengeance."[215] In the early 1850s, Bidwell was their enemy.

Recalling the Butte Creeks' campaign to kill Bidwell's Indian workers and destroy his property, he explained that "the [Mountain Maidu] Indians conceived a great hostility toward me. They seemed to think that if I were out of the way, they would have a free pass to do almost what they wanted. I seemed to be in their way."[216]

Tradition prohibited Valley Maidu from entry to Mountain Maidu territory, let alone staying there for months on end, working for a white man. So in early 1850, Kimshews, a Mountain Maidu tribelet, ambushed and killed a Mechoopda worker in Bidwell's mountain mining camp. In response, Bidwell formed a twenty-man pursuit party. Because of its large size and his use of Valley Maidu workers in a pursuit party two years later, this one also probably included ranch Indians. Pressed for manpower, he also recruited Michael Nye, even though he had spread a falsehood that Bidwell killed Indian workers. The party found the Mountain Maidu Kimshew camp and a fierce fight ensued on a thin trail between Butte Creek and the West Branch of the Feather River. Bidwell "had a narrow escape from death" and his party lost a second ranch Mechoopda. An arrow injured but did not kill Nye. Bidwell's party killed "seven or eight" Indians, of whom "two or three" were women. The unequal loss of Indians and settlers continued into the next decade and would always trouble Bidwell.[217] This event, and the Mechoopdas' rebellious behavior at his ranch in late 1851, tested Bidwell's local reputation as a skillful manager of Valley Maidu workers.

Repercussions of the Defeated Treaty

In May 1852, now Indian agent Wozencraft reported an increase in the number of Indians "stealing through necessity" while they waited for the U.S. Senate to ratify the treaty. With their families going hungry, Mountain Maidu were irate that farmers not only denied them access to oak trees they relied on, but fed the acorns, their staple food, to hogs. Mining tailings were filling mountain streams, killing fish, another staple. Miners' tents and shacks covered Indians' prime creek-side campsites. Gold miners along the Feather River that May noted Indians hovering nearby, ready to snatch their supplies or shoot arrows at them to drive them off.[218]

Bidwell Responds to Cattle Thefts

When mountain snows receded and the sun was drying out the valley grasses in 1852, Bidwell's Indian and white workers drove his American cattle to the grazing camps in Sierra Nevada meadows where they fattened up for market—and some were stolen by Indians. On June 15, Bidwell's head vaquero there, James Callen, appealed for help, "The Indians are doing mischief here more and more every day and are threatening the members of this settlement and something must and will be done ... you will please send me word what you can do when and how."[219] Callen, aware of Bidwell's conciliatory approach to disputes with the Indians, suggested he visit the camp (since he had some grasp of the tribelet dialects) or send an interpreter such as Rafael to negotiate a return of the stolen cattle. If they could just "punish the guilty," Callen ventured, it might save the lives "of some good miner and many Indians."[220]

As in the murder case on his ranch, mentioned in Chapter Two, Bidwell would have preferred the sheriff act so that the Indians could adapt to the jurisdiction of the American justice system. However, apart from arrests of Indians who committed infractions in towns, sheriffs and deputies refused to respond. This left Bidwell, once again, on his own to recover his property. Nevertheless, he was determined to be deliberate, show restraint and model a peaceful resolution of the problem.[221]

On the same day Callen requested Bidwell's help, Mountain Maidu entered the grazing grounds on his ranch and stole "a lot of American cattle" the vaqueros had not yet moved to the mountain meadows. While Bidwell ignored most of the thefts of "Spanish" or wild cattle, "American" cattle from the plains and Midwest were a different matter—they were worth up to six times more than Spanish cattle because they came from finer stock and offered superior breeding opportunities. Their theft was too costly for Bidwell to ignore.[222]

California Indians knew their thefts undermined the viability of ranches. According to Sherburne Cook, between 1830 and 1845, Indians across interior California stole between twenty thousand and seventy-five thousand cattle from ranchers, who sometimes lost "everything, even to their saddle horses."[223] Under cover of darkness, thieves drove cattle and led or rode horses away from the ranch fields, then butchered them, leaving carcasses strewn along their path.

Standing by his principles, Bidwell contrived a pseudo-law enforcement approach: he would make a "citizen's arrest" of the culprits and deliver them to Justice of the Peace Thomas Wright.

According to Chico old-timer Frank Crowder, a resident and Indian fighter from the later 1850s, since legal institutions were not fully developed in California, Bidwell was not unusual in acting in place of the law: "Everyone was a peace officer in those days when it came to breaking the law of men."[224]

In order to avoid punishing innocent Indians and worsening his problems with the Mountain Maidu, Bidwell decided to show them the "American" version of investigation, trial and punishment. First, Bidwell had to identify the thieves. He had his men hold two Mountain Maidu suspects who "came down" to the ranch and interrogated each separately.[225] He learned that one and probably both had participated in the theft and they revealed the identify of the other thieves.[226] Savvy Indians could be devious and sly, but they did not lie.

With only two "defendants" in hand, Bidwell decided to "go out and get those [other] Indians."[227] But, as he recalled later, "For some time I could not persuade anyone to assist me."[228] The farmers he approached for help refused because they believed an arrest attempt would only put them at greater risk to hostile Indians who had no notion of, let alone a regard for, the settler legal system. Finally, in late June, Bidwell organized a pursuit party of men from his ranch. They included thirty "well-armed" ranch Indian men and employees Amos Frye, Charley Taylor, Jacob Updegraff, "Mr." Soule (a miner who sometimes worked for Bidwell), Casamiro Fabela, Alex Barber and Duncan Neal. Nye probably participated as well.

Bidwell's party also included the witnesses for his case, the two Mountain Maidu whom the Mechoopdas had brought in and he had arrested. When the two admitted their guilt, Bidwell's attention turned to 150 Mountain Maidu, the "Chico [Creek] Indians" from the Sulemshew tribelet east of his ranch on the north side of Chico Creek. When the large party moved east into the foothills, the Mechoopda scouts ahead of them spotted the Sulemshew rancheria near the head of the creek. Bidwell ordered his men to silently camp overnight in Iron Canyon [upper Big Chico Creek]. Bidwell planned to make a sudden, noncombative appearance at the rancheria at sunrise—essential because Bidwell's party was heavily outnumbered by the Sulemshews. He expected them, caught off guard and grateful not to

Standoff

Iron Canyon along upper Chico Creek was the vicinity of Bidwell's 1852 sortie that failed when Mountain Maidu forced his party to retreat to the valley.

have been attacked, to hear out his complaint and evidence, then to hand over the collaborators his captives had identified. He planned this civics lesson to introduce the Mountain Maidu to American legal accountability and to force Wright to try the defendants Bidwell would deliver to him.

Before dawn, however, a weapon suddenly went off in the pursuit party's camp. Although later that month Bidwell insisted to reporters the shot was an "accident," in his memoir decades later he called it a "betrayal"—a ranch Indian man had shot his gun to warn the Mountain Maidu. While no white employee would have alerted hostile Indians to the party's presence, recent problems with his ranch Indians indicated that a few were more loyal to their larger tribe than to Bidwell.

This author believes when Bidwell publicly interpreted the shot from a member of his party not as a warning but accidental, he was protecting ranch Mechoopdas from his neighbors' general suspicions of Indians and their particular resentment of his Indian workforce. Mistaken firing of weapons was unlikely in deep darkness because the loading and firing of cumbersome muzzle loader rifles and pistols were complicated, requiring several steps in a fixed sequence.

As the shot's crack reverberated and Bidwell's groggy men scrambled to figure out what was going on, about one hundred Sulemshews and their Nimshew neighbors appeared on the ridge above Bidwell's camp and showered arrows on them. The attackers killed Frye, the prisoners escaped in the mêlée and Soule took an arrow in his hand. Although decades later Bidwell recalled he ordered his men not to return fire, a source in 1852 said the armed Indians in his party "fought bravely."[229] The Mountain Maidu's principal target was their old enemies, the Mechoopdas, who had aligned with the hated Bidwell against them.[230] The Sulemshews and the Nimshews, superb archers, killed eleven men from the small Mechoopda tribelet whom Bidwell had tapped for pursuit duty.

The Mechoopdas had already lost two men to Butte Creeks in Bidwell's 1850 clash, another one or more in the murders on the ranch and now, eleven more. The loss of so many deepened their survivors' dependency on him. The cumulative cost to Bidwell in ranch labor was considerable and would increase the pressures on him to attract Indians from other tribelets to work at Rancho Chico.

The Mountain Maidu attackers followed the Bidwell party back to the valley, taking "potshots" at them with arrows and taunting them. As the party picked its way back on foot along the uneven and boulder-strewn banks of the creek, its members tended to Soule and carried the dead. This failed arrest attempt had turned into Bidwell's second "Indian-killing expedition," the term he used to criticize others' pursuits.[231] Bidwell's 1890s memoir named no Indian or white victims in this clash and he disparaged as unjust the outcry over the death of one white man (Frye), when compared to the far greater number of Indians who perished in that and other clashes.[232]

When the pursuit party's defeat became known, the settlers who had refused to join it blamed Bidwell for Frye's death. Although not well-liked, Frye was still a fellow settler. Valley settlers in general feared the Mountain Maidu's fierce fighting tactics and were convinced Bidwell's failed sortie would further fuel the Indians' rage. At the time, the six hundred settlers identified in the Butte County census were greatly outnumbered by Indians. While there were only a few dozen Butte Creek warriors, without their war garb they were undistinguishable from peaceful Indians. Settlers resented Bidwell's dismissal of the dangers Indians presented and ridiculed his visionary claims that Indians could be arrested, tried and punished under American law.

BIDWELL CONSIDERED REGAINING HIS NEIGHBORS' confidence by organizing another pursuit of the thieves. Although he knew how to find the Sulemshews, he wrote his employee D. M. Bean at his Butte sawmill to ask the whereabouts of "Ned's tribe," the Maidu Nimshews.[233] When Bean, reacting to the letter, mentioned the rancher's name within earshot of fifteen Nimshew men, the Indians became agitated and pressed him for information. Bean wrote to Bidwell, warning him of their threat to kill him.[234]

Bean believed the Indians' boasted intent was real. A former Butte Creek miner later recalled, "We never went out without our guns or revolvers, as we were liable at any moment" to an ambush.[235] Tensions were so high that, when rival Butte Creeks burned down a Nimshew rancheria, local miners hastened to provide "good will" gifts to the tribelet's survivors. Their attempt to appease the Indians reduced tensions, albeit only for weeks.[236]

To impress on Bidwell the danger the Nimshews presented, Bean also wrote it was a good thing a lone miner working down a nearby trail had not come to the mill that day because, when the Indians who threatened Bidwell left, they headed down the same trail and likely would have killed him had they crossed paths.

Bean offered his boss some frank advice. In order to gain the respect of the Sulemshews and Nimshews and other Butte Creeks, Bidwell must fight back and win: "If you go out into a fight with these Indians you must go through with it and conquer all of them before you quit otherwise I won't have anything to do with it, the Concows, Nimshews and Tigers [Kimshews or Tigus] are all the same if you fight one you fight them all—I think I could get 25 or 30 men."[237] Despite Bean's offer, Bidwell decided against another pursuit.

Arson Attempts Against Bidwell

Bean's warnings troubled Bidwell through the summer of 1852.[238] Around this time, Butte Creeks entered the Mechoopda rancheria where they shot Dupah, "one of [Bidwell's] favorite Indians."[239] An arrow tip protruded through his chest, according to ranch Indians. No local doctor was on hand so Bidwell sent to Sacramento for a physician who successfully removed the arrow and treated the wound. Ranch Indian descendants recalled hearing that Dupah's recovery angered the Butte Creeks.

In June, July and August, as the doomed treaty proposal languished in a U.S. Senate committee, Sulemshews made three or four surprise raids on Bidwell's ranch headquarters and set two fires there. Bidwell's men spotted the flames; some put them out, while others unsuccessfully pursued the raiders. A year later, Nelson Blake remembered a night on guard duty with Casamiro Fabela and Jake Updegraff: "We slept side by side by the old haystack with our weapons by us."[240]

After the first July arsons, Barber wrote Bidwell from the grazing camp: "I am informed that there has been another attempt to fire your premises and also that you look to the mountains for the depredators. Allow me to advise you to look to those who live near you if not in your own immediate household for your enemies. Would not the same dispositions do you personal and bodily injury if an opportunity arose? Reflect a little on these things. They appear to me of some importance."[241] Because Barber also worked on Rancho Chico, he understood its operations and had a close knowledge of the white and Indian workers. Bidwell's employee and friend Blake would write Annie Bidwell more than fifty years later that, in the early 1850s, Bidwell was "too confiding and unsuspicious, believing everyone to be as honest as he himself was, and as unselfish."[242]

In his 1890s memoir, Bidwell made no mention of Barber's alert and was cavalier about the fires: "We always put [them] out."[243] However, any blaze was a serious threat because even moderate winds could quickly spread a summer fire throughout the tinder-dry valley.

Bidwell was in San Francisco when he learned the Sulemshews

had struck the ranch again on August 24. Although Bidwell's ranch buildings bordered Chico Creek, buckets filled from its low-flowing stream were no match for the fast moving blaze. Flames raced through a 100-foot-long structure that included, at the front facing the road, the large frame hotel and saloon he had just completed. It also took the row of buildings attached to the back of the hotel, extending along the creek bank. These were his residence, the equipment storehouse and the carpentry shop. It also destroyed his granary filled with freshly harvested wheat and barley crops. It consumed 5,000 feet of sawn lumber, doors, framed windows and other building materials for the large house Bidwell was ready to erect as his new residence and business office. Before his stable burned to ashes, his men saved the horses, feed, tack, pack saddles and five riding saddles. Less fortunate were guests' trunks, a "great quantity of provisions: blankets ... dry goods, farming & other utensils, kitchen & Household furniture and many other things." In Bidwell's estimate, the losses exceeded $26,000: "They burned me out. My life was in danger."[244] When Bidwell's wife later asked ranch Indian elders about this fire, they agreed it was set by Sulemshews. Bidwell later remembered them as among those "wild Indians," the Butte Creeks, who "hated me for a number of years."[245]

THAT SAME YEAR, EIGHT HUNDRED Maidu died from cholera, tuberculosis and possibly influenza. Despite the losses, some survivors continued to join Butte Creeks in their raids against miners and farmers. Barber, in Bidwell's grazing camp, was worried: "Indians <u>bad</u>. Very much inclined to steal."[246] Neighbors advised him to corral the cattle at night. He asked Bidwell to send a second white man to help protect the camp, assuring him he would do what he could in the meantime. In response to such incidents, miners sent an ultimately unsuccessful demand to the governor that he remove five hundred Indians from the area.

In May 1853, Butte Creeks again attacked the Mechoopda rancheria across Chico Creek from his new mill and the employee house behind it.[247] Bidwell sent an urgent summons to Justice Wright to investigate "a murder." The victim must have been an Indian because press accounts featured crimes against settlers and would have printed the valley victim's name. An occurrence on Bidwell's widely known ranch around that time would have been newsworthy. That also explains Wright's reply to Bidwell's call, "I doubt if any apprehension of the murderer could be affected by my coming up. However, I could be up in a few hours.... P.S. I have just learned I have no horse up and will not be up as above stated."[248] Presumably, Wright, whose stable was among the best, dispatched his note by a rider—on a horse. Under California's 1850 Act for the Government and Protection of Indians, justices of the peace had jurisdiction over Indian civil and criminal matters, a jurisdiction Wright and others in his position most often ignored. They were no different from other justices reluctant to involve themselves in conflicts with Indians they considered wards of the federal government.

The Greatest Horse Race

Despite Butte Creek raids on the ranch, in July 1853, Bidwell prepared for hundreds of spectators to descend on his ranch for "the greatest [horse] race that California north of Sacramento [had] yet seen."[249] He and his employees laid in dozens of gallons of port, beer, brandy, whiskey, wine and claret. He made sure the store was stocked with sugar, halters, picks and other popular items; additional supplies crowded the new hotel's kitchen. Miners and farmers began arriving at Rancho Chico days before the July 29 race. Melons from the ranch's fields were best sellers in the heat, while liquor fueled the betting of sums well above the $10,000 purse, an extraordinary sum at the time.

Justice Wright's mare "Pocahontas" was the favorite by noon of race day. But William Williamson's "Bay Stallion" had captured the crowd's enthusiasm by the 3 p.m. start. Bay Stallion's powerful charge from the gate was his last impressive move—frightened by shouts from the crowd, he ran straight off the track. Once back on the course, despite his lost time, Bay Stallion was catching up with Pocahontas. He was a couple hundred feet behind her when the bell caught him short and Pocahontas was declared the winner. The bystanders credited her performance to the "good management and care" trainer and rider, Conrad "Coon" Garner, 35, had "bestowed on her."[250]

Conflict in the Foothills and Construction in the Valley

Cattle thefts continued in 1854. In the high country near Yankee Hill, Concow Maidu killed two Chinese miners they thought were from rival Indian tribes and left two others wounded, producing a rare collaboration: white miners joined the Chinese to chase down the perpetrators.[251] The *Butte Record* called for more such cooperation: "[Indians] have sense sufficient to distinguish between justice and revenge, and the white man should not be the first to practice the latter when the former is required."[252]

That same year, Bidwell had replaced the hotel and its workshops with adobe structures.[253] The shops, storage buildings and a two-story stable pushed the headquarters' other buildings north and east into adjacent fields. However, he sited structures close to the headquarters' enclave which doubled as a "fort." By the mid-1850s, in the area north of Chico Creek around the headquarters of Bidwell's rancho, still also referred to as Rio Chico and increasingly as Rancho Chico, a busy hamlet sprung up that people called "Chico." During this period, Bidwell consolidated the various Mechoopda rancherias into a single location near the other ranch buildings.

In late 1855, workers at Bidwell's Bar looked forward to the upcoming Christmas activities, but when word arrived that "Ned," the Nimshew headman, his brother Jack and their large Indian party were in the vicinity, the miners set off after them. With a history of confrontations between Nimshews and themselves, the miners were keen to kill Ned. In the battle that ensued, five Indians died, but Ned escaped.[254] There were no white fatalities, although one man suffered serious wounds and may have died later.

Butte Creeks Attempt to Assassinate Bidwell

On January 25, 1856, several of the ranch's Mechoopda Indians allowed a Butte Creek war party, intent on killing Bidwell, to enter their rancheria and hide in their sweathouse. The next

Bidwell: Siege and Pursuit

This late 1850s view of Bidwell's Rancho Chico headquarters, on the Oroville-Shasta Trail, resembles its appearance when the Mountain Maidu attempt on his life took place in 1856. In the left foreground, his store marks the ford on the north bank of Chico Creek. Next to it is his adobe hotel and saloon. Across the trail, on the right, is his 1854 mill. One peaked roof just visible behind the store is Bidwell's farmhouse. In the foreground the fence across the road sets off John Potter's estate. The trail—Old Chico Way— continued at right around the Potter ranch, then south again at (later) Olive Street.

morning, someone, likely a loyal Mechoopda, alerted Bidwell, who summoned men from his mill, store and hotel and, armed with rifles and pistols, they all headed for the sweathouse. There, Indian guards alerted those inside to their approach. Although they had lost the advantage of secrecy, the Butte Creeks were still in luck: leading the oncoming group was their target—the big, dark-haired man. They waited until he was within range, about seventy-five feet, then shot all their arrows into his chest, killing James Schaeffer, the ranch miller who resembled Bidwell.[255] At the end of the encounter, no other white man had been killed or wounded, but Bidwell and his men had killed a mix of five Mechoopdas and Butte Creeks.

Bidwell later told Annie the Butte Creeks entered the ranch to trade that day, but contemporary press and later ranch Indian

Standoff

accounts agreed the warriors' purpose was to kill him. In his 1890s memoir, he inferred that, among the Indian men he and his workers killed, was the Mechoopda ranch hand whose pre-dawn gunshot had "betrayed" him, alerting the Butte Creeks to the presence of Bidwell's Iron Canyon party in 1852.[256] That this unnamed, disloyal Mechoopda was still in his workforce in 1856 and collaborated in the assassination attempt suggests Bidwell considered him a principal member of the tribelet he hoped to win over and hesitated to confront.

While Bidwell mentioned only the one untrustworthy Mechoopda, others were in the sweathouse with the warring party.[257] In his memoir, Bidwell recounted the assassination incident immediately after the Iron Canyon incident. By placing the two events together and inferring the same Indian was the betrayer in both of them, it appears Bidwell had been aware for years that one or more Mechoopdas placed loyalty to their larger tribe, including tribelet rivals, ahead of loyalty to him. This incident also recalls Barber's warning to Bidwell in 1853: that he should be suspicious of Indians who might be in his "immediate household."

The assassination attempt tested Bidwell's idealistic vision of

This later Maidu Mechoopda sweathouse resembled the one in 1856 where Bidwell's men defeated the attempt to assassinate Bidwell.

goodwill and peace between the two races. During this period, he escaped death once again when he came upon a white man, known as "Kentucky Blood," trying to take "liberties" with a Mechoopda woman seated in a circle at his mill sewing grain sacks. When the man ignored the rancher's order to get out, Bidwell cracked him on the head with a wooden shingle, and, thinking the man was standing up to leave, Bidwell turned to go. However, Kentucky Blood drew his pistol and shot at him, the ball passing through his hat. Sheriff E. K. Dodge happened to be nearby and managed to deflect a second shot. Bidwell, faced with the bother of legal proceedings, decided not to press charges when the man agreed to leave the area immediately and never return.[258]

By the end of the 1850s, the Mechoopda population had shrunk to about half its number when Bidwell acquired their territory. Despite such critical losses, eight months after the Butte Creeks tried to assassinate Bidwell, the Mechoopdas entered a formal battle with a tribe from across the Sacramento River.

When the battle began, settlers near a mound above Rock Creek, about seven miles north from Bidwell's ranch, hid themselves to watch the fierce but choreographed fight. Both sides were "shooting at long range" poisoned arrows that were "flying thick as hail" between the opposing sides.[259] After the battle had ended, the Mechoopdas carried two dead and about a dozen wounded back to their rancheria on Bidwell's ranch. The onlookers said an arrow that penetrated the chest of one of the injured Mechoopdas was poisoned and predicted he would also die.[260]

A witness to a similar battle between two Maidu tribelets described how "the arrows pass through the air so swift that a white man cannot see them, yet the practiced eye of the Indian discovers them in time to dodge them. Often times the [Indians] bound in the air six or seven feet while the arrow would pass under them, then again they would spring off to one side with the rapidity of lightening and from the fact that there was only five or six killed and wounded on a side during a two hour fight amply proves their dexterity in dodging."[261]

No one used shields, although Maidu fighters sometimes

wore stick vests with high necks into which they ducked their heads for protection. "Hideous" war cries added to the drama.[262] The bystanders watched as young children from each side, by mutual agreement, ran into the opposing ranks to recover stray arrows.

Settlers understood the Indians' rage against them but were puzzled by the cross-tribelet hostilities. After a battle similar to the two described above, rancher James Keefer asked a tribelet headman he employed at his Rock Creek flour mill why the Maidu fought among themselves. The Indian told Keefer that ranchers with Indian laborers such as himself and Bidwell had deepened the already existing resentment between Mountain and Valley Maidu.

The Mechoopdas still enjoyed an easier subsistence living on the fertile valley floor than the Mountain Maidu, who were forced to stay on the move to escape the snow and supplement the meager resources on their mostly unproductive land now overrun by strangers. To their eyes, the Mechoopdas, though subjugated, had become even more materially privileged because of Bidwell's patronage. In exchange for their submission to the "white enemy," the Mechoopdas at least received food and supplies at a time when the Mountain Maidu faced starvation and were welcome nowhere. With the traditional balance of power between Valley and Mountain Maidu in collapse, their raids were desperate attempts to reestablish the "natural" order that had prevailed throughout their history as a people.[263]

AFTER THE BUTTE CREEKS' FAILED 1856 attempt to assassinate Bidwell, they stopped raiding his ranch and clashes with miners between Mud Creek and the North Fork of the Feather River declined. This occurred when Robert Anderson, Harmon "Hi" Good, Frank Crowder, Simeon Moak and others, who would later become the area's most well-known Indian fighters, arrived in southern Tehama County and the Rock Creek area of northern Butte County. According to the later memoirs of Anderson, Crowder and Moak, they were unaware of, or had forgotten, the extent and cost of earlier Butte Creek battles against Bidwell and foothill ranchers prior to their own arrivals in 1856 and 1857. Possibly due, in part, to the lull in fighting, they and other "late arrivers" erred in their recollections that the settler-Indian troubles began in their time.[264]

If Butte Creeks were to advance their chances of ousting the intruders from their lands, they had to find a new base of operations. Their only viable option was Mill Creek and Deer Creek canyons, controlled by the small but aggressive Yahi tribe in eastern Tehama County. Those sparsely populated and exceedingly rugged canyons could not provide a new home or refuge for the Mountain Maidu as a whole, but they could benefit their Butte Creek warriors. While tribelet leaders reviewed their strategy and tactics in 1857 and 1858, Butte County miners, settlers and peaceful Indians in the mountains, foothills and valley believed this decline in violence meant the Mountain Maidu had "declared" a truce. However, unprecedented events associated with an increase in raids on Tehama County foothill farms led residents there to suspect they had become the new target of the Butte Creeks and other raiders out of Deer Creek Canyon.

4

The Butte Creeks Become Mill Creeks

After the Mill Creeks' costly raid on Bidwell's ranch failed in 1856, they made no further attempts on him, his valley property or the Mechoopdas living there. Bidwell refused to capitulate and immediately rebuilt everything the raiders destroyed. Particularly grating to the Butte Creeks must have been the sight of the loyal Mechoopdas still at work behind his plows and on guard at his wheat field borders.

This chapter and the next present evidence that the Mountain Maidu revised their strategy in 1857 and 1858 to satisfy several objectives: First, they had to restore winter access to the valley's foothills. At present, going out on raids and returning to the canyons in Butte County necessitated weaving their way around armed miners, whose campsites fanned across Mountain Maidu territory. Second, they had to find replacements from other tribes for Butte Creeks killed in conflicts. Third, they had to procure a safe haven and staging ground for their raiders. Having given up retaking access to the valley to replenish their food stock in northern Butte County, they had to identify a substitute location with similar resources within a reasonable distance from their rancherias. Location was also important because Butte Creeks traveled by night, raided at daybreak, quickly slaughtered and butchered captured livestock, then carried what they could on their backs to their camps.[265]

While no sources reveal how Mountain Maidu headmen and leaders of their Butte Creeks deliberated on these problems in 1857, the dramatic changes in their subsequent actions suggest they formulated a plan.

The Mountain Maidu and Miners

The Mountain Maidu and miners lived among one another from the late 1840s through the 1850s. With their tribal economy decimated and few alternatives to survive other than working in the mining camps, most Maidu did their best to adapt to their situation. Having always lived at risk to rival tribelets and tribes, now they were also subject to abusive miners in the Sierra Nevada.

Although aware they were outnumbered by the Indians around them, miners continued to work the streams, overlooking the occasional disappearance of food, tools or even acquaintances. Although most Mountain Maidu were not aggressive, their warriors, the Butte Creeks, were mixed in among them and settlers could not distinguish which individuals were dangerous.[266] In 1857, when miners realized the steep decline in clashes with Butte Creeks was holding steady, they welcomed what appeared to be an informal "truce."

Nonetheless, occasional infractions still occurred. Two miners disappeared soon after leaving Concow Valley. When challenged about their role in this, Maidu Concows blamed Maidu Kimshews located in the Feather River region where the men were headed.[267] (No retaliation is on record.) Some miners and their suppliers assiduously courted the Indians' goodwill during this period. After a miner named Downs at Spanishtown, near Oroville, harassed an Indian woman, other Whites intervened because "the Indians are at present very kind to the miners and disposed to be friendly, but there is a danger that ... Downs ... will cause them to become exasperated and cause trouble."[268]

A forerunner of such attempts to keep the peace had taken place in 1854 when Mountain Maidu Kimshews and Whites together pursued Paiutes (the "foreign Indians" mentioned in Chapter Three) who had killed miners.[269] In September 1859, at Honcut, near Oroville, when a white man tried to kidnap an Indian woman, her mate killed her rather than let the white man take her. While Indians beat up the predator, white onlookers not only stood back, they restrained his friends from going to his aid.

Mountain Maidu were aware in early 1857 that the Army had removed Feather River Mountain Maidu (who lived just south from Valley and Mountain Maidu) to the Nome Lackee Reservation near Red Bluff. When settlers expelled the "Colusi," a Glenn County tribe, some headed for the Sierra Cascades, where they camped among other homeless Indians and "renegades" at Eagle Lake and other areas around Lassen Peak. Renegades was a term Whites used and peaceful Indians adopted for those who fled their own tribes to avoid punishment for infractions. According to Homer Speegle, an early twentieth-century resident on Deer Creek, where Indian survivors were an elusive presence on the fringes of his family's everyday life, "Indian law was very strict," with their penalty often "an arrow to the heart." By the late 1850s, he said, Mill Creek bands, formerly made up solely of Yahi, included "outlaws from every tribe within a hundred miles."[270]

While cross-tribal conflicts periodically flared in the Lassen Peak camps, some Indians turned their anger on settlers. These Indians, many of them experienced raiders, joined "pickup" bands that sprung up to steal from, and sometimes kill, isolated Whites in remote Sierra Cascades locations, thus prolonging Indian resistance to outside settlement.[271]

During the mid-1850s, in the Cascades just north of the Sierra Nevada mining camps, violent incidents kept settlers, isolated and outnumbered by Indians, uneasy. However, because these settlers also worked among Indians as they milled lumber, built cabins, set up ferries and drove drays stacked with pine and fir to Red Bluff, they expected Indian hostility to abate. Instead, as the decade's end neared, raids became more deadly and terrified settlers began to move their families down to the Sacramento Valley for safety.

Settlers Call for Help

By 1856, Californians, as residents of the new American state, felt entitled to public protection from outlaws and dangerous Indians. That year, after Captain Henry Judah's Fourth Infantry, Company E, pursued hostile Indians around the Antelope Creek headwaters, he observed, "The Indians are so exceedingly wild, evidently on the lookout for the approach of white men and upon discovery are enabled to take themselves to localities where it is impossible to pursue them with any chance of success."[272] Upon his return to San Francisco, Judah recommended that Brevet Brigadier General Neuman Clarke authorize a military post in the area, but the proposal fell victim to other priorities.

In the fall of 1857, settlers appealed to the governor for help against raiding parties in the Sierra Cascades. In response, the Army dispatched Lieutenant George Crook and his company to make a "relentless pursuit of Indians on their own territory."[273] However, Crook made his sole focus the Indian camps around Lassen Peak. While Crook later became known for his willingness to negotiate, this was not an option he pursued with tribes in the vicinities of Antelope Creek, the Pit River and Hat Creek. He was wounded by an arrow in one of his unit's clashes with them. In another Pit River engagement, his men killed eight warriors and wounded others.

Crook recalled such Indian sorties with regret: "When they were pushed beyond endurance and would go on the warpath, we had to fight when our sympathies were with the Indians."[274] Army correspondence expressed several officers' low regard for many of the settlers who took land in the Cascades. Crook's unit was ordered to pull out with the approach of winter, the end of the Indians' fighting season.

In late May 1858, after another settler petition for help went to the governor, the Army again dispatched Judah and thirty-six men to Lassen Peak. There, they made arduous pursuits and entered into hard-fought clashes on both sides.[275] Settlers in the vicinity, such as Dr. E. W. Inskeep,[276] owner of the Antelope lumber mill, near the hamlet of Antelope, and farmer James Patrick tried to ingratiate themselves with the Indians around them in the hope of lessening tensions. However, their efforts were fruitless because, as Inskeep reported: "All of the surrounding [creek sides] are infested with warlike and thieving tribes of Indians."[277]

The Butte Creeks' New Base of Operations

In the meantime, south of Lassen Peak, Mountain Maidu

headmen and their Butte Creeks decided to make the Yahi's Deer Creek and Mill Creek canyons their safe haven from which to launch raids on the Sacramento Valley in Tehama County.[278] Yahi had long raided this Wintu tribal territory adjoining the northern border of Butte County. To secure a base in the Yahi's canyons was worth the risks to Butte Creeks because the Yahi, while fierce, had limited manpower. In the valley adjoining their canyons, raids were feasible because weakened Wintu had lost their territories to settlers and widely scattered farms sprawled in reach of impenetrable canyon havens.[279]

Evidence of the Butte Creeks' incursion into Deer Creek Canyon appears in the observation of A. M. Sadorus and other farmers along nearby Rock Creek.[280] He reported, in late May 1858, that they had frequently spotted bands of Maidu Sulemshews (the "Chico Indians" who tried to assassinate Bidwell) and Maidu Kimshews from upper Butte Creek Canyon. Sulemshews and Kimshews were "regulars" in bands of Butte Creeks.

Sadorus reported seeing the "entire force" of Indian warriors, fully armed with bows and arrows and guns, crossing his Rock Creek ranch, heading north toward Deer Creek.[281] They ignored the white onlookers who looked away when the Indians snatched some chickens. The canyons across Deer Creek Ridge were so rugged and inhospitable that, until then, they had presented no temptation to Mountain Maidu, apart from quick raids. In 1858, the Butte Creeks' weaponry, the direction they took, their timing (a large portion of the Yahi would already have moved to Lassen Peak for the summer) and subsequent events addressed in Chapter Five support the view that this was when Mountain Maidu gained a foothold along Deer Creek and Mill Creek canyons, out of which their Butte Creeks would now operate.

Yahi villages were across a ridge from Mountain Maidu territories. Once in Deer Creek Canyon, the Butte Creeks could descend on numerous Tehama County farms and then escape to the canyon to hide from pursuing settlers before returning to their Butte County rancherias. The Yahi's canyons were also valuable to Butte Creeks because, unlike their home territories, they were solely occupied by Indians and contained no gold or other resources of value to miners or farmers. Furthermore, settler pursuit parties had difficulty moving through the tall, dense underbrush carpeting the boulder-strewn ground below caves, caverns and ledges that punctured the sheer canyon walls. As Yahi scholar Jerald Johnson put it, the Yahi had "a deep-seated pattern of seeing, but not being seen."[282] Those canyons became an asset to the Butte Creeks and Lassen Peak renegades.

Yahi warriors, known to other Indians and Whites as Mill Creeks, may have been defeated by the Butte Creeks. Or, one anecdote suggests, by the winter of 1858–1859, the Yahi had invited them into their bands. According to the *Red Bluff Beacon*, when food supplies were dangerously low in the canyons, a Yahi from Deer Creek, "the Old Doctor," crossed over the ridge to Chico Canyon, where he pressed Maidu Sulemshews to join with his men in raids on valley livestock. "A large majority" agreed to participate; those who stood back were poisoned. Poison—from rattlesnake venom, millipedes, black widow spiders, various mushrooms, and snakeroot—was an important tool for the tribelets.[283] The Yahi's invitation to join their raids may have alerted the Mountain Maidu to the Yahi's vulnerability, and supports Steve Schoonover's assertion that, by this time, the Yahi could no longer survive in isolation.[284]

While the Yahi were known for their boldness and courage, their small population of two hundred to four hundred people, including captives, in the late 1850s could marshal warriors from only a dozen or so extended families. Their survival had always necessitated valley raids to supplement their minimal food sources. By this time, the Yahi were "hardly in a position to attack any significant party of Wintu and Maidu...."[285] Under these circumstances, and in light of the frequency and effectiveness of the raids from their canyons that began in 1858 and built to a peak in 1859, Johnson raised the question, "Is it possible that some or even most of the violence attributed to the Yahi was the result of activities by others?"[286] Both Schoonover and anthropologist Orin Starn, who examined Yahi life in his research for *Ishi's Brain,* expressed similar doubts about the small tribe's ability to carry out, on their own, the extensive campaigns of 1858 and after.[287]

That other tribes gained entry to Yahi territory finds support in the birth of Ishi in the mid- to late 1850s. He would become one of the last surviving Indians with links to that area. If anthropologists Stephen Shackley and Johnson are correct, Ishi was likely a Yahi and Wintu mix. Evidence that some Wintu had access to the Yahi canyons surfaced in 1857.[288] Someone in an early pursuit party in Mill Creek Canyon spotted an Indian he recognized from Red Bluff where he appeared "in quite an advanced state of civilization": he was a drayman who dressed in settler clothes and understood some English.[289] Seeing him in the canyon was unsettling because it confirmed that Valley Indians, while generally trusted, were consorting with canyon Indians they formerly feared. This observation supports the Yahi's weakened control of the canyon by 1858. This was also when the Butte Creeks made it their new base of operations—one they shared with Yahi, Wintu dissidents and warriors from the Cold Springs Valley and around Lassen Peak.

While new foothill farms deprived Mountain Maidu of their accustomed winter refuges among rancherias east of Chico, the Yahi continued dividing their time between winter canyon sojourns and the Lassen area summer camps at Childs Meadow and Morgan Valley. According to Schoonover, they considered those two mountain valleys their principal residences from spring through fall. The Yahi were not welcome in the Sacramento Valley west of Mill Creek and Deer Creek canyons, their winter quarters.[290]

Therefore, in contrast to the Yahi's Mill Creeks, in 1858, the "new" generation of Mill Creeks included men from other tribes. Whatever the participants' origin, in the late 1850s, any who raided out of the canyons were called Mill Creeks. Like earlier Yahi Mill Creeks, the initial raids of the new, multi-tribal Mill Creeks, beginning in 1858, immediately scored ample booty with little risk to themselves.

After Theodora Kroeber argued in 1961 that Yahi were the sole raiders on the Tehama County and Butte County foothills, her analysis gained public acceptance through the early twenty-first century. Notwithstanding her valuable work on Ishi, she not only exaggerated the Yahi's role, but also included the aggressive Mountain Maidu in her flawed assumptions about the relatively more peaceful culture and history of the Valley Maidu. This confusion led her to ignore or dismiss contemporary

Tehama County residents' factual, direct observations and suspicions that Maidu played a significant role in those valley raids. As Chapter Five demonstrates, those suspicions were born out. While Kroeber's work remains important for sustaining interest in these events, her publications distorted the roles of Indians and settlers in both counties during the Indian-settler wars of the mid-nineteenth century.

An Aside: The Nome Lackee Reservation

The larger context of these developments would be incomplete without attention to the situation at the post-treaty Nome Lackee Reservation, which was of particular importance to all the tribes of Mountain Indians and some Valley Indians during this period (Chapter Two touched on its formation). The Army still held captive there four thousand homeless Maidu, Wintu and other Indians. Soldiers supervised their charges and protected reservation Indian workers from settler abuse when sent to work at outlying farms. However, in late 1857, the Army announced its plan to shut down all its California reservations, which meant, over the next four years or so, Army troops would leave Nome Lackee to wind down, short of funds and vulnerable to predators.[291]

By the end of winter in 1858, as the reservation's staff was shrinking, those still remaining increasingly lost control over the reservation's Indians. By the decade's end, food shortages left the male captives who worked the reservation's farm and cattle operations so emaciated and weak they were no longer able to produce sufficient crops to feed their people. In order to preserve what little food there was for the male workers, the staff sent the women, traditional food gatherers, out to collect edibles for themselves and their children. Increasingly desperate and on the verge of collapsing, some men began to menace reservation staff and destroy property. Indians who escaped often made their way to the headwaters of Antelope, Deer, Mill and Battle creeks. Although shared suffering on the reservation quelled some of the old tribal rivalries, clashes still occurred and sometimes carried over to the Lassen Peak camps.[292]

In conclusion, when the Butte Creeks moved into the Yahi's

canyons and, along with homeless and renegade Indians from other tribes, joined the Mill Creek raiding parties, the Mountain Maidu achieved their goals. They regained their strength and secured access to badly needed (and undefended) valley food stores scattered along southern Tehama County's foothills. They also gained new opportunities to make the lives of more valley settlers unlivable. Successful raids on Tehama County livestock in 1858 and 1859 vindicated the Butte Creeks' decision to operate out of the Mill Creek and Deer Creek canyons.

While Butte Creeks continued occasional raids in Butte County mining country, their primary raiding targets across Deer Creek Ridge in the Tehama County foothills became so established that, after 1860, their original name, Butte Creeks, practically disappeared and they became known as Mill Creeks in both counties. If readers find this mix of tribal names confusing, so it was for settlers. This name change originated with Tehama County farmers in 1859 when they alleged that Butte Creeks were core members of the extensive raiding parties on eastern Tehama County.

That discovery led the settlers to speculate that Butte County gold miners had encouraged, even rewarded, Butte Creeks who raided Tehama County farms. It was thought the miners' motive was to deflect the Indians' aggressions away from the gold camps and, instead, toward the Sacramento Valley. Chapter Five examines the role of Tehama County's private pursuit parties which entered the Mill Creek and Deer Creek canyons to retaliate against Mill Creeks. It also examines the pursuers' search for evidence that miners were in collusion with the Mill Creeks they tracked into Butte County mining country.

5

Settlers Avenge the New Mill Creeks

Seasonal attacks on farms and businesses were ongoing around Lassen Peak in 1858 when the newly reconstituted parties of Mill Creeks burned down Sacramento Valley homes and outbuildings, destroyed fences and stole livestock in southern Tehama County. These raids out of Deer Creek Canyon onto the foothills began in April and so alarmed settlers that local leaders began to consider the county's farm economy in peril. While some livestock thefts could be the work of Whites, valley farmers recognized Indian tracks they traced back to the canyons. Ranchers in the nineteenth-century West considered American cattle theft such a serious crime that suspects of every race were vulnerable to lynching.

The raids in 1858 differed from previous attacks on settlers. According to the *Beacon*, this time the raiders also stole prized horses, lariats and riding gear. A *Red Bluff Beacon* article is the earliest reference to settlers' suspicions that the raiders were either solely Butte Creeks or they had joined the Mill Creeks.

According to the *Beacon*, farmers deduced that the raiders were not Yahi because Yahi had never singled out high quality livestock or tack when they raided. They shifted their suspicion to Mountain Maidu, well known for their regular contact with miners. The newspaper's editor described the culprits as "a mere fragment of a tribe that lives by plundering and murdering defenseless persons."[293] The editor used the term "fragment of a tribe" because, at that time, unlike Pit Rivers or Hat Creeks, the Maidu in Butte County south of Deer Creek had, as yet, no unifying name that embraced every tribelet. It was not until the 1870s that observers concluded all the tribelets comprised a single fragmented tribe and subsumed them all under their common word for "the people": Maidu.[294]

Standoff

Second, the editor's use of "fragment" spoke to the Maidu's starkly different Valley and Mountain branches, each of which was further splintered into dozens of rival tribelets. Third was the editor's use of "plundering" and "murdering."[295] The Butte Creeks were known for thefts and killings of miners and other Indians. By contrast, Tehama County residents would have known that Valley Maidu—the other fragment, just south of them on the Oroville-Shasta Road—were, by then, dependent and harmless farm workers.

When Rock Creek farmer A. M. Sadorus reported the May 1857 sightings of Butte Creeks dressed for war and heading toward Deer Creek, the *Beacon*'s editor concluded the Yahi had lost control of the canyon and that Butte Creeks were using that route for raids on Tehama County livestock. As he put it, "It is determined beyond a doubt that Ned's party' [Maidu Nimshews] has been the source of the late troubles" in Tehama County.[296] Therefore, when foothill settlers filed an (unsuccessful) petition to the governor that year, they sought the removal of Mountain Indians not only in the Sierra Cascades of Shasta and Tehama counties, but also in the Sierra Nevada of northeastern Butte County.

SUSPICIONS ABOUT THE RAIDERS' AFFILIATIONS intensified during the following season of heavy raiding. In April and March 1859, the *Beacon* expanded on the previous year's allegations: "We boldly assert that White men [Butte County miners] are connected with the Indians in these robberies, for what wild Indians [who did not ride horses] would come seven miles into the valley, passing hundreds of cattle to steal a fine mare worth $400, within a pistol shot of a house occupied by four or five persons...."[297]

Complicity in Indian Raids

In Butte County between 1852 and 1856, there had been no doubt that Mountain Maidu were conducting raids against John Bidwell and other foothill farmers. While Bidwell would recall that miners resented him, he never alleged they instigated Butte Creeks to raid his ranch.[298]

By contrast, years later, Robert Anderson, a former Tehama County Indian pursuer, recalled that, in 1859, suspicious settlers wanted "proof that Mill Creeks received support from either Butte Creek Indians or the miners or both, and that the arms and ammunition procured in this way was used to murder white people...."[299] The allegation that Butte Creeks were collaborating with Whites was taken seriously in the valley. However, without evidence and for convenience, all the raiders, regardless of their tribal affiliation, were now being referred to as Mill Creeks. This chapter examines what roles, if any, miners and the Mountain Maidu's Butte Creeks played in the raids on Tehama County in 1859.

Another reason Valley farmers suspected miners were collaborating with Indian raiders was because the number of Indian thefts in Tehama County's foothills had soared since the "truce" began between Butte County miners and the Mountain Maidu. Farmers suspected the miners wanted to prolong the peace by redirecting the hungry Indians' thefts from the mining camps to the Sacramento Valley.

Initial suspects were miners—forty to fifty "white brutes" who had "crossed over" to camp with Indian women and renegade Indian men near the Butte Creek headwaters.[300] One was Pat Daugherty, who had lived with Mountain Maidu since 1841 and was indicted in 1854 for inciting Indians "to commit depredations."[301] Another was murder suspect Charles Blair, who had merged into the Pit River Indian camps to escape execution. White collaborators were also an issue in Plumas County in 1857, when Peter Lassen and one hundred others sought prosecution of Whites who sold guns to Indians.[302] In addition, the Army officer in charge of the Nome Lackee Reservation spoke of white employees who joined the Wintu in a fight there against the Maidu. He recommended the regular turnover of Whites in reservation jobs, "lest they form ties with one tribe or another."[303]

Tehama County settlers also suspected their neighbors' Indian farm workers. Some, given to unexplained or unannounced departures and reappearances, might be collaborating with Indian raiders. After all, the *Beacon* pointed out, ranch Indians "are not only cognizant of the time these parties are to make a descent on the farmers in the valley, but, they give their mountain brethren information of the best places to make an attack, where they are the least liable to be caught in the act."[304] Capt. Henry Judah cautioned a subordinate he sent to the valley in 1858: "[Protect] yourself from the mischievous results of the secret cooperation of Indians belonging to ostensibly friendly ranchos with their hostile brethren...."[305] Although valley farmers denied their Indian workers collaborated with Mill Creeks, this suspicion persisted.

A Volunteer Pursuit Party

In response to the Indian incursions on the foothills, two parties of volunteer pursuers left for the canyons on April 20, one heading up Deer Creek Ridge and the other, Mill Creek Ridge. The former made John Breckenridge its captain and the latter Jack Spalding. When neither party spotted any Indians, they merged and continued their search.[306] How could the canyons appear so devoid of people? Pursuers of Mill Creeks and other Mountain tribes found that, like the Plains Indians, they could "disappear" when threatened. For well over a decade, pursuers in the Sierra, like those in Texas, were aware Indians kept them under surveillance from canyon ridges and caves. Frank Crowder, a Rock Creek farmer and Indian pursuer, later recalled they would "only attack those they met on their pathway who were unprotected. They seemed ever ready for murder of the white man or woman, when they could do so without risk to themselves."[307] While settlers considered hiding both dishonorable and frustrating, it was a reliable tactic for Indians.

The 1859 sortie reached an upper canyon camp before "a large number of Indians" allowed the pursuers to see them.[308] Some of the Indians continued their daily work, ignoring the bullets that fell short across the deep, wide and fast moving creek, while others moved to favorable positions and fired off rifle shots and arrows at the outsiders. Rifles, lacking later weapons' ease of handling and quick response, were cumbersome and often inaccurate. Although the Indians' shooting and skilled handling of bows and arrows yielded no casualties, the pursuers retreated from the canyon.[309]

When the pursuit party reentered the Sacramento Valley two

weeks later, they reported they had seen few Indians and no white collaborators because the puffs of smoke they had spotted on entering the canyons came from Valley Indians warning the Yahi's Mill Creeks. In later canyon sorties, they began to recognize simulated bird calls and distinctive rock piles signaling canyon locations. But in this sortie, the pursuers had not yet deciphered the smoke codes. Therefore, as they moved through the foothills toward their homes, they shot and killed random Indians they guessed had sent up the earlier signals.[310] The pursuers alerted neighbors that their flight from the Mill Creeks would "embolden" the Yahi to retaliate by raiding the foothills.[311] It evidently did not occur to the pursuers that their invasion might also compel the Yahi to break with tradition and ally with Indian fighters from other tribes. The settlers, disappointed by the sortie's failure, decided a full Indian campaign was in order, although state funds would be necessary to keep volunteers in the field for an extended length of time.[312]

The Last Straw: The Killings of the Stevenson and Cronk Families

Near the end of April, in the area of Antelope Creek, northeast of Red Bluff, a settler pursuit party, searching for horse thieves, entered an Indian camp and killed fourteen Indians, including women and children. This shocked valley residents, who feared retaliation, and the *Beacon* called for cooler heads.[313] On May 3, attention returned to raids on the valley where a party of thirty Indians stole horses from a foothill ranch. Then, on Thursday, May 16, three miles southeast of Red Bluff, Indians struck again. The home of Colonel Edward A. Stevenson and his family was not a random pick. A newly announced candidate for the State Senate, Stevenson had been director of the Nome Lackee Reservation. Although in 1856, a white man had shot and wounded him when he refused to hand over an Indian woman, in 1858, he led a party in pursuit of Indians who had fled the reservation. In the ensuing fray, three Indians were killed and three other men, including a reservation employee, were injured. When Nome Lackee was slated for closure, Stevenson was assigned to search for a new reservation site near the Pit River.[314]

In the early morning, while Stevenson was away, his wife Harriet's helper, Tom, 10, a Pit River Indian, quietly left the house, locking the only door behind him and taking its key. The boy (or an accomplice) then set fire to the house and escaped to the countryside on horseback. The Stevensons' hired hand, Mr. Cronk, who, along with his own family, also lived in the house, managed to escape, but his wife, Catherine Cronk, their three children and Harriet Stevenson and her two small children burned to death. Because Tom was so young and the arson somewhat complicated, neighbors were convinced adult Indians, who had been seen loitering in the vicinity of the house for several days, had planned the attack and used the boy. The next day, two more attempts on nearby households were thwarted when barking dogs alerted the residents who warded off the attackers.

Few ranchers and farmers were frontiersmen and so most community men, although eager to pursue and avenge the Stevenson and Cronk deaths, were unsuited to the task. They were neither skilled nor rugged enough to crawl through brush, climb canyon walls and live off the land for weeks at a time in remote and unforgiving territory while outnumbered by hostile Indians. Their personal "arsenals" of pistols and rifles were unsuited to confront dozens of Mill Creeks, who could suddenly appear out of nowhere, attack and then vanish.

The Petition

In response to the Stephenson/Cronk killings, on May 21, 1859, valley men petitioned Gov. John B. Weller to fund an extended campaign by local pursuit parties. They described the farmers' dire situation: "The close proximity of the mountains to the settlements enables these Indians to make nightly excursions to the valley, committing their depredations upon the farms, driving off the stock and in a few hours, unless … pursued, [to] hide in their mountain fastnesses. The peculiar ruggedness of these mountains enables them to hide from the most vigilant to escape from the most wary and oftentimes to make good battle against the bravest."[315]

The petitioners characterized the raiders in terms similar to

Oliver Wozencraft's 1851 general description of the Sierra Nevada (Mountain Maidu) and Cascades tribes: "[They] are very different [from the Valley Indians] as they are athletic, wild, brave, independent, and measurably intractable beings; their physical and mental organization is far superior to those in the valleys. These Indians cannot be subdued by waging a war on them. The rugged face of the country forbids it, and the Indian can pursue this course without halt, whenever he will, and live upon the indigenous product of the soil, where the White ... cannot tread or transport his food."[316]

The petition asked Weller to dispatch help from the head of the State Militia, Adj. Gen. Kibbe, an Illinois Democrat. By 1852, his interest in California politics had already brought him, first, a membership in the new Assembly and, then, a stint as quartermaster. From there, he became the state's adjutant general in charge of the Militia.[317] In that capacity, he had recently authorized a state-backed volunteer unit, "Kibbe's Guards," to fight the Coast Range Indians.

Tehama County's petitioners were adamant: they did not want the governor to send soldiers. While Theodora Kroeber later dismissed this stipulation as a churlish insult to the Army (an ideological attitude reflective of her own mid-twentieth century), that was not the case. Residents respected military training and regulations, but they considered its protocols useless for surreptitious, extended canyon sorties only possible on foot or bellies.

Red Bluff businessman and foothills rancher J. Granville Doll, who had suffered losses in the raids, carried that petition, and a second similar one from farmers near Deer Creek, to Sacramento.[318] While community leaders' properties in villages like Tehama and towns like Red Bluff were safe from Indian raiders, their businesses depended on trade with rural farm customers who were vulnerable. According to Sherburne Cook, business leaders feared continued large-scale livestock thefts would lead growers and cattlemen to "abandon their farms and ranches."[319] In Texas, for example, settlers fleeing Indian attacks emptied whole counties. In Tehama County, therefore, a major objective was to restore public confidence.

The governor's response was mixed. He ignored the appeal

for state funds to back local volunteers. He did not send Adj. Gen. Kibbe, who was embroiled with legislators over allegations that his pursuers in Mendocino and Klamath counties used excessive force against Coast Range tribes. Instead, he turned to the Army, which sent Capt. Franklin Flint and Company A, Sixth Infantry.

The unit reached Red Bluff on May 26. In a meeting with town leaders the next day, Flint explained Brig. Gen. Clarke had not ordered him to deal with raids on the valley. Instead, he was to proceed to the Cascades east of Red Bluff, where his men would evaluate dangers in the area around Lassen Peak.[320] Travel there had become so risky that some stagecoach companies suspended service and freight wagons moved in long trains for protection. The region between the Lassen Peak headwaters of Butte Creek and those of the Pit River further north provided a base for raiders made up of Pit Rivers, Hat Creeks, Yahi and renegades from other tribes.[321]

Clarke defined Capt. Flint's mission at Lassen Peak: "You will take energetic measures to secure them [violent Mountain Indians] and, as before instructed, deliver them up to the civil authority."[322] He also prohibited the soldiers from any military engagement with Indians "until open war is declared by competent authority."[323] In other words, the Army ordered Company A to operate only in the mountainous part of Tehama County where Flint's company was to *arrest*, not kill, hostile Indians. Experience had made the Army leery: again and again, troops had responded to settlers' calls for help, only to find the accused Indians had acted in self-defense against the very settlers who demanded military protection.[324] Flint had seen examples of that while on recent duty in the Coast Range. However, his compliance with any orders was suspended because, within days of Company A's arrival in Red Bluff, one soldier after another was stricken with "chills and fever"—malaria—the bane of valley residents. The troops were in no condition to head into hostile territory.

While foothill residents were dumbfounded to learn that, while Capt. Flint expressed his own willingness to do all he could to protect settlers, he emphasized that the governor had issued orders not only preventing his men from initiating violent confrontations with Indians, but also dismissing their pleas to fund local volunteers.[325] Residents, understanding his orders were those of his superior, continued to treat him with respect. However, they remained determined to protect their foothill farms against Mountain Indian raids. As a courtesy, they requested Flint's "permission" to appeal again for funding to hire local volunteers. Subsequent actions made it clear they considered his opinion irrelevant.

On May 29, Tehama County merchants, artisans and farmers gathered at James Mayhew's Crossing, a stagecoach stop in the Deer Creek Canyon foothills, between Bidwell's ranch and the village of Tehama, the farmers' commercial center. They were on high alert because Mill Creeks were setting what appeared to be small warning fires between Mill Creek and Deer Creek canyons, a six-mile expanse of foothills east of the Sacramento River. Farmers "got the message": with hay crops drying, wheat crops next to dry for summer harvest and visions of fire racing across the fields, the threat of bankruptcies was paramount.[326] The April sortie's failure and the governor's refusal to fund volunteers left residents to defend themselves. Farmers raised money on their own for a second local pursuit party: "their only hope to protect their lives and property."[327]

Tehama County attendees in the Mayhew's Crossing meeting drafted an appeal to Gov. Weller to reinforce their May 15 petition for the state to fund a volunteer pursuit party. A committee reviewed the lengthy draft meant to impress on him the personal dangers and financial losses valley settlers faced from raids. The writers explained that, because standard military training and protocol were not suited to sorties in the area's rocky canyons, it was imperative that local men, familiar with and capable of navigating its unique topography, conduct the raids. The men they had in mind were the local Indian pursuers who had just made the most recent attempt. Doll also carried to the governor a letter from farmer J. C. Bradley describing the plight of foothill farmers: "On Friday night the house of Mr. Seth Hooker was burned to the ground with all the household furniture, provisions that he owned. Last night they [Indians] were prowling around my house and attempted to steal my horse. On Saturday evening they were at Mr. Hickman's attempting to steal his horses. Since last Friday night we have been compelled to guard our houses and property all night for the security of our families, as the only means of safety. Our harvest is now so close and in fact our haying has commenced and it is impossible to pursue them into the mountains without irreparable loss."[328] On June 2, the governor replied that, if Company A's efforts proved ineffective, he would provide additional assistance.[329]

A Local Pursuit Campaign Takes Shape

Attendees at the Mayhew's Crossing meeting issued a plea to valley employers to fire "domestic Indians."[330] Their attention was even more keen that day because an armed guard had just repelled a suspected Indian raid on Mayhew's stagecoach stop. The men raised about $4,000 among themselves and their neighbors to cover wages, supplies and bounty money for a volunteer private pursuit party to conduct a two-month sortie against the Indian raiders.

But the ranchers were suspicious about the motives of men who would volunteer for such a dangerous job. To collect the bounty money, the settlers demanded the men return with "scalps" or "some other satisfactory evidence they had killed [Indians]."[331] (Scalping, common among the Mountain Indians, was already being adopted by some Tehama County settlers.) Captains of pursuit parties had first choice and could take all the scalps, but probably shared at least some of the bounty. Scalps with long black hair dangled from saddles, representing the pursuers' stature and bravado as Indian killers.

Tehama County leaders calculated that additional state funding could extend their two-month sortie by one month. The group of men selected for the sortie were referred to as "the Breckenridge party," "the valiant party of volunteers" and other similar descriptions. Here they will be referred to as the Tehama Volunteers or the Volunteers.

Capt. Flint attended the Mayhew's Crossing meeting. Afterward, he and his soldiers rode east to survey the entry to Deer Creek Canyon. According to Robert Anderson, when Mill Creeks revealed themselves along the cliff tops, well out of rifle range, the soldiers pulled back and headed for their Red Bluff camp.[332]

Anderson and his neighbor, Harmon "Hi" Good, were veterans of the April sortie and played key roles in other Indian pursuits through 1865. Anderson's later book recording their experiences contributed to this account. After Anderson's 1857 arrival in Northern California, he and his partner, Joseph Rountree, had cabins about a mile-and-a-half from Good's place where Deer Creek enters the Sacramento Valley foothills. Good, who arrived in 1855, had clashed with Indians on his journey west and in Tehama County, where some of his livestock was stolen.

Within a year of their meeting, Anderson and Good, both in their early twenties, had committed themselves to learn how to "outplay the savages at their own game."[333] They, and allies like John Breckenridge, Bully Bowman, Jack Spaulding and George Carter, wanted to do away with "seat-of-the-pants" sorties. Instead they wanted to execute disciplined, well-planned offensives that would take the war to their enemies' own turf.

By spring 1859, no matter the weather, Good, Anderson and their partners explored Mill Creek and Deer Creek canyons, where they watched for clues to Indian messaging and closely observed terrain, game, weapons, cave locations and tribal identifications.[334] They learned that when they could not make it back to their camp for provisions, a pinch of sugar from their pouches sweetened manzanita berries enough to quiet their hunger. With the help of experienced frontiersmen such as Obe Field and Breckenridge, they refined their scouting and tracking skills. They became adept at moving and camping under cover, and learned to travel at night and sleep by day.[335] They copied the Mill Creeks' early morning attacks when there was just enough light to shoot at groggy targets. They learned where best to ford creeks and how to steel themselves against frigid mountain streams, in which slick stones slowed their crossings and icy water nearly paralyzed their legs and feet. Good and Anderson observed how Indians handled their bows to project arrows accurately at high speed with extreme accuracy and calculated how conditions, such as distance and incline, affected the arrows' flight and accuracy. While others were only intermittent pursuers, Good and Anderson became mainstays. Both respected their adversaries' fighting ability and never relaxed their vigilance.

Hi Good and Robert Anderson, young Tehama County farmers who became skilled trackers and organizers of numerous Mountain Indian pursuits.

Hi Good's role comes into fullest view through Anderson's memoir, letters, other public documents and press items. The two men became close friends, trading roles as tracker, scout and lookout. Later Butte County pursuer Simeon Moak would remember Good as "one of the best Indian trackers in Northern California," "a great Indian trailer."[336] While Good and Anderson sometimes disagreed on issues like whether to leave or remove Indian women, their intense self-training, self-discipline and coordinated teamwork with other intermittent pursuers produced the settlers' first serious challenges to the Mill Creeks. More and more, instead of safely escaping quick encounters with sleepy settlers, canyon raiders now faced retaliations from pugnacious, fit white men who had adopted Indian tactics as their own.

Anderson's and Good's experience with Mill Creeks qualified them to assess the suitability of Capt. Flint and his men. They noted the pains the soldiers took to camp according to standard regulations unsuited to war on foot in the canyons. They conceded the fully provisioned company of well-mounted marksmen would be formidable against the Sioux or Lakota, but were adamant that regular soldiers had no chance against mountain and canyon Indian raiders because military equipment, reliance on horses, protocols and conventional maneuvers were impediments to canyon foot pursuits against fighters they could rarely see, let alone approach. Breckenridge, Good, Anderson and their cohorts considered themselves the only white men who, on their own and with no backup, could find, kill or at least identify what tribes had joined the recent Mill Creek raiding parties. Area residents understood most of these foothill farmers were still raw talent with a rocky record from their just completed first campaign, but they were the best the area could come up with for such grueling work.

Captain Flint and Company A Leave for Lassen Peak

By mid-June, enough of Capt. Franklin Flint's men were in remission from malaria that he ordered Company A to Lassen Peak. As they rode off from Red Bluff on June 16, farmers in town were still discussing the latest incursions: those foothill fires set in May between Mill and Deer creeks.

As Company A headed toward Lassen Peak, Hat Creeks and Pit Rivers watching them ride up the public road must have recalled Capt. George Crook's soldiers during his 1857 Pit River expedition. In contrast, it appeared the present soldiers were reserving their shots for target practices or game rather than Indians. Settler flight from the mountains for the safety of the valley was credited as a "win" for the Indians. Reaching Red Bluff, the settlers reported that "Indians followed [the soldiers] all the way up and back, but at a respectful distance. ... The night the soldiers were encamped at [Dr. Inskeep's] mill the Indians were prowling around the premises watching for a chance to attack."[337]

The Indians decided not to provoke the soldiers, preserving their fighters for another opportunity with the advantage of surprise, favorable terrain and numbers. While Kibbe did not acknowledge the Mountain Indians' savvy in lying low, he understood this was a calculated tactic rather than cowardice, recalling other raids on soldiers' camps, during which they displayed no fear of death, capture or punishment.[338] In 1857, Capt. Judah similarly noted both the Cascade Indians' stealth and aggressive posture in conflicts in the Lassen area. He, like Capt. Michael Morgan before him and Flint and Lt. Archibald Harrison after him, was eager for a transfer out of the area.[339]

A year earlier, in 1858, Dr. Inskeep had sent alarms to the valley about Indian thefts around his mill, apparently hoping Capt. Morgan, then on duty at the Nome Lackee Reservation, would ride out to help him. Morgan complained that any mischief around Lassen Peak was more likely made by "Mexicans or by white men as bad as" the complainers.[340] Although Morgan discounted Inskeep's complaints on the grounds that he had not suffered any losses, a twenty-man unit was sent out but encountered no hostile Indians.

When Flint's company stopped at Inskeep's mill, they learned Mill Creeks had just scalped and slit the throat of "bull puncher" William Patrick, 28, who "considered Indians his particular friends."[341] He had been delivering hay to Inskeep's place from his farm in Cold Springs Valley just south of the Deer Creek headwaters, a magnet area for fugitive and displaced Indians. The Indians hid Patrick's body in the brush, pushed his wagon over a cliff and left with his team. The soldiers also learned that the Indians had chased and shot at a man named Judd the same day. The Indians withdrew when Judd neared Inskeep's mill, busy with workers and customers.[342] Flint did not initiate a pursuit.

Dr. Inskeep, familiar with Pit Rivers and Hat Creeks throughout the Lassen Peak area, had just returned to his Antelope mill from trapping near Lassen Butte. He was not surprised that Flint was aware Indians were stationed along and above the roads and trails on which his company had traveled. Inskeep informed the captain that Indians from diverse tribes told him they planned to "combine" and take on the Whites "in a general battle."[343] It was well-known in the area that the Mountain tribes "were exceedingly expert in the exchange of telegraphic signals, by which they could communicate between distant portions of the same tribe, the approach and number of an invading force ... [and] the direction of march indicated."[344] Mountain residents expected the soldiers to stand up against the Indians, but Flint explained this trip was only to reconnoiter the area for his report to headquarters.

After one day there, assuring the people his unit would return for the rest of the summer, Flint and his company arrived in Red Bluff on June 19. There, his men convalesced and fought new onsets of malaria. In his report, Flint discounted the seriousness of Indian threats to settlers around Lassen Peak. He estimated that only thirty to forty Hat Creeks were dangerous; of course, settlers would not have considered his estimate reassuring.[345]

In late June, Flint and his men, as promised, returned to set up camp near Inskeep's mill.[346] By the end of August, however, new onsets of sickness felled forty-eight of the company's sixty men, requiring another return to Red Bluff for treatment, with Lt. Archibald Harrison's unit filling in for them at Lassen Peak. Within a month, Flint's men returned and stayed until winter set in—the end of the Indian fighting season. While the soldiers were not active in pursuits, their presence offered a measure of calm over that mountainous area of Tehama County. But their military focus so far northeast meant they were of no help to foothill residents at risk to other Indian raiders out of Deer Creek and Mill Creek canyons.[347]

The Tehama Volunteers' Tehama County Campaign

In mid-June, disappointment at Flint's restraint in the mountains and the governor's lack of concern for foothill farmers led them to raise more money and send the new unit, Tehama Volunteers, into the canyons, this time for a two-month campaign.[348] While their April sortie had failed, the settlers hoped this party would benefit from the information the earlier pursuers had gained about the Mill Creeks' tactics and territory. According to press accounts, of particular credit to the Volunteers, in the thinking of their neighbors, was their willingness to reenter the deep, dangerous canyons, even though the Indians had previously run them out of there.

Breckenridge, a leader in the April sortie, accepted that role again in the second one. Little is known about him, but members of pursuit parties must have respected his skills and judgment because they elected him their captain twice. The editor of the *Red Bluff Beacon* spoke of him with respect.[349] Although Anderson's memoir infers reluctance to credit Breckenridge's leadership in pursuits, he acknowledged he was "very deliberate in his movements ... [and was] possessed of great strength."[350] Breckenridge could handle himself in dangerous situations, was at home in harsh terrain and his thinking in the wild was strategic. However, Robert Anderson sometimes resented him and once left him exposed to great jeopardy: after Breckenridge accidentally fired his gun in a mountain camp and then got into hand-to-hand combat with an Indian captive who was his match, Anderson refused to let the other Volunteers rescue him; he narrowly prevailed. Breckenridge's party of nine men included Ohioan Hi Good.

AWARE THE GOVERNOR WAS RELUCTANT to back the Tehama Volunteers and having learned they were about to leave for the canyons on a private Indian pursuit, Kibbe was determined not to repeat his mistake in Klamath and Mendocino counties where he unwittingly sent out abusive local men as pursuers. This time he dispatched Army Captain William Burns, "a renowned Indian fighter," to assess the men's character and fighting skills.[351] Understanding a favorable review from Burns would help the Volunteers secure the funding they needed for a longer campaign, Breckenridge stood aside as captain in favor of Burns.

On June 15, the Volunteers entered the canyon on foot with pack mules carrying their food and ammunition. One destination was the Antelope lumber mill, whose owner, E. W. Inskeep, was the leading complainant.

While canyon Indians had not been fearful previously when they watched Flint's troops enter and quitely exit Deer Creek Canyon, this approach of a dozen armed Tehama Volunteers, some of whom had combed their territory over the past year-and-a-half, could present a challenge.[352] From their positions along the cliffs, Indians could also see to the northwest, across the Sacramento River, heavy smoke rising from flames consuming the village of Tehama. By dusk, the Volunteers were deep in the canyon.

It is remarkable how much ground these men gained within days of leaving the valley's foothills. According to Anderson, it was not unusual to trail their quarry for ten to twelve hours, as light permitted; their fast pace was aided by their ability to ignore the winding routes of roads and trails, instead crossing the ridges "as the bird flies."[353] They had, by now, learned how to "read" piles of stones: their number stacked represented how many ridges away from the pile the Indians planned to rendezvous. Only when the Volunteers neared the rendezvous site did they slow down "to work" a path to it. Anderson and Good were considered to be the settler's most expert trackers.

The Volunteers had been in the canyon a short time when Burns fell sick and returned to Red Bluff. In his place, the pursuers again elected Breckenridge captain. His men included, in addition to Good and Anderson, William Simmons, John Martin, John McCord, "Slim" and "— Cartin" [possibly George Carter] and about four others. While their makeup and numbers would shift over time, the Tehama Volunteers were characterized by remarkable physical strength, endurance, marksmanship, knowledge of Deer Creeks' and Mill Creeks' terrain and determination to kill any male Indian "of age" believed to be dangerous.

However, at an early point in this campaign, without informing their backers, their actions revealed their own intentions. They postponed their assignment to kill Indians and instead decided to track a likely war party to determine whether the members were Butte Creeks who had joined Mill Creek parties, which, backed by miners, were suspected of raiding Tehama County farms.

The Volunteers, deep in Mill Creek Canyon, eventually spotted signs of an Indian camp and stopped for the night some distance from it. They knew those Indians were aware of them when sporadic rifle shots landed in their vicinity during the night. They suspected they had come upon a raiding party because they believed those were the Indians who used guns. The next morning they found the empty camp of about a dozen Indians and set out to follow, allowing one to two days' distance. Here was their opportunity to attack them than to find out who the men were. Were they Butte Creeks? The Indian party, observing tradition, avoided group hostilities by moving on, leading their pursuers across Lassen Peak in the direction of the Pit River, territory of their fierce rivals. On approaching it and realizing their pursuers continued on their path, the Indians decided not to cross, but instead circled back toward the headwaters of Deer and Mill creeks.[354] The Volunteers also, therefore, circled back south but they diverted in the direction of Inskeep's mill. On the basis of their subsequent actions, it appears the Volunteers wanted to know whether any of the Indians would head for Mountain Maidu territory; if so, it would confirm their suspicions that that tribe's Butte Creeks had joined Mill Creek raiding parties.

Confident they could later pick up their tracking of the large party of Indians, the Volunteers turned off at Inskeep's mill on June 19. Their support unit had moved to a pre-arranged site they had been unable to reach.[355] Ordinarily, they would have hunted game, but this time they arrived at the mill "out of sorts" and "demanded" the mill workers fix them a meal.[356] Dr. Inskeep repeated to them what he had just told Flint: all the tribesmen he met while hunting spoke of a pending attack on settlers.[357]

The Volunteers learned the Indian party they were tracking evidently "sent them a message." At no point did the war party turn back and attack the Volunteers. Instead, they attempted to intimidate them by killing wagon driver William Patrick and their attempt on Judd. The Volunteers held to their first priority: to learn the Indians' destination and thus their identity. According to an ambiguous remark by Anderson, "Believing the [Mill Creek] Indians were reinforced not only by miners, but also by Butte Creeks, we used every precaution in trailing them."[358] After a day at the mill, the Volunteers picked up the Indians' tracks again and moved in tandem with them.

AFTER THE TEHAMA VOLUNTEERS LEFT Inskeep's mill, their course from June 20 through July 27 is unclear. Anderson treats their actions between the stop at Inskeep's mill and their entry into Butte County as linear. However, according to a *Beacon* item, on June 26 they had set up a camp between the Mill Creek and Deer Creek headwaters. Because Anderson later spoke about knowledge of Butte Creeks in Cold Springs, the same location they returned to for a later attack, that was likely the next stop to which the Indian party led them after turning south from the Pit River. In Cold Springs Valley the Indian men in the party scattered and melded into the multiple camps of mixed tribal Indians that lined the banks of the valley's creeks and lakes. The Volunteers stayed near the hamlet of Cold Springs for almost a month, gambling that the twelve Indians they were tracking would regroup and leave for their nearby tribelet rancherias. If members of the Indian party returned to Deer or Mill creeks, they were likely Yahi. However, if any crossed into Butte County—Mountain Maidu territory—most likely they were Butte Creeks whom the miners were furnishing with weapons as encouragement to raid Tehama County farms. The local white community, anxious over the death of Patrick and shooting of Judd, was relieved to have the well-armed Volunteers camped in their vicinity.

Adding to evidence for the Volunteers secret tracking was Breckenridge's conduct. On June 26, he returned to the burned village of Tehama and the hamlet of Mayhew's Crossing for provisions. He delivered reports to the Volunteers' backers and checked on his and his colleagues' property, vulnerable to Indian retaliation. When the *Red Bluff Beacon*'s editor asked for information about Indians they had killed, Breckenridge said they hadn't seen Indians, but he assured the editor they would by the end of the summer.[359] Valley backers, believing the Volunteers' sole mission was to kill Indians, would not have understood camping, surrounded by desperate and angry Mountain Indians, in the relative comfort of a cool mountain community, waiting for certain Indians to move out.

The State Launches a Volunteer Pursuit Campaign

Gen. Kibbe was making regular stops in Red Bluff on his way to the Coast Range to monitor units of local Indian fighters there. Because those companies had been abusing Indians, he had become skeptical about backing independent local Indian pursuit parties. He used his stays in Red Bluff, therefore, to test the validity of the claims Tehama County settlers made in their petitions to the governor for state funding for an extended campaign by local Indian pursuit parties. If he found a new campaign was justified in the Cascades and Sierra Nevada, he wanted it led by professional officers from the California Volunteers whom he would personally command. In Red Bluff, allegations that Mountain Maidu's Butte Creeks participated in Tehama County raids led Kibbe to include Butte County in the scope of a possible campaign.

Kibbe knew Gov. Weller would be hard to convince because the State Legislature was reluctant to allocate money for Indian pursuits, and federal funds were also hard to come by. When Edward Beale became Indian Superintendent for California in 1852, he focused federal expenditures on southern California, the location of most cattle ranches with which the agency contracted to feed the state's Indians, and he discounted reports about the clashes between Northern California Indians and settlers.[360]

On the other hand, the governor could not ignore the losses ranchers suffered from Indian raids. By the late 1850s, raids had cost settlers about $150,000 (over $4 million in 2016) and, in Tehama County alone, raiders had killed at least twenty-five white men, three farm wives and four children. Indian lives lost and the decimation of their economy were ignored. In the end, Kibbe's reports to the governor about the settler losses in Tehama County and the supposed connection of Butte County's Butte Creeks to raids there reinforced the credibility of the local petitions for state help. With Kibbe's support, the governor deemed Tehama and Butte counties qualified as priorities meriting state intervention.

By contrast, the Army had dispatched Flint's unit to address Tehama County raids under useless orders, such as arresting hostile Indians. Gov. Weller ordered Kibbe to recruit local volunteers but refused to fund the Tehama Volunteers, still in the canyons. However, he did not specifically exclude Breckenridge or his men. Kibbe was to personally command all the volunteers to assure their proper conduct.

While Kibbe was much criticized for his recent experience with abusive volunteers in the Coastal Range, he was an expert in the use of volunteer fighters. In his 1856 appeal to Washington,

D.C., for Indian fighting funds, he praised volunteers who fought "well armed, bold, and daring warriors, pursuing a system of warfare which is little understood by our regular [U.S. Army] troops."[361] Only experienced local volunteers understood California's mountain terrain and had at least some idea of Indian culture. In such situations, Kibbe said, volunteers had proved more successful and cost effective than regular troops.[362]

In the Coast Range, the Army had some history of negotiations between settlers and Indians. By contrast, Capt. Flint and Lt. Harrison would not or could not conduct successful negotiations in the Sierra Nevada-Cascade ranges. In addition, unlike their predecessor Capt. Henry Judah, Flint and Harrison had not served long in these mountains and did not believe white miners' complicity with Indian raiders was a significant factor in valley raids.

Now that valley residents had organized their own pursuit party—the Tehama Volunteers—and Gov. Weller had ordered a state campaign against Indian raids, residents' fears and frustration, which had sometimes spiraled into calls for extermination of the Indians, subsided. The governor, drawing on funds from bonds the Legislature issued in 1857, ordered "the suppression of Indian hostilities," not through violent confrontations and killings, but through the collection and removal of Hat Creeks, Pit Rivers and Mountain Maidu to reservations. However, Kibbe explained to Red Bluff citizens he would require another month-and-a-half to organize the removal campaign because resources were still committed to campaigns in Mendocino and Klamath counties.[363] On July 11, Kibbe wrote Flint from Red Bluff, inquiring whether his unit, although still under Army command, would be willing to recommend to his superiors a share of command with California Militia officers for the Indian removal.[364] Kibbe sent the governor Flint's response: "I have no reliable means of judging of the number of hostile Indians in this vicinity. The Country between Butte and Mill Creeks and as far back as Antelope Mills has been thoroughly examined by various detachments of my company and thus far neither Indians nor Agents have been met with ... I consider [my unit] and the orders I have received as sufficient to check the incursions of any Indians in this vicinity."[365] He ignored the Sacramento Valley.

Meanwhile, on July 20, when Kibbe reached Red Bluff, returning from the Coast Range, another of several stops there that summer, he fell ill. As soon as he rallied, he left for Lassen Peak. There, when he met with Lt. Harrison, the officer replacing Flint who was on sick leave, they discussed the Army's orders that its units stand back from a State Militia removal campaign. While the presence of soldiers in that area had created a modicum of peace, Kibbe was struck by how resistant "Federal soldiers" were to an expansion of their role, particularly to address valley raids.[366] While in the hamlet of Antelope, near Lassen Peak, he met with Inskeep and others, whose fear of hostile Indians in their vicinity presented a stark contrast to the dismissal of any Indian problems by Flint and Harrison. Kibbe's Indian removal preparations indicate he and the governor lacked confidence in the Army officers' observations.

While Kibbe concluded both mountain and valley settlers had legitimate needs for state help, he recognized that members of most Mountain tribes, like those of most Valley tribes, were peaceful. He estimated that the number of principal raiders across the mountains and the valley were forty-five to one hundred men from several tribes. Although adversaries, he respected them: "They are probably the largest, most athletic, and healthy race" of Indians in California.[367] After leaving the Cascade mountains and stopping in Red Bluff, he went to Mendocino County, this time not only to check on his volunteer units, but also to determine whether the Nome Cult Reservation in Round Valley could accommodate hundreds of Indians from Butte and Tehama counties.[368]

The Tehama Volunteers' Butte County Campaign

The Volunteers waited near the hamlet of Cold Springs until July 26 when the Mill Creeks they had tracked there left the Indian camps. That day, as the Volunteers got underway, they killed another party of four Indians and a white man. Anderson later inferred this fight was a random act, not one against Mill Creeks or Butte Creeks. The Volunteers despised white men associating with Indians, so the white man's presence may have infuriated them. Exercising his prerogative as captain, Breckenridge claimed the right to scalp him.³⁶⁹

The Indian party they were tracking led them into Butte County approximately at the Cohasset Ridge: their gateway to gold country and the Mountain Maidu's rancherias. The Indians' return to their tribal territory had justified the Volunteers' lengthy tracking.

The Volunteers' decision to follow the Indian party there caught the attention of writer Theodora Kroeber, who was puzzled by it. She speculated they had advanced through the Lassen Peak area without killing Indians because they did not want to confront the "dangerous Indians," the Yahi's Mill Creeks, whom she asserted were the sole raiders on the foothill farms in Tehama County. She declared the Volunteers "felt they must find *some* Indians to kill, even if they could not catch any Mill Creeks."³⁷⁰ When she declared they veered off into gold mining country to scalp-hunt for bounty money among the "easy-going" Mountain Maidu, she confused the more aggressive Mountain Maidu with the peaceful Valley Maidu. The Volunteers' actions throughout this sortie reveal they understood the Mountain Maidu were hungry and homeless people who depended on their Butte Creek warriors for food and protection, and that they were up against adversaries possibly backed by Butte County miners.

When Robert Anderson recalled the Indian party headed straight into "Butte Creek country," he was referring to Butte Creeks, the warriors.³⁷¹ Anderson's description of his party's tracking was consistent with the thinking of their fellow farmers in Tehama County: "We had always felt certain that the Mill Creeks procured arms and ammunition through friendly relations with Whites...."³⁷² Collusion between miners and Butte Creeks in raids out of Deer Creek canyon was plausible to Tehama County residents because, while the Yahi had little or no contact with Whites, Mountain Maidu and their Butte Creeks worked for or lived in close proximity to gold miners.

When the Indian party continued across Keefer Ridge in the foothills northeast of Chico, the Volunteers stayed behind for a brief respite near M. T. King's Vermont mill above the ranch headquarters of James Keefer, who ran a stagecoach station on the Oroville-Shasta Road, as well as a lumber mill and grist mills in the foothills along Rock Creek.³⁷³

Irvin Smith and a fellow gold miner at their Butte Creek camp.

Late on July 26, leaving some men on guard, Anderson and others set off for Keefer's store on the Oroville-Shasta Road and then to Chico, about nine miles away in the valley, for provisions. From there, they canvassed the Butte County foothills where they gleaned information about Mountain Maidu and the terrain from Rock Creek to Butte Creek and the Feather River. The farmers they talked to, who lived in close proximity to Mountain Maidu rancherias, welcomed their arrival because all they had to rely on for protection from raids was the fragile truce between the miners and Indians.

Settlers between Deer Creek Ridge and Chico shared their suspicions about Butte Creeks raiding with Mill Creeks and having backing from miners. According to Indian pursuer Crowder, who lived near Rock Creek: "It was a common remark among settlers that the Mill Creek Indians were receiving aid from either the Butte Creeks or miners, or both, on Butte Creek and I think those suspicions were well-founded."[374] Crowder cited a quarrel he overheard between Rock Creek farmer Ed Bryson and a miner. Their exchange, he said, "satisfied me that some of the miners on Butte Creek were furnishing the Mill Creeks with arms and ammunition."[375]

Referring to Butte Creeks who had raided his ranch until 1857, John Bidwell noted, "Even the miners would sometimes pretend to be friendly to the [Mountain Maidu] Indians and unfriendly to me, because they were afraid of [Butte Creek] Indians whom the miners knew disliked me."[376]

The miners' attitude toward the Volunteers' arrival at King's Vermont mill was a different matter. Anderson later recalled that, during their quick stop in Chico, the Volunteers received an

Butte Creek was a principal drainage, choice gold mining site and the location of clashes between miners and Mountain Maidu. Valley Maidu and settlers referred to warriors from the Mountain Maidu tribelets as Butte Creeks until the 1860s when they had merged with Mill Creeks.

anonymous letter claiming fifteen miners "would be waiting for us if we persisted in the pursuit."[377] The timing and source of this warning supported the pursuers' suspicions that Butte Creeks were raiding in Tehama County and that this conflict was also between farmers and miners. The warning also was direct evidence that the Indians they had pursued were English speakers who went directly to the miners to complain. The miners' prompt letter and the Indians' later actions suggest that between the truce, which reduced miners' hostility, and their backing, the Indians had counted on security against miners' retribution when they raided the valley from the mountains. But the white Volunteers' tracking of the Indian party suggested they might be white miners who were ignoring the truce and, so, were betraying their trust.

The Forest Ranch Attack

In response to the threat in the anonymous letter, by July 27, the Volunteers added Robert Anderson's brother Jack and another man to their ranks. Butte County settlers were alarmed that the Indian-set fires, initially between Mill and Deer creeks, were now being ignited near Rock and Mud creeks northeast of Bidwell's ranch. This endangered the dried wheat crop under harvest.

Breckenridge, Anderson, Good and their cohorts filled the gap Wozencraft had noted in 1851: "There are but few of the Caucasian race who can endure the native men's hardships and privations … and *none* who can chase them down."[378] Theodora Kroeber, although a critic of the Indian pursuers, conceded that Anderson and Good were "large, shrewd, and fearless" and that both "were natural trackers and scouts…."[379] They and their cohorts were now free from the constraints of surveillance. They were ready to attack their targets.

The tracks the Volunteers followed from Keefer's Ridge led them across a steep section of Chico Creek Canyon and, from there, "very close to" an established trail that approached Forks of Butte, a mining town of three hundred settlers on Butte Creek.[380] The trail took them to the Butte Creek Ridge above Forks of Butte and then to an Indian camp near Forest Ranch where the tracks merged with those created by a large group of sleeping individuals they observed. It was comprised of Indians, who were gold mine workers, friends and family members. It had become common practice for Butte Creeks in flight "to intermix with those who have the confidence of the Whites, and by so doing to avoid detection."[381] Concluding that was the case here, the Volunteers pulled back, hid themselves and waited out the night.

The next day, July 28, as the Volunteers approached the camp before dawn, they killed and scalped an Indian they considered a likely scout. They spread out around the perimeter of the camp at intervals of seventy feet and fired on the sleeping occupants as they struggled awake, staggered to their feet and fled through the circle of shooters and into the forest.

Anderson considered the attack successful but flawed. First, he used his six-shooter and an inaccurate muzzle loader that could not rapidly deliver successive shots. Second, the Indians' defensive actions at Forest Ranch explain, in part, why the death toll was far less than the forty Anderson recalled later. Indians who understood English heard Good, following Breckenridge's orders, call out to the pursuit party not to shoot the women or children. This allowed the men to shield themselves behind women or grab children for cover—or to rescue them—as they all fled. It was later confirmed that the "firm" death count was about five men and one or two women and two children whose bodies they found lying over dead men.[382]

After the attack, Breckenridge scalped the second white man killed in this campaign. He was Malo Joe, a "Butte Creek squaw man" or "White Indian," whom Volunteers shot four or five times.[383] By the end of August, when the campaign ended, Breckenridge would claim that over the entire summer campaign, the party killed twenty-nine Indians.

When Breckenridge and his men went through the camp, they found dishes, sugar, flour and $60 to $70 in cash. They also found a half dozen six-shooters, as well as rifles and ammunition. Anderson's own booty was three six-shooters he found on one corpse. Since Indians still preferred bows and arrows for hunting game, the men concluded these guns belonged to the Butte Creeks who had joined Mill Creeks in settler attacks. The Butte County Grand Jury's annual report that year concluded

Indian crimes were traceable to white men who supplied them with rifles.

While the Volunteers were returning from Forest Ranch to camp near Vermont mill on July 28, erroneous news that Butte Creeks had killed several Volunteers in the Forest Ranch attack reached the valley. In response, Rock Creek rancher Conrad Garner (whose horse had won the 1852 race at Bidwell's ranch) organized a pursuit party to avenge the killings. For Garner, an Illinois native who enjoyed good relations with his neighbors, Indian raids were always a possibility and now seemed imminent.[384] He recruited fifteen Butte County men, including cowboys Simeon Moak and Pleasant Guynn and Chico wainwright (wagon builder and repairer) Daniel Sutherland.[385]

The Volunteers no sooner set up camp at the mill than they saw Perry McIntosh, a friend of Anderson, running toward them, yelling for help. He and farmer William Lindsey were driving a wagon up Cohasset Road to pick up a load of posts and rails from Keefer's mill. When arrows struck Lindsey, who collapsed, McIntosh took off. The Volunteers made an unsuccessful pursuit and Lindsey eventually recovered. Breckenridge and Anderson considered the attack retribution by the Indians they had just fought while returning from Forest Ranch to Keefer Ridge.[386] Anderson faulted Breckenridge for rejecting his suggestion they set up patrols along Cohasset Road to protect such travelers.

The rumor about dead Volunteers at Forest Ranch had been scotched by the time Garner and his recruits met up with them. However, the Volunteers told them that during their return from Forest Ranch, Indians and others the Volunteers thought "weren't Indians" watched them from the north wall of Chico Canyon.[387] They also said they saw Indian target practice spots along the way and told about dodging close-hitting bullets from six to seven pursuers they thought were Butte Creeks who had escaped their Forest Ranch attack. The use of rifles supported the Volunteers' suspicion that miners had supplied them to the raiders. Indians also stole weapons and were becoming more skilled in their use of rifles and pistols. Anderson remarked the best had reached the proficiency of an average white man.[388]

Breckenridge accepted the offers from Garner and several of his men to join the Tehama Volunteers' pursuit party, a valuable opportunity for the Butte County men to learn the tracking and offensive and defensive methods the Volunteers had perfected. The party sent word to Red Bluff they were returning home by way of Cold Springs, where they had unfinished business, having disappointed some settlers by not making an earlier planned raid there.

On July 31, they made what they intended to be a quick detour to the Forest Ranch Indian camp to check whether any Butte Creeks had shown up. While on the night of their attack they had tracked some to Forest Ranch, the larger party they tracked dispersed. The few Indians collecting remains on the raid site, upon seeing them, fled toward Forks of Butte. Intrigued, the Volunteers postponed their return to Cold Springs to look for more of the original party of Butte Creeks and followed these Indians who headed for the hamlet at Butte Creek.[389]

The Volunteers were probably unaware that right after they left their campsite near the Vermont mill to check on Forest Ranch, Butte Creeks burned down that mill, after which owner M. T. King moved his family to Mayhew's Crossing. Anderson would learn that the same night Indians had burned down his and Rountree's cabins and stole their livestock. In light of the random fires threatening wheat crops and because word of the mill arson followed news of the clash at Forest Ranch, Rock Creek and foothill families gathered together in guarded cabins ("forts") or, like the Sadoruses, moved closer to the Sacramento River. Yet another blaze took place that same day: Dr. Inskeep watched from the cover of a haystack as other Indians danced around as they burned down his Antelope house. (Inskeep moved to Cold Springs.) At this time, Kibbe was en route to Red Bluff to interview volunteers for the removal of Mountain Maidu, Hat Creeks, Pit Rivers and renegade Indians around Lassen Peak.[390]

As the Volunteers approached Forks of Butte, Breckenridge ordered his men to kill any suspicious Indians they encountered, but they were not to pursue those who entered cabins where miners might protect them. Whites and Indians could get away with killing in the wilderness because, as a practical matter, there was no way to prosecute remote murders. However, with law enforcement within reach of Forks of Butte, Volunteers could

Standoff

not kill Whites there, even those suspected of collaborating with hostile Indians.

Because Indians the Volunteers were following from Forest Ranch to Forks of Butte had alerted the village of their approach, they found the village seemingly "empty." However, at George Lovelock's general store, manager Richard Wallace, 52, was up front, while Indians crowded in the back room, hiding. Wallace dismissed Breckenridge's accusations that miners helped Indians who raided valley farms. Breckenridge, "not a pleasant man to have as an enemy," informed Wallace that his party had trailed armed Butte Creeks (whom he began calling Mill Creeks) to the Forest Ranch Indian camp. Breckenridge alleged miners sold rifles to these Mountain Maidu raiders who, with Mill Creeks or on their own, used them to kill Tehama County residents and destroy property such as cattle.[391]

In return, Wallace vented his rage at the Volunteers' attack on the Forest Ranch camp where his own Indian consort, the mother of his children, was injured.[392] According to Breckenridge's later account, by making this threat in the hearing of the Indians crowded in his back room, Wallace was demonstrating his allegiance to them. While the two men exchanged verbal blows in the front, in the back room Anderson was checking the wound of a man he had shot at Forest Ranch.

The extent of the anger the Volunteers encountered in Forks of Butte disconcerted them. Their Forest Ranch attack had aroused fury because some considered their actions unjust and many believed they threatened the fragile late-1850s truce with the Mountain Maidu. Miners were already alarmed because the local Indians considered the Forest Ranch attackers, not as a specific coterie of valley farmers, but rather "white men" in general. The Indians could not distinguish between white men coming "from the direction of the valley" and ever-changing white miners.[393] The Volunteers also learned that a miner had lodged accusations against their conduct in the *Red Bluff Beacon*, the newspaper their donors read. This and other letters are treated in another section of this chapter.

Faced with furious miners and the scrutiny of other skeptical Whites, the Volunteers had to, as Anderson put it, "straighten out affairs with the Indians of Butte Creek"[394] by demonstrating that the Butte Creeks who escaped them at Forest Ranch still remained around Forks of Butte.

After almost two weeks in the vicinity of Forks of Butte, the Volunteers finally narrowed their focus to seven well-armed Mountain Maidu there whom they considered Butte Creeks. When confronted, the suspects, trying to prove they were not connected to the raids, vowed they would hunt down and attack the Mill Creeks on their own with bows and arrows. Breckenridge accepted their proposal, but held their headman hostage pending the party's return. After the suspects departed, guards thwarted the headman's escape attempt.

When the accused Indians did not return, the Volunteers tracked them to a camp and brought them back to Forks of Butte. The men protested they had fought the raiders but had been defeated and, shifting the subject, offered to lead the Volunteers to the "hiding places of the renegades" among homeless Indians around the headwaters.[395] It must have struck the Volunteers that these Mountain Maidu were quite familiar with the Lassen Peak Indian camps, even though Butte Creek gold miners claimed the Indians were workers who did not travel and stayed "on the creek."[396] This time, several Volunteers accompanied the Butte Creek suspects, arranging to meet the rest of their party at the Sadorus place on Rock Creek. However, as the suspects and their escorts moved north, the Indians managed to flee. Anderson was convinced they had "escaped to join another party in Deer Creek [Canyon]."[397]

In late July they intended to resume tracking the party they suspected included Butte Creeks. On August 15, however, the Tehama Volunteers postponed heading home in order to return to Cold Springs. But, first, they agreed to punish Indians thought to have killed a settler in the Concow Valley sixteen miles east of the village of Tehama. Using the same method Breckenridge ordered at Forest Ranch, they surrounded the Indians' camp at intervals of about sixty feet and shot at those who tried to break through, killing nine.[398] Then they carried out the raid on Indians they had promised Cold Spring's white residents, but had postponed when waylaid by Forks of Butte residents on their detour there after checking on the Forest Ranch site of their raid. This last battle cost at least ten Indian lives.

As they were leaving Cold Springs Valley for home, on August 19 the Volunteers captured "Billie," a "dangerous and troublesome customer" who had earlier escaped during their "test" en route from Forks of Butte to the Sadorus place. Evidently a Mountain Maidu who lived among miners, the young man understood English and had taken an English name.[399] After Billie confessed twice to two questioners that he shot William Lindsey on Cohasset Road, Breckenridge killed him. A Volunteer killed another captive, the "Old Doctor," in an escape attempt. Likely he was the Yahi elder who, the previous winter, had crossed into Butte Creek territory to recruit fighters to join Mill Creek raiding parties. The "Old Doctor" put up a game fight against the odds in a running exchange of shots. According to Anderson, the series of encounters convinced Breckenridge that Butte Creeks played significant roles in valley raids.[400] By late 1859, having combed the canyons and the headwaters above, the Volunteers were finally able to recognize individual Mountain Maidu visible to them along Butte, Deer and Mill creeks.[401]

On August 21, valley farmers reported seeing Good and Anderson driving a wagon carrying thirteen Indian widows and children, survivors of the Volunteers' final campaign attack at Cold Springs. Anderson and Good delivered the survivors to Yumalacca, a temporary reservation east of the Sacramento River in southwestern Tehama County. From there, they headed for their farms on Deer Creek.[402]

War of Words

It is unclear when the returning Volunteers learned the extent of the newspaper coverage of their Forest Ranch attack, which started with the earlier mentioned anonymous Forks of Butte miner's letter to the *Butte Record*, reproaching their conduct. A similarly anonymous letter written on August 20, appeared, by style and content, to be from a different Forks of Butte writer. One author challenged anyone to identify men in Forks of Butte keeping Indian women. Both authors conceded that there were dangerous Indians in the Forest Ranch camp. One mentioned Butte Creek Malo Joe and then blamed "Deer Creek" or Yahi Indians for the murders and arsons, which the writer characterized as "mischief" in the valley and around Lassen Peak.[403] Both authors condemned the Volunteers' "painting" of their faces before the attack. The second writer was emphatic about the wrong the Volunteers had done in killing Forest Ranch's gold mine workers and family members.[404] Both authors were adamant that the killings were excessive and uncalled for to handle the problem. Both insisted that had Whites been alerted, the mining community would have cooperated in making peaceful arrests.

Since the Volunteers were still en route home when the two critical letters arrived, the editor of the *Red Bluff Beacon* printed the first Forks of Butte letter and, in the same edition, wrote his own editorial negating the charges he considered inconsistent with his impressions of the good character of Breckenridge and the other pursuers he knew. He challenged the doubters: "Are not the people of Butte Creek leagued in with them as has been reported here, and do not the 'squaw men' of that creek furnish them with arms and ammunition, provisions &c. and assist them in carrying on their depredations and plundering excursions against the settlers of the valley?"[405]

By late June 1859, the *Red Bluff Beacon* editor no longer mentioned Pit Rivers or Hat Creeks as principal valley raiders. It is also important to note that, by August 1859, there were no more statements in the newspaper reflecting the original understanding that Yahi were central to the valley raids that year. Nevertheless, twentieth-century writers reconstructed these events with a singular focus on the Yahi's Mill Creeks and overlooked, or dismissed, the roles of Butte Creeks or others in the 1858 and 1859 raids in Tehama County.[406]

On August 17, the editor wrote another defense of the Tehama Volunteers, then engaged at Cold Springs. He noted the anonymous writers' acknowledgments that armed Indians were mixed with peaceful Indians in the Forest Ranch camp. He chided one writer for denouncing the Volunteers' seizure of guns from the Indians and dismissing as "mischief" the Indians' killings and property crimes. After the Volunteers returned from their campaign, Breckenridge, in conversation with the *Beacon*'s editor, took exception to the accusation that his men blackened their faces to hide their identities,[407] because, to Whites, that inferred a criminal intent. The Volunteers first denied, then admitted they had darkened their light faces prior to the break-of-dawn attack, but were emphatic they had not done so to hide their identities and considered their actions just.[408] Facial blackening was a common practice among Maidu mourners, who were, consequently, called "tar faces" by early miners.[409]

In response to one letter writer's assertion that no Forks of Butte white men lived with Indian women, Breckenridge emphasized miners' rampant sexual abuses of Maidu women, pointing to the example of Wallace's Indian companion and their children.[410] An exception that supports his observation took place six years earlier, when Frenchtown miners in the Concow area resolved that, if the law did not crack down on the "frequent" sexual exploitation of Indian women and girls as young as ten, they would become vigilantes and punish such acts themselves.[411] Breckenridge believed that, forty to fifty miners were determined to control the Indian women they treated as "concubines."[412] Breckenridge's observation is confirmed in the research of Cook, who concluded the miners' exploitation of Maidu women in Butte County was extensive, ongoing and brutal. From the Indian perspective, the situation may have been unbearable, but it was also complicated to resolve, had anyone tried, because Maidu culture accepted some forms of abusive behavior toward women by Maidu men.

Despite rampant exploitation of Indian women, men like Rich Bar miner Alfred Burr Clark and Yohema (or "Kitty," as he called her), the daughter of a Concow headman, created stable families. When Indian and settler relations in Butte County reached another nadir, this one in the mid-1860s, Clark named two of their sons George Washington and John Adams, staking the children's claim to the well known and respected presidents. Other prominent multiracial families included those of Martin Gramps, John Gramps, Horatio Leggett and William Pinkston. Descendants of those families, some of whom still reside in the vicinity of present-day Concow, served in world wars and have made other contributions across the nation. However, in the 1850s and 1860s, Anderson, Rountree, Breckenridge and the other Volunteers who observed pervasive and flagrant abuses of Indian women could not envision a positive outcome for some.

Settlers Avenge New Mill Creeks

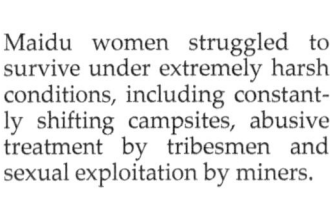
Maidu women struggled to survive under extremely harsh conditions, including constantly shifting campsites, abusive treatment by tribesmen and sexual exploitation by miners.

IN EARLY SEPTEMBER, SEVEN MEMBERS of the Tehama Volunteers signed a letter stating, "We believe all the depredations that has been [sic] committed in the mountains and on the valley in the vicinity of Deer Creek [in southern Tehama County] has been [sic] done by the Butte Creek Indians." Therefore, the miners "are wrong about the Butte Creeks' innocence and their claim that the Indians never leave Butte Creek."[413] As Anderson remembered it, "The Mill Creeks received support from the Butte Creek Indians or the miners or both and that the arms and ammunition secured ... was to murder white people of the country further north."[414] His partner Good died too young to reminisce, but his actions inferred this also became his position. While their remarks here named only Butte Creeks as the principals in Mill Creek raiding parties, they were aware of other dangerous white men and renegade Indians from several tribes living in the Lassen Peak camps. Had those Indians' roles been significant, however, the pursuers—who loathed them—would have acknowledged they participated.

The Tehama Volunteers' case against the Maidu's Butte Creeks vanished from late twentieth-century history because of the influence of Theodora Kroeber, long the leading writer on Ishi, a Yahi. She was convinced Mill Creeks were always solely

Standoff

Yahi, who raided valley farms out of desperation. In contrast, she described the Volunteers as unstable adventure seekers carrying out personal vendettas. However, by the end of the Volunteers' campaign in the canyons and forests, Breckenridge and his men confirmed, to their satisfaction and that of their backers, that Butte Creeks, backed by miners, were the principals who raided with or as Mill Creeks. Letters from Breckenridge, Good and Adj. Gen. Kibbe, as well as Anderson's and Crowder's memoirs, fixed chief responsibility for the valley raids on the Maidu's Butte Creeks.

The Volunteers considered themselves vindicated in their focus on Butte Creeks as Mill Creeks by (1) personal experiences and observations while tracking the Indian party first encountered on Mill Creek to Forest Ranch; (2) the Butte Creeks' bad faith at Forks of Butte when challenged to prove they had not collaborated in Mill Creek raids; (3) the discovery that Butte Creeks from their Forks of Butte and Forest Ranch clashes were the same men they recognized in headwater Indian camps, including one Butte Creek who confessed to an Indian shooting; (4) Wallace's display of outrage at the Volunteers that was meant to placate listening Indians who might otherwise turn on the miners; (5) multiple guns carried by a few Indians in the Forest Ranch camp who did not belong to that rancheria but were hiding among its members; (6) Wallace's and the two letter writers' denials of facts and trivialization of the valley settlers' suffering in farm raids; and (7) the Forks of Butte letter writers' acknowledgements that dangerous Indians were present in the Forest Ranch camp. Finally, these reasons add meaning to nineteenth-century Deer Creek settler Homer Speegle's criticism of Theodora Kroeber's account in an aside to his son Claude: "And oddly enough, Dad starts out mentioning Deer Creek and Butte Creek [Indians]." Claude had only heard about Deer Creeks and Mill Creeks with respect to the wars. He reflected: "We have to assume that Dad and Uncle Mel [Speegle] know a helluva lot more about it than we do."[415] Taken together, such findings deepened existing strains between canyon miners and foothill farmers.

The Tehama Volunteers' attacks at Forest Ranch and Cold Springs shattered the "truce" for good while the Butte Creeks continued their hold on their raiding bases in Deer Creek and

Mill Creek canyons and shifted their attacks back to Butte County gold mining camps and adjoining foothills where local pursuers were neither organized nor adept at the task. These Indian raiders stole food, blankets, clothing and, occasionally, attacked settlers, creating terror they hoped would drive them out.

For their part, Tehama County leaders evaluated the Volunteers' briefing at their campaign's close and concluded that, despite the information confirming the roles of miners and Butte Creeks in the raids, there was no solution in sight and raiders remained a threat to public safety. Feeding this assumption, sporadic raids on foothill farms continued.

In 1859, Tehama County residents were unaware that the outcome of the Volunteers' attacks on the Mountain Maidu at Forest Ranch and the renegade Indians clustered at Cold Springs had amounted to their county's "victory" over Butte Creeks, who ended their raids on the Sacramento Valley foothills of Tehama County. Therefore, leaders still pushed for Kibbe's plan to remove all the Mountain Indians before winter. While some settlers would have welcomed the Indians' extermination, they were satisfied with their transfer to reservations so far away they could not make their way home. To that end, in late July and early August, while the Volunteers were following the Butte Creeks, Kibbe was launching his "Pit River Expedition" to remove Indians from the Sierra Cascades and the Sierra Nevada as far south as Butte Creek and the North Branch of the Feather River. Chapter Six addresses Kibbe's campaign with a focus on gold mining country's part in it.

Because Mountain Maidu raiders continued to anchor their operations out of Deer Creek Canyon, the term "Butte Creeks" largely disappeared from the vernacular and, by the 1860s, whoever raided in Butte County from Deer Creek Canyon became known as Mill Creeks, *regardless of tribal affiliation.* That said, even Anderson, in his 1909 memoir, interchanged the terms Mill Creeks and Butte Creeks.

6

Kibbe's 1859 Pit River Expedition
The Butte Creek Flank

In late July, Adj. Gen. Kibbe returned to Red Bluff to sign up local recruits for Indian pursuits in the mountains and canyons. He estimated he would need eighty to one hundred volunteers for each of two flanks or "fronts": the Butte Creek and northern. While men from the Tehama Volunteers were obvious candidates for Kibbe's newly-formed Rangers, they missed the August 17 interviews because they were still on the trail after their clashes at Cold Springs near the Deer Creek headwaters.[416] Kibbe assigned recruits to companies led by three lieutenants from the California Militia.

Capt. Burns, who had briefly accompanied the Tehama Volunteers, was to lead the Butte Creek flank of Kibbe's campaign,[417] suggesting Kibbe respected the intelligence the Tehama Volunteers provided on the Butte Creeks' role in valley raids.

As mentioned in Chapter Five, Robert Anderson and Hi Good delivered captive Indian widows and children to the Yumalacca Reservation after their final assault on the Butte Creeks. On August 20, while returning from there to Tehama County with other Volunteers, they had crossed Mud Creek in Butte County when they happened upon Kibbe and Burns' company en route to Rock Creek. Anderson later remembered Kibbe's close interest in their account of events at Forest Ranch and Forks of Butte. The general praised John Breckenridge and his men, whose names he took down, offering assurances they were worthy of regular military status with pay.[418]

Anderson and Good, still skeptical about regular soldiers' ability to pursue Mountain Indians, declined Kibbe's offer to join the campaign. However, he enlisted the services of other former

Volunteers, including Conrad Garner, who agreed to serve as the equivalent of a lieutenant in Burns' unit.[419] After Breckenridge returned from delivering another group of Cold Springs Indian captives to the Nome Cult Reservation, he caught up with Burns' company and accepted Kibbe's offer to serve, like Garner, as a "lieutenant." Dan Sutherland, M. T. King of the razed Vermont mill, Henry Sadorus, Chicoan Hank Sunderland and others also joined Kibbe's Rangers.[420] Each was assigned the rank of private and assigned a government rifle, a pistol, five pounds of ammunition, three days of "grub" and a couple of blankets.[421]

The former Volunteers were now subject to the general's order to spare women and children and not kill male Indians, except when their own lives were threatened or the Indians tried to escape. They were to try to persuade the Indians that life in a reservation would be safer than among hostile settlers. Kibbe summed up the situation: "Humanity requires that no more human blood should be shed than is indispensable to give security and protection to the people."[422]

Kibbe wrote his superiors that the experienced former Tehama Volunteers could "read" the remote and rugged terrain, vital to detecting Indian parties, provide tracking tips to the officers and new recruits from the Cascades and advise them about suitable tactics for the Sierra Nevada. As a result, Kibbe's officers relied heavily on the former Volunteers' experience in the canyons during the earlier weeks of the campaign.[423] They knew, for example, that while the Indians' advantage of high ground on ridges helped them spot adversaries, their accuracy with guns suffered when they had to aim downhill or were taken by surprise. The number of Mill Creeks lost to gunfire in a clash might seem high, but, taken as the proportion of fighters lost, it would actually be modest because Indians almost always outnumbered their pursuers. Frank Crowder, who took part in Indian pursuit parties out of Butte County, attributed the Indians' relatively low death rate to their skilled escape methods: they were fast and would "run and scatter like deer," referring to the characteristic zigzag pattern developed to dodge their rivals' arrows.[424] Pursuers were at a disadvantage because they continuously had to reload cumbersome weapons. Even before the Indians' facility with guns improved, the Volunteers respected their skill with the bows they swiftly raised, shooting arrows sometimes poisoned with snake venom. Miners in isolated camps were more likely to die from arrow wounds than Indian pursuers, who used considerable caution to stay out of arrow range.

The Volunteers admitted they never felt confident they could recognize which Indian individuals were their adversaries. Mountain Maidu, Pit Rivers, Hat Creeks and renegades regularly recruited new fighters. Only after multiple encounters were the Volunteers able to recognize Billie and the "Old Doctor" in Butte Canyon in the summer of 1859. Because the Volunteers were never "off-guard,"[425] they lost none of their men to the adversaries they now called "the boys in the hills." In sum, the Volunteers were valuable for being able to convey to the new soldiers what they had learned and what they had yet to master.

Kibbe's Rangers Head Out

Adj. Gen. Kibbe set up his headquarters near Cold Springs on Butt [not Butte] Creek.[426] He ordered the companies to fan out from Little Cow Creek in the north through the Pitt River and Hat Creek territories. Capt. Burns' company would search the Mill Creek and Deer Creek headwaters and then head for Butte Creek (understood to include creeks between Deer Creek and the Feather River branches). Kibbe had no plans to send the Rangers into the hostile Indians' principal havens, Mill Creek and Deer Creek canyons, because, as he explained in a letter to the governor, those were impassable "for [white] man or beast."[427] A significant flaw in Kibbe's plan, therefore, was that none of his companies even attempted to enter the canyons that provided key hideouts for violent Indians. The Indians they were able to find could not be identified as raiders, so his men were ordered to capture as many men as possible on the assumption that some warriors would be in the mix.

Because the Rangers primarily moved by daylight, they broiled in the hot summer sun as they hacked their way through greasewood, underbrush and chaparral.[428] On August 22, Capt. Burns' company reached Rock Creek Canyon, where their mules, laden with provisions, began "turning summersets, rolling down declivities and upsetting all our paraphernalia, goods, etc."

Kibbe wrote Gov. Weller: "This is the worst country to hunt Indians in the State."

Meanwhile, the truce between the miners and Indians had ended. The Rangers, on the advice of valley residents, searched recently abandoned gold miner shacks along Rock Creek, south of Deer Creek Ridge, for farm goods they believed miners persuaded Indians to steal.[429] The miners had begun fleeing the area because formerly peaceful Mountain Maidu had turned hostile after the attack at Forest Ranch. A former Volunteer identified the area as territory of the Maidu Kimshews or "Tigers," who had "committed the latest depredations on the valley" in Tehama County.[430] As the company continued toward Butte Creek and the Feather River, the Rangers, unable to recruit Indian scouts or informers, relied on Breckenridge and the other Volunteer veterans to identify enemy fighters and guide them to the rancherias of Concow, Kimshew and other Maidu tribelets.

Along the way, Breckenridge pointed out the corpses of two Indians his Volunteers had killed. After Burns' company set up camp on a ridge above Butte Creek, he dispatched Garner's men to round up Indians in that vicinity and along Chico and Rock creeks. Burns and some of his men escorted Kibbe to Rancho Chico, where they opened a line of credit at John Bidwell & Co. for ammunition, clothing and food. Bidwell also provided a campground to temporarily house the Indians Burns' men had rounded up for removal.[431]

The Mountain Maidu at large were aware they were the targets of a removal, but they could not distinguish among the Whites and, therefore, could not identify their "collectors." And so, in defense, they turned on all Whites. According to a Forks of Butte writer, the Tehama Volunteers' attack on Forest Ranch had served as a rallying cry for the Mountain Maidu tribelets: "The war tocsin has been sounded, and the remnants of the Diggers [Mountain Maidu] are collecting, armed and equipped, and arrayed in Nature's full-dress uniform. Their very looks and manners indicate revenge."[432] The treaty was gone; war was on.

Miners Arrest Farmers

At dawn on July 24, the Rangers surprised the members of a

Mountain Maidu rancheria at Cox's Flat on Butte Creek, about a half mile from the cluster of cabins called Centerville. However, according to Ranger veteran Henry Landt, this time, unlike the Tehama Volunteers, Kibbe had "no disposition to exercise cruelty towards the Indians; but, on the contrary, he always gave orders to the men not to kill any Indians that could be taken alive."[433] The Rangers seized twelve to fourteen Indians. However, after some fled, and "call[ing] several times for them to stop," they took shots at three or four, wounding two, while Garner's unit continued up the creek.[434] Indians and miners in the vicinity of Forest Ranch were understandably fearful of another attack. Garner and Breckenridge were the last men they wanted to see again, especially carrying orders from a general.

A miner approached the Rangers guarding the prisoners and demanded they turn over an Indian woman to him. When they refused, he headed for nearby Diamondville, where a crowd of miners were downing free liquor at a county sheriff's campaign rally. Forty-five men rushed back with him to Cox's Flat, where they forced the Rangers to release the prisoners. The miner who demanded the Indian woman took her away, leaving behind her husband, one of the men a Ranger wounded when he and the others tried to escape.

The miners from Cox's Flat and Diamondville were still not satisfied. Recognizing former Tehama Volunteers from the Forest Ranch attack in the Rangers party, they threatened to lynch them. Breckenridge recalled the scene: "No white man will use such insulting language as was used to us."[435]

Also present in the crowd at Cox's Flat was at least one candidate for public office, Deputy Sheriff David W. Cheesman, a Republican, then or later a lawyer. When he arrested the four Rangers on murder charges, the crowd backed down.[436] No sooner had he removed the men to Diamondville, than a mob there made the same threats as at Cox's Flat. When he assured them he would personally deliver the prisoners to Kibbe, a guest at Bidwell's rancho, the miners relented.[437]

Once at Bidwell's place, Cheesman explained his arrests of the Rangers and described the threats made against them at Cox's Flat and Diamondville. This predicament illustrated to Kibbe the tensions between Butte County's miners and farmers and the

Indian problems with both groups.[438] Kibbe's order to Cheesman to free the Rangers provided the deputy political cover for his election campaign during the controversial removal: his arrest of the Rangers, hated by the miners, appeased those angry voters, while their release suited law-abiding constituents.

Kibbe returned with Burns and the four Rangers to Cox's Flat where, on August 29, the entire company again surrounded the Mountain Maidu rancheria and, like the Garner unit had done, rounded up its residents. Taking the Indians with them, they continued to the area around Forks of Butte where they met no resistance as they removed another one hundred or so Indians, although several miners objected to the removal of their children and female Indian companions. Kibbe gave them a choice: if the men would marry the women with whom they had families, all their dependents could remain. This proposal produced three weddings.[439]

With the roundup at Forks of Butte complete, on September 17, miners there sent a petition to the superintendent of Indian Affairs to use his influence to discontinue further removals, which deprived miners of Indian labor they needed to haul supplies and equipment to their mining camps to finish the season. They received no response.[440]

Burns and his men moved on to collect Mountain Maidu from the Kimshew and Concow rancherias. Among them were three Concow headmen, Tippee, Moolah and, chief among them, Yumyan. He was also known as "Tome-ya-nem or "Maker of All Things," and, among Whites, as William Pete. The men's influence extended beyond their own tribelets. Of the three, Tippee was the "most dangerous" and "daring." In late September, Ranger Capt. S. D. St. Johns discovered dozens more Mountain Maidu at points along the Feather River who had hidden from Burns' men. When his company delivered the Indians to Rancho Chico, Bidwell sent over a wagon of watermelons to ease their misery.[441]

About fifty miners wrote a letter to the *Butte Democrat*, objecting to the removal of the Indians. Since the issue containing the letter was already in circulation when Kibbe and Burns' company reached Butte Creek, the letter's authors evidently hoped to influence the general to release the Indians. The letter pointed to

Garner and his men as the former Volunteers who had attacked the Indians at Forest Ranch and defended the Indians at Cox's Flat as harmless workers who had not been "off the creek for awhile."[442] The letter reiterated the belief espoused during the Forks of Butte controversy that the area was not a haven for "squaw men ['White Indians']... as commonly understood." It declared local Whites were wrong about Mountain Maidu valley raids and that the "creek" Indians were, in fact, only "packing our provisions, tools, lumber &c." Then the writers acknowledged that, while the Forest Ranch camp included a few dangerous Indians when the Tehama Volunteers attacked it, they could have made a peaceful arrest by calling on the help of four to six miners to assist them.

Kibbe either did not hear about the letter or he read and dismissed it as contradicting the former Volunteers' reports he considered more trustworthy. By contrast to the aftermath of the Forest Ranch incident, when the Forks of Butte miners wrote a letter challenging the Volunteers (see Chapter Five), this time Breckenridge and his men anticipated their criticism and wrote a rebuttal to the newspaper. They asserted that, while with the Rangers at Cox's Flat, they recognized the Maidu's Butte Creek warriors, whom they had recently fought at the armed Cold Springs camp.[443]

The Northern Flank

With the Butte Creek flank of his campaign successfully completed, Kibbe shifted his attention to the northern one, which also engaged in some violent clashes. From "Fort Kibbe," his Butt Creek headquarters (not to be confused with Butte Creek), a few miles from the Deer Creek headwaters, he rode out to check on his units collecting hundreds of Pit Rivers, Hat Creeks and renegade Indians.

Because Kibbe's objective was to place the Indians on reservations so distant they would be safe from vengeful settlers and could not find their way home, the Nome Lackee Reservation, west of Red Bluff in Tehama County, had to be excluded. However, the governor disagreed, thinking its proximity to the collection points and the remains of its infrastructure ideal.

Kibbe sent urgent letters pressing the governor to reconsider and approve alternate locations.

Although the governor agreed to place two hundred Indians in the Mendocino (County) Reservation on the coast, he insisted Kibbe send two hundred others to Nome Lackee. Considering this idea "worse than useless," Kibbe again explained that Nome Lackee captives and neighboring farmers shared a mutual loathing. He emphasized that his prisoners included angry, vengeful men who would flee the reservation and return to the mountains at first chance. Eventually the governor agreed to send some of the captives to other reservations, including Nome Cult in Round Valley, also in Mendocino County.

Kibbe hoped that, by December, six hundred prisoners would be sent to the Tejon Reservation in Kern County.[444] He delivered approximately seven hundred Indians and their children to the Mendocino Reservation, where living conditions were poor and local residents antagonistic. After the snow receded in 1860, most were moved to the Nome Cult Reservation, bringing its population to about four or five hundred.[445] In all, about twelve hundred Indians were delivered to reservations by Kibbe and his men. In the 1860s, Nome Cult Reservation was renamed Round Valley Reservation to conform with popular usage. Coverage of events that follow through Chapter Twelve will reflect that change.

Because winter weather had closed roads and trails, a large group of the Indians heading for the Mendocino Reservation went by the river boat steamer *Sam Soule* from Red Bluff to San Francisco. The boat at first frightened, then confused and finally fascinated the Indians. Nine babies were born along the way. Upon arrival in San Francisco, they camped along the Bay, awaiting the next ship's arrival for the trip up the coast. Their apparel was so inadequate for the city's cold that a local newspaper urged donations of warm clothing. Citizens responded in droves and then stayed to stare at the captives, described by a reporter as "handsome" though "dangerous" people.[446]

Aftermath of the Pit River Expedition

Kibbe's report to the State Legislature on his Pit River Expedition stated his Rangers had killed thirty to forty Indian men and two women and a child caught in the line of fire.[447] During the later weeks of the removal, an Army unit at Eagle Lake, in September 1859, recognized local Indians who had escaped collection and "renegades from Shasta, Tehama and Colusi counties."[448]

By mid-December, Indians, including at least nine considered warriors, had already escaped from the Nome Lackee Reservation and headed back home. By then, Kibbe's companies had delivered their last captives to Red Bluff and disbanded.

Recognizing he was responsible for plunging Mountain Maidu Indians deeper into helplessness and destitution, Kibbe wrestled with his conscience over the capture of the hundreds of Maidu, Hat Creeks and Pit Rivers for whom he had the greatest respect: "Probably the best and finest race of Indians—athletic and healthy—in California and [they] possess more intelligence than any race I have yet seen."[449] His admiration for the Mountain Indians of the Sierra resembled that of federal Indian agent Oliver Wozencraft in his 1851 report to the Interior Department.

In Kibbe's final report to the Legislature, he stated that most of the settlers' calls for help were justified and, without naming the Tehama Volunteers, mentioned the value of local volunteers' knowledge regarding the locations of dangerous Indians. A newspaper account by a member of his expedition noted problems that impeded their collections and motivated Mountain Indians to escape the reservations: "Three more months of determined assiduity will not rid these mountains of their aboriginal inhabitants. The rough country over which the Indians are scattered is too extensive, the number of men employed to capture them too few and facilities afforded inadequate to accomplish so much in so short a time."[450] Some Indians had escaped, usually those who posed the greatest threat: the most physically fit with no family ties who now were even more hardened and willing to join violent bands fighting against the settlers. Nevertheless, Kibbe believed his men had removed the bulk of the most dangerous Mountain Indians from northeastern Butte and eastern Tehama counties.

Kibbe's report focused on the Pit Rivers and Hat Creeks in the Lassen Peak area, concluding that, at any one time, the perpetrators probably numbered sixty to eighty warriors from six to eight tribes who "roamed from Butte Creek on the south to the head of the Pit River on the north; from Eagle Lake on the east and the Sacramento River on the west." His mention of Indians along the Sacramento River meant he included the scattering of Valley Maidu and Wintu ranch workers widely believed to have collaborated with raiders from the canyons. Kibbe emphasized that, although his men did not collect Valley Maidu or Wintu, "all ... the surrounding and intermediate tribes were implicated [with the Mountain Indian warriors] in the various depredations."[451]

Kibbe's report, however, omitted specific mentions of the Butte County flank of his campaign, even though he had accompanied Burns' unit and launched his campaign there, and statements at the time reflected his agreement with Red Bluff leaders about that flank's importance.[452] It appears that, in the interest of garnering legislative funding for his expedition's expenses, he emphasized the Pit River and Hat Creek fronts, where Whites put up no resistance to the removal. It would not have been politic for him to implicate Sierra Nevada miners—especially their citizens' arrest of his Rangers. Miners, after all, were national heroes and the constituents of legislators. His exclusion of the Butte County front from his report explains its omission from subsequent studies which had relied on it.[453]

Kibbe emphasized how his volunteers' restrained use of violence contrasted to the widely disparaged brutal tactics of Walter Jarboe's "Eel River Rangers" on the Coast Range. Kibbe initially backed that volunteer campaign and then struggled to bring it under control. Gov. Weller had denounced it as an attempt to exterminate the Indians and, therefore, an abuse of the public's trust. Within months, Jarboe's spreading disrepute led the governor to disband his unit. After Governor John G. Downey assumed office in January 1860, he terminated state support for all armed volunteer Indian pursuits.[454]

Kibbe's report claimed, in general terms, that "the tribes of Indians engaged in [the war] whose frequent acts of violence and atrocity had rendered them a terror to the region ... are completely vanquished and subdued."[455] Kibbe also expressed his hope the expedition would discourage other Indians from avenging their grievances by attacks on settlers.

Even while the Kibbe removal was still under way, Indians

who escaped collection were competing for food with Mountain Maidu south of the Feather River and Indians who had escaped the Nome Lackee Reservation. According to newspaper accounts, starvation forced some to steal.[456] Mountain Maidu warriors, determined to renew their vengeance against settlers, could not raid from their own rancherias which were surrounded by angry Butte County miners. Instead, they reestablished their uses of "isolated haunts in the mountains": Deer Creek and Mill Creek canyons, the last all-Indian territory.[457]

Anderson and Good remained in the Sacramento Valley foothills as independent volunteers in occasional canyon pursuits of Indians. Good continued to improve his mastery of Indian dialects, useful for gathering information from the women and children survivors he delivered to reservations or farms.[458] Veterans of Kibbe's Rangers went back to their jobs and family life. Kibbe dispatched John Breckenridge to Indian pursuits in Tulare County and, from there, to Arizona where Apaches killed him. In his absence, Good and Anderson became the principal leaders in canyon pursuits.

Late February 1860 was marked by seasonal peace from Lassen Peak to Butte Creek, freeing Kibbe to battle with the State Legislature over his campaign expenses. However, in eastern Tehama County a new round of livestock thefts were perpetrated by desperate Indians whose displaced families were stranded and starving in snowbound mountain caves. A group of settlers from the Lassen Peak area decided to avenge the thefts by attacking the Indians in Mill Creek Canyon. The following overview is from Steve Schoonover's discovery of a scrapbook copy of an original newspaper account, no longer available in archival collections.

"As the headwaters pursuit party moved deep into the canyon, a cluster of Indian men atop Black Rock watched their approach. Theirs had been a winter-long wait. When the pursuers spotted smoke from a small village over a rise in the distance, they stopped to consider their next move. Then, they spotted an Indian man who walked alone toward them. They were unsure what to do. Was he aware of them? He was unarmed. When one of their party raised his rifle to shoot, his companions protested; they wanted more time. However, in the commotion his gun fired and the Indian man fell dead. This launched fire from the surveillance Indians and their backup, men who emerged from the nearby cave."[459]

After the Black Rock conflict, the witness who authored this recollection became the guardian of an orphaned boy, a survivor, who much later told him his people's (apparently Yahi) account of the clash. The previous summer, in 1859, when their leaders heard about Kibbe's removal campaign, they decided they wanted him to take them all to the reservation for their safety. Through the winter, the Yahi posted sentries on Black Rock who watched for Kibbe. They expected he would be accompanied by an Indian emissary to whom they could explain their peaceful intention. The sentries were in place the day the settler party entered the canyon. According to the boy, "The men at the top of the rock were the chiefs or big men of the tribe, including [the orphan's father]."[460] When they heard the rifle fire, others, waiting in a canyon cave, emerged and joined the elders in the fight. All the pursuers survived, but seventeen Indian men, women and children died. Also dead was the peaceful Yahi's hope of safety on a reservation. After 1860, other Indians, like those Yahi, also sought the protection of reservations from white pursuers.

In 1860, before the seasonal conflicts between Butte County Mountain Maidu and settlers reignited, Maidu tribelets resurrected their own intra-tribal wars. In late May, according to the *Marysville Appeal*, about five hundred Mountain and Valley Maidu had met north of Oroville to negotiate a treaty. However, their efforts failed and buggy driver John Tremont of Marysville stopped to watch them battle about half a mile from the rural Prairie House Hotel. The Mountain Maidu wore breech clouts and red face paint; he noted head feathers on the Valley Maidu. After a man ran back and forth waving a bear skin, combatants shot bullets and arrows at each other. Three or four men died and several were wounded. Which side won was unclear to the observers. The Valley Maidu then entered the hotel, and seized the owner whom they dragged through the rooms, looking for a man they believed was hiding. Not finding him, they left without further harming the owner. Although the Indians were not hostile toward the Whites at the battle scene, within a few hours, a band of race track attendees arrived and killed several Indians with whom Tremont stood talking. His efforts to save one of them was unsuccessful.[461]

By 1862, according to Frank Crowder, local men who remained skeptical of the military credited the let-up in hostilities not to Kibbe, but to Breckenridge and his Tehama Volunteers. While Robert Anderson did not credit either the Volunteers or Kibbe's Rangers for the let-up, he and others blamed the removal campaign for the increased number of embittered Indians. The miners resented Kibbe's removal of Indian workers and their family members and remained convinced the Volunteers' attack at Forest Ranch had broken the trust the Indians had placed in Butte Creek miners during the truce.

In 1860, with Indian raids on the rise in the foothills east of his ranch, John Bidwell purchased his late neighbor John Potter's adjoining ranch. On that open land south of his headquarters and across Chico Creek he surveyed a new "Chico Village" along both sides of the Oroville-Shasta Road where it crossed the creek. Until then, Potter had shut off use of the road where it passed through his ranch, forcing a detour around it. This bypass, a farm road called Old Chico Way, followed east along Chico Creek, then turned south along present Olive Street, which rejoined the main road somewhere south of Little Chico Creek.[462]

In 1862, Bidwell, moved his store from his ranch to a brick building he erected on the new village site at Front and Broadway streets (today's First and Broadway streets). By then, he had gone into partnership with his former store manager, George Wood. He gave married ranch workers lots for homes there and welcomed entrepreneurs and professionals, many of whom accepted the easy terms he offered for land parcels. He began to remove or level the clutter of old buildings around his house and across the road—the hotel, granary, saloon, stable, workshops, storage sheds and workers' quarters—a project that took more than a decade to complete. The front and side yards of his Rancho Chico headquarters gradually transformed into the lush grounds of his former residence (predecessor to the present mansion). With this, the ranch was no longer the site of the "company town."

As early as 1862, when the first two houses went up in the new Chico Village, complaints circulated that Indians in the

Standoff

foothills north and east of there were killing and stealing from miners. After miners, angry about thefts of horses, retaliated by lynching five Kimshew Maidu, the Indians killed white women and children in the Butte County foothills, inflaming the settler community and drawing Bidwell into the fray once again. Although no one expected Indian issues to compete with those of the Civil War, in both cases Bidwell became a lightning rod and growing Chico Village, a hot spot. Chapter Seven addresses the renewed outbreaks of violence.

7

Child Killings in Civil War Politics

In the early 1860s, as the Civil War unfolded, thousands of California men headed east for the front while some Easterners took off for California. Others were avoiding enlistment or deserting, some had been injured in service and found nothing left to keep them at home. Regardless of the reason, most who showed up in northern Butte County shared the same desire to start over. But life in northern Butte County was not a panacea—Indian and Civil War issues ran along parallel tracks that crossed from time to time with dramatic and sometimes tragic results.

In its new brick building at Broadway and Front streets, the telegraph machine at John Bidwell & Co. supplied updates on frontline engagements in the Civil War. Many days, word of battlefield results fueled fighting words, fisticuffs and fatalities. The north and south stagecoaches—road conditions permitting—delivered letters and home-state newspapers that passed from hand to hand. John Bidwell recalled devouring the content of year-old papers. Oroville's *Butte Record* copied war coverage from the San Francisco and Sacramento presses. Whether residents had arrived in the 1840s or were fresh off overland trails, the Civil War shaped personal relationships, business patronage and responses to the war with Indians. For example, after tribesmen killed a teamster and three children in 1862, valley residents conflated their rage at Indians, their jealousy of Bidwell's private Indian labor force and their anger against his pro-Union politics.

This and later chapters reconstruct the ways Civil War passions influenced the Army, which took command of the State Militia for the war's duration. Now called the California Volunteers, they continued to address Indian-settler clashes in the Sacramento Valley and in the Cascades and northern Sierra Nevada ranges.

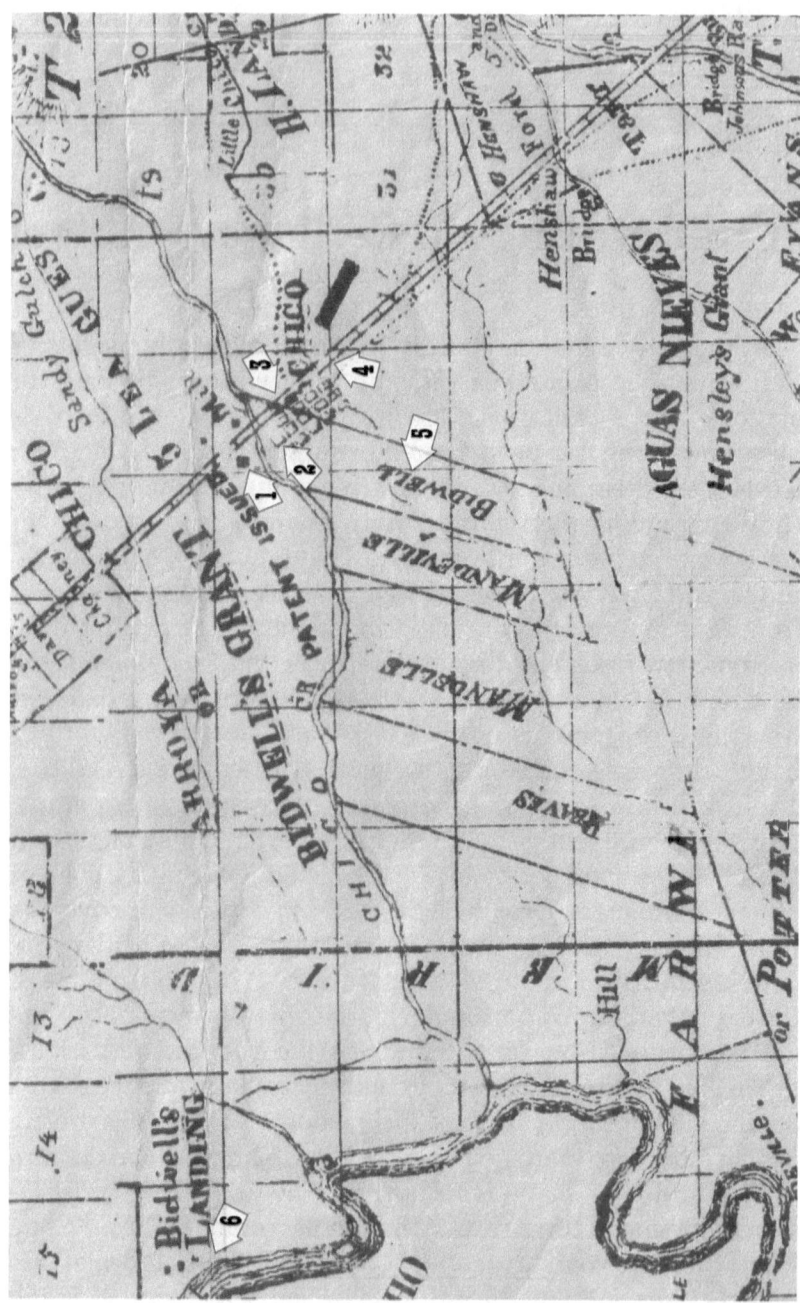

Chico Village layout, 1862. 1) Bidwell ranch headquarters, 2) Bidwell's new store 1861, 3) First Village houses rising 1862, 4) Bidwell moved road straight through Chico, 5) Potter's Half-League until 1860, 6) Bidwell's Landing: vicinity of temporary Indian camp.

Civil War Politics: 1861 and 1862

In 1860, a dispute within northern Butte County's Democratic Party presaged the war strains to come. That year, Bidwell, a Union Democrat, joined the effort to preserve his party from a takeover by California's Chivalry Democrats, who embraced the South's demand for states' rights to preserve slavery. This possibility also concerned General Albert Sydney Johnston, the new commanding officer of the Army's Department of the Pacific. Loyal to the Union and aware that most Californians were as well, he said "secessionists are much the most active and zealous party, which gives them more influence than they ought to have in their numbers." Whenever he sent troops on missions, their appearance was also meant to "overawe ... disloyal leaders."[463]

Bidwell was a delegate that year to the national Democratic convention in Charleston, South Carolina, where supporters of moderate Stephen A. Douglas challenged the Southern Democrats' favorite, John C. Breckenridge (no relation to the Tehama Volunteers member), for control of the party. Bidwell, the only California delegate who supported Douglas, opposed his own U.S. senators, William Gwin and Milton Latham, both of whom were "State's Rights Democrats" or Confederacy supporters. After the convention, Bidwell later recalled, "Stephen A. Douglas ... sent for me. He wanted to see the man who dared to differ with Gwin and the rest of them from California."[464] Because Douglas and Breckenridge each campaigned as the Democratic Party's true nominee for president in 1860, they split the party's national vote. In Butte County, part of a sprawling but thinly populated congressional district, this division between Democratic Party factions helped Abraham Lincoln's Republican Party eke out a victory there.

In response to the challenge, according to Civil War historian Alvin Josephy, "California secessionists isolated in small groups ... throughout the war angered local citizens and troops with their demonstrations of sympathy for the South."[465] This was the case in Butte County, where, in August 1861, rural partisans collided at Daniel Gibson's store, near present day Nord. Gibson punched Union Democrat Miles Harper, who had killed

"Secesh" Turner the previous day.[466] Throughout the following winter, Chico readers of Oroville's *Butte Record* followed the trial and last minute reprieve of Fred Wagner, charged with killing Jacob Girr, who had cheered for Jefferson Davis on election day. The court concluded Wagner acted in self-defense.

As trials and appeals played out, two Union men boasted they had whipped seven local Confederates in a fistfight.[467] Such incidents most often reached print in the Northern-leaning *Butte Record* when men sympathetic to the South were on the losing end. Meanwhile, Bidwell had to put up with "Reb" rowdies who rode back and forth in front of his hotel "hurrahing for Jeff Davis." Indian-settler crises were intensified even more by this politically charged environment.

When the 1861 State Democratic Central Committee met in San Francisco, Butte County's Chico delegation included former congressman and Southern-courting Joseph "Mac" McCorkle, who had helped Bidwell oppose the 1851 Indian treaty in Washington. Mac included Chico in his campaign rounds as he tried to resurrect his political career, which had foundered when his mentor, Governor David Broderick, died in a duel with Mac's former law partner, Stephen Field. Perhaps because rivalry between the party factions could split votes he needed at the San Francisco meeting, McCorkle urged Butte County's Southerners to tone down their rhetoric.[468]

A few months later, Bidwell made a futile attempt to persuade local Chivalry Democrats to cross over to the Union cause. At the party's state convention, he competed with McCorkle and others for the party's gubernatorial nomination. Over the course of eleven ballots, McCorkle vied with Bidwell for the lowest vote in the tally.

Because Butte County delegates denied their own Bidwell twenty-two of their twenty-three votes, he denounced their action as a "kind of contempt" for him personally and considered it, in effect, a Confederate takeover of the county's Democratic Party.[469] A few months later, Bidwell gave up and joined the Republicans. Under its new war name, the "Union Party," backers vowed to counter the influence of Southern-sympathizing Democrats.[470]

In Chico, well-organized Chivalry Democrats could keep up

pressure on Union Democrats and Bidwell's new Union Party because, while 63 percent of Chico Township's white, American-born males were Northerners, 37 percent were natives of the South or the border states. Dense clusters of the South's backers also lived in surrounding townships which supplied trade to Chico businesses. Referring to their collective political clout, Bidwell said, "There was a large majority of southerners here."[471] Near his ranch, significant landowners included David Reavis from Missouri and Virginia natives James Morehead and John Tatham, whose former slave, Joseph, 30, tended his farm.[472] Bidwell knew "one or two" southern men who supported slavery, but objected to secession.[473] While there may have been Union Democrats among local men from the South, no evidence points to them as either organized or documented. From the war's start until its end, residents' home-state politics embroiled Chico and its surrounding townships.

Indians and Farmers: Combustion

In the fall of 1861, according to an Oroville family, "Indian Jim" peered at the evening sky and pointed up at tree limbs to indicate the height of the snow and depth of water he foresaw.[474] The effects of extreme weather competed for attention with war-centered tensions through that winter. When floodwaters swept across the valley, drowning thousands of cattle, bankruptcies rose.

Meanwhile, because spreading white settlements in the foothills denied Mountain Indians access there for winter refuge, they again huddled in the Cascades-Sierra Nevada ranges' frozen canyon caves. To survive, they broke into settlers' cabins, stealing food, weapons and clothing, sometimes killing individuals who crossed their paths. One of those was the Chinese cook of the Mountain House, a hotel, who left Berry Creek for work, but never arrived. Evidence suggested Maidu from the rancheria there killed him. Although his Chinese friends posted a reward, no settler pursuit ensued.

Over the winter, Mountain Maidu in the higher regions attacked so many mail carriers that, in April, the postmaster general shut down overland service and ordered all California mail to go by sea. Pursuit parties began finding Overland Mail rifles in Indian camps they attacked. With no hope of reviving the Indian truce of the late 1850s, miners around Forest Ranch met in a saloon to swap information and talk about ways to end the thefts and killings. In June, miners who knew three slain men and had heard about two others formed a committee in Forks of Butte to solicit men, arms and money "to suppress further depredations."[475]

Indians also were victims of anonymous killers in remote areas, but their casualty counts are elusive. For those individuals, there can be no identification, no record of their fates and no historical accountability for their killers. Surviving accounts agree, however, that settlers avenged their losses by killing multiples of Indians. For example, when one White was killed, settlers might kill ten Indians. Even though official records of such disproportionate Indian killings are thin, ample archival accounts left by settlers document this pattern.

Like the incident on Cohasset Road in 1859, set out in Chapter Five, settler killings by Mill Creeks near Rock Creek on June 25, 1862, were consistent with acts of vengeance. However, in that case, no information suggests what, if any, particular offenses accounted for their actions.[476] After burning cabins and slaughtering livestock, the Indians crossed Keefer Ridge to Cohasset Road, which follows the broad curves of the fast creek below it. They spotted James Keefer's teamster Thomas Allen, accompanied by Tom, Rebecca Keefer's young Indian helper, as they drove a wagon of fencing from the Morrill mill. The Indians shot both of them, then swarmed the wagon. Tom, though injured, had managed to jump out and run toward a house, darting back and forth like a deer to avoid being hit. Two young hunters who had seen the attack also ran to that same house where they pressed Elvira Hickok, whose husband, Frank, was away mining, to flee with her small children and them to Keefer's grist mill, a mile down Cohasset Road. But she refused because she had sent her three older children with their dog and pony up Rock Creek to pick blackberries.[477] When Tom arrived and she saw his bloody arm, she relented. Tom then ran north to Keefer's headquarters and the two men and the Hickoks ran south to the nearby mill for help. Meanwhile, the Mill Creeks had left

Killings in War Politics

James Keefer, Rock Creek farmer, mill owner and adviser to trackers of hostile Indians.

Allen and his wagon behind and crossed Cohasset Road in the direction of Rock Creek.[478]

When the boys and Mrs. Hickok arrived at the Keefer mill and delivered the news about the attack, the miller said he could not leave his wife and newborn infant alone to help Allen. He, three customers and the two hunters resolved his dilemma by carrying his wife in her bed to Tom Gore's place a mile away, where Frank Crowder and Gore, Robert Anderson's brother-in-law, left work to assist Allen. They arrived to find Keefer and his men had already arrived and found the teamster dead and scalped. While some of the rescuers tended to Allen's remains, his wagon and team, Crowder, Gore and others left to find the Hickok children. By nightfall, the searchers had only found scraps of the two girls' dresses, their arrow-pierced dead horse and family dog. They had to tell Mrs. Hickok that her three children "are doubtless in possession of the Indians."[479]

Early the next morning, a search party walked the creek banks and fields for signs of the children. They discovered the body of Minnie Hickok, 13, in creek water, and that of her sister Ida, 16, crumpled and nude in a nearby tree hollow. According to Crowder, who found one of the girls, the arrows in both bodies had been so accurate that the arrow tips clustered in each girl within the diameter of a quarter. They did not find the girls' brother, Frankie, 12. They took the bodies to the Hickoks' place and then on to the Chico cemetery, where a gravesite service drew an emotion-packed crowd whose anger was tempered somewhat by hope that Frankie survived.

With seventy-five men ready to carry the search for Frankie north into the Deer Creek country of the Mill Creeks, residents along Rock Creek gratefully accepted Dr. Willard Pratt's offer of his house as a guarded "fort" where families could gather. Before parents packed their families' possessions, they assembled provisions, guns and ammunition for the search party.

The pursuers narrowed to thirty of the fittest neighbors who hacked their way through the thick underbrush, clambered around and over immense boulders and climbed canyon walls along Deer Creek. They killed any Indians they could spot, but most stayed out of sight or range, watching their every move. Within a day or so, they were outnumbered, out of provisions and overwhelmed by the terrain. The exhausted and famished men headed back to Keefer's ranch, where they told him they killed eleven Indians, without finding Frankie.[480] The rancher replied that only men from the Tehama County Volunteers had the skills to confront Mill Creeks in those canyons, and arranged for Hi Good and Bully Bowman to take over the search. With Breckenridge gone, the pursuit party's leadership had fallen to Good, whom Keefer paid $75 as a gesture of good faith and with assurance of fuller compensation later. Good recruited veteran pursuers William Sublet, Bully Bowman and Obe Field to lead the Butte County men in a second search for Frankie Hickok. (A family crisis kept Good's partner Anderson at home.[481])

The Recovery of Frankie Hickok

Once Good and his men reached Chico, they prepared the town's local volunteers for the grueling conditions that defeated the initial searchers' attempt to find Frankie. There was broad agreement in town that this must be the opening phase of a full campaign against the Mill Creeks. Wages and provisions were required to send the Good party into the canyons, so Dr. Samuel Sproul took an appeal to the governor for help.

In response, Governor Leland Stanford turned to Brigadier

General George Wright, a West Point graduate who was "every inch the soldier and a gentleman."[482] Wright sent the volunteers crates of smooth bore, "rusty" muskets—accurate only to eighty yards—and authorized no additional ammunition or money.[483] This cavalier response contrasted to that of the Tehama County men who, when called on to help in Butte County, had dropped everything to head for Chico. This fed public skepticism about the state government's reliability. The offended pursuers shipped the "rusty muskets" back to Sacramento.[484]

Despite the lack of state help, Good and his search party headed out. In just under two weeks after Frankie was kidnapped, Good's men found his mutilated remains at the bottom of a cliff. According to search party member Pleasant Guynn, 35, a Missouri native who worked on Rock Creek as a Sadorus ranch cowboy, they found the child's corpse covered by rocks near Mill Creek's headwaters.[485] By examining tracks in the area, the pursuers concluded he had been led around inside a circle of rock-throwing children until fire caught the tufts of dried leaves they had attached to him. It was customary for Mountain Indians to torture and kill male captives, often with rocks and sometimes fire.

Good's party collected eight scalps from Indian men they killed at a nearby camp.[486] The pursuers made a litter from their clothing and carried the boy's remains to Good's cabin and then to Chico, arriving July 11. Reports of the boy's torture intensified emotions in the already distraught and anxious crowd, which walked to the cemetery for his burial next to his sisters. Demanding vengeance, there were calls to massacre all Mountain Indians.

Confederate Chico Turns on John Bidwell

Bidwell later noted that, after the funeral, "throngs of people from all sections" surged back across Chico Creek and "refreshed" themselves in Broadway's clutter of jerry-built saloons, where the larger bachelor populace regularly gambled, ate and drank up front or dallied with prostitutes in lean-tos in the rear.[487] From there, the men headed for John Bidwell & Co., where they climbed the store's wide center stairs to Bidwell Hall, the spacious community meeting room. They filled the rows of

The Rancho Chico cattle gate from which livestock were herded down Broadway en route to summer pastures in the mountains. To its right is John Bidwell & Co. Upstairs is Bidwell Hall, where Hi Good's 1862 Indian pursuit was planned during a public meeting.

pine benches and, in need of more room, folded back the shutters and opened the long windows. The overflow spilled onto the deep balcony around two sides, jockeying for space.

As the "Hickok" meeting got underway, it became clear that more was at stake than avenging the Hickok children's murders. The Union flag at the front of the room would not stir unifying sentiments in the hearts of Confederate supporters who made up a significant part of the crowd. They arrived primed to lay out their convictions about Indians, the Civil War and Bidwell's influence on both. Among them was Virginia native, Missouri resident and '49er John Guill, who would remember the crowd as "the largest I have ever seen."[488] Scattered through the crowd were local figures such as Bidwell, Justice Thomas Wright, Yankee Hill hotel owner Michael Wells and Judge Warren Sexton of Oroville. As an old man, Crowder looked back on this meeting as the "angriest" he ever attended.[489] However, in its early moments, the success of Good and his men in locating and bringing home the Hickok boy's remains unified the participants behind a full campaign against the Mill Creeks.

Contributing to their initial common purpose was the Hickoks' grievous losses and the experience of close calls by others present: foothill farmer Sunedecker had escaped multiple shots and bow and arrow-wielding raiders had killed foothill farmer Guill's neighbor, Michael Walsh, as he tended his sheep on the land swales southeast of Chico. As a result of the Hickok killings, foothill farmwives and children required armed escorts even to outhouses; parents spelled one another on watches and family dogs became sentries.

Rural wives felt especially unsafe because the need for additional income forced their husbands to find jobs elsewhere, such as Chico, mining camps or Oroville for days or weeks at a time. (This left the women with the added responsibility for their husbands' farm work while they continued making virtually everything their families used. Mary Murdoch Compton was so busy with work at her home on the Llano Seco ranch, where Indians were not a threat, that, over eleven years, she went to Chico only a few times.[490])

The need for security unified the community behind Good and his men's objective: to kill so many Mill Creeks that other Indians would fear joining such bands. For its part, the crowd also agreed to apply political pressure by organizing a follow-up petition to the governor, this time with signatures from Tehama County, to fund a volunteer campaign.

During the meeting, men offered to join Good on the new campaign, but the attendees were hard pressed to scrape up sufficient money to provision an immediate, extended sortie. Even if the governor would help, state funds would not arrive in time. In mid-nineteenth-century Chico, whenever influence or money was required to meet an important objective, the hope was that Bidwell would pick up the tab.[491] The crowd decided he should step forward with "cash in hand."

Bidwell refused and fell victim to their boiling resentment over his support for the Union. The "Rebs" turned on Bidwell, making him the target of all their Indian and Civil War grievances.[492] In this they had the assistance of the men they elected to run the meeting: R. H. O'Farrell, a Maryland native, was their secretary, and Alabaman Washington Henshaw, 54, was the meeting chairman. Old hands at politics, the Southerners knew how to "count votes" and use intimidation to turn a meeting their way. A prominent farmer, Henshaw and his family still claimed the labor of Matilda Henshaw, 24, a young black woman they had brought west when she was a child slave. As a Chivalry Democrat, Henshaw resented Bidwell's politics and complained the Mechoopdas stole fruit from his orchard.[493]

A brief overview of Southerners' influence in northern Butte County will explain the difficulties Bidwell and others loyal to the Northern cause encountered, even in this Indian war crisis, from their Confederate-sympathizing neighbors.

Southerners Turn on Bidwell

When the Northerners and Southerners in Bidwell Hall that day made their way west in the early 1860s, they brought with them their convictions about slavery. While Chico settlers of the 1850s arrived with divided opinions on the issue, they avoided divisive discussions in the interest of keeping good relations with neighbors. According to Crowder, who hailed from North Carolina, Lincoln's 1860 election plunged northwestern Butte County into "bitter strife," with Union- and Confederate-leaning residents "pretty much at one another's throats." Crowder added, "Everything was at a fever pitch and men were willing to believe most anything."[494] The Crowders, residents since 1856, were Chivalry Democrats who lived in the Rock Creek voter precinct. Frank Crowder was 18 when he found the body of one of the Hickok sisters. The version of these events in his later memoir is largely consistent with the recollections of contemporaries such as Bidwell, Simeon Moak and Anderson.

Tensions between Southerners and Northerners rose with the soaring July heat during the Hickok meeting in the upstairs room of Bidwell's store. Chairman Henshaw did not intervene as men shouted accusations that Bidwell's Indian ranch workers were "in league with those of the mountains, or at least [they] form a blind for the Mountain Indians to get into the valley."[495] Contributing to the suspicion, when Bidwell needed temporary help in the late 1850s, he hired Mountain Maidu to back up his

Mechoopda workforce. At the end of harvest or planting seasons, they returned to their territory, where settlers suspected they shared what they had learned about the valley farms. Settlers also were sure they stole weapons while at Rancho Chico and gave them to Butte Creeks (now part of the Mill Creek bands) to curry goodwill when Mountain Maidu accused them of collaborating with Bidwell.[496]

Their accusations were based on local memory that some ranch Mechoopdas helped the Mountain Maidu in their attempt to assassinate Bidwell in late 1856. Residents were also aware that some Mechoopdas, upset over the private treaty with Bidwell in 1851, disobeyed him and came and went from the ranch at will.[497] By this time Mechoopdas were in an impossible position: both settlers and Mill Creeks considered some of them untrustworthy.

Even though Northern- and Southern-born residents respected Bidwell, many also envied him and resented his control of a large, steady Indian workforce. In 1862, almost any criticism of Bidwell by Confederate sympathizers linked labor complaints to their war-related resentments. For example, men charged that Bidwell was an Indian slaver and, therefore, a hypocrite in his opposition to black slavery. It will be recalled that as early as the late 1840s and the early 1850s, miners resented him for the large parties of Valley Maidu who mined his gold. Other ranchers watched Rancho Chico Indians drive header wagons that collected harvested grain, demonstrating "precision, attention and skill ... requisite to catching the grain in their wagons, carried from the mower up a draper into these wagons while they were all moving, which obliged each wagon to fall immediately in behind the one that had just been filled and was passing out. They could plow mile long furrows practically by sight."[498] War partisans on both sides fumed at the irony that Bidwell, the preeminent Indian "master," was the most ardent local opponent of black slavery.

Northern Butte County's Chivalry Democrats not only denounced Bidwell, but, to some extent, Keefer and Robert Durham as "black abolitionists," equating the term to the southern pejorative "Black Republicans," which, back East, referred to northern white abolitionists. While both terms disparaged opponents of black slavery, in the particular context of Butte County politics, "black abolitionists" were those who opposed abolition only as it applied to black slaves in the South, but not to Indians whose lives and work on local ranches approximated that of slaves.[499]

Contributing to their conviction that ranch Indians were equivalent to slaves, immigrants to Chico from the Deep South also saw in them a physical resemblance to slaves back home. Even William Brewer, a New Englander, whose survey party camped at Rancho Chico in 1862, spoke of a physical resemblance between Indians and Blacks. Brewer added another racist twist—the Valley Indians he saw in Chico appeared to him as "very dark, black as our darkest mulatoes...."[500] Sherburne Cook considered "serf-like" a more accurate description of California's ranch Indians' status. He said Bidwell and Pierson B. Reading maintained "serf-like bands of Indian retainers" who "were reasonably contented and worked steadily."[501] Bidwell denied any similarity between his Indian laborers and the slaves of plantation masters.

All these issues erupted during the Hickok meeting when Bidwell responded by challenging the rural men's accusations that his ranch sometimes harbored dangerous Indians. An antagonist advanced to the podium and, shaking his fist in Bidwell's face, shouted "Shut your mouth. If you open it again in defense of those [Mechoopdas] outlaws I'll strike you!"[502]

CONFEDERATE SUPPORTERS AT THE MEETING also hammered Bidwell for his support of the Union. In this, he stood in solidarity with the slight majority of township residents. Most on both sides were Methodists because no other denomination's circuit-riding pastors made regular visits to the area. The national Methodist Church already had experienced such turmoil over slavery in the 1850s that, well before the war broke out, it split into northern and southern branches. In contrast, as the war commenced, all Butte County Methodists, regardless of their political leaning, continued to gather for the sermons of circuit preachers at the Pine Creek school north of town. John Bidwell & Co.'s store clerk and Union loyalist, Charles Stilson, would stay home from church when "a [antiwar Democrat] Copperhead preached."[503] After Pastor George Gray's sermons blamed northern abolitionists for the war, angry Union members formed the Methodist Church North, which met in a schoolhouse on the southern bank of Little Chico Creek.[504]

Chico's Southerners followed their lead to town, establishing the Methodist Church South, the better funded of the two branches. According to Hubert Howe Bancroft: "The methodist church south formed a factor in antiwar ... and pro-slavery politics and held its emissaries in the rural districts north to Oregon."[505] After the war, Chico's Southern Methodists would build a handsome church at least five years before their northern counterparts could afford more than a shabby parsonage where they also held services. And, also before the Northern Methodists could build, Bidwell gave the town's few Blacks a lot on which his carpenters erected the African Methodist Episcopal Church.[506] (The present Bethel A.M.E. Church on Linden at East Ninth Street inhabits the original building of the Methodist Church South, which was moved to that location.)

John Guill, a member of the Methodist South congregation, who was present at the Hickok meeting on July 11, 1862, remembered twenty years later that "during the most exciting time of our civil war ... everything else was absorbed by the war news, when neighbor was suspicious of neighbor."[507] The Southern supporters must have noticed that, in the uproar of the meeting, Bidwell's fellow Union supporters hesitated to denounce the local Rebs' accusations that Bidwell was an Indian slaver who harbored dangerous Indians. They also may have been worried that ranch Indians were forerunners of a potential California slave workforce that would compete with them for work. With Chivalry Democrats in charge of the meeting, the "radical and fiery speeches" about Bidwell's Indian "slaves" evolved into a call to kill every Mountain and Valley Indian. However, later, when their rage subsided, they acceded to the appeal from Frank Hickok, the child victims' father, to leave the peaceful Indians alone and they voted for a resolution to remove every area Indian to a reservation.

Just to be sure Bidwell was clear about their opinions of his operations, they doubled down with a second, blanket resolution to end Chico Township's "Indian slavery." They topped that with a vague threat to all ranch employers of Indians who persisted in attempts "to defeat the wishes of their neighbors and fellow citizens."[508] Years later, when Bidwell recalled the Hickok meeting, he characterized his attackers' accusations as the ravings of "infuriated drunken men" who envied his success. He also considered them ignorant about the burden he carried in his support of the rancheria Indians, regardless of their ability or willingness to work.[509] As his subsequent actions attest, Bidwell did not discount the threats he heard then and elsewhere. Indeed, his scrutiny of the Rebs' operations in northern Butte County's townships increased.

Bidwell was aware that Chico fielded a chapter of the Knights of the Golden Circle, or American Knights, a national organization that promoted the expansion of slavery and kept a close watch on its activities: "Whenever the Unionists were defeated, [the Knights] became very bold. I employed a man to join that

Sandy Young, Jay Salisbury, Harmon Good and "Indian Ned," Good's young killer who was later killed by Young, Good's close friend. Young was John Bidwell's head vaquero who trained and supervised Mechoopda cowboys.

society; paid his initiation fees, etc. Every night after they had a meeting he reported to me. He reported their secret signs and passwords. At one time they had under consideration and actually did resolve that every man of them should kill one Republican. Two men were selected to kill me. Things went on that way until the Union began to be victorious and until the soldiers came up."[510]

According to Bidwell, support for the South remained strong, in part because prominent California politicians continued to campaign for the Confederacy. Although voters had thrown them out of office, they waited in the shadows for a Confederate victory to restore them to power. When Brigadier General Edwin Sumner, commander of federal troops in California, prepared to send state residents east to join the war, San Francisco financiers and other leaders objected: "To deprive us of the military support of the Government at this time is to hold out a direct encouragement to traitors."[511] While this sentiment was most intense in Southern California, experience in Butte County convinced Bidwell and others to launch Union League chapters in Chico and Oroville. His store clerk, Charles Stilson, became an officer. Fellow member and Indian pursuer Moak recalled, "We pledged ourselves to uphold the Union at all hazards...."[512]

AFTER THE HICKOK MEETING, ATTENTION shifted back to preparing for the pursuit party to remove local Indians to reservations. Bidwell also found a chance to mend fences with his opponents. He announced he would dispatch his "chief vaquero," Alexander "Sandy" Young, 26, to accompany Good's party, in which Good and his partner Bowman would alternate as tracker and spotter. Young had trained Bidwell's Mechoopdas to ride horses and handle livestock at his summer grazing grounds. In 1862, Young was running the mountain camp and was especially alert to preventing Mountain Maidu attacks on cattle, himself and the Valley Maidu vaqueros, whose presence in their rivals' territory remained an affront. When raids appeared imminent, he would send word to Bidwell to send up an extra rifle or, when he distrusted ranch Indians with him, he would ask Bidwell to provide an additional white colleague as backup.[513]

Young's participation in Good's 1862 pursuit party was

valuable to Bidwell because it could prevent a repeat of 1859, when Kibbe's Rangers picked up Rancho Chico Indians in the removal sweep through the mountains. Young would be valuable to Good because he was one of the men most knowledgeable about Butte County's Maidu. Although he didn't share some of the other party members' hatred for Indians, he respected the danger some of them presented.

In addition to Bidwell's offer of Young, he also won the foothill farmers' goodwill when he convinced Kibbe to replace the rusty muskets the governor had sent for the volunteers. Kibbe sent Bidwell "a couple of boxes of U.S. rifles in good order," capable of striking targets at 200–300 yards. Bidwell passed them on to Good, whose men were to return them at their mission's end.[514] Bidwell also bought the surety bond required to secure their return.

That the weapons were sent to Bidwell added a new dimension to the unease of local Confederate supporters: the rancher's Southern opponents could not miss the fact that only he, the biggest Union supporter and Indian employer in the area, had inside access to weapons from the U.S. Army's Pacific Division.

Before Good's party left for the canyons, Bidwell offered a third and especially welcome contribution to its success. After the petitions to the governor from Butte and Tehama county residents had been signed, he promised he would personally deliver them to Gov. Stanford. Signers took this to mean he would persuade the governor to fully fund their campaign. Unlike the first petition, which asked, in general terms, "for men and means," this petition specifically called for the state "to raise and equip a campaign of thirty men to Mr. H. E. Good."[515] It also originally asked for support for sixty men, but someone scratched out that number and inked in half as many.

ALTHOUGH MID-TWENTIETH-CENTURY WRITERS ON THE California Indian wars compared some local men who volunteered for pursuit parties to psychopaths and mercenaries, nineteenth-century rural settlers called them heroes. In order to understand why Indian pursuers were so venerated, it must be remembered that no effective public entity at any level was charged or equipped to protect settlers from Indian attacks, whether in the valley, the foothills or the mountains. In a sense, the foothill settlers' and mountain miners' isolation and lack of outside protection was a kind of equalizer because Indians could only sometimes secure temporary help from rivals in other surrounding tribelets or tribes.

The Hickok killings were significant because the terror of raids already experienced by gold miners and settlers around Lassen Peak now revisited Butte County farm country. Settlers considered Indian pursuers to be especially courageous individuals who risked their lives to defend total strangers against predators. Those men considered Indian pursuits their duty, one that called them from their homes for indefinite lengths of time and required them to confront danger while poorly paid, fed, provisioned and outnumbered, in remote areas and with no rescuers at hand.

Although Mill Creeks rarely managed to kill pursuit party members in the field, they learned where volunteers lived and regularly retaliated on their premises. It will be recalled how, in 1859, Mill Creeks set fire to Anderson's buildings and stole or killed his valuable livestock.

While the current use of the word "volunteer" refers to private work for public purposes without wages, modern soldiers who volunteer their services expect pay for their risk and sacrifices. During the Indian wars, pursuers' families and business partners had to carry the load during their extended absences: "These volunteers are called from harvest fields where help is scarce, and have no resources to sustain them."[516] Modest wages were necessary.

In July 1862, the volunteer Indian pursuers, headed by Good and provisioned by Adj. Gen. Kibbe, left Chico, confident in Bidwell's promise to deliver the petitions to Stanford and convince him to fund their pursuit party.

Bidwell Goes His Own Way

On July 15, 1862, Bidwell carried the citizens' petitions to Sacramento for his meeting with Stanford. Although Stanford and the State Legislature had eliminated laws that provided state support for volunteer Indian pursuers, he retained the power to designate and fund a special type of militia to confront squatters. But even that option had been suspended when the State Militia, now called the California Volunteers, fell under Army control for the duration of the war. Therefore, Stanford sent Bidwell directly to Brig. Gen. George Wright, head of the Army's Pacific Department. A veteran of American wars with Indians and Mexicans, he had commanded Fort Reading, north of Chico, as a young officer in the early 1850s.[517]

In Bidwell's later account of his July 16 meeting with Wright, his careful wording inferred it was a success: "The Indian difficulties were fully explained by me, and he [Wright] resolved to order a company forthwith from Humboldt County to the scene of troubles."[518] However, the "troubles" referred only to problems in Tehama County, not Butte County. Wright also ignored the petitioners' request for state backing of Good and his volunteers. Instead, he sent two companies, headed by Capt. David B. Akey and Capt. H. B. Mellen, both of the Second Cavalry, California Volunteers, to patrol the area around Antelope Valley in eastern Tehama County, where the military had addressed conflicts through the late 1850s. While the evidence is incomplete, in addition to presenting the petitioners' requests for help, Bidwell probably played his own particular Confederate "card" in his meeting with the general. That is, he "fully explained" his need for soldiers at Rancho Chico because Southerners had threatened his Indian workers and him as a penalty for his services to the Union cause. In stark contrast to Bidwell's opposition to federal reservations to protect Indians in the early 1850s, particularly Mountain Indians most at risk to settlers, he now wanted the government to protect his own private Indian workforce against other settlers.

While Bidwell's report sounded as if he were satisfied, without soldiers his Indian workers remained vulnerable to the Confederate backers' threats. When he arrived home, the petitioners concluded he must have purposely misrepresented them since all their requests had been denied: instead of volunteers, Wright sent soldiers; instead of help for both Butte and Tehama counties, Wright sent all the help to Tehama County.[519] And finally, Bidwell was denied protection for his Mechoopda ranch workers. Suspicions that Bidwell had purposefully misconstrued the petitioners' wishes in his meeting with Wright, undermined public regard for him at home.

Bidwell had failed to sway the governor or win over Wright. However, looked at in light of events a year later, when Wright would consider no local opinions but Bidwell's, it appears Bidwell had impressed the general with his personal knowledge of Indians and conditions in his area.[520] At the least, the Chico rancher had demonstrated enough influence to secure both weapons and troops from the Army's commanding officer, albeit to the wrong front. Despite the outcomes, Bidwell derived some benefit: while California Volunteers were no threat to Mill Creeks, their presence in the North State helped to rein in Chico Rebs who had been harassing him.

The Good party's gratitude for Bidwell's help evaporated a week after they left the valley when word reached them at Deer Creek Flats that he failed to secure help. They learned that his meeting had not been with the governor, but was with Wright, who ordered troops to an area where they would be of no help to the volunteers from Chico Township. And, the governor had declined to fund their campaign.[521] Exasperated, half the men left Good's party, leaving only fifteen.

On July 22, Good sent the *Red Bluff Beacon* a plea for donations from Tehama County residents, who had backed the 1859 volunteer pursuit party and were joint petitioners with those from Butte County in the present one. He explained: "For some unexplained reason Gen. Wright, unsolicited by petition, has preferred to send us the promise of regulars."[522] Common opinion, he went on, was that "regulars [soldiers] ... are generally conceded to be more efficient in guarding Indians than hunting Indians."[523] Without mentioning Bidwell, Good condemned the "treachery or criminal neglect of those in power, or those entrusted with the citizens' petition for the organizing and commissioning of a company of volunteers."[524] He described "a deep sense of injustice [which] pervades the minds of the petitioners. Different causes and persons are blamed...."[525]

A century or more later, Good was despised for his vendetta against the Mill Creeks. In his own time, however, he was a champion, albeit a somewhat quirky one. When Good went to town, some saw a dandy who was "odd in his dress, which though scrupulously neat was composed of many colors, differing from prevailing fashions and well adapted to the showing of his well developed and symmetrical proportion."[526] Not only was he something of a peacock, he was also known for the bulging strings of long, black-haired Indian scalps that dangled from his saddle horn, symbolizing his success in "the hunt."

From another angle, while Good, a master marksman, could be a brutal avenger in his war against Mountain Indians, once he dismounted at a hitching post in town, he appeared articulate, well-spoken and reasonable, a contrast which must have complicated his reputation in the settler community. His smoother side appears in his letters to Stanford in 1862. They demonstrate that, by contrast to his reputation as an independent Indian fighter, he also pressed the governor for guidance. For example, he was in the canyons on August 8 when he wrote, "Being without a Commission or instructions ... I am at a loss to know to whom I should report; therefore trusting that if you are not the proper person you will do me and those I represent the favor humanity requests by forwarding this to the proper authorities, who will no doubt forthwith some instructions at least respecting prisoners whom I shall continue to respect until a reasonable time for an answer. One more favor I crave is to know why our citizens' petition was unheeded, and what became of it?"[527]

In Good's attempt to win Stanford's support and to make his unit, in effect, a temporary California Volunteers company, he laid out his credentials. He described his expeditions to date, estimating he and his men had personally observed about one hundred Mill Creeks of the two hundred or so who joined and left raider parties; he identified the location of two camps at the head of Mill Creek, with the rest divided between the heads of Antelope and Cow creeks; he and his men had attacked one of those camps, where they found an Overland Mail rifle and other guns and ammunition; his men killed eighteen Indians there, counted six wounded (many who escaped often died later); and he took to Nome Lackee six children, the prisoners he had mentioned in his letter to the governor. The toll his campaigns took on the Indian side might have been even greater had a warrior party not been out at the time on a raid of the Tehama County farm of George W. Kelley. (The one hundred raiders Good estimated were then active exceeded the number of men the small Yahi tribe could have fielded on its own.) Good twice sent appeals to Stanford from Deer Creek, in each case describing his unit's actions and specifying what he thought the governor needed to know to make proper decisions. The governor did not respond to either appeal.

Good probably never learned that Kibbe read his appeals and proposed to the governor that he should either present Good with a specific assignment and so bring his operation under state control, or order him "to desist from further actions."[528] Stanford acted on neither suggestion. Good and his company were on their own.

Meanwhile, the two California Volunteers companies Wright dispatched to Tehama County in response to the petitioners' request for help made passes through mountainous areas where Mill Creeks camped, but soon withdrew and moved on to other assignments. It would be another year, 1863, before Wright would dispatch companies of troops to set up camp in Chico itself. By that time, his confidence in Bidwell had grown.[529] While events in 1863 were so critical they require separate treatment, years later their proximity to events in 1862 would muddle old timers' memories about what happened in which year. One element their memories retained in common, however, was the weight they all placed on Bidwell's conflict with local supporters of the Confederate cause while in the midst of conflicts with Indians.[530] Certainly, the contest between Bidwell and local Rebs probably explains why, in 1862, he again moved the Mechoopda rancheria to a more defensible location across the creek from his headquarters.[531]

A review of the state's preference to confront Butte County's Rebs rather than Indian troublemakers or restive settlers is in order. Chapter Eight expands on the military's presence in Chico from 1863 to 1865, when its priority to provide security for Indian workers on ranches contradicted its other more vague or unworkable orders to protect settlers from Indians in canyons and foothills far from Rancho Chico. Chapters Nine through Eleven explain the roles of several military companies in the 1863 Indian removal from Chico.

8

Harassing Rebs, the Indian Soldiers' Pastime

Southerners who arrived in northern Butte County in 1862 and 1863 included "squads of demoralized rebels from [Sterling] Price's shattered army."[532] They had fled Missouri after years of violence between supporters of slavery and Northerners determined to secure the state for free labor. Most of the new arrivals settled in clusters along Rock and Mud creeks, pathways for Mill Creeks entering and exiting the Butte County foothills. Other arrivals from Southern and Border states settled around Dayton, southwest of Chico, where references to "the Dayton crowd" became interchangeable with the popular term Copperheads. While Copperheads elsewhere were pro-Confederate Northern Democrats, local newspapers and Charles Stilson, Bidwell's store clerk, considered them any Confederate supporter or secessionist. This section employs this common, albeit erroneous, usage.

Union men who groused about their new neighbors' politics found no support in the *Butte Record*. Its Oroville publisher, George Crosette, a New York native and fervent Democrat, was skeptical about the rightness of the war against, in effect, a faction of his beloved party. He welcomed the Southerners to Butte County, confident they were "tired of the war [and] wanting to settle down away from destruction."[533] On the other hand, as discussed in the last chapter, Union Democrats feared the influx of Southern voters would shift the control of the county's Democratic Party to its Chivalry or Southern faction. The narrowly divided election returns in September 1863 temporarily relieved their fears. As Bidwell & Co. clerk Stilson gloated, "The County ticket is safe. Copperheads are miserable as they ought to be but Union men are jubilant."[534] Before his early 1863 arrival in

California, Stilson had taught school in Missouri where he tried to stay clear of its blood-soaked politics.

Chico's Southerners—often called Rebs—could not have been happy in 1863 when the Union Army's commander, in response to the settler-Indian conflicts, sent Captain Augustus W. Starr's Company F, Second Cavalry, California Volunteers, to Chico. (The next chapter discusses this and other Indian-related military issues.) Even worse for the Rebs, the company did not leave after their stint at guarding Indians during the Indian removal that year ended. Anticipating ongoing problems between John Bidwell and the farmers, given ongoing clashes with Indians, they remained at Camp Bidwell on Rancho Chico.

Bidwell, who later took credit for the military decision to move against the local Rebs, said they were an annoyance "until the soldiers came up. Then we arrested every fellow who hurrahed for Jeff Davis and kept him under guard...."[535] Bidwell's use of "we" referred to Brig. Gen. Wright's August 1, 1863, order to Starr "to consult frequently with Major Bidwell.... You will find the major reliable and extremely loyal."[536] Starr passed this instruction along to Capt. Alfred Morton, whose Company K, Second Infantry Division, California Volunteers, arrived the second week in August to assist him with the Indian removal.[537] Those companies' roles in the removal receive full attention in later chapters.

While Starr's men were guarding Bidwell's ranch Indians from foothill farmers, they found plenty of time to address Union men's complaints about local Confederate affronts. Hubert Howe Bancroft's description applied to Chico: "There was never a moment when the advocates of secession ... did not assert their freedom from any allegiance to the government."[538] Until the troops arrived, packed crowds in Bidwell Hall had cheered rousing speeches by Reb speakers and debaters. Stilson, staying late for the south stage mail pouch, grumbled at the enthusiastic shouts upstairs. However, once soldiers arrived, Confederates became more circumspect.

With the onset of winter in 1864, Camp Bidwell troops put up a "liberty pole" in support of the Union.[539] Two months later, Stilson wrote in his diary: "Surely today was an unlucky one for some ardent secesh sympathizers who under the influence of liquor gave vent to their resentments in the presence of some Soldiers who were guarding horses near Sandy's Corral—the result was they were arrested and are now incarcerated in the guard house, will probably remain on duty awhile...."[540]

A few days later, unrest erupted in Evansville, a mining town, where voters in the 1864 election were evenly divided between Union and Confederate supporters. The two factions broke into a squabble about which flag—Union or Confederate—should be displayed on the public school's flag pole. At first, Union men seized control of the pole and ran up "the stars and stripes." But once they relaxed their vigil, the Rebs stole and desecrated the flag.[541]

As complaints multiplied about Southerners championing the Rebs, Capt. Starr's men "arrested" the agitators and strapped ninety-pound gunnysacks of bricks or sand to their backs and ordered them to pace the yard. The gunnysack injured Arkansan Charles Barham, a mason, who, thereafter, kept his politics to himself. Stilson was gleeful: "The secesh are indignant to think that their friends are 'packing sand' at the camp."[542]

Mary Silsby, a new arrival in 1864, had never observed such war tensions in her New England hometown where everyone backed the Union. She reported, "There is not that unity of interest [in Chico on the war] that we find in the East. This is not to be wondered at if we take into consideration that California ... is made up of people from all parts of the country ... who have no interests in common & perhaps even a jealousy of each other, like the people [here] of the North & the South."[543]

On April 13 of that year, Starr's company was ordered to leave Camp Bidwell and head for Camp Union in Sacramento. However, in late July, when clashes with Indians in northeastern Butte County again led Chicoans to call for help, Wright ordered Capt. James C. Doughty and Company I, Second Cavalry, California Volunteers, to Camp Bidwell for a sixty-day assignment. Once there, the company found it impossible to respond to Indian raids hours away on the upper Humboldt Wagon Road in the foothills east of Chico. Capt. Doughty, therefore, kept his men busy with Civil War duties on the Chico "front." Stilson noted in his diary that, by contrast to Starr's relatively restrained approach to problems with the Rebs, Doughty's soldiers "are more ready to deal with all our exultant copperheads—and in consequence they [local Southerners] are very angry to see them come."[544]

DURING THE LATER WAR YEARS, because Southerners were numerous and vocal in California, the Army, having federalized the State Militia, organized local militias to suggest Union strength and readiness should Rebs consider uprisings. These militias were separate from the ongoing California Volunteers, the state's professional soldiers and officers who continued to handle the Indian wars and other serious problems. Once Gov. Stanford appointed Bidwell commander of the new Northern California district of local militias, Bidwell established the Chico Light Infantry in the fall of 1863. The Oroville Guard, the Lassen Rangers of Susanville and others fell under his purview.

While Bidwell's position carried no independent authority to call even his home brigade into action, his promotion to the honorary rank of brigadier general added to his status for the rest of his life.[545] After he turned Bidwell Hall into the Armory, it operated as a kind of clubhouse for the most devoted Light Infantry members. Membership in the local militia carried a special allure because recruits sported uniforms, poured over drill manuals, jockeyed for election to officer ranks and carried government rifles. When California Volunteers at Camp Bidwell were not out on missions, they participated with local militiamen in occasional joint activities: parades, a fancy ball and the Chico Light Infantry's Private Daniel Sutherland, an occasional Indian pursuer, bested all but one of Capt. Doughty's men in a competitive shooting match. Militiamen not only organized rallies and marches, but one of their cannonades to celebrate a Union victory went on so long that the sick called for them to stop.[546] Chivalry Democrats gave up on public rallies.

Stilson joined the Light Infantry in September 1864 because he was eager for action and thought the drills would give him exercise. After an Indian raid in March 1865, he hoped his unit might assist the California Volunteers on Indian duty, but the Army never called on them.[547]

Enlistments for the national draft spiked with the rumor that California men were about to be drafted and "put on the front ranks to receive the enemy's fire, while those who volunteered could stand in the rear."[548] Chico men considered exemption from the draft as the most attractive benefit of the militia.

When Confederate sympathizer Ridgely Greathouse showed up in Butte County, the effect was electric. After a widely publicized federal arrest in 1863 for his part in the purchase and arming of a San Francisco-docked schooner, the *J. M. Chapman*, Greathouse was put in military prison on Alcatraz Island in the San Francisco Bay. Greathouse and his cohorts had been planning to capture forts around the Bay. Although their arrests occurred the moment they raised anchor in port and seized nothing, avid Union supporters demanded harsh penalties. According to Frank Crowder's memoir, Greathouse's and his partners' actions convinced Chicoans, like others across the state, that a Confederate invasion of California was imminent.

In February 1864, Stilson was simultaneously indignant and fascinated to find himself in the same Oroville-to-Chico stagecoach as Greathouse, who recently had been released from Alcatraz because he accepted President Lincoln's offer of amnesty in exchange for his declaration of loyalty. After the trip, Stilson deemed Greathouse a "personal" acquaintance and pronounced the Kentucky native's vow "a farce."[549] He was jubilant on April 9 when Capt. Doughty's men arrested the "noted pirate [who] was taken thru town in irons—on a new charge." Best of all, he wrote in his diary, "it makes the secesh boil with rage."[550] Greathouse eventually escaped a New York prison and moved on to other adventures.

According to Bancroft, advances by Union Army forces into Southerners' home states heightened tensions in California in 1864. Determined not to let the state's Southern Democrats regain power, in late spring, Bidwell left Chico for the Republican Party convention in Baltimore. Afterward, during a side trip to Washington, D.C., he expressed to Secretary of War Stanton his "intense desire to see General Ulysses S. Grant."[551] Stanton agreed to reward him for his support. Bidwell waited at the White House, then open to the public, until Gen. Grant's couriers arrived with instructions. Once he was granted permission to serve as the return courier, soldiers escorted him to the Union Army headquarters in Virginia.

While his ship from Washington to the front was under sail, Bidwell was surprised to learn many prominent Confederate Californians on board had made numerous trips to the war zone. Their commitment to their home states' defeat of the Union deepened Bidwell's determination to advance the North's cause back home.

Bidwell wrote of his brief visit with Grant: "Where I was going I did not know, but finally came to Grant's tent. I did not see an Army. Grant took my dispatches. He asked me to dinner, and in about half an hour he told Quartermaster Ingalls that we would start in half an hour. In 15 minutes, every tent, everything was out of sight and in the wagons. I asked Grant how far it was to the front. He said about half a mile. 'How far is it to where Lee is encamped?' They are about 40 feet from our advanced line. We mounted and were off. We went about 15 miles but in such a cloud of dust that we could scarcely see ourselves. But I could see Grant's shoulders and kept watch of him. At sundown we came to a stop; but did not see the army then. We built a campfire and lay there until 5 in the morning. The baggage wagons had not come up yet. About one o'clock they arrived and in fifteen minutes every tent was in its place. I slept in Grant's tent that night in an iron bedstead. In the morning he arranged for me to go back. He told the quartermaster to hurry up or the troops would take the road from us. Finally the troops came along. Grant knew just where each column was. During that night I don't think he slept more than 15 minutes at a time. Dispatches were arriving constantly. His composure under those circumstances led me to have great confidence in him, altho' he was so entirely different from what I had expected. No drawing of his sword; no orders given through a trumpet; no pomp or noise."[552]

Upon Bidwell's return to Chico, he launched his campaign for nomination as the Union Party candidate for a seat in the House of Representatives. Stilson, 21, a staunch temperance man, was uneasy about the generous bar his boss laid out in the Armory for the thirsty crowd of prospective voters who become increasingly boisterous over the course of the evening. Although only a social drinker himself, Bidwell deferred to the voters who considered an open bar their due.[553]

Political passions drove this election and secessionists could not contain their frustration over news of Confederate losses in the East. Fisticuffs were so frequent that Crowder recalled Chico Village, as Bidwell called it, was in a state of "small civil war."[554] In mid-August, Capt. Doughty dispatched a Camp Bidwell sergeant and private to look into complaints about a rowdy secessionist. Another assignment took soldiers to a Reb rally where his men arrested speakers denouncing "black abolitionists," their word for abolitionists like Bidwell who relied on Indian workers. On another occasion, when the California Volunteers returned from an unsuccessful Indian sortie, a normally "quiet and polite" soldier beat up a noisy secesh in a saloon. When Capt. Doughty called him to account, the soldier explained he had joined to fight Confederates and that is what he did.[555] About the same time, soldiers rode to Oroville where they arrested a "Copper" and took him to the guardhouse at Camp Bidwell. Discipline problems along the way led their sergeant to arrive there not only with the Reb, but with three of his own men in custody.[556]

Gunfire exchanges over war issues cost two Butte County men their lives. In one of these incidents, a participant in a Union Democratic Party meeting escaped to Oregon after he killed "Irish Copperhead" Phillip Farrelly, an Oroville saloon keeper. When he was captured and returned for trial, the justice of the peace acquitted him on grounds of self-defense.[557] But such Chico events rarely reached print in Oroville's Union supporting *Butte Record*. One reason may have been the resentment in Oroville at Chico's attempts to secede from Butte County and create a separate county, which the newspaper's publisher opposed.

CHICO'S UNION MEN FLOCKED TO the Armory for rallies and to hear traveling orators champion the North's cause. Crowds cheered each time the Light Infantry fired its cannon to celebrate Sherman's capture of Atlanta and other victories. Northern supporters raised $1,000 "in coin" for the Sanitary Commission, a national organization for the health and safety of Union soldiers. In an Oroville fundraiser, supporters sold the same bag of wheat at each stop across the state, raising hundreds of thousands of dollars.[558]

Throughout the war, Charlie Stilson fretted over the safety of his Union soldier brothers, Thomas and James, gleaning news of their units' campaigns from his mother's letters. On October 1, he received word that his brother, Thomas Hart Benton Stilson, of Company A, 7th Wisconsin Volunteer Infantry, died on July 31 in the battle of Petersburg: "Oh how can I express my feelings upon ... the sad sad news of tonight—my own Dear Brother Thomas is Dead yes was killed when his time to return to dear friends had so nearly arrived & this blow is my first great affliction ... there is one great consolation that he lived & died a christian. Oh that I were one also."[559]

The next day in church, when the Reverend James M. Woodman included Thomas Stilson in his prayers, Charlie "could not prevent the scalding tears flowing," his friends comforting him as he wept.[560] Meanwhile, fellow Light Infantryman Sutherland waited for news from home about his three brothers. Two became disabled and a third died from battle wounds at the battle of Pea Ridge.

Having won the nomination for a seat in Congress, Bidwell entered the general campaign where he faced stiff opposition from both Union and Chivalry Democrats. Their political strength extended south to the farmers around Colusa County, where he stumped during late October. Upon his return to Chico, Bidwell made a "sound and logical" speech at a political rally there, while a second speaker "urged all to maintain that Union which cost us so many precious lives & that ... our Brothers shall not die in vain—."[561]

On October 24, an election debate took place upstairs, now the Armory. In his diary, Stilson seethed about the evening's "Dem-Copperhead Traitorous meeting" in which a Bidwell opponent, Jackson Temple, fanned "secesh sentiment ... a rich treat for Traitors."[562] The death of Stilson's brother moved him to work even harder for the Union League, for which he created a list of every "loyal" man in every precinct for "get out the vote" drives.

As the campaign neared election day, members of the Chico Light Infantry marched in an Oroville parade to promote Lincoln's re-election. Militia units from Butte and Yolo counties carried "mottoes ... and banners" accompanied by marching bands. Stilson made large "transparencies" (early photographs made with gelatin and silver on glass) that accompanied the Chico unit. Reverberations from the unit's "12 pounder" shattered the courthouse windows. Stilson was proud because "the procession ... was certainly ahead of anything ever known in Butte...." And, when his boss Bidwell exhorted the voters to support the Union and his candidacy, the crowd responded with "long continued cheers."[563]

With reports of Union Army advances, California's Southern supporters realized Confederate armies alone could not win the war—they needed to oust Lincoln. Their only chance to drive the incumbent president from office seemed to rest on the Democratic Party's nomination of former Union Army General George B. McClellan, who was reluctant to end slavery in the South. Democrats in his camp were convinced that only he could draw support from both the Democratic Party's Union and Chivalry factions. While Lincoln carried Butte County in the November 5 election, McClellan captured 46 percent of the votes cast in Chico, where saloons, observing the state mandate, closed for the day. Union Party candidate Bidwell, riding on Lincoln's "coattails," defeated the Democrat, Temple, and made ready to serve in the 39th Congress.

Over the remainder of 1864, Union supporters flocked to the Sanitary Commission's lecture series. At one, Stilson heard graphic accounts of battlefield conditions and vivid descriptions of sad scenes in hospitals: "Oh, how freely tears flowed as I tho't of my Dear Brother."[564] Chico women sold tickets to a benefit dance and regularly solicited donations door-to-door to benefit the Commission. Oroville women also did their part. When a preacher declared he would not accept wages his female parishioners had raised by holding a dance, the women went ahead with the event anyway, withholding his wages and donating the entire proceeds to the Union cause.[565]

While most of Chico's Reb supporters had to be careful what they said about the war, they employed other means to express their opposition to the Union. Politics was personal in nineteenth-century Chico, influencing social life and where residents spent their money. Chico's growth meant new places to shop, so some Southern supporters refused to patronize the general store of Bidwell and his partner George Wood. Even though Stilson noted in one of his 1863 entries that "soldiers have kept us busy all day and trade is lively," his diary was replete with references to slow trade.[566] Stilson, whose wartime diaries reveal him as prickly and quick to judge, was indignant when he encountered Southerners. Although he noted daily sightings of local Rebs in front of the store and around town, he did not mention them as customers.

After 1862, Stilson's diary mentioned intense business meetings between Bidwell and Wood. Stilson described one and made other remarks on the store indicating that, despite population growth and lucrative military trade, the store's patronage suffered during the war. Despite the apparent "boycott" of the general store, the war provided Bidwell other sources of revenue: federal warrants payable in gold for rentals of the Armory, the parade ground behind his store, the California Volunteers' corral and campgrounds and purchases of Indian and military provisions.

While Wood and store manager Gus Chapman were on the record as Union men, war issues seemed of little concern to either man, which may have been a factor in their close friendship. Chapman left Michigan for California when the war began. A lawyer and merchant in his home state, he handled the legal work to set up the Chico Light Infantry. However, Chapman's rare attendance at its drills irritated Stilson, who suspected his boss, still a Democrat and not active in Union pro-war events, was more interested in promising business opportunities that took him out of town.

Throughout the war, Wood, a Massachusetts native whose wife was a former Georgia belle, was a California correspondent for the *Mobile* [Alabama] *Advertiser*. Somehow he maintained an exchange of letters and documents with Mobile lawyers, which ultimately resulted in halting the Confederate government's confiscation of his late in-laws' large store. Once Wood received the proceeds from its sale, he and Chapman broke from Bidwell to open a rival store on Main Street at Second Street.[567]

After the War

In 1865, Capt. Starr's company from Camp Union in

Sacramento arrested rowdy Colusa County Confederate sympathizers and then rode to Camp Bidwell, where, on April 10, his and Capt. Doughty's units learned of Lee's surrender from Bidwell's telegraph machine. The Chico Infantrymen celebrated the news by firing their cannon one hundred times as its members and both companies of California Volunteers marched down Second Street to cheers.[568] The township's Southerners could only commiserate in private, but their grief and resentment would smolder over the rest of the century.

On April 14, a Camp Bidwell soldier, Pvt. Frank Hudson, shot Lieutenant D. W. Livergood through his stomach as the officer walked from Camp Bidwell to his Chico cottage at 9:00 in the evening. Hudson was angry because the lieutenant had caught him drunk and ordered him to march at "double quick time." After Starr and his men left camp, Capt. Doughty aborted an Indian patrol so that the men could oversee the search for Hudson, who had escaped, and supervise Camp Bidwell in place of the unit sergeant who was sick.

As Livergood's friends maintained watch over the young officer, the news of Lincoln's assassination and the critical wounding of Secretary of State William Seward spread. Stilson wrote in his diary: "The most terrible calamity that ever befell a people has been made known to us to day & such a gloom & sorrow was never felt in any community. President Lincoln was assassinated yesterday evening in Washington and tonight we are mourning the loss of the greatest man the world ever knew. Sec. of State William Seward was also wounded & little hopes are entertained for his recovery. I cannot have time to express my feelings."[569] Stilson's spirits rose with later news that his surviving brother's company in the Fifth Michigan Cavalry had captured Jefferson Davis and his family in Georgia.

While Union supporters were grieving for Lincoln and Seward, who survived his injuries, they welcomed news that San Franciscans had vandalized the offices of secesh-leaning newspapers. Chicoans joined a national vigil for Seward's recovery. Stilson and Joseph Eddy, his friend and captain in the Light Infantry, headed for Livergood's home where they shared the latest news. On leaving, they agreed he seemed "past hope"; he died not long after their visit.[570]

On April 19, the funeral at the lieutenant's cottage attracted an overflow crowd. The International Order of Odd Fellows and the military presided over services for the officer, who had received a promotion to first lieutenant only the previous December. Livergood's membership in Chico's new Odd Fellows chapter provided about $10 a month in life insurance for his widow.

Pvt. Hudson's brief flight ended with his capture in the countryside by a local man who recognized his military boots. Hudson waited in custody for the arrival of seven officers from Sacramento to conduct his court martial. Stilson made friends with the officers, who felt welcome at the store and kept him abreast of the hearings. The worldly confidence of the officers, who were somewhat older than Stilson, made him uncomfortable at times, but, according to his diary, their teasing about his prospects with one of the town's young women encouraged him to overcome his shyness and ask her out.

News of the capture and killing of Edwin Booth, Lincoln's assassin, inspired Stilson's bitter reaction: "It only causes regret that he was permitted to die so early—I would like to be one who would take his life by inches."[571] In April, after anti-Union men in Colusa County fired guns to celebrate the assassination, Wright dispatched Starr to take the troublemakers to Camp Bidwell. His unit was still there in early May, when Stilson noted local Southerners were "blue" after soldiers placed Chico farmers Al Stewart, 27, an "Irish Reb," and Oliver P. Gregory, a Virginian, in Camp Bidwell's brig. Although in custody, Stewart managed to appear before the justice of the peace to defend his lawsuit against another "Reb." Starr's final arrest, while at Camp Bidwell, was that of B. F. Baker in Forbestown, east of Oroville. Capt. Doughty arrested Butte Creek resident Lucius W. Thomas, known as "Three-Fingered Jack," a "man of secession proclivities," who was in Colusa County when Doughty arrested over a dozen like-minded men.[572]

In late May, Starr set off with his prisoners for Sacramento. The captain and his men added an unnamed "prominent traitor" to their party in Yolo County.[573] All Starr's prisoners received sentences of confinement at Alcatraz, where Chico's Three Fingered Jack was the cellmate of "Long Primer" Hall, editor of the *Amador Dispatch*. A Democrat, Hall advocated slavery in California

The Humboldt Road opened a new trade route through Mountain Maidu territory to Idaho mines.

and considered Lincoln a dictator. The two men shared a mat and food Three Fingered Jack considered superior to his meals at home.[574] On May 23, not long after Starr's departure, Capt. Doughty and his company also left Chico. By May, all but two of the ten companies in Wright's Second Cavalry were in conflicts with Indians around the state.[575]

On June 1, 1865, Chico's businesses, like those across the country, closed for the day in celebration of the Union's victory. According to Stilson, some residents assembled for a sermon by Rev. Woodman, while others preferred private reflection.[576] In a unifying gesture as 1865 came to a close, local people set up a "Union Commission" that raised funds to benefit both Whites and Blacks in the "war devastated Southern states."[577]

One sign of a return to normal life that summer appeared on May 26 when the Idaho Stage carried the first mail to Chico over the just completed Humboldt Road, which linked local trade to Idaho's mines. However, residents' hopes for an economic boost from the road were dashed by Mountain Maidu attacks on travelers.

While Civil War battles no longer divided neighbors, the war's effects lingered. For example, in the 1880s, Frederick Clough's Southern-born grandmother Libby Stansbury refused to serve yams, watermelon or catfish—black folks' food, she explained. Clough remembered how she once flipped through his history text and penciled an "X" across Lincoln's photograph. During the same period, a proposal to install a statue in Chico to commemorate Confederate soldiers found support. In response, Bidwell threw himself into an effort to place the statue of a Union soldier in the cemetery. With each side determined to deny the other its statue, or uneasy at the prospect of opposing statues, neither prevailed. In the early twentieth century, an ambiguous statue of an unidentified Civil War soldier appeared in Chico's cemetery, where it currently overlooks the graves of soldiers from both sides.[578]

Civil War issues in northern Butte County influenced new outbreaks in the conflicts between Indians and settlers, settlers and settlers, and between Valley and Mountain Indians. The next chapters go back in time from the present chapter to follow the evolution of Indian and settler conflicts between 1863 and 1865. For example, Chapter Nine examines the 1863 crisis that began when miners lynched five Indians in a mountain village. This led Indians to retaliate by kidnapping and killing settlers' children and the Army to dispatch Capt. Starr's company to Rancho Chico, where the men set up Camp Bidwell to remove Indians to the Nome Cult Reservation.

9

The Military Response to New Child Killings

Through the fall and winter of 1862–1863 settlers nursed their disappointment that a lack of funds the previous summer had cut short Hi Good's and his men's pursuit of Mill Creeks. Meanwhile, in response to an Idaho mining boom, John Bidwell and his partners launched the Humboldt Wagon Road with a financial allocation from the California State Legislature, backed by Bidwell's credit.[579] Because the road's route from Chico across the Sierra Nevada to Idaho would impinge on Oroville's trade monopoly, it further divided the already strained relations between northern and southern Butte County.

In addition to Bidwell's ongoing need for ranch employees, now he had to hire road construction crews. The Mechoopda population's decline from ninety in 1851 to sixty in the early 1860s meant there were too few men to cover either need, let alone both. Therefore, for several years, Bidwell had been supplementing his workforce by hiring Indians from other Valley and Mountain Maidu tribelets.

General Kibbe's Indian Captives Flee Nome Cult Reservation

In September 1862, problems festered in the Coast Range that would affect Butte County over the next year. With winter's approach, starvation loomed for the Mountain Indians delivered to reservations there by Adj. Gen. Kibbe in 1859.[580] In addition, the Mountain Maidu, Hat Creeks and Pit Rivers in the Round Valley (formerly Nome Cult) Reservation, were targets of Coast

Range Wylacki and other tribes native to Mendocino and Klamath counties. The Kibbe captives informed James Short they were leaving for their homes in the Cascades and the Sierra Nevada. They included Indians moved to the Mendocino Reservation and then transferred to Round Valley where they joined others he had captured.

James Short, recently fired as the Round Valley Reservation superintendent and not yet replaced, sympathized with the captives and did not challenge their departure. He informed the superintendent of Indian Affairs, agent George Hanson, that, due to settler attacks on the reservation Indians, hundreds had "pulled up stakes yesterday evening and left ... for their old homes in Butte County."[581] Short added that Concow Maidu Tome-ya-nem was among them.

This communication must have rankled Hanson because the previous year, 1861, his predecessor had only started the process of firing Short. When Hanson became superintendent, while preparing to carry through with Short's termination, he persuaded Wright to station troops in Round Valley to improve order at the reservation. In October, Capt. Charles D. Douglas and Company D, Second California Infantry, established Fort Wright and placed the surrounding area under martial law. Douglas banned liquor sales and held a hearing on Short's administrative record. When Douglas concluded Short was incompetent, he notified Hanson, who fired him in 1862.[582] However, while an extended search to replace Short was underway, he continued to reside near the reservation through 1863. His presence there would have consequences for Indians he had helped to escape and hundreds more.

THE THREE HUNDRED INDIANS WHO had decided to leave Round Valley Reservation were exhausted by their descent down the precipitous mountain trail to the Sacramento Valley. Made up mostly of Mountain Maidu with some Hat Creeks and Pit Rivers, they stopped near Red Bluff at the familiar remains of the closed Nome Lackee Reservation. Company E of the Second California Cavalry, U.S. Army, under Colonel Francis J. Lippitt, arrived to resume custody of them as they recuperated from their journey and prepared to wait out the winter in the valley. While they intended to return to their old homes in the Sierra and the Cascades, they might starve and freeze there as winter was setting in, so they postponed the rest of the trip until spring.[583]

Their conditions and circumstances upon arrival were so dire that surrounding farmers brought them food. However, without an ongoing arrangement for provisions, the farmers realized the Indians would eventually have no other option than to raid their farms. By November, with that prospect in mind and rumors that soldiers raped a ranch Indian woman, the settlers wanted to know, "Where is Hanson?"[584]

Before Hanson became the Indian agent for California's northern district, he had been a Marysville leader whose relative prosperity and education distinguished him there. He had organized the town's Methodist Episcopal Church in 1850 and was considering becoming a pastor when he signed on with the federal Indian Affairs Department. Although new to such work, fast-moving events, such as his arrival at the closed Nome Lackee Reservation, now full of Indians from Round Valley, quickly brought him up to speed. In Red Bluff, Col. Lippitt, like the farmers, pressed him to transfer the reservation Indians somewhere else.

Because no reservation had room for hundreds more Indians, Hanson appealed to Bidwell for space on his ranch where the Indians could await transfer. Four years earlier, in 1859, Bidwell had allowed Kibbe to place many of the same Indians on Rancho Chico before soldiers delivered them to Round Valley and other reservations.

Hanson explained to Bidwell that if the freed Mountain Maidu, Pit River and Hat Creek captives sought refuge in the Sierra Cascades, the increased numbers of multi-tribal refugees there would not accept them. According to Hanson, they "would all be killed and they fear it also, but some would risk it."[585] He also played on the rancher's Union sympathies: "The secessionists drove [them] from Round Valley after wiping out their crops. ... I am determined to place them on your land and a man to remain with them all the time to protect them and see they did not interrupt any person's property. ... This thing of Whites and Indians living in the [Round] valley is 'played out.'..."[586]

Hanson's urgent appeal to Bidwell to harbor the Round Valley

Reservation Indians was critical because tensions remained throughout Butte County's townships along the Deer Creek Ridge. In the valley, the addition of hundreds more Mountain Indians to Bidwell's ranch might spark his neighbors' objections.

Based on Hanson's promise that the government would remove the Round Valley Indians from Rancho Chico in the spring of 1863, "when I can in safety return them to the reservation in Round Valley,"[587] Bidwell acquiesced and designated a site near what was called Chico Landing or Bidwell's Landing, where steamships docked on the Sacramento River. This location on the western boundary of his ranch distanced the displaced Indians from his ranch Indians and foothill settlers. Hanson sent special Indian subagent James Franklin Eddy to supervise the reservation Indians.[588]

The significance of these developments can best be understood by keeping in mind that, from late 1862 through the summer of 1863, four distinct groups of Indians would be located on Bidwell's ranch: (1) Mechoopda Maidu, permanent residents; (2) seasonal employees from other Valley tribelets who worked for Bidwell; (3) peaceful Mountain Maidu; and (4) Kibbe Indian captives from Round Valley Reservation, including Pit Rivers and Hat Creeks among the large number of Mountain Maidu, whose Butte Creek warriors had raided the Mechoopdas and Bidwell in the 1850s.

Special Indian Subagent James Eddy at Rancho Chico

Because James Eddy's decisions played a key role in events, it is appropriate to consider influences that had shaped his character. About two hundred years had passed since James Franklin Eddy's New England forebears experienced conditions such as he grappled with in everyday California. The Eddys' purpose when they arrived in 1630 was to join Gov. John Winthrop's Massachusetts Bay Colony. After flawed paperwork scuttled this plan, Miles Standish escorted them to Plymouth where they settled for about forty years. Eddy's forerunners experienced such severe hardships that, at one point, Winthrop ordered the

Eddys to temporarily place their children with other families. Puritan authorities cited one of Eddy's maternal ancestors twice for washing clothes on Sunday and she received an admonition for traveling on Sunday. Like other Puritan dissenters, the family found refuge in the tolerant theology of the Congregational Church in Rhode Island, where James Eddy's grandfather married a descendent of Roger Williams, the leading advocate of religious tolerance. In 1777, the Eddys moved to Dudley, Massachusetts, where James was born in 1833.[589]

California's Gold Rush boom was in decline when Eddy arrived from Dudley during the late 1850s. Taking up residence in the village of Tehama in 1860, he made many acquaintances as a bartender at the Tehama House, a hotel near the Sacramento River. A good marksman, he won third prize in the pigeon event of a shooting match.

In mid-1862, forty-five straight days of rain turned inland California into a vast lake. The next summer, drought led to financial losses that imperiled not only workers like Eddy but ranchers like Col. Edward A. Stevenson, whose family was killed by Indians in 1859 (discussed in Chapter Eight) and who now faced economic collapse.[590]

Therefore, that October, conditions for Eddy were uncertain when he accepted Hanson's appointment as special Indian subagent in Chico. In hiring the young bartender, Hanson probably relied on the recommendations of prominent Tehama Village residents familiar with Eddy's character and reputation. Two of them were his employer, S. Willis Knotts, who owned the Tehama House near Nome Lackee Reservation, and Col. Stevenson, that reservation's former supervisor.[591]

Eddy's new job required him to live among his Mountain Indian wards in the primitive conditions at the Chico Landing camp. Despite the fact that he had "consumption" (tuberculosis) and was fighting its symptoms, his new responsibilities immersed him in life and death issues that required his good judgment, frugality and sense of fairness. As the product of New Englanders, he respected the importance of personal integrity and civic responsibility. While his wages were paltry, it gave him a chance to exercise independent authority on behalf of a worthy purpose.[592]

Hanson's budget for 1863, already strained by Congress's Civil War cutbacks, did not cover Indians away from the Round Valley Reservation. He called on San Franciscans for donations to sustain their "desperate fellow-beings ... the suffering Indians."[593]

Hanson opened an account at John Bidwell & Co. for Eddy to purchase rations such as flour to supplement the berries, game, fish and acorns the Indians collected. While a thick canopy of oaks and cottonwoods sheltered them from sun, winter meant they would need shoes, clothing and blankets. In need of cash to pay for supplies, he sought local donations and contracted out some of the reservation Indians' labor. Bidwell, longtime employer of Indian farm workers and former contractor of Indian workers to gold miners, was in a position to advise Eddy on this part of his job.

Farmers who called on Eddy for workers found him cooperative but cautious. He dispatched work parties with notes identifying which men and women could do the harder or more skilled work and who, because of age or infirmities, must do light work. While the able-bodied and more skilled workers were to be paid in cash to support the whole group, he also required some ranchers to pay "in kind" for workers without shoes or blankets.[594] Eddy's provision of useful Indian workers quieted most farmers' objections to the presence of Mountain Maidu in the valley. In addition, work kept Indians busy and out of trouble. Eddy's camp included children, the old, those of limited skills and the frail, so even though Eddy found paying work for many adults, the Indian Department's bill to John Bidwell & Co. climbed.

Lacking a workforce sufficient to maintain his ranch and build the Humboldt Road, Bidwell drew on the reservation Indians Eddy was supervising at Bidwell's river camp, but he needed even more workers. In the spring of 1863, a San Francisco labor recruiter cautioned him that, unless he covered their travel fares, workers would refuse to consider Chico. However, Bidwell considered it risky to pay their fares without any guarantee they would enter into or remain in his employ. Other local employers, who sometimes lost their Indian and other workers to Bidwell, resented his expanding Indian workforce.[595]

Bidwell hired Henry Landt, a neighbor and veteran of Kibbe's 1859 campaign, to recruit and supervise Mountain and Valley Maidu, including Indians from Eddy's camp, who worked on the Humboldt Road's construction. Sandy Young took over guarding the road builders from hostile Indians, who were determined to stop the roadwork cutting through their territory. Bidwell's readiness to hire peaceful Mountain Maidu for both projects points to the potential he saw for them in the settler economy. As early as 1852, Granville Stuart had recognized Mountain Maidu's strength, ability and reliability; by the 1860s, they worked in a variety of jobs in mining towns.

However, Bidwell's correspondence with Landt at Big Meadows infers some vetting of Mountain Maidu for their possible roles in raids. Landt assured Bidwell that, if any Indians he sent to the ranch should prove "incompetent or are unwell, send them back. ... I will keep recruiting and send down as fast as I can get them to go. I have given out word that they can go to Chico and get all the fruit they can eat, work or not but once get them down there you will have no trouble keeping them."[596]

Mountain and Valley Maidu's Rivalry Erodes at the Ranch

George Crosette, publisher of the *Butte Record*, described settlers' uneasiness about Mountain Maidu crossing back and forth between the valley and the canyons. He recalled Bidwell in the early 1860s as a busy man and optimist who looked on the best side of Indians, even though he, like his neighbors, had experienced Indian violence. With Bidwell always in need of workers, Crosette noted that Rancho Chico had become a regular destination for Mountain Maidu looking for work and some were renegades who abused Bidwell's trust as they used their access to make trouble for Valley Maidu and settlers. Although Eddy, and then Crowder, acknowledged settler abuses as the main cause of most Indian offenses, both men agreed with Crosette. This explains why settlers in 1863 called Bidwell's ranch an "elysium to outlaws."[597]

An important side effect of Bidwell's efforts to expand his

labor force emerged that summer. The Mountain and Valley Maidu now lived, although not together, in close proximity to one another, and both in subjugation on Rancho Chico: Mountain Indians to Eddy and Bidwell and Valley Indians to Bidwell, contributing to the erosion of their traditional enmity. The new situation recalls the 1851 comment by treaty commissioner Oliver Wozencraft, who worried that Mountain Maidu were "interchanging visits [with Valley Maidu] of late and meeting in council."[598] He and Bidwell worried then that "they were confederating against the Whites."[599] Similar concerns resurfaced in the 1860s.

The contact on Bidwell's ranch initiated a bond between Mountain and Valley Maidu. That the new commonality would grow into a permanent connection appears in a 1908 comment by William Conway, a Mechoopda Maidu leader from the Bidwell rancheria. He spoke of as normal the contacts "Bidwell Maidu" and Feather River Mountain Maidu maintained with one another and with "Indians of the Deer Creek district [who] are the remnant of the tribe [Mill Creeks] that was subdued in the last great fight" against Hi Good and other private Indian fighters in 1865.[600] Similarly, D. B. Lyon of Tehama County would explain to interviewers in 1915 that, by the end of the nineteenth century, the Mountain Indians, who had long been "very warlike, all of the small neighboring tribes being afraid of them," mostly associated with "the Indians of the Bidwell rancheria at Chico and the Hat Creek Indians north of Lassen Peak."[601] In other words, decades of contact since the 1860s would turn Deer Creek from a periodic base for raids into an ongoing haven for some Mountain Maidu and survivors of other Mountain tribes unwilling to live among Whites. Lack of understanding about earlier rivalries central to Maidu culture and about how events of the early 1860s forged new links between Mountain Maidu and Deer Creek Indians has compromised analyses by twentieth-century observers.

However, the key Mountain Maidu issue dividing Indians and settlers in 1863 remained their warriors' participation in Mill Creek raids on farms in the valley foothills. Therefore, Bidwell's agreement with the government to temporarily place hundreds of Mountain Maidu, Hat Creeks and Pit Rivers on his ranch made local residents anxious. They were aware that the violent

Mountain Maidu's Butte Creeks had conducted raiding parties through the 1850s. As Robert Anderson and Hi Good confirmed during their Indian pursuits, Butte Creeks had joined with Mill Creeks in the late 1850s.

In early March 1863, settlers near the Pence ranch between Oroville and Chico remained concerned that some Indians among the hundreds of Mountain Indians on Bidwell's ranch were dangerous. Their fears increased when foothill shepherd George Hayes arrived at his cabin one day and found fifteen Mill Creeks, whose families were freezing and starving in the high country, removing his food and clothing.[602] As the raiders ran off, Hayes ran behind them, grabbing what they dropped. The Indians turned and fired, wounding him twice.

When Bidwell heard about this, he quickly rode out in pursuit with twenty of his ranch men, including Indians. His response blunted the revival of accusations that his ranch Indians were complicit and that he had no concern for settler safety. Because so many additional Indians now camped on his property, he was even more vulnerable to such claims than he had been in 1862. Within a week of the Hayes incident, settlers near Mud Creek, about eight miles above Chico, killed three Valley Indian ranch workers, claiming they were Mill Creeks.[603] About this time, Bidwell wrote a San Francisco associate about his despondence over financial problems and other unnamed reverses.[604]

While most Indians in Eddy's camp posed no danger, local people had a valid reason for concern about others. Although it appears settlers were unaware of it, a dozen or so of the Mountain Indians in Eddy's camp had recently been involved in a violent attack. In September 1862, just before they left the Round Valley Reservation for the Sacramento Valley, eighty Maidu, Pit Rivers and Hat Creeks assisted William G. Chard, a prominent Tehama County rancher, in avenging the Wylacki tribe's cattle thefts from his summer grazing fields near the Mendocino Reservation. Wylacki had been clashing with the Maidu, Pit Rivers and Hat Creeks since their 1859 arrival at the reservation. Chard's Indian party located the Wylacki who stole the cattle, then hid and painted their faces so Chard and twelve of his men, who were to shoot from the sidelines, could distinguish them from the Wylacki. Headed by Maidu Concow leader Tome-ya-nem, the Indians advanced, undetected, on the Wylacki camp. When they reached its outskirts, where about 1,000 people mingled, they leaped seventeen feet from a precipice onto the Wylacki men below who were slaughtering Chard's cattle.[605]

According to Tome-ya-nem's later account, although he and his men were outnumbered, they threw themselves into such a ferocious attack that he lost control of himself. They killed dozens of men, women and children, only stopping when they ran out of arrows. As planned, the rancher and his men on the edge of the battleground picked off scores of Wylacki trying to escape until they ran out of ammunition. Then, the Round Valley Indians waited and killed forty more who returned to recover their dead. The Round Valley party then attacked another Wylacki camp, with similar vicious results. In a later interview, Tome-ya-nem expressed regret.

As mentioned previously, Tome-ya-nem was a title the Concow leader named Yumyan assumed. His English name was William Pete, according to an 1859 account about Capt. Bill Burn's unit, which had captured him in Kibbe's campaign. The writer described Tome-ya-nem as "a very intelligent Indian chief, he speaks English fluently, and … has never manifested much hostility to the Whites. Yesterday, within my hearing, he observed to Capt. Burns: 'now Captain since you've got me, you won't have much difficulty in getting all the other Indians—they will all follow me to the Reservation.'"[606] Tome-ya-nem later spoke of the camp on Bidwell's ranch where his leadership must have been of considerable value to James Eddy.

Eddy worried about how Hat Creeks at the Chico Landing camp were influencing Bidwell's Mechoopdas. Although the two Indian factions were camped a good distance apart, none was restrained from travel, resulting in occasional contact. For example, Eddy chided Bidwell about ignoring the considerable time "Hat Creek Liz" was spending with ranch Indians. Then about 26, she was a "tall and well-formed Indian" woman with "large, dark eyes; jet black luxuriant hair, small hands and feet." According to a journalist who saw her firsthand in 1859, she carried herself with a confidence and pride that attracted other Indians to her. Her "wild and defiant look" and "impatient, half-disdainful air" distinguished her. What concerned Eddy was her

Military and the Removal

Shave Head, a Hat Creek leader in Tehama County, was severely wounded attempting to drive settlers off tribal territory. In 1859, General Kibbe captured him for removal to a reservation.

reputation of wielding "more influence [on other Indians] ... than any surviving member of the Hat Creeks."⁶⁰⁷ Her captors' local sources had identified her as "the main counselor for the tribe" and "instrumental, if not actually the leader, in most of the murders" by Hat Creeks when they fought with settlers in Plumas and Shasta counties.⁶⁰⁸

Another Kibbe captive at Chico Landing who would have worried valley residents was Hat Creek Liz's brother Shave Head, who found her at the Chico Landing camp and wanted to take her away. A man of medium height and "well-built ... [with] piercing eyes," he had led parties that killed mountain settlers, including stage coach travelers.⁶⁰⁹ After one incident, pursuers who entered Shave Head's camp found booty from the store of a murdered settler. He had reason to resent Rancho Chico Indians in 1863 because three years earlier they killed both his brothers when they entered Bidwell's high country camp.⁶¹⁰

In another clash, Shave Head became permanently disabled after a settler shattered his arm. Eddy admonished Bidwell: "It will not do to allow the Hat Creeks to roam about," and urged him to send Hat Creek Liz away with her brother "and tell her not to come back [to the Chico Landing camp]."⁶¹¹

An incident that Eddy could not have predicted, but one that supports his concerns about Hat Creeks, took place three years later. In 1866, Hat Creek men, described then as Round Valley "reservation stragglers," who "practice no mercy, but deal out death and destruction to the border settlers," killed some Tehama County Indians who worked for Whites.[612]

Even though contact between Mountain and Valley Maidu at Rancho Chico might jeopardize Bidwell's control, he honored his promise to help Hanson through the winter. However, when the spring of 1863 arrived and Hanson was to move the hundreds of Indians from the Chico Landing camp back to a reservation, the Indian agent informed Bidwell that settlers recently had killed Indians at Round Valley, where provisions would not support additional arrivals, and that he had been unable to secure reservation space elsewhere.

Another of Hanson's problems was his recent termination of Round Valley's superintendent Short, a personal friend of sitting president Abraham Lincoln, who considered him "as honorable [a] man as there is in the world."[613] The president had been Hanson's neighbor in Illinois and Hanson had nominated him for president at the party convention in 1856. In a lengthy letter to Lincoln, he explained that Short, a widower, had become obsessed by an Indian woman who had left her Indian consort for him. As a consequence, he wrote, Short had neglected reservation responsibilities at a time of ongoing crises. Furious at his dismissal, Short refused Hanson's demand to give up the woman and leave the area. In the meantime, Hanson had yet to fill the still-empty position and his ongoing search meant a new hire could not take over until September.[614] Tensions between Short and Hanson would soon affect Indians and settlers between the Sacramento River and the Sierras.

Miners Inflame the Uneasy Peace

As Chapter Seven set out, miners who worked the creeks east of Chico continued to grapple with Indian thefts and killings of colleagues. Nevertheless, despite their fear of hostile Mountain Maidu and the absence of any local law enforcement or military protection, they continued to work their claims.

Because the state had ignored the miners' 1862 appeal for help, in the spring of 1863, a group of them met at a Forest Ranch saloon to discuss how to protect themselves. They believed that miner parties could launch reprisals so costly to Indians in property and life, they would be intimidated and stop their aggressions. This bears on the events of June 9, when a small group of miners, to avenge the theft of horses, captured five Maidu Nimshews at random and confined them for days in a Helltown barn near Butte Creek. Village residents were apprehensive about the miners' intent for the Indians and whether other Mountain Indians would intervene.

Neil and Anna Campbell Sorenson of Helltown knew one of the Indian captives and were sure he was not a troublemaker. From time to time, "Old Captain" had appeared on their doorstep to trade for fresh eggs. Like others in Helltown, the Sorensons were more afraid of the miners who guarded the barn. While the five men languished under guard in the barn, another Nimshew approached Sorenson to ask what was going to happen. Sorenson reassured the man that, once the miners made their point (although he did not know what that point was), they would free his people.

The Nimshew showed up at Sorenson's place again to tell him white men had lynched the five captives from a hydraulic lumber flume.[615] Local Whites wanted to believe that outsiders, not local men from their community, were responsible for the hangings. "Despairing Indians came down from the hill wailing, crying for their lost tribesmen. The weeping and mourning cries of the Indians were heard for several days by the residents of Helltown."[616] While Anna Sorensen remembered the townspeople's horror, she also recalled the boast of a saloon patron: "I grabbed Old Captain's legs and I hung on until he was dead."[617] Even as the settlers listened to the Kimshews' wails throughout days of mourning, they knew the Indians would act on tradition and avenge the murders.

During this period, Indians and settlers retaliated against one another across Tehama and Butte counties' common borders. Robert Anderson and Hi Good continued their independent Indian sorties in Deer Creek and Mill Creek canyons and thus remained Indian targets. For example, in response to a theft and attempted arson at his place, Anderson's pursuit left one Indian mortally wounded. In a June 1863 incident, when two horses were stolen from his father-in-law Solomon Gore, Anderson and two others followed Indian tracks into the canyons. Before the three returned to Good's cabin near Deer Creek, an Indian woman in their vicinity stopped by and told Good that Anderson's party had killed seven Mill Creeks and severely wounded two.[618]

Anticipating more attacks, Bidwell made ready. Having only recently impressed on Bidwell the necessity of keeping his reservation charges separated from the ranch's Mechoopdas, on June 24 Eddy moved the reservation Indians from Chico Landing to a camp "a few rods" down Chico Creek from the Mechoopda rancheria behind Bidwell's farmhouse. Eddy treated the situation as dire and sent farmer and state representative Isaac Allen a message: he must return to Chico the Mountain Indian crew—three men, a woman and a ten-year-old girl—Eddy had sent to help him thresh wheat.[619]

At this same time, a malaria epidemic at Eddy's camp broke out with the deaths of three children; the numbers would rise through June, July and August. In the meantime, settler antagonism toward the Indians on Rancho Chico was intensifying, trumping the disease threat for Eddy and Bidwell. (This crisis is discussed later.)

In mid-July, about a dozen Mill Creeks moved across Deer Creek Ridge, crossing into foothill and canyon areas northeast of Chico, They stripped, for a second time, the cabin of Mr. Sunedecker, a member of some Indian pursuit parties. On Sunday, July 19, near Forks of Butte, they seriously wounded a miner in his Butte Creek camp and killed the three Indian women who worked for him. Later that day, the Indian party seriously wounded John Strommer at his claim above Dogtown (later Magalia).

The next day, the Mill Creeks killed miner Richard Morrison on the West Branch of the Feather River. During the morning of Tuesday, July 20, they reached the Magalia Road about three miles from the Pence ranch and shot a pregnant farm wife as she gathered beans from her garden while her husband, Mr. Blum, was away. Despite heavy bleeding from a deep wound to her thigh, she managed to run a mile to a neighbor's home. Rather than pursue her, the Mill Creeks stole her food and supplies. Mrs. Blum gave birth in January but died the next day from complications related to her wound.[620]

That afternoon, the Mill Creek party, now moving back toward Deer Creek, spotted Sam and Mary Ann Lewis' three children on their way home from school. The Mill Creeks shot and killed Jimmy Lewis, 11, as he drank from Dry Creek, then they kidnapped Johnny, 6, and the boys' sister Thankful, 9.[621] When they did not come home, their parents were concerned but assumed they had stopped overnight at their grandmother's house. Still uneasy, early the next day, July 21, they searched separately and Mary Ann found Jimmie's body shot in the back with arrows. A search party of forty men set out to look for the other two children. News spread fast about the Lewis children. Travelers delivered the first version of events to John Bidwell & Co. on the 21st. The store's clerk, Charles Stilson, wrote in his diary: "Another Indian massacre had taken place. One boy and a girl were murdered—parties have gone in search...."[622] The initial pursuit parties turned up nothing.

Meanwhile, on the same day, while crossing foothills along the eastern edge of the Sacramento Valley, the Mill Creeks, irritated by Johnnie's weeping, killed him. The next day, Thankful escaped from the kidnapper guarding her. She disappeared into the upper foothills east of Chico where she hid, listening to her kidnappers' voices as they searched for her. After a time they gave up and continued north toward Deer Creek Canyon, breaking into cabins on Little Chico Creek and near Richardson Springs.

Thankful happened onto Hardy and Margaret Thomasson's farm, near Rock Creek in the lower foothills adjoining the Sacramento Valley, where she saw Hardy and his brother Nate working in a field. After telling them her story, she agreed to guide a search party to recover Johnnie's body. Her memory was exceptional, given that previous to her trek with the Mill Creek kidnappers across the foothills, the nine-year-old had no knowledge of the route, yet was able to retrace her path right to her brother's remains.

Thankful Lewis' extraordinary memory is important because of consequences following her report to the rescuers. She recalled some of her captors "could speak good English."[623] Her account of the incident includes references to her verbal exchanges with the kidnappers in English. For example, she mentioned a moment when they slipped into their tribal language so, she thought, she would not understand their talk about killing her brother.[624] This suggests her kidnappers were not Yahi, who did not speak English, but rather Mountain Maidu Butte Creeks, who picked up English in their close association with miners, and who were becoming known as Mill Creeks for their raids out of those Yahi Canyons. The settler community latched onto this clue and another of the child's memories: after she and her kidnappers reached a point north of Nance Canyon, one of the Indians bid the party "Good-by," then walked off toward the valley, visible from their stopping place. That location was within range of several Indian rancherias: Bidwell's and Eddy's or Durham's. She also said the departing Indian "was not a Mill Creek Indian, but was supposed to have been one from the rancheria."[625]

Thankful's account corresponded with local experiences with Mountain Indians. Crosette explained that settlers believed Mountain Indians, most of them Maidu, in Eddy's camp, as well as those free Mountain Maidu in or near the Mechoopda rancheria who came for Bidwell's seasonal jobs, included troublemakers among those laborers using their access to Bidwell's ranch to "plot disruptions."[626] Thus Thankful's account about the Indian kidnapper who headed for the valley shifted attention to Bidwell.

Historian Hurtado found it was not uncommon for Indians who had been employees of Whites to take part in raids.[627] A. G. Tassin, an Army officer markedly sympathetic to the Indians' plight at Round Valley, said that Indians who worked as "servants, acting ... in the capacity of feudal retainers ... came and went as they pleased, and it may be readily inferred that their contact with [renegade Indians] tended to increase, rather than diminish, whatever dissatisfaction they may have had against the Whites in the intercourse between them."[628]

Bidwell Seeks Indian Removal and Indians Seek Protection

On July 21, news that Mill Creeks killed the Lewis boy raced through the Indian rancherias along the mountain creeks and the branches of the Feather River. With the 1859 removal a fresh memory, peaceful Mountain Maidu immediately understood they were about to be hunted down again. Many decided a reservation was preferable to being killed by crazy, armed white men.

The most dramatic evidence of their efforts to save themselves took place in Maidu Concow territory. The same day Mary Ann Lewis discovered her elder son's remains in Little Dry Creek, a party of about forty to fifty Concow Maidu in Yankee Hill Township approached Michael Wells' store and hotel where one of them worked. Wells, who had mediated between Indians and miners for years, agreed to hide them until he could figure out the best course. However, probably the same large search party of mostly miners looking for the children, showed up and ordered him to hand over the Indians and then threatened to kill them.

Wells was ready with his own threat: if they killed innocent Indians, he would personally have the vigilante party members charged with murder. Since this would be credible, given their stated intentions, the men narrowed their focus to four men who stood out as different from the rest. According to later Chico mayor O. L. Clark, the pursuit party's "commissary," the

Michael Wells' Concow hotel. Wells protected Indians in 1863 when they fled attacks by settlers after Indians killed two white schoolboys and kidnapped their sister (who escaped).

Concows acknowledged those four were not members of their tribelet. Wells persuaded the settler party to leave the rest alone and give the four men a chance to run for their lives. On a signal, they raced off and, after a brief lead time, the pursuers fired their guns. They killed two and the other two escaped.[629]

Once word spread about Wells' protection of the Concows, he accepted more Indians and, on July 23, led them to Chico, where the sight of whole Indian families trudging up Main Street headed for Eddy's camp aroused not only sympathy for them among the town's four hundred residents, but also empathy for the Lewis family. Bidwell's anxious staff telegraphed him to return from a mountain trip immediately.

Meanwhile, after angry foothill farmers attended the Lewis boy's funeral, they headed for the valley, where they set up camp on Butte Creek a few miles south of Chico. On the morning of July 24 they formed a delegation which rode to Rancho Chico to confront Bidwell with their demand that he hand over all Indians on his place for removal. According to Bidwell's 1890s memoir, "everyone expected them [the farmers] to shoot me down, but I talked to them, and in half an hour they went off."[630]

However, primary documents from the Bidwell archives contradict this account. The following reconstruction weaves together aspects of Bidwell's recollections with those of Stilson's diary and the contemporary account in a letter to Bidwell from his neighbor Robert Durham.

According to Durham and Stilson at the time, when the delegation of farmers arrived at Bidwell's office on the 25th, his employees explained he was still away and they left. However, by traveling through that night, he reached his home before dawn on the 26th. Because his housekeeper and her family were asleep inside and he knew everyone was on edge about the mob in town, he covered himself with a blanket he carried and slept outside on his office stair landing.[631] His staff briefed him on the farmers' demands and Eddy filled him in on Wells' delivery of the large party of Concows who sought his protection. The two men wired George Hanson, urging his immediate departure for Chico. In San Francisco, he understood the urgency and made a swift departure.

Bidwell and Eddy learned that after the farmers left Rancho

The mob in 1863 went to Bidwell's farmhouse (long misidentified as "Bidwell's Mill") to confront him. The building's first-floor shed roof sheltered those waiting to enter the office at left. The portion at right and above was his residence. In this photograph from about 1870, the house is vacant and the front entry porch, where he slept rather than frighten his niece's family when he arrived home at night to face the mob, has been removed. A brick border of his elaborate gardens and the waterfall that irrigated them is at right. Above the roof line, is the water tank Bidwell erected after Mountain Maidu burned down his headquarters in 1853.

Chico, they rode to Durham's Esquon Ranch, located between Chico and Butte Creek, where the Indian workers were from a different Valley Maidu tribelet than that of Bidwell's Mechoopdas.[632] The men demanded that Durham cooperate in the removal of all his ranch Indians. Durham tried to discredit Thankful Lewis' allegation that a farm-based rancheria was the destination of her captor who had left the kidnapping party and headed for the valley. According to a letter from Durham to Bidwell, he tried to deflect the men's attention from them by emphasizing Hanson's authority over Eddy and the reservation camp. He insisted the Indian Thankful said left for the valley must have gone there. His introduction of Hanson's role also underlined the distinction between innocent, permanent rancheria laborers and possibly dangerous Mountain Indians among the peaceful captives from Round Valley Reservation for all of whom Hanson was responsible. However, no distinctions appeased the men. Durham later explained he was trying to stall the men until Bidwell returned and Hanson was summoned.

Realizing he had failed to distract or calm the men, Durham assured them he and Bidwell would cooperate in the removal.[633] When his concession appeared to diffuse the men's anger, he queried whether, if he and Bidwell acceded to the removal demand, they might "keep out some of the best [workers]."[634] The delegation's leader agreed that his men would permit Durham and Bidwell to "burn out the rancherias and make [the remaining few Indian workers] live at the house."[635] This remark seems based on the democratic model of the Midwest, where bunkhouses were rare and bachelor farmhands often lived in the homes of their employers. When the foothill men left, Durham was convinced that, if he and Bidwell did not comply with the farmers' demands, a crowd would descend on their farms and "massacre the whole or all they can find before they leave the valley."[636] Because Durham had spoken for Bidwell without his permission, the next day, the 26th, he rode to Rancho Chico, where, told Bidwell was "at the [Masonic] lodge," apparently inviolable to nonmembers, he left him a letter emphasizing this was a "crisis" situation in which "[we] must act for our safety."[637]

So well did Hanson patch together transportation by ship, train and stagecoaches that he reached Chico from San Francisco that evening. As he approached the town, "at almost every house along the way" he spotted handbills advertising a public meeting the following evening at the Pence Hotel, between Chico and Oroville, to consider a response to the murders of the Lewis children.[638] The killings of Richard Morrison and Mrs. Blum were also mentioned, but the killings of three Indians in the valley as retribution that summer were not an issue. When Hanson's stagecoach reached Chico at 10:30 p.m., all the talk at his hotel was about the mob's revenge killings of two Indians a few blocks away that night.

Drunk and bolstered by Sam Lewis' presence, the foothill

farmers had set out from their Butte Creek camp to avenge his children's deaths. Stilson summarized the event in his diary: "The mountain boys that were camped below town got drunk came up this afternoon &, after making an attempt to get up excitement enough to lead them to kill all the Indians in the valley, they finally compromised the matter and were content with killing two. Shot them & if they get a little more whiskey will no doubt kill them all."[639] He was referring to men in that mob convinced the two Indians were the survivors of the four who ran for their lives at Wells' hotel. One, who had been shot through his mouth, was in agony. The miners tied their hands and set them in a cluster of trees where Lewis, backed by others, shot and killed both. Onlookers cut away slices of their scalps for souvenirs.

Bidwell met Hanson the next morning and they agreed the situation was beyond their control. Each telegraphed Brig. Gen. Wright for federal military intervention: "Great excitement here. White people killed by Indians. Volunteers in arms and threats of extermination. Please order a company to send troops to 'Bidwell's [Chico] Landing' immediately to aid me in protecting, collecting, and removing Indians to the reservation."[640]

Even though Hanson's telegram to Wright had mentioned the murder of white people as the immediate cause of the crisis, as superintendent, his first priority was the protection of Indians. At

Brig. General George Wright sent three companies of soldiers to guard Rancho Chico's Indian workforce from settlers and to remove all other Indians on his ranch to the Round Valley Reservation.

Standoff

the same time, once the Indians were removed, he was certain the settlers would feel secure and regain their confidence. Bidwell and Hanson both scanned a letter scrawled by a Pine Creek farmer north of Chico on July 26. One of his Indian workers had left to join the removal; he wanted Bidwell to send him back. He included a tip: "The people is forming a company to clean out Bidwell's rancheria...." and "be on your guard."[641]

HANSON AND BIDWELL ATTENDED THE July 27 meeting at the hotel near the Lewis place, about twelve miles from Chico.[642] When Hanson took the floor and encountered "300 of the most infuriated men I ever met,"[643] he tried to convince them that the Lewis murders were not the beginning of a new Indian campaign, but were retaliation for the Butte Creek miners' lynching of the five Nimshews at Helltown.[644] Because Hanson was obliged to Bidwell for the reservation camp ground on his ranch, he only mentioned removing the reservation Indians. When challenged about his intentions for Bidwell's Indians, he explained he did not have enough funds to remove all the Mountain and Valley Maidu. He offered to remove "the tribe or tribes whose Indians had committed the Lewis killings."[645] The crowd would have none of it.

By now, it was considered common knowledge, based on word from farmers on the Deer Creek Ridge and the Butte County men in the Tehama Volunteers, that Mill Creeks were now principally warriors from Butte County's Mountain Maidu tribelets, supplemented by other Mountain tribes. They also suspected that some Indians linked to Eddy or Bidwell participated in or facilitated raids. And, because the settlers could not differentiate members of individual Mountain or Valley tribes or tribelets, they insisted all Indians, including Bidwell's Mechoopdas, must be removed. They appointed Dr. J. G. Moore, Thomas McDaniel and W. N. Smith to oversee their removal.

Settlers then and their descendants through the twentieth century would believe the Pence Hotel crowd forced the removal on the reluctant Bidwell and Hanson. However, when Hanson announced to the men at the hotel he had already decided to organize an Indian removal, he did not mention he had done so in agreement with Bidwell. Consistent with this, in his 1890s memoir, Bidwell claimed sole responsibility for the removal decision: "I had the Indians moved over to the Round Valley Reservation."[646] Yet, preceding that quote was his remark that he needed troops because his life was in danger. Those who have read Bidwell's later account assumed his phrasing referred to a threat from Indians. True, many Indians would have celebrated his death and a few had tried to kill him more than once. However, the principal reason Bidwell called for troops in Chico in July 1863 was because of the settlers' threat to his core Indian labor force.

With soldiers on their way, Bidwell assumed a defiant tone with the settlers: he would never allow the removal of Rancho Chico's rancheria Indians.[647] While Bidwell had come to know and care about Mechoopdas as individuals, history's mistake has been to sentimentalize this relationship. Because the Indians remained central to his cattle, field crop, mill and orchard operations, settler threats to those workers endangered his entire ranching and farming operations and his already strained finances. Large farms operated on borrowed money secured by future harvests which were subject to pests, droughts and floods.

The crowd did not back down, perhaps remembering the previous year's Hickok murders, when Bidwell called for military help solely to defend his ranch Indians against Reb threats and not, as the farmers had expected, to protect farmers from Mill Creeks. Although the previous summer Bidwell had agreed with local residents that volunteer pursuers were superior to soldiers, now that his ranch workforce was again at risk to settlers, he ignored the need to protect farm families from Mill Creek attacks and opted instead for troops to protect his Indian workers. He found no support when he denied Indians on his ranch were complicit in the Lewis children's killings.

Attendees at the Pence Hotel meeting concluded with a resolution that, over the next thirty days, every Indian must "go to settlements to be removed ... or be killed."[648] They demanded Hanson hold at Eddy's Chico Landing camp all the Indians they planned to collect. Also, Hanson and the military must deliver "all" the Indians to any reservation so remote they could not make their way home. The settlers' many references to "all" are significant because removal was no longer the issue. Indeed, the whole settler community, including Bidwell, wanted the federal Indians removed. Instead, the subtext for the farmers' insistence on removal of all Indians was a mix of their desperation for security and their determination to dismantle Bidwell's envied Indian labor force. They remained convinced it harbored dangerous Indians.

Bidwell's handling of their previous petition in 1862 led them to suspect that, since his influence outweighed theirs, he would again try to sabotage their demands in lieu of his own needs. Therefore, in order to keep control of the removal, the crowd agreed to meet again in a month to assess how many Indians had been collected and the location of any, including Valley Maidu, still on ranches. While the men were less concerned about the few ranchers who had Indian workers, Bidwell's large operation infuriated them.

Bidwell was stubborn and used to getting his way. On his drive to Chico he had plenty of time to mull over what he had heard. He also had reason for hope: soldiers were coming to protect his ranch. To Bidwell, that meant he could exempt from removal his essential workers without risking their lives.

During the stagecoach ride to Sacramento, it was clear to Hanson that "the enraged citizens of Butte were prepared to force Bidwell to send away the rancheria Indians."[649] He was now convinced the Indians of Rancho Chico were at such risk to extreme violence that, despite his gratitude for Bidwell's help, he must convince him to give up his Indian workers to the removal. Their lives were as much at stake as the Mountain Indians in federal custody. As Indian agent, Hanson's first priority was to protect their lives; not Bidwell's business. His correspondence demonstrates this was when he began distancing himself from the rancher.

ON JULY 25, EDDY CALLED in the five Indians he had sent to work in June at the Allen ranch near Rock Creek. When they did not arrive on the 26th, he assumed they had stopped at Keefer's ranch where the Odawi Maidu rancheria was located. However, the Indian work party, which had stayed to finish some work, did not leave Allen's place for Chico until July 27. Witnesses who spotted the men, woman and girl noticed they had tucked the "passports" Eddy sent them in their caps. Late the next day, Eddy received word the bodies of all five Indians had been discovered in a cabin near a slough. The following morning, when he arrived there in a wagon to recover their bodies, he found Allen had left a note at the cabin about their deaths before he left, perhaps in pursuit of the killers. When he reached Rancho Chico with the remains, Eddy reported the murders to Hanson in San Francisco: "More harmless persons do not exist and a more cowardly murder was never perpetrated."[650] He advised his superior that any investigation and prosecution could only be achieved with the backing of a "strong military force as [northern Butte County] is the most inflammatory district we have."[651]

Bidwell found little support for excluding his Indian workers from the removal. He had provided jobs, good deals on land and help for local residents in need; in return, he must have believed townspeople would rally behind him. However, Bidwell was also known for his cold demeanor and hot temper. A bachelor of wide acquaintance, he was, at his core, a loner with few, if any, close personal friends during this period.

While Bidwell's immediate neighbors were not overtly hostile toward him, records suggest he could count on only a few "friends," and those men had financial ties to him. The area's numerous Southern sympathizers were at odds with him as a Union man, and even those who shared his Union sympathies commiserated with the vulnerable foothill families. The *Oroville Union* leaned toward sympathy for the families, but its August 8 editorial was discrete: "Whether they [the soldiers] are intended for the protection of citizens or Indians does not yet appear fully. We are told, however, that they are sent to receive the surrendered Indians of Butte County."[652]

In the 1860s and later, Bidwell was convinced the real reason less prosperous farmers objected to his ranch Indians was not fear of Indians but envy of his success. This found reflection in Lt. Colonel Ambrose E. Hooker's assertion in a late 1863 report (discussed in Chapter Eleven) that Chico's Indian problem had less to do with Indian offenses than resentment against Bidwell for his large Indian workforce other farmers could not afford.[653] In a variation on this, Bidwell's wife Annie would later dismiss her husband's detractors from that time as "wicked men who had come into the locality as laborers in his mill or on his ranch."[654]

Because of the threats directed at him and his ranch Indians by angry settlers, Bidwell sent all of them to hide with the reservation Indians in a heavily forested area across the Sacramento River.[655] Indian oral history recalled how Bidwell's Maidu aide, Rafael, then about 21, would cross the river to warn the Indians about "soldiers" attacking innocent Indians.[656]

This version of Rafael's warning, which also appears in standard historical accounts, has produced unwarranted criticism of the California Volunteers. Bidwell never sent the Indians to hide from soldiers and none had arrived in Chico when he sent the Indians away or when the attack Rafael spoke of took place. Bidwell sent the Indians away to hide from marauding settlers. The "soldiers" Rafael spoke of included privately armed white men in pursuit parties collecting Indians for the removal that, to the Indians, looked like military companies. For example, a private pursuit party delivered sixty Mountain Maidu to James Eddy on July 30, a day before the California Volunteers arrived to carry out the removal. Rafael's description also applied to the local militia unit, the fifty-man Oroville Guard, Company A, headed by Capt. H. B. Hunt. Although they had no orders to do so, Hunt and his men collected Indians in the foothills before the California Volunteers arrived. Presumably its officers should have known better than to act on their own initiative because only the previous May they had trained at a special state camp. However, in response to the Lewis killings in 1863, this unit showed up at the Hupp mill's butcher shop where one or more of its members killed two Indian men and a fourteen-year-old Indian boy, despite the butcher's attempts to save him.[657] (The Chico Light Infantry was not formed until months after these events.)

While the foothill farmers were seeking retribution, Company F of the California Volunteers, led by Capt. Augustus Starr, was being dispatched "for Bidwell,"[658] wording that implied protection of the ranch Indians and Bidwell was their first priority. The soldiers were volunteers who earned paltry wages and had to provide their own horses or mules. They also paid their own bridge tolls, river boat fares and stage coach fees, even in dangerous areas. While their performance in the 1850s had been uneven, regular drills and lessons, as well as difficult assignments, had honed their discipline and performance by the 1860s. Starr was the son of a prominent Marysville family which built flour mills over the later nineteenth century.[659] He had served since August 1861, most recently at Bear River in Utah Territory, where his Company H and others engaged in a battle devastating to both Indians and soldiers.

With the arrival of Company F—about "forty sleek looking soldiers"—on July 31, Bidwell had armed protection. However, the public saw Company F proceed from the Chico Landing to set up camp on his ranch. Then, on August 10, only days after Starr and his men arrived, Bidwell flaunted his "alliance" with them by joining the company in a showy ride south along Main Street, en route to Humboldt Road. In a visual sense, Company F must have resembled Bidwell's personal posse.

Ostensibly, this sortie was in response to a request from Henry Landt, the Humboldt Road's construction supervisor. Due to reconnoitering Indians, Landt had asked Bidwell for two more rifles because "there is no telling what will happen."[660] Over the years, when a request for rifles arrived from his mountain grazing camp, Bidwell would dispatch a worker to deliver it. This time, he took advantage of the soldiers camped across the road, asking them to accompany him to deliver the rifles. With hostile Indians covertly watching the party pass through their territory, the long ride gave Bidwell time to brief Starr about his views of the Indians, settlers and the removal. After delivering the rifles, the soldiers and Bidwell brought a few peaceful Mountain Maidu back to the ranch for removal.[661]

As Company F rode through the foothills, miners and farmers observed Bidwell and the captain at the head of uniformed, well-armed soldiers. While this reinforced their impression of Bidwell's influence, the journey also impressed on Capt. Starr the rural settlers' antagonism toward Indians and Bidwell. By journey's end, Starr understood that the rancher's determination to keep his Indians out of the removal would incite settlers to attack the Mechoopdas and his other Indian workers left behind.

Capt. Starr was troubled by the implications of those threats for his company. Should settlers attack the soldiers' Indian charges, as commanding officer he would have to order his troops to shoot American citizens. For guidance, Starr wrote the Army's Lt. Colonel R. C. Drum, who became assistant adjutant general for the California Volunteers and Wright's chief aide for Army operations in the state during the Civil War.

Soldiers were on duty at Rancho Chico to protect the Indians from settler attack and Eddy's reservation Indians had moved their camp near Bidwell's headquarters, but still separated from the Mechoopdas. Officers stationed pickets there and in the fields around the clock. Although Starr's company's August 10 ride up the Humboldt Road with Bidwell made a show of force for the settlers' benefit, from Company F's first arrival in Butte County, the safety of the Indians against settlers—not settlers against Indians—was their priority.[662]

This interpretation of the soldiers' role at Chico is supported in contemporary sources. Stilson, Bidwell's store clerk, for example, was sympathetic to his boss's position and to the ranch Indians. He soon became a confidante of the soldiers and his diary entries hint at neither soldier animus nor threats from townspeople to Indians. Support for this view also comes in the firsthand memory of Tome-ya-nem, the Maidu Concow headman in Eddy's camp. He later recalled what the new arrivals from his old home in the mountains had told him about the Indian collection in the Yankee Hill area. They spoke about their terror of private parties' conduct, but mentioned no soldiers' misconduct.[663] In addition, while twentieth-century versions savaged the soldiers, no references to abusive conduct by California Volunteers while in Butte County appear in contemporary Indian oral history, press accounts, letters or other archival materials.

An event southwest of Chico near the village of Princeton on the Sacramento River around the time of the Lewis killings represents the uncertainty shared by Valley Maidu and settlers. As Kate Furnell, a farmer's daughter, and Mona, her family's Maidu helper, placed quilts into tubs of soapy water, they froze at the sight of two breech-cloth-wearing Indian men racing toward them. Mona grabbed her child and Kate yelled for her mother, an accomplished target shooter. The men reached them and stopped, their bodies "shining with heat and breathing heavily."[664] They told the women they came from Rancho Chico to warn settlers and Indians to flee to safety because "bad Indians come from the mountains and kill all white mans and good Indians...."[665]

The situation throughout the area was intense. Indians unwilling to leave for the reservation hid or moved elsewhere and settler parents kept children home from country schools. Armed fathers escorted family members to tend gardens. Levi Moak moved his wife and children from their farm to a place near Chico. He and his brothers "packed" pistols between their houses and barns.[666] Foothill resident O. L. Clark relied on his wife to stand watch, his loaded revolver in her hand, while he milked their cow. Through a house window they glimpsed an Indian man watching them several times. When he realized they spotted him, he would "skulk" away. B. B. Brown wrote Bidwell that foothill settlers felt unsafe outside just in the time it took to bring their cows in from pasture. Ordinarily at ease with Indians on the move around them, country residents now feared every Indian in the nearby "woods, ravines, caves &c."[667]

Businessmen were uneasy because, if conditions did not improve, they were sure "women and children ... will quit forever their present homes" in rural Butte County.[668] For example, like the Hickoks who abandoned their Rock Creek cabin, Thankful Lewis's mother never returned to her home on Little Dry Creek and the Sunedecker family eventually sold their farm after numerous Indian attacks. Jacob Moak bought it, but was soon beset by clashes with Indians. In the July meeting at the Pence Hotel, participants predicted that, without increased security, the ongoing conflicts would collapse land values and increase bankruptcies. Failures that year were already predicted, due to a year-long drought that had devastated many, including Chico physician Dr. John Barnett Smith, whose "Sunflower Farm" on Little Chico Creek was sold at auction.

Indians Killed amid the Removal Collection

By August, Bidwell, Hanson and the military officers were convinced settlers posed grave dangers to any local Indian and agreed that removal was the only way they could protect them. This contradicts later assumptions that the four officials' commitment to the removal stemmed from punitive attitudes toward Indians. The only issue they could not agree on was whether the Bidwell rancheria Indians must join the removal. Bidwell never waivered from his position that the military's priority must be to protect his ranch Indians in place.

In June, the Indians in Eddy's camp were succumbing to malaria, launching the perennial "sickly season." The Sacramento Valley was a prime breeding ground for mosquitoes: dotted by wetlands and crisscrossed by creeks and sloughs, its annual mountain snowmelt created spring floods that filtered into a vast aquifer or flowed to the Sacramento River.

While mosquito bites were usually benign, in the spring of 1863, a deadly species thrived, spreading pernicious, or mortal, malaria along the lower spans of the river's feeder creeks, where Eddy's lightly clothed Mountain Indians camped by Chico Creek. In contrast, the Mechoopdas on Bidwell's ranch now wore full western clothing, slept in huts and apparently had built up a genetic resistance to the disease. Evidently Mountain Indians carried no immunity since their higher territory was inhospitable to this most dangerous species of mosquitoes.[669] This could explain why, in 1863, the Indian deaths on Bidwell's ranch concentrated in Eddy's Mountain Indian camp, not in the Mechoopda rancheria.

Malarial symptoms first surfaced in June with the death of Indian children. Dr. Sproul initially attributed the cause to digestive problems from eating too much fruit. However, as the number of deaths mounted, he diagnosed "ague," another name for malaria.

As the disease spread, frightened but healthy Indians of all ages were arriving from the canyons for removal, only to fall sick. The cost of providing them medical care exacerbated Bidwell's financial problems because government funds had not been budgeted to cover Eddy's charges in such a crisis. While Bidwell had long done business with the federal government, it had taken him seven years of negotiations to be reimbursed for damages to his property from the Mountain Maidu arsons in 1852. How many years would it take Washington to reimburse him this time and how much would the government even pay?

Like the Mountain Indians in Eddy's camp, new settlers that

summer also suffered a significant toll from the disease. Stilson noted the tally his first malarial season in Chico: "There is a great deal of sickness around for 'healthy Cal'" (September 15, 1863) and "This country has been more unhealthy this year than any country I ever saw. For instance, tonight I hear of three deaths & ... Mr. Reed is nearly gone" (November 20, 1863). John Bidwell & Co.'s store manager, Gus Chapman, became bed-ridden with a severe attack. Although he recovered, he would suffer reoccurrences the rest of his life.

Indians of the Sierra Nevada and the Cascades were used to aggressive mosquitoes. In the Cascades, during 1859, they were so fierce that drivers drove their horses at full speed to "get clear of the swarms that collect around their ears."[670] However, those mosquitoes were a non-dangerous species, different from the infected swarms in the valley in 1863.

ALTHOUGH AT THIS TIME SETTLERS maligned Bidwell for harboring dangerous Indians, he agreed with their characterization of Mill Creeks as nothing more than "a hostile, roving murderous band living in the Sierra Nevada mountains."[671] Complicating matters with his neighbors in 1863, they remembered how, in 1862, he backed Hi Good's pursuit of the Mill Creeks who had killed the Hickok children, carried settlers' petitions for protection to Brig. Gen. Wright, and then betrayed them by urging Wright to send troops to protect only his own Indians and property. Now, they concluded, he again tried to protect his own property at the expense of valley farmers' safety. As the events of August 1863 moved toward their climax, Bidwell's, Hanson's and the soldiers' relations with settlers reached new lows.

10

John Bidwell Outfoxes Soldiers, Bureaucrats and Settlers

Mountain Indians headed for Rancho Chico throughout August 1863 joined the (Round Valley) reservation Indians brought there in 1862 and together they waited for removal to the Round Valley Reservation. At the same time, John Bidwell's ranch Indians probably were unaware they were subject to a tug-of-war between his determination to keep them and other settlers' determination to include them in the removal. While Mountain Maidu of all ages walked toward Chico and Capt. Starr's Company F of the California Volunteers were bringing in a couple of groups of Indians held for them between Oroville and Quincy, tradesmen in Chico were in a frenzy. Foothill farmers so resented Bidwell they avoided trips to town or, when possible, did business with his rival tradesmen. In the hope they could restore the foothill farmers' trade, Chico businessmen met on August 17 and elected Gus Chapman, formerly a lawyer in Michigan and now Bidwell's store manager, to chair a strategy meeting.

Two days later, the group circulated a resolution drawn up by pharmacist Wesley Lee and Indian subagent Eddy, with the advice of businessmen Charles Pond and C. J. Doty. It declared Chicoans' sympathy for the country people's plight and vowed unity with them in seeking a faster removal of "the Indians now gathered in our midst."[672] That phrase was ambiguous enough that Bidwell could construe it to mean his ranch Indians were exempt from the removal because no one had "gathered" them. When the farmers also concluded the vague wording gave Bidwell an opening to keep his Indians on the ranch, they continued to limit their trade in Chico.

Standoff

The public soon realized that Starr and his men, when not practicing drills or guarding the Indians in Bidwell's fields, rarely left Rancho Chico. This, of course, conformed to Brig. Gen. Wright's orders to "remain in the vicinity of Chico" and protect "friendly Indians, particularly those residing on the ranches of citizens against the brutish assaults of bad white men."[673] Lt. Col. Drum, Wright's chief aide, ordered Starr "to consult frequently with Major Bidwell, both on account of his large experience in these difficulties and also from the fact that he is the representative of the Indian Department in that part of the State. You will find the major reliable and truly loyal."[674] Therefore, despite the troops nearby, farmers and peaceful Indians in the foothills and mountains of Butte County remained without protection against Mill Creeks holed up in the canyons of Tehama County.

Had settler protection been his company's priority, Starr would have camped in the Mesilla Valley between Chico and Oroville, the site of multiple Mill Creek raids. However, his men's daily rounds, restricted to Rancho Chico, confirmed local suspicions that his company's mission was to protect Bidwell's property and workers against citizens' threats, not to protect foothill farms against Indian raids. This vindicated the farmers' initial plan to collect the Mountain Maidu themselves.

AS PREVIOUSLY MENTIONED, THE ACTIONS and communications of Bidwell, California Volunteers officers and Indian agent George Hanson confirm they agreed the threats made at the Pence Hotel meeting in July were genuine and would result in attacks on Indians. For example, during the second week in August, Eddy's camp took in additional Indians and, in response to ominous rumblings around the township, stayed on alert for a raid by foothill farmers. Charles Stilson wrote in his diary: "The soldiers who came to town Sat. are [miserable]. Some are fearful of a collision as the mount[ain] boys are coming in. The soldiers are bound to keep the Indians here and to drive ... [the foothill farmers] out. I hope nothing will occur."[675] One of the soldiers' havens was John Bidwell & Co., where they mingled with other Union supporters. The store's location near Camp Bidwell was also convenient because Stilson kept it open evenings while he waited for the north stage's mail drop. Company officers repaired there to banter and exchange "all the news" with Gus Chapman, Charles Stilson and their Union-leaning customers.[676]

Bidwell was adamant that, when Starr's company left on the removal, another company must remain on duty at Camp Bidwell to fend off the settlers' threatened attack on his ranch. Wright obliged him by dispatching Capt. Alfred Morton and Company K of the California Volunteers to Rancho Chico with orders to "protect peaceable Indians and to consult with Major Bidwell as to the proper course to pursue."[677] After Company K arrived on August 16, Morton met with Bidwell and Starr. On the basis of their assessment of likely conditions once Starr left with the removal Indians, Morton requested a third company be sent to assist him at Camp Bidwell in defending the Rancho Chico Indians. Like Starr, he wrote to Lt. Col. Drum at the Army's Pacific Division headquarters for guidance on "how to proceed in the case of a collision."[678] Were his soldiers authorized to shoot citizens? After Morton and Starr met with Bidwell, the rancher left for San Francisco where he met with Wright, supporting Morton's claim that two companies were not sufficient to simultaneously conduct Indians to the Round Valley Reservation in Mendocino County and defend his ranch Indians against 150 settlers.[679]

Capt. Augustus Starr and Company F conducted the 1863 removal of Indians from Butte County to the Round Valley Reservation.

By August 22, Hanson had given up trying to persuade Bidwell to include his ranch Indians in the removal. He was aware of the Chico rancher's close links to the military and his influence with politicians and Hanson's own Interior Department superiors. Therefore, anticipating he might be blamed for subjecting Bidwell's Indians to killings or injury by a settler mob if he did not remove them with the rest, he wrote federal Indian Commissioner William P. Dole requesting it to be placed on record that he wanted to include all Bidwell's Indians in the removal: "Should I not remove [all] those Indians immediately, there can be no doubt but an effort to carry out the effect so unanimously adopted at the [Pence Ranch meeting] will be made, and the consequences will be a bloody affair."[680]

"The Sickness"

Weekly funerals for Indians provided a somber counterpart to the political jockeying on removal issues. Stilson wrote in his diary, "The Indians are having a terrible pow-wow tonight and in fact all day over the death of some of their members. It is horrible mournful wailing—and it continued all night."[681]

While other accounts have noted there was sickness among the removal Indians, time has obscured its cause and the extent of its impact. For example, Dorothy Hill, in explaining allusions to sickness, postulated that "many of the Indians were already sick from being rounded up, marched [to Chico], and corralled there awaiting removal."[682] Described this way, the sickness could be simply exhaustion or a common cold.

Although children, elders and the frail were among the Mountain Maidu who walked to Chico, they made their journey at a steady pace. There are no reports that any collapsed or died on the way to Eddy's camp. Distances were no problem for hearty people who, for centuries, had traversed even more difficult terrains on foot. Once they arrived at the camp by the creek, however, mosquito-borne malaria descended on them.[683]

Mosquitoes, both anopheles and culex types, require human blood meal to develop their eggs. However, only the female Anopheles mosquito can transmit malaria. When infected females bite a human, they inject the *Plasmodium* parasite, which grows and reproduces in the victim's blood. The parasites then move to the liver to feed on blood cells and subdivide, multiplying as they disperse throughout the body. For some victims, this process requires as little as eight days, but for others months can pass before full-blown malarial symptoms appear. The malaria moved quickly in Eddy's camp, where the mosquitoes continued the cycle of ingesting parasites from the infected and implanting them in healthy arrivals. Because malarial mosquitoes usually do not fly beyond roughly a one-half mile radius, they continually hovered over Eddy's camp.[684]

How could it be new information today that, in 1863, malaria was the cause of the Indian deaths in Chico and later? Because "malaria was such a common factor [in the lowlands along the Sacramento River], few people thought it worth comment."[685] Settlers referred to it as "ague," "the chills and fever" or "the seasonal sickness" and physicians called it "bilious intermittent fever." So common was it that people were resigned to its appearance as fate; just another of life's tragedies.

According to Stilson, store manager Gus Chapman was a victim that year. Like other Whites, he had limited exposure to mosquitoes because he wore full clothing and slept and worked inside. By contrast to the Mountain Indians who lived outdoors at the Rancho Chico camp, when symptoms struck, he stayed inside, slept, drank fluids, swallowed quinine and could either cool or warm himself until he recovered. Even though such treatment did not spare all victims from death, some of those who survived had periodic flare-ups throughout their lives, including Chapman.[686] Pestilence, not violence, caused the high Indian death rate in 1863 around Chico and en route to Round Valley Reservation.

Through that summer, Eddy and Dr. Samuel M. Sproul treated the Indians for malarial symptoms: recurrent headaches, extreme fatigue, muscle aches, nausea, vomiting and diarrhea. Victims regularly succumbed to chills so violent their teeth chattered and they could not lift their hands to their mouths. When the chills subsided, they collapsed in exhaustion and sweat from high fevers drenched the little clothing they wore. Some in advanced stages became delirious; other consequences were seizures, kidney failure, mental confusion and comas.[687]

Many victims of "pernicious intermittent malaria" found relief when their bodies' immune systems; temporarily subdued the parasites. However, as parasites continued to reproduce, in a day or so, new rounds of symptoms appeared. They found little relief in these battles for survival. Eddy warmed the chilled with blankets and cooled the fevered with rags soaked in creek water. When quinine and its alternative medication "chinca" (a cheaper powdered bark from the South American cinchona tree) failed, as they often did that year, malarial blood cells clogged arteries, leading to severe anemia and death. In the disease's mid-course, victims experienced weakness so extreme they could hardly hold up their heads or feed themselves, let alone sit up or, for the removal Indians, walk a hundred miles—and half of that up a mountain—to Round Valley.[688]

Eddy and the healthier Indians nursed their sick under the direction of Dr. Sproul, who also treated newly-arrived soldiers who came down with malaria. In an 1870s interview at Round Valley Reservation approximately a decade after the removal, the Maidu Concow leader Tome-ya-nem recalled his people's sickness in Chico: "Many ... became very sick with chills and fever, and when the time came for us to go back to [Round Valley Reservation] they were so weak that they could scarcely walk, and many died on the trail, lying down sick and dying all the way to the reservation...."[689] His use of "chills and fever" identifies malaria as the killer.

Eddy Tends Indians While Hanson Arranges Their Removal

With subagent Eddy, subagent Bidwell, who had held that position since the early 1850s, and military officers all at work on the removal preparations, Hanson left for Mendocino County to prepare Round Valley Reservation for its new arrivals in another month. While as recently as late July he had planned to remove the Indians to the Smith River Valley Reservation, he concluded conditions there were even worse than those at Round Valley, making the latter his only option.[690]

Hanson faced considerable hurdles. The new reservation

supervisor who was to replace James Short had not arrived.[691] A day after Hanson reached the reservation, a settler torched 2,000 bushels of wheat, more than two-thirds of the reservation Indians' recent harvest. They would not want to share the meager remainder with new arrivals, so Hanson had to find and buy sufficient wheat not only for the new arrivals, but also for the Indians already on the reservation.[692]

Second Pence Hotel Meeting

Hanson had little time for his preparations at Round Valley because he had to return to Butte County for the August 28 follow-up meeting at the Pence Hotel. To accommodate a dance scheduled that evening, the start time moved up from 10:30 P.M. to the afternoon. Without the extra travel time for distant miners and farmers, Hanson only faced fifty or so reasonably sober men, rather than the hundreds of inebriated men who had attended the July meeting.[693]

Chairman Washington Henshaw, Secretary R. H. O'Farrell and George Hanson zeroed in on their only agenda item: the number and identities of Indians in the removal party. They reported that private parties such as that of R. C. Rose and four others collected 435 Indians from Yankee Hill, Cherokee, Johnson's Ranch, Dogtown and Rock Creek.[694] In 1918, this version of the settlers as effective collectors appeared in Mansfield's *History of Butte County* and, after that, in successive accounts of the Round Valley removal.[695] These overlooked the hundreds of Indians who decided to volunteer for the reservation rather than be hunted down by settler pursuers like the Oroville Guard's Company A, who killed innocent Indian workers in the Hupp mill butcher shop.

The figure of 435 *collected* Indians announced to the crowd was misleading because it inferred Michael Wells actively pursued and collected, like the others, 220 of those Indians. As discussed in Chapter Nine, Wells was never a collector; instead, since the day after the eldest Lewis boy's killing, he had been protecting Indians from angry settlers. The Mansfield account featured a Maidu Concow descendant's praise for Wells' success in limiting settler killings in one instance, but the reach of Wells' protection has escaped credit due him. He eventually received limited backup from Starr's unit, which rode to his Concow hotel to escort forty of the hundreds of Indians who sought his help.[696]

This role placed Wells in a delicate position, but he was no political slouch. Although the Indians' best known protector, he also represented himself to the Pence Hotel committee as their partner. This not only gave him valuable access to their plans, but by feigning his cooperation, he deflected potential hostility toward him and the Indians he protected. In this, as a merchant, he balanced humane principles with practical business considerations. The number of Indians who surrendered to him alone would comprise about one-half of the entire removal party.[697]

The largest group of Indians captured by a private party appears to be sixty-five Mountain Maidu whom Robert Rose delivered to Eddy's camp, about the same time Bidwell's aide Rafael cautioned Eddy's Indians in his river camp to hide from such collectors, whom he mistakenly called "soldiers."

It appears that, apart from Rose, private collectors delivered altogether about 150 Indians. Despite initial enthusiasm for rounding up Indians, it is likely some lost interest when they realized they could be killed or how difficult it was to capture Indians who could rapidly disappear into Deer Creek and Mill Creek canyons, the headwaters camps around Lassen Peak or, like Maidu Kimshews, who escaped into Plumas County.[698]

Another group in Eddy's camp awaiting removal comprised a few dozen Indian workers for local farmers who respected their decision to leave. The twelve Indians on James Keefer's ranch arrived at Eddy's camp without incident. When Robert Durham's twenty Indian workers decided to leave, he urged Bidwell to order his chief vaquero Sandy Young to use his influence to change their minds. Durham's appeal was unsuccessful and he finally acknowledged his twenty workers' right to leave. He wrote Bidwell: "I find all my Indian boys want to go to the reservation and I for the present let them go up with the balance to your place."[699] In the end, two Indians stayed with him. After that, when Durham found himself shorthanded, he borrowed Indian workers from Rancho Chico. No evidence indicates the preferences of Indians who worked for Bidwell or suggests he offered them a choice.

In the end, despite settlers' bravado, the best evidence of their limited collection prowess appears in the final makeup of the removal body. In addition to Wells' 220 and Rose's 65 deliveries of Mountain Maidu and the roughly 40 Valley Maidu farmhands from small farms, it is probable Bidwell released a few Rancho Chico Indians who had started families with Mountain Indians from Eddy's camp over the winter of 1862–1863.[700] The balance comprised the people in Eddy's camp who still survived the onslaught of malaria taking two to three of them a day all summer.

Because interest was intense and rumors traveled fast, the August 28 Pence Hotel meeting participants were more or less aware of or suspected these developments when George Hanson spoke. He did not reveal he had changed his mind and now agreed with them that Bidwell should release his Indians to the removal. While Bidwell vowed to disregard the mortal threats and keep them in place, Hanson's responsibility as Indian agent was to protect them—*by moving them to a reservation* (discussed below). Nevertheless, he deferred to Bidwell by telling the men that, while all of the Mountain Indians at Chico would leave in about a week, Bidwell's Indians would stay on his ranch. He failed to enlist his listeners' mercy when he described the mounting death toll among the Rancho Chico Indians and mentioning another fifty gravely sick with the "bilious intermittent fever."[701]

Instead, about a dozen men vowed that, if the soldiers did not remove Bidwell's Indians with those in Eddy's camp, a party of 150 armed men would advance on Rancho Chico and drive them away by force.[702] The relative sobriety of this crowd made their threat all the more compelling. If they could intimidate Bidwell into releasing his ranch Indians, they would diminish his public standing and dismantle his "privilege" of a private workforce. After the meeting, Hanson opted not to return to Chico to oversee the removal and instead returned to San Francisco.

Removal Preparations

In preparation for the early September departure, Eddy spent hours in John Bidwell & Co., where he and Stilson assembled foods, supplies and medications, including quinine and chinca for 600 Indians. That number reflected Hanson's hope Bidwell still might change his mind and send the Mechoopdas and other Indians in his charge. At Eddy's camp, the Indian death toll from malaria continued to rise and, at Camp Bidwell, nine of Capt. Starr's men were sick by the end of the month.[703]

Over the course of that August, Hanson turned over significant responsibilities to Bidwell. On August 11 he ordered Bidwell to rent neighbors' wagons to transport parties of twenty or so sick Indians per wagon. Bidwell was confident that, because the wheat harvest was complete and the removal plan had broad support, farmers would rent sufficient wagons and teams for the removal.

On August 29, a day after the second Pence Hotel meeting and only five days before departure, Hanson reached San Francisco. Assuming that Bidwell had made good on the wagon rentals, Hanson ordered him to soften the harsh late summer sun by draping the wagons.[704]

As the deadline for the removal's start neared, Wright's officers at Camp Bidwell learned the rancher had not secured enough wagons. To Bidwell's embarrassment, local farmers refused to rent their wagons or teams. In desperation, he telegraphed the San Francisco residence of a local farm owner, who ordered his ranch manager to rent out three wagons. Eleven wagons probably came from Rancho Chico's sixteen.[705] Camp Bidwell's one wagon brought the final count to fifteen—insufficient to carry both supplies and sick Indians.

Eddy combed the countryside in search of farmers willing to lend drivers and rent him mules to pull the wagons. However, he had no cash for deposits on the teams so the owners refused. Eddy telegraphed Hanson for advice. In a letter to Bidwell, Hanson expressed his frustration: "If the people of Butte won't trust the government [for the rent] that much, I think their great parade about Indians was a humbug." When Hanson asked Bidwell to stand for the team rental fees, the rancher immediately offered to advance the cash.

Because Hanson had tried to make the removal as comfortable for the Indians as possible, it seems odd that he absented himself only days before the departure. Bidwell had finally convinced him he would not release his Indians and would take his chances with the settlers' threats against them. Evidently, thinking about the effect dead Indians in his care would have on his professional reputation, Hanson wrote a letter to Bidwell on August 29, urging the rancher to act on the "urgent necessity for [the Bidwell Indians'] immediate removal" to avert "a bloody affair." He impressed on the rancher that, if he continued to keep his Indian ranch workers and their families out of the removal, he jeopardized not only their lives but Bidwell's.[706] He said he was prepared to remove every one of Bidwell's Indians with the rest before Wright transferred the soldiers to other duty: "Otherwise I will be censured in the event of any or all of them being killed. Tell the Col. for me to be on his guard late and early."[707] Hanson was bluffing, of course, because he was in San Francisco and, although as an Indian agent he was senior to subagent Bidwell, he wielded less political influence than the rancher.

Hanson's absence during the final stage of the removal's preparation was a boon to Bidwell. It favored him that the soldiers had worked with him on a daily basis, their camp and parade ground were on his land and they socialized with his staff. Then, too, with insufficient wagons and teams to carry out their mission properly, the exemption of Bidwell's ranch Indians meant the soldiers and Eddy had fewer Indians to transport and provide for.[708]

The Camp Bidwell contingent prepared on two levels. Starr's men assigned duties, put up supplies, planned the route and laid out a schedule. Lt. Col. Hooker's and Morton's companies maintained pickets on the ranch. Taking advantage of the three companies of soldiers still at Rancho Chico, Hooker, the camp commander, implemented a plan of "strategic deterrence": to discourage post-removal attacks on the ranch once Starr's unit left. He mounted a display of force in a public, formal review of the companies: 121 enlisted men and five commissioned officers.[709] In a decision farmers and miners must have found alternately provocative and intimidating, he invited Bidwell to review the parade with him "as one of my Staff."[710]

Hooker conducted the review on the parade ground behind Bidwell's downtown store. This was "front and center" property Bidwell had rented to the California Volunteers since they first arrived in Chico. Since Starr's August 1, 1863, arrival, soldiers had become a common sight for residents and farm customers as they passed daily from their camp, between Bidwell's mill and the cemetery, across the bridge to the parade field for drills.[711]

The final tally of 461 Indians faced a grueling journey to the Round Valley Reservation. They were, for the most part, Mountain Maidu. From the original three hundred who had arrived from Round Valley Reservation in 1862, about 170 were the Mountain Maidu malaria survivors and some Hat Creeks and Pit Rivers. Their reduced number was confirmed in a December 1863 letter from Bidwell to the Secretary of the Interior in Washington. As part of his appeal to the federal government to remove the Indians in Eddy's camp, Bidwell noted they had been dying from malaria over the summer at the rate of about two per day. Confirming this estimate, on August 30, a newspaper reported thirty Indians had died there in the previous two weeks and fifty more were "deadly sick,"[712] underlining the sick Indians' frailty in every stage of the disease when they left Chico on the removal.[713]

As Chapter Eleven explains, the 461 Indians who left Chico moved as best they could, depending on one another, trusting Eddy and supervised by a company of soldiers, sick themselves, who bore them no ill will but had few options to relieve their misery. But in their haste to remove them from Chico's armed settlers, Indian Department officials and military officers sent them away with inadequate transport. In contrast, as the removal began, John Bidwell was well prepared: he had two companies of well-provisioned California Volunteers protecting his ranch's Indian workers against angry farmers.

11

The Death Trail

Brig. Gen. Wright ordered Capt. Augustus Starr to deliver the Mountain Indians safely to the Round Valley Reservation. He was to see that "no violence is to be used in bringing in the Indians and if any should be resorted to the general desires you to protect the unoffending Indians to the extent of your power."[714]

Correspondence between Superintendent Hanson and James Eddy prior to the removal reflected their apprehension about settler threats against the Indians and confidence in Company F's ability to safely deliver the Indians. The following sections address Company F's conduct in light of their orders, the conditions of their mission and its aftermath.

Whether John Bidwell would carry out his vow to exempt the Rancho Chico Indians from the 1863 removal remained an open question until departure day. While he had been adamant about keeping the ranch's Indian workers behind, his caution, aversion to violence and pride had led Indian Affairs superintendent and agent George Hanson to hope he was bluffing.[715]

On September 4, however, when Indian subagent James Eddy, the California Volunteers' Company F, led by Capt. Starr, and 461 Mountain Indians left for the Round Valley Reservation, Rancho Chico's Indians stayed behind. Round Valley Reservation was one hundred miles away, requiring the Indians to walk across the Sacramento Valley and climb the Coastal Range, with its highest elevation at 6,000 feet, through what is now known as the Mendocino National Forest, a harrowing challenge for even the able-bodied.[716]

Sickness had winnowed Starr's company to only twenty-three men well enough to travel. Soldiers and ranch workers guided the children to the fifteen wagons waiting at Camp Bidwell. They delivered the most helpless Indians on litters and fitted them among barrels and boxes stacked along the wagon beds; the rest walked or were carried. Soldiers helped the drivers, local farmers, harness their mule teams.

At the last moment, Bidwell denied Dr. Samuel Sproul's offer to accompany the removal party. His friend, who tended Rancho Chico Indians and oversaw the "infirmary" area of Eddy's camp, understood how difficult patient care would be for Eddy, whose tuberculosis was worsening. While Bidwell could be sympathetic and helpful, it was in his interest to keep Sproul behind because an attack on the ranch might cause injuries (and death) to himself and his workers. Because Eddy had worked with Sproul over the summer tending to the malaria victims, he and his Indian helpers had experience treating and caring for the sick Indians.[717]

The Journey

As the removal wagons and Indians on foot headed north to Mendocino County, Starr avoided towns and traffic. Turning west from the Oroville-Shasta Road to camp at Colby's Ferry, near modern Nord, the party made ready to cross the Sacramento River.[718] The walkers' physical conditions dictated the pace, but even with stops for burials and wagon repairs, they covered about ten miles a day. Starr's men spelled the farmers at the wagons' reins, while he and others scouted the route ahead, arranging for a ferry or finding a ford. Tehama County Indians watched as soldiers shepherded the rival tribesmen through their territory, with strings of horses and mules bringing up the rear. In that long parade of Indians, who had once been lightening runners and tireless walkers scrambling up cliffs, many now stumbled.

As the party made its way across the Sacramento Valley, one of Starr's challenges was to keep moving. Aware that water was essential to relieve malaria's symptoms, he rode ahead to negotiate with farmers for campsites near springs or creeks,[719] relying on William Baldwin, 31, who had so impressed him as a private that he promoted him to first sergeant, to keep order.[720] One family, which had lost members to Indians, allowed Starr's party to set up camp, but at a considerable distance from the spring near their house. Intermittent crises also created delays. When the removal party crossed into the foothills of the Coastal Range, Indians on higher ground showered them with arrows, without effect.[721]

Along the way, Eddy administered quinine and chinca to sick soldiers and Indians, two or more deaths occurring each day. Afflicted soldiers carried on to complete their mission.[722]

The Chico area farmers had agreed to drive their wagons on the condition they would turn back at the Coastal Range. There, Starr was told, military personnel from Fort Wright in Round Valley would meet him with fresh supplies and a full complement of replacement wagons. When the removal party reached the base of the mountains, fourteen of the fifteen wagons turned back to Chico, taking with them sick Pvt. Richard Loder, to join five men from Capt. Alfred Morton's company in Camp Bidwell's sick bay. While Starr waited for the wagons, the Indians rested and dried beef for the next leg of the journey.[723]

From Fort Wright, Capt. Charles Douglas sent a wagon train with provisions to Starr's waiting party. Accompanying it were Lt. Noyes and an unidentified civilian aide who rode ahead to find Starr's camp.[724] Once there, Noyes told Starr that the wagons were still a couple of days up the difficult trail and that Douglas had ordered the drivers to leave the provisions—*but not the wagons*. Starr moved his party on foot and litters about three miles above the Mountain House, a hotel, and made camp. (Hereafter called the Mountain House camp.) No information explains why Starr chose that site or whether he was ordered to do so. It was long thought the camp was on hotel grounds rather than three miles beyond. Apparently the site was a streamside meadow large enough to accommodate several hundred Indians and was the "takeoff" point for the steeper climb on the trail just above it. In any case, the wagons delivered their freight there and returned to Ft. Wright empty. The stranded party would have to continue up the mountain with only the Camp Bidwell wagon.[725]

The next phase of the journey would be even more challenging because well over a third of the Indians were sick. Starr and Eddy agreed that, with the Indians in such weakened conditions, they could not climb the perilous trail to the reservation. They turned the camp into an infirmary where Eddy would remain and tend 150 of the sickest. Company F would move on with the rest of the relatively fitter Indians, gambling they could manage the arduous fifty-mile balance of the journey.

Meanwhile, Back at the Ranch

After the removal party left Chico on September 4, Charles Stilson felt relieved but remained anxious: "The great event today was the starting of the Indians who are to be removed to the reservation...." Then, he added, "Still, Bidwell's remain & [we] fear it may cause trouble...."[727]

With the two companies of captains Morton and Davis, under Lt. Col. Hooker, picketing Bidwell's sprawling property, the crisis at Chico subsided. The rancher's refusal to accede to Hanson's pressure to remove his Indian workers meant he had again, as in 1862, outfoxed his antagonists. And he had cleared his ranch of Hanson's sick Indians. Bidwell indulged himself in a moment of vindictiveness. Although he sent Hanson two letters in the week after the removal began, in neither did he mention what the superintendent most wanted to know: whether he had kept his Indians from the removal. Hanson restrained his curiosity. Finally, on September 9, when the removal had been under way for five days, after responding to Bidwell's complaints about slow federal payments, he added a postscript: "I suppose your Indians are not gone are they?"[728] While the two men had cooperated in the removal, they could not reconcile their differences over Bidwell's insistence to exclude Rancho Chico's Indians. There is no little irony in the common twentieth-century assumption that Bidwell had kept the ranch's Indians from the removal to protect them from it. He was its initiator and mainstay. As he told the Secretary of State in Washington, D.C., the removal Indians "were fed, taken care of, and finally sent to the reservation all at my expense."[729]

While Starr's party was still crossing the Sacramento Valley toward Round Valley, in San Francisco Hanson learned that Humboldt County settlers, resenting his efforts to protect Indians, had convinced Indian Affairs to fire him. As he wound up his affairs, he responded to Bidwell's plea for advice about how to expedite federal payments. Despite his urgings that George Wood, Bidwell's partner, keep prices low to forestall questions about their Chico store's billings, Hanson pointed out it submitted "exorbitant charges" for items Eddy bought for the Indians. The prices, he said, were double those a Redding store charged for the same items. Bulk purchases, such as pants, soap, flannel shirts, medications and bran for Eddy's Indian camp and Camp Bidwell made the government John Bidwell & Co.'s biggest customer in 1863.[730] No longer protective of Bidwell, before Hanson left office he opened a federal account with W. Lee & Co. as the alternate Chico supplier of reservation goods.

Legislation the previous spring had repealed the legal status of Indian peonage under which Bidwell had long operated his ranch. Hanson urged Bidwell to formalize his Indian labor arrangements with a contract that would grant Rancho Chico Indians recognized status as workers, but the rancher ignored Hanson's advice and continued to operate as before.[731]

ALTHOUGH THE REMOVAL WAS UNDERWAY, foothill residents still could not relax. Only a day before Starr and his men arrived at Camp Bidwell, Indians had killed three Butte County miners on Dry Creek.[732] Settlers living around Nimshew and Dogtown were already uneasy about the increasing number of male Mountain Maidu whom, they suspected, were a mix of removal escapees and others who had avoided being captured by hiding out in Deer Creek Canyon.

The removal party had not even reached Round Valley before miners in the Sierra Nevada and farmers were already figuring out where to turn for help to remove the rest of the troublesome Mountain Maidu. This time they adopted Bidwell's approach: political pressure. Having given up on the governor and state legislators, who relied on Bidwell for advice, the petitioners appealed directly to Brig. Gen. Wright, the Army's wartime commander of the California Volunteers, and Indian Affairs' Superintendent Hanson, who had yet to be replaced.[733]

The miners and farmers appointed Thomas Wells, 39, as their advocate to continue removing all Valley and Mountain Maidu Indians from Butte County. This Missouri native and newly elected school trustee had held elected positions in eastern Butte County since the 1850s. As justice of the peace in at least two mining communities, Judge Wells had "dealt evenhanded justice."[734] And he was a locally famed orator: a year later he would be president of the Oroville town trustees and deliver the speech welcoming the railroad's arrival.

In San Francisco, Wells contacted Joseph McCorkle, the northern district's former state assemblyman and former member of Congress. He persuaded Hanson to set aside his low regard for Wells' constituents and meet with him and Wright. The Army's Lt. Col. Drum, doubling during the war as the state's acting assistant adjutant general and Wright's chief aide, joined Wells and Hanson on Wright's behalf.[735]

Drum offered Wells no help with the new proposed removal and Hanson made it clear Round Valley Reservation had no budget to feed additional Indians. Anxious to derive some benefit from this meeting, Wells agreed the settlers would drop demands for the removal of the Valley Indians.

With this concession, Drum agreed the California Volunteers would deliver to Round Valley Reservation all the Mountain Indians locals collected and Hanson granted them space on the reservation. Because Wright's order for wagons big enough to transport twenty people each had been ignored in the removal underway, Drum and Hanson specified that all the Indian transfers must be "in small parties" that could fit into available wagons.[736]

While in his public report, pubslished in the newspaper, Wells expressed satisfaction with the meeting, he had only persuaded the military to continue minimal transfers to the reservation. Having promised Hanson and Drum he would immediately publicize their agreement, Wells wired a lengthy message to the *Butte Record*, which published it on September 19. This speed enabled Wright to gauge the public's reaction before he recalled the two companies from Camp Bidwell. Apparently, however, Wells was still counting on the military's help, claiming "immunity is guaranteed to us from a reliable source against savage theft, incendiarism and murder."[737]

When Col. Hooker at Camp Bidwell learned about Thomas Wells' meeting with Drum, his note to Bidwell reflected surprise that his superiors had issued orders on the advice of a man unknown to him. Later, Hooker's letter to Army headquarters discounted Wells in vague terms. As northern Butte County's settlers wearily and warily resumed their daily routines, Morton's and Hooker's soldiers continued to picket Rancho Chico.

The Death Trail Continues

On September 14, 1863, Starr and his men departed from the Mountain House camp with 277 of the healthier Indians. Of the 461 who set out from Chico, 32 had died crossing the valley and 150 had stayed behind with Eddy. With only the lone Fort Bidwell wagon left behind, the Starr party immediately encountered "impossible trails." On the second day, facing deep ruts in the crooked path and sharp turns at steep angles, the wagon broke down, beyond repair. Leaving behind all the supplies the party could not pack on the mules, their horses and people's backs, they started out again. The difficult road conditions required an exertion which, hour-by-hour, day-by-day, debilitated even the healthier Indians. One individual after the next became nauseous, feverish and shivered violently. Most were too weak to walk back to the Mountain House camp for Eddy's care or continue to the reservation.

Recognizing the reservation was the closest source of provisions, wagons and medicine, the captain decided to continue on. Starr later reported to Hooker that his men placed sick women on their own horses and mules and led them "the greater part of the way."[738] Because Indian women had never ridden an animal, the soldiers tied them in place to prevent falls. Although ill, the women still considered riding such beasts foreign, offensive and frightening. As a descendent explained, the soldiers "tied [them] right on the mules so they so they couldn't, you know, couldn't move, couldn't do anything else for themselves."[739] Eddy did his best to mediate between the proud Indians and well-meaning soldiers.

Rescue from the Death Trail

On September 18, Starr's unit reached the Round Valley Reservation, with only eighty Indians out of the original 461 and the 277 he led from the Mountain House camp. Strung out on the trail behind him were almost two hundred people—corpses and others still clinging to life. Maidu Concow leader Tome-ya-nem recalled the survivors' arrival at Round Valley Reservation: "The head men on the Reservation had gone to the big city near the great waters [San Francisco], & there was no one here to do anything for us—only the White Chief Douglas at Camp Wright, who sent his medicine men to take care of my sick and whites [soldiers] and mules ... to bring my people left dying on the trail—and here we have remained ever since."[740]

The Indians who made it to the Round Valley Reservation encountered more problems there. The reservation had recently fallen under the direction of Dr. William P. Melendy, the reservation's esteemed physician, whom Indian Affairs had just promoted to fill James Short's former position as reservation supervisor. (Melendy was still expected to continue his medical services at no extra pay.) When told about the removal party's impending arrival, he was alarmed because settler arson had destroyed the reservation's crops, leaving provisions inadequate to sustain the Indians already there, let alone the eighty new arrivals and the hundreds still on their way. Although prior to his termination George Hanson had submitted a large order for cattle to feed the new arrivals, Elijah Steele, his replacement as superintending agent of the Indian District of Northern California, had placed a stop on the payment.[741] While Starr and the Indians were en route to the reservation, Melendy left for San Francisco to secure authorization for funds from Steele to pay for the cattle. However, when Melendy reached San Francisco, he learned Steele's authority to grant his request would not become official for five more days. While Melendy waited, he persuaded Steele to return with him to assess the situation at Round Valley Reservation. As a result, they did not arrive there until early October.[742]

Therefore, although Starr expected to hand over the Indians to the reservation when his party arrived on September 18, he found no one authorized to take over their care, much less rescue the remaining 150 infirmary camp Indians and the 200 strewn along the trail. Starr rode to Fort Wright, a mile away, where he briefed Capt. Douglas. Although Starr told him about the 350 sick Indians left behind on the trail, Douglas initially authorized the use of his fort's personnel and supplies only for the eighty

Indians Starr had delivered to the reservation.

WITH NO ORDERS TO STAY, Starr and Company F left the reservation on September 21 for Camp Bidwell. As the soldiers rode down the mountain, planning to make a stop at Eddy's camp, evidence of their mission's failure—the smell of decaying corpses and the sight of Indians ravaged by malaria—faced them at every bend.

At Eddy's camp, they discovered he and his Indian assistants had kept alive all the sick. Some who recovered had already left for the Sacramento Valley on their way back to the Sierra. After Starr apprised Eddy of the situation up the trail and at the reservation, Eddy returned to Chico with him and his men for medical supplies and provisions.

When the men arrived on September 24, Bidwell provided Eddy a room at the new Chico Hotel around the corner from his store. He and Stilson stuffed medicines and provisions into Eddy's carryall and a pack they secured behind Eddy's saddle. The next day he headed back to the infirmary camp. After dropping off supplies, he headed up the trail. At every turn, he came upon clusters of Indians, stopping to console, cover, cool, medicate and bury.

Captain Douglas Takes Charge

Arriving at Round Valley Reservation, Eddy learned from Capt. Douglas that after he left for Chico with Starr's company, travelers who had seen the corpses and sick and dying Indians on the trail made detours to Fort Wright where they insisted his company act. When Douglas wrote his own report he did not mention that he only had tended the eighty Indians Starr delivered, ignoring those demands for almost a week before he relented and rode out to assess the situation. His subsequent actions indicate that when he returned to his post, now aware of the tragedy's extent, he was determined to divert responsibility from the California Volunteers to Indian Affairs. Douglas wrote his superiors: "I found all the Indians that were sent or brought on the reservation from Chico, about 10 days ago in an almost dying condition, through sickness and the gross neglect of duty of the present supervisor [Melendy]. I was also informed by Starr, then confirmed by passersby that nearly two hundred sick Indians are scattered along all the way for forty miles, and that they are dying by the tens for want of care and medical treatment and from lack of food."[743] Of that two hundred, he estimated that 150 of those were dead or dying at a rate of two to three a day. He added: "The object in view is the proper care & treatment of the sick Indians, the shameful neglect of which has brought the Government of the United States into disrepute."[744] Because Indian Affairs was the government agency charged with Indians' "care and treatment," but its reservation manager was absent, Douglas found himself Round Valley Reservation's de facto supervisor. To diminish the significance of this role, he placed on the record that Indian Affairs' reservation staff was responsible for the removal's failure. It is noteworthy that Douglas also failed to mention that he had denied Starr wagons to replace the fourteen that had returned to Chico, stranding the Indians en route to Round Valley Reservation at the Mountain House camp.[745]

Douglas dispatched Fort Wright's physician, men and provisions for temporary duty at points along the upper trail. According to Tome-ya-nem, they had been conscientious in treating the gravely sick Indians who first arrived and now they did their best for the Indians who collapsed just short of the reservation.[746] Transport for the sick and burials of the dead along the steep trail were logistically demanding and the military's botched execution of the removal in general had the makings of a political scandal. While Douglas attempted to extricate himself and the California Volunteers from any liability, he was still faced with a practical problem: the reservation had no competent or reliable personnel to complete the removal.

Douglas was so intent on divorcing Fort Wright from any association with the removal disaster that, after he returned there from his tour of the trail, he sought out former reservation supervisor James Short, the only man in the area who could credibly manage the Indians' retrieval and understand the dialects of the Maidu. During Short's stint as the Round Valley Reservation's superintendent, he had come to know many of the Indians he was now charged to rescue. They had been among the starving

The Death Trail

James Short, superintendent of the Round Valley Reservation, had been fired for incompetence but was rehired to relieve the military by collecting bodies on the trail.

Indians he had helped leave the reservation in 1862 when they informed him they were returning to their Sierra Nevada and Cascade mountain territories.[747] For Douglas, making Short responsible for the retrieval helped shift blame for the removal's failure from the military to Indian Affairs.

As touched on above and in Chapter Nine, in October 1861, after Douglas instituted martial law in Round Valley, Brig. Gen. Wright suspended his order but appointed him to head an inquiry into Short's reservation mismanagement.[748] At the hearing's end, Douglas concluded Short's leadership reflected "entire want of zeal and gross mismanagement.... Mr. Short exerts himself to hinder, embarrass and delay" the work of his staff.[749] Also mentioned, in a letter to President Lincoln, who had appointed Short to that post, Hanson explained one reason he fired him was an obsession over an Indian woman that led him to neglect his duties.

Why would George Hanson explain to the president of the United States his reasons for this ordinary personnel decision? Short had made it known that Lincoln and he were personal friends in Illinois when he lived on the farm next to that of the family of Lincoln's love Ann Rutledge, whose mother was Short's housekeeper. A regular visitor to Short's home, Lincoln helped him pick corn and Short helped Lincoln with a financial predicament. Short had pressed his case against Capt. Douglas at a meeting with Lincoln in Washington as recently as the summer of 1862.[750] The informal tone of Hanson's letter was based on his own personal relationship with the president, and he closed with "Your old friend, G. M. Hanson."[751]

Douglas was worried Short might collect removal information deleterious to him and Starr. However, he could no longer claim ignorance of the Indians' plight and requested that Short transport the survivors to the reservation and bury the dead. Aware Douglas had no one else to call on, Short agreed to take the job, but on his own terms: he demanded Douglas write Lincoln, praising his service as reservation superintendent.[752] Douglas agreed and the expansiveness of his letter's positive remarks, in light of his key role in Short's recent firing, speaks to his desperation to enlist the man's help.[753] More important for the present study, Short's letter to Lincoln matters because it confirmed the Indians were sick and dying from malaria, not from abuse by the soldiers. Although Douglas assured Short that "food, medicines and supplies will be sent with you from this post,"[754] he did not order his dozen or so soldiers to help Short.

THESE DETAILS AND ADVERSARIAL CORRESPONDENCE between Indian Affairs officials and officers of the California Volunteers reveal how long-standing tensions between their agencies contributed to the removal crisis. Had the conduct of either side become a public issue, each was prepared to defend itself and deflect blame to its rival.

Although Short only worked a couple of weeks before Melendy returned and replaced him, his October 1863 letter to Indian Affairs provided a firsthand glimpse of the tragedy he came upon when he set out on the trail on September 27, presumably with Indian helpers from Round Valley Reservation. He had rented, at his own expense, twenty pack mules and, later, oxen, that pulled a reservation wagon about 250 miles up and down the trail. Short's observations about trail conditions resembled those of Douglas: "Everyone that come by [the reservation told] of the great suffering, entirely destitute situation, nothing to eat, no medical treatment, and positively the hogs eating them up either before or after they was dead."[755] After he came upon one young mother, dead from a "wild boar" attack, he surmised that, while this boar might have come upon her corpse, it more likely killed her because, before she died, she had managed to place her baby, who survived, in a tree, out of its reach. Although a modern resident who lives near the site of the Mountain House denied there were currently any boars in the area, they were common in the removal period and after in the Sierra Nevada. Forty-niner Charles Pancoast recalled wild boars as "more fierce and savage than any animals I ever set my eyes upon."[756] Accounts by removal descendants Leland Scott and Thelma Wilson, as well as those by firsthand witnesses Douglas and Short, support the survivors' awareness of wild boars roaming the Coast Range.

In Short's first two days on part of the upper trail, he oversaw the burial of thirty fresh corpses Douglas' men had not yet reached and he brought up sick and emaciated survivors to Round Valley Reservation. When Melendy arrived at the reservation with his boss, the new Indian superintendent Elijah Steele, who was replacing Hanson, he was furious to discover Short back at work there. However, Steele could not fire him again because no Indians were qualified to drive the reservation wagon along the steep mountain trail. However, when Eddy returned to Round Valley Reservation with supplies from Chico, he was ordered to take over the recovery from Short. Eddy was likely helped by the reservation Indians. Had Douglas been able to overlook his personal resentment of Short, and had the Indian Affairs officials continued Short's employment, all of them—Starr, Douglas, Short, Eddy, and the soldiers—could have worked together to speed up the transport and treatment of the victims.[757]

Steele signed off on the bill for the needed cattle on September 29, before he left for Round Valley Reservation. Once there, he and Melendy turned on Douglas, whom Steele accused of "usurpation of Power" for hiring Short. After being fired this second time, Short wrote bitter letters to President Lincoln seeking compensation.[758] He continued his appeals through the following summer, concluding in one, "I am Low Spirited among Strangers without a dollar and not able to work."[759] However, despite his personal reasons to resent both Steele and Douglas, Short never said, nor implied, that Indian Affairs personnel or the California Volunteers soldiers had assaulted or killed any Indian between Round Valley and Chico.[760]

BECAUSE OF THE LARGE NUMBER of sick Indians being treated, Eddy quickly depleted his medical supplies and needed to make another trip to replenish them. While the village of Tehama was a more convenient destination for medications and other provisions, he still traveled to Chico for bulk supplies from John Bidwell & Co. On his trip back to Round Valley, Eddy rode Bidwell's horse Dan, leaving word at Bidwell's office that he wanted to purchase him. He quickly filled his order and returned to the reservation. By mid-October, the last removal Indians, still alive on the trail, were waiting to be collected from their camp near the mountain's summit. Eddy brought them down to the reservation barely ahead of the snows.[761]

Captain Starr's Report

When Capt. Starr's company returned to Camp Bidwell on September 24, he was debriefed by Lt. Col. Hooker, his commanding officer, to whom he gave his journal of the trip. Starr, his men and the Indians had received inadequate support at every stage of the removal. They had been denied a physician and sufficient wagons to carry the sick Indians. They had been deprived of replacement wagons at the Mountain House camp for the balance of their journey, including their treacherous ascent into the Coastal Range. As the two men talked, hundreds of the Indians they were ordered to protect and deliver still had not reached the reservation because they had died or were stranded and dying. And, now, Starr, Douglas and their superior officer Hooker might face disciplinary actions for the mission's failures.[762]

Should that happen, Starr's journal would be called on as evidence. A transcription of the journal was later attached to

Hooker's own report, which appeared in the military's *Official Records* of the Civil War years. That "official" published version of the journal has been relied upon for virtually every rendition of the removal since. However, its contents contradict two other first person accounts. The following analysis of the journal in the context of other contemporary documents demonstrates that Hooker's published version is most likely a heavily edited account—one riddled with omissions, distortions and mistruths.

The content and tenor of the edited version of Starr's journal that Hooker submitted points to an implicit intent to use its entries to shift responsibility for the disastrous removal from the California Volunteers to federal Indian Affairs staff at Round Valley Reservation.

Of the two men, Starr and Hooker, who had possession of the journal, Starr had neither the motive nor political savvy to shape his entries in anticipation that he, Hooker and his other Army superiors might face future inquiries. The authentic parts of Starr's journal included entries like this example of his general record keeping and writing: "September 17: Left Log Cabin and traveled westerly thirteen miles and encamped between South and Middle Forks of Eel River. First three miles was ascending. Next ten miles was steep and descending. Some water about halfway down the mountain, north side of road. Spent one night at government camp."

In his journal, Starr's position on the removal resembled that of Capt. Douglas' at Fort Wright, whose letters to his superior officers about its collapse alluded to information gleaned while Starr's unit stayed at Fort Wright prior to its return to Camp Bidwell. Their brief stay there exonerates Douglas from revisions of Starr's journal.[763]

Hooker's edited version of the journal reflects his decision to contain the potential damage from Starr's original writings. The following analysis is necessarily speculative since Starr's original journal is no longer available. Assertions and nuances in the surviving version of the journal raise questions that compel its reinterpretation. Starr's original entries remained: recorded terrain, camp locations and water quality. They provided the edited version's "spine" and lent the entire journal an aura of authenticity. However, when Hooker rewrote some of the entries, or had Starr do it, individually dated entries were merged into a single narrative stream that invited skimming rather than close scrutiny. While Starr's concerns about water quality at stopping points remained, there was no mention of the Indians' dire physical condition or that an average of two to three died every day, resulting in thirty-two deaths just in the first ten days it took to reach the foothills on the west side of the Sacramento Valley. Starr himself might have considered this information inappropriate to include, but in light of more obvious edits that followed, it appears such information was pruned from his original journal.

As an example of Hooker's probable editing to hide the Army's responsibility for the removal's failure, entries from September 8–12 are of special concern. Starr's journal noted Douglas' Lt. Noyes and an unidentified man "from Fort Wright" arrived at Starr's foothills camp on September 8 where, anticipating the arrival of replacement wagons from Fort Wright, Starr had already released the Butte County wagons, which were on their way home. However, Noyes must have alerted Starr that Army wagons would not arrive until the 12th, when they would unload the promised provisions at the Mountain House camp. The apparently edited section of Starr's September 12 entry stated that the wagons arrived at Mountain House camp from "*Round Valley Reservation*" [emphasis added]—not Fort Wright—inferring Indian Affairs' reservation personnel alone had dropped off the provisions and then had driven off with the empty wagons. The wording exempted the Army's Fort Wright and, by extension, Douglas from responsibility for the botched delivery so harmful to the sick Indians.

Although leaving office, Hanson had readied the reservation for the Indians' arrival. He knew Superintendent Melendy as yet had no authority to requisition or pay rent for civilian wagons or pay for food—let alone wagons and mules. Nor would settlers in Round Valley, who loathed the reservation and resented Fort Wright, have loaned the reservation wagons and mules of their own volition to bring in hundreds more Indians.

No available information explains why Douglas did not order the wagons and mules to transport the Indians from the Mountain House camp to the reservation. Since opening Fort Wright, he had already demonstrated a proclivity for peculiar interpretations of his authority. Early in his command there, he shut down all Round Valley saloons for excessive drunkenness in the civilian population (an order Gen. Wright later ordered him to rescind). After his review of James Short's reservation management, he recommended Short be terminated, rather than ordering him to reform his policies. If an investigation of the removal failure took place, Douglas, already controversial at Army headquarters, would be the target of an inquiry and his career ruined. Therefore, in combination with later suspect entries, it is likely that Douglas edited the journal.

While the edited version of Starr's journal that Hooker sent to Army headquarters reported a successful mission, its September 18 entry raises questions about that claim. It specified the soldiers delivered 277 Indians (they actually delivered eighty), that thirty-two died over the whole journey (that was the number of deaths crossing the Sacramento Valley alone) and reported two Indians escaped (the number was at least five). The journal was correct that Starr left 150 Indians at the Mountain House camp. However, the journal did not mention that, at the time Hooker was debriefing Starr, 150 of the 200 Indians still strung out along the mountain trail were dead or dying (by now at a stepped up rate of three a day.)

The final entry—*made at Camp Bidwell*—differed from all of Starr's other ones in its length, style and content. Right after the erroneous summary of deliveries and deaths, the entry abruptly changed course, launching into a litany of complaints about Round Valley Reservation's inadequate food and poor housing for the Indians. While the reservation's condition was deplorable, this editorial diversion attempted to shift readers' attention away from the Army's failed charge to provide the removal Indians with adequate transportation and safety. Instead, it diverted attention to Indian Affairs' purported mismanagement of the Indians' care. While the questioned entry's phrasing and content are at odds with Starr's style and content in his other entries, they match the passion, venom and focus that characterize Hooker's report.

That same entry closed with fulsome praise for conditions at Fort Wright and a notation that Company F's men returned to Camp Bidwell in excellent condition. However, according to the unit's "Post Returns," ten of its twenty-three men checked into the sick bay.

In the mission report Lt. Col. Hooker, as Camp Bidwell's commander, sent to Lt. Col. Drum at Army headquarters, he turned on Butte County settlers who had worked with him. He disparaged George Wood, acting for Bidwell in his absence, as "an alarmist," "wanting to keep troops" in Chico to protect his ranch Indians against threats by angry crowds that had "not the shadow of a foundation of truth in any one instance."[764] This overlooked the execution of two Indians in Chico proper the previous month. Hooker claimed Wood and other petitioners had called for troops when there were problems with only a dozen or so Mill Creeks. According to Hooker, Camp Bidwell had no purpose but to "quiet the imaginary fears of a few timid citizens"; that is, Bidwell and his local business associates were less concerned about Indian raids than about losing the patronage of settlers.[765] His allegations ignored his own collaboration with Bidwell, Superintendent Hanson, Brig. Gen. Wright, Capt. Starr and Capt. Morton when they anticipated an imminent mob attack on Bidwell's Indians. Because Hooker arrived to command Camp Bidwell on August 26, only days before the removal's September 4 departure, he was, in effect, denying all the settler-Indian conflicts prior to his arrival.

In an aside on the San Francisco agreement Thomas Wells made with Lt. Col. Drum and Hanson about continuing to collect Indians for another removal after Starr's removal had departed for Round Valley Reservation, Hooker pointed out in his report that foothill citizens and James Eddy had collected few of the Indians in Starr's party. Although factual, it omitted important information of which he was aware: most Mountain Maidu in the removal had surrendered themselves from fear of settlers. Hooker's reference to settlers as collectors who started prior to Starr's departure was misleading because Starr's Company F and the Indians had already reached Round Valley when Butte County settlers learned, on September 19, they would have to collect additional Mountain Maidu on their own for removal by the Army. They had no more enthusiasm for that dangerous role then than they had had in late July through August. Hooker's remarks infer his report was a defense Wright, as commander, could use against any direct challenge to the California Volunteers.

Hooker's report ignored the Indians' grave medical condition and desperate circumstances. He only raised the subject to credit the soldiers for giving up their horses to transport the sickest women.[766] Then, Hooker never mentioned that, without the promised military wagons, Starr's unit and their Indian charges had to walk fifty miles from the Mountain House camp to the Round Valley Reservation. Hooker made sure to blame Bidwell and Eddy for the wagon shortage in Chico at the removal's start: "The means of transportation of those in charge of the Indian affairs here [Chico] was entirely inadequate to the demand."[767]

Hooker's boldest deceit in his report, his most original feint in this political subterfuge, was his retroactive redefinition of Starr's mission. He claimed he "had sent [Starr] to *assist*" [emphasis added] Eddy in the removal.[768] In reducing Starr to the role of aide to a civilian, however, Hooker contradicted Starr's August 11 orders from Drum, on behalf of Wright, which explicitly stated he was to "take charge of" the reservation-bound Indians in Chico and deliver them to Round Valley Reservation.[769] Hooker's (edited) "official" version of Starr's journal on the removal became the bona fide historical evidence for the removal. Therefore, the editing alleged here in that sole surviving version, deemed as fact by Hooker in his report, has, until, now compromised the accuracy of all subsequent removal histories.

Under other conditions, Hooker might have won credit for the peace in Chico after the Mountain Indians were removed. After all, the colonel mounted a showy review presenting the three well-armed, mounted companies as a single disciplined force. The sight of this likely intimidated onlookers and thwarted the uprising he and others expected if Bidwell excluded his Indians from the removal.[770] However, the removal proved so disastrous that, as soon as Hooker realized its magnitude, he concentrated his effort on drawing attention away from the roles played by Captains Starr and Douglas and himself. By doing so, he sacrificed the credit some might say he deserved for protecting the careers of Starr, Douglas and himself as their commander.

The blame Hooker placed on Indian Affairs is ironic because Eddy and his boss Hanson were dedicated Indian Affairs workers. In the end, neither side had to defend its role because Indian Affairs never challenged the Army's California Volunteers on the failure of the removal. For one thing, the ubiquity and lethal nature of malaria was already the reason behind the Army's policy to avoid basing troops, when possible, in the Sacramento Valley during hot weather and this factor alone explained the removal's death toll to their satisfaction. For another, correspondence between Hanson and Steele and Army headquarters in 1863 and 1864 reveals that Indian Affairs' problems with the military already extended well beyond the issues at Round Valley Reservation.[771] As a result, Hooker's criticisms of the agency were merely one more volley in the two opponents' ongoing conflict.

According to author and historian Colonel Herbert M. Hart, "The Civil War battles at Fort Wright ... usually were fought between the Army and the Indian Bureau. With few exceptions, tribesmen were on the sidelines."[772] The soldiers at Fort Wright believed their presence was essential to "the saving of the Indians" at Round Valley Reservation from its management.[773] Conversely, reservation administrators considered the soldiers "a nuisance."[774] As recently as August 22, while Hanson was at Round Valley readying it for the removal arrivals, he reported Douglas for not consulting with him, as Indian agent, before he executed five Coastal Range Indians who had preyed on reservation Indians.[775] In Hanson's opinion, "the military posts are worse than useless," a waste of the money needed for support on the reservations.[776] In 1864, Round Valley's superintendent Melendy prohibited any military personnel from entering the reservation. In response, the California Volunteers' headquarters instructed Douglas no Indians "or squaws" were to enter Fort Wright's grounds "under any circumstance."[777]

AFTER HOOKER'S REPORT DISCOUNTED BUTTE County settlers' latest claims of Indian threats, Brig. Gen. Wright withdrew the two companies which had arrived in mid-to-late August but ordered Capt. Starr's Company F to remain at Camp Bidwell to protect area Indians and settlers from one another. Northern Butte County residents, convinced the California Volunteers had, as in 1859, deferred to Bidwell at their expense, looked the other way as Companies A and K departed on October 25, 1863.

Over that fall, a few local collection parties in the Sierra Nevada, following the terms of the Wells agreement in San Francisco, picked up random Mountain Maidu, mostly women and children. With Eddy's help, Starr's men brought in some escapees from the reservation. In December, Company F escorted two parties of twenty each to Round Valley.[778] Because a couple of miners' Indian women made up some of the December captives, they trailed the military party, watching for a chance to grab them. That few male Indians were among those collected seemed to explain why attacks on miners continued.[779]

While slow trade was the worry at John Bidwell & Co. during the winter of 1863–1864, Butte County miners were observing growing numbers of Mountain Maidu around their camps. Indian raiders killed five miners at Potter's Bar nine miles from Oroville. When miners petitioned their state representative to stop the escapes from Round Valley Reservation, he forwarded their demands to Elijah Steele and William Melendy, who ignored them. Although similar killings continued sporadically into 1865, no local, state or federal agency provided either protection or prosecution.[780]

The Indians' Account: Oral Histories

The analysis above cannot stand alone because archived transcriptions of descendant Indians' oral histories variously ignore, endorse and contradict it. Influencing the historical transcriptions in archives were traditional storytellers' versions that passed along impressions of the removal's tragic events from one generation to the next. As a consequence, because soldiers were in charge of the removal, Indian descendants, several generations removed, deduced that only killings by soldiers could explain so many deaths. Also, all modern interpreters have overlooked or missed entirely the role of malaria, probably because references to it in removal documents are vaguely worded. Compounding that, with the disease's later eradication in California, awareness of its perils disappeared. Therefore, the twenty-first century white and Indian communities treat as fact the allegation that men of Company F killed removal Indians who did not make it to Round Valley Reservation.

The continuance of Mill Creek raids in the wake of the removal led Butte County settlers to consider it a failure and, evidently, unworthy of mention or such a bad memory that, in otherwise fulsome accounts of Indian incidents, Bidwell and local historians ignored it. It was the late Dorothy Hill's 1978 interviews with Rancho Chico Indians' descendants that restored awareness of the tragedy. In 1980, she edited and published Annie E. K. Bidwell's essays, written about fifty years after the removal, which provided additional Indian descendant anecdotes.

For example, even though William Conway, a later Rancho Chico rancheria member and respected leader, mixed up the chronology of incidents, some of his memories matched information from other sources.[781] He attributed his knowledge to three vaquero elders: Jack Frango, Bill Preacher and Chico Tom. Each was Conway's senior, but none was in the removal. Jack Frango, or Otila, was a Valley Maidu born about 1845, who was working for Bidwell by 1863. Bill Preacher, who was 23 when the removal took place, worked for Bidwell with young Frango at that time. Chico Tom, who moved to the Bidwell Ranch three years after the removal, worked there until he died in 1918.[782] If these vaqueros were tending cattle at Bidwell's summer camp, they were not witnesses to the removal events and if they remembered Eddy's camp on Rancho Chico, none mentioned it to Hill.

Despite differences between Indian and settler accounts, both peoples spoke about the slow pace, the high death toll, the wild boars and the soldiers' placement of women on their horses and mules. Analysis that follows has reconciled the most important contradictions between settler and Indian reports by recognizing how Indian removal descendants explained the extreme suffering in terms of tribal culture.

For example, in an interview with Hill, Mountain Maidu removal descendent Thelma Wilson was puzzled because, before leaving their rancherias for Eddy's camp in the valley, her people had been in good health, putting up a "tremendous store of acorns" for the winter of 1863–1864: "So, how in the world then could … people suddenly die on the trail, even if they were older people, unless they had some sort of brutal treatment?"[783] Descendent Henry Azbill surmised that the walk from Yankee

Bill Preacher, member of a Southern Maidu tribelet, became a longtime Rancho Chico employee.

Hill to Chico left his ancestors sick from exhaustion.

The settlers relied on 1860s' medical science to explain what caused the Mountain Indians' rapid decline at Eddy's Rancho Chico camp. Settlers had also lost friends and family to ague or malaria, which they considered the product of bad air along Chico Creek that behaved like, in later terms, "an infectious disease does when introduced into a completely nonimmune population, becoming an acute disease that spread rapidly and had a high mortality rate."[784]

In contrast, Maidu looked to their traditional use of poison to explain the casualties. To kill or sicken rivals, deer livers, either putrefied or infused with rattlesnake venom, were attached to arrows. Four years before the removal, Mountain Maidu claimed Yahi from Deer Creek poisoned their men who refused to join them in a raid on valley farmers. Even in the late nineteenth century, some of Bidwell's Indians considered Chico Tom "a poisoner" who had killed both his own son and Joe Shoe Fly.[785] Leland Scott, descendant of removal participant Oregon Charlie from the Cherokee rancheria near Oroville and other Mountain Maidu believed Bidwell's Mechoopdas poisoned the Indians in Eddy's camp. Bud Bain, who was born in Tehama County after the removal and lived on Rancho Chico as the husband of a

Mechoopda, also spoke of the poisoning allegation to Dorothy Hill. Bain's tribal beliefs were undiluted by education; as a ranch laborer, he understood the world in terms of traditional Valley Indian culture, mixing fact, custom and imagination. For example, when his uncle entered rival Indian sites at night, he would, "like an owl ... go from one tree to another and, of course, they thought he was an owl. He would put poison on door knobs."[786] Two starving women who escaped the removal party accepted food from a settler woman, but later discarded it because they suspected she meant to poison them. That "different tribes poison one another" was a regular part of the natural cycle of life and death for Maidu.[787] The use of poison as a murder weapon goes back thousands of years and readers of Sherlock Holmes' murder mysteries will recall it was common in nineteenth-century England.

While Mountain Maidu from the removal generation reported Mechoopdas poisoned their removal Indians, the significant use of poison in Valley and Mountain Maidu conflicts faded from descendants' memories and so it made more sense to them that Company F soldiers killed their ancestors.[788]

Removal Indians who had observed soldiers on picket duty on Rancho Chico and then in charge of the removal journey understandably came to the conclusion that military soldiers, rather than local vigilantes, collected their ancestors for the removal. However, the soldiers were California Volunteers who arrived in Butte County *after* most of the Mountain Maidu had already arrived at Rancho Chico, whether voluntarily or by force. The powerful imagery their stories initially provided became the basis for successive generations' versions of the tragedy.

The Maidu were a wary and contentious people. Modern Maidu have acknowledged that dimension of their ancestors' tribal life and the place violence once played. For example, Maidu Concow matron Marie Potts explained that tribelets sought vengeance against those who offended them. Leland Scott gave this example: normally peaceful Mountain Maidu avenged a Mill Creek kidnapper by holding him flat on a rock, smashing his toes and fingers with rocks and then pounding him to death. Despite such incidents, Potts and Thelma Wilson explained their Mountain Maidu ancestors' natural inclination,

The Death Trail

After Bud Bain married a Mechoopda woman, he became a Rancho Chico employee. His impressions regarding the Army's conduct of the 1863 Indian removal, preserved in oral interviews, became an important source for later Indians' beliefs.

when unprovoked, was "not warlike in any way whatsoever."[789]

Over time, descendants added new allegations that soldiers used Indian war methods to kill the removal Indians. They accused Company K's men of bashing them with rocks or wood, as well as shooting and bayoneting them. They accused soldiers of arson and corpse abandonment, with particular targeting of women and children. Removal descendant William Conway explained the deaths this way: "In taking the Indians to the reservation the soldiers were very cruel. If one fell by the wayside, exhausted, the soldiers thrust the bayonet through their body and they were left there to die."[790] Descendant Azbill also told Hill, in 1969, that soldiers killed Indians with bayonets.

What about the bayonet allegation? Before the removal, some Rancho Chico Indians may have observed Camp Bidwell soldiers carrying the 1861 .58-caliber Springfield rifled-musket. Although the Chico Light Infantry was not organized until a month after the removal, some Mechoopdas may have seen its members carrying them with bayonets affixed in drills and Civil War parades—their only approved use in California. Bayonets, were inappropriate for picketing and escort duties. It is also possible that descendants learned over the years about bayonets from schoolbook illustrations. However, in 1863, the year of the removal, Capt. Starr's Company F, a cavalry unit, was armed with Sharps Model 1853 carbines. It would have been highly irregular for a cavalry unit, mounted on horses, to use bayonets or sabers in the field in the West, according to John Spangler, a mid-nineteenth century weapons specialist and military field historian. In August 1863, it would have been particularly strange because Starr's men faced no threat for which an officer would have considered bayonets necessary. Company F needed stretchers and wagons, not bayonets. Despite such contradictions, the accusation that Starr's men used bayonets to kill removal Indians became a staple of removal descendants' anecdotes over the years.[791] In addition, the vigilante collectors the removal Indians confused with soldiers never threatened to "machine gun" the Indians, as a descendant once insisted, because such weapons were not in use on the West Coast at the time.

Soldiers' weapon of choice was guns, a focus of their training and pride, their resort in crisis. It taxes common sense that American soldiers would commit messy, bizarre murders using bayonets when they could have much more easily and more quickly arrived at the same end using guns.

Azbill, accounting for the rarity or absence of shooting accusations in the removal stories, speculated that soldiers resorted to other types of violence to save ammunition. Through the end of the Civil War, forty rounds per man was the standard for ammunition issued to California Volunteers. Starr's men, therefore, set out with 920 rounds, but because most of the removal Indians were helpless and unarmed, they posed no threat to the troops who, therefore, had no need to save ammunition.[792]

A curious aspect of such removal accounts is that the crimes they attributed to soldiers were uncharacteristic of them. For example, according to Azbill, a soldier whipped an Indian to get him to walk faster. With hundreds of sick Indians struggling to keep up, the decision to punish one with a heavy whip seems at the least improbable and even counterintuitive, if the purpose was to make him move faster. Curiously, neither the removal Indians, whose experience was firsthand—Oregon Charlie, Tome-ya-nem and the two young women who escaped—nor later removal descendants, mentioned crimes commonly associated with soldiers, such as rape and battery.[793]

Another accusation at odds with military practice was corpse abandonment. Descendant Roy Scott, Leland Scott's younger brother, described how "the road from here [Chico] to the reservation was strewn with the skeletons of the Indians...."[794] Scott's impression is consistent with settler accounts that Indians died the whole way between Chico and Round Valley Reservation. However, while Maidu burials of their own tribelet members were important ceremonial events, it was a Mountain Maidu war practice to leave attack victims where they fell, usually scattering rocks over them or tossing them into nearby streams. In 1862, Mill Creeks, who, by then, included Mountain Maidu, after killing one of the Hickok girls, discarded her corpse in Rock Creek. Later, after killing Frankie Hickok, they hurled his body over a cliff above a stream bed. In 1863, Mill Creeks killed and then left the elder Lewis boy's body in the stream where he had been drinking. The same band left the younger brother's body by a canyon creek where they had killed him.[795]

Had a rogue company of soldiers collaborated in the killing of Indians along a public trail, would they have left the mutilated remains of their victims—evidence of their crimes—strewn about as if no one would notice or care or report them? It makes no sense that Starr, a disciplined, experienced and conscientious officer, would have allowed his men to kill and abandon, in public sight, large numbers of Indians whom they had been tasked to protect. In fact, formal reviews of Company F's enlisted men after the removal were so positive that fourteen of them were promoted to officers—men who, in no other instance, were known to disobey regulations, let alone offend their own culture's standard of decency by leaving corpses unburied.[796]

When Leland Scott accused soldiers of burning down rancheria structures while they collected the Mountain Maidu, he was, in fact, describing an action soldiers might have taken. For instance, Capt. John Feilner burned down a rancheria in the area of Shasta while in pursuit of Pit River Indians who had killed settlers.[797] In Butte County, settlers who were brutal and vengeful likely did the same in the Sierra Nevada. However, Indians also traditionally burned down rival rancherias and the property of settlers, including Bidwell's ranch in 1852, grain fields in Tehama and Butte counties in 1859, as well as the cabins of Indian fighters Robert Anderson in 1859 and Daniel Sutherland in 1865.[798]

According to oral histories, soldiers used knives to stab Indians. Soldiers carried knives and might have resorted to stabbing as a last resort. While there is no mention of such use during the removal, stabbing seemed plausible to the Maidu since their hunters and fighters were expert in the use of penetrating weapons such as spears and arrows. In their mythology, "Nature struck his victim with a stone, cut out her heart with a knife, and carried her head to camp on a spear."[799] But the point of storytellers' oral histories was not necessarily to be factual. Instead, their delivery was intentionally emotive and meant to impress on listeners the larger truth—that during the removal, hundreds of removal innocents experienced terror, suffering beyond words and death while under the control of soldiers.

Descendants' oral histories placed special emphasis on the suffering of women and children during the removal. Bud Bain told Hill in the late 1960s that he "was brought up on stories" of the removal to the Round Valley Reservation. In one, "if a woman and child could not keep up with the group, she was killed or relieved by a soldier of the baby she might be carrying. The baby would be taken by the feet and killed by swinging or hitting its head against a tree trunk, or rock."[800]

According to Stephen Powers' Mountain Maidu study, based on interviews with elder descendants, their warriors "did not generally make slaves of female captives, but destroyed them at once."[801] There were exceptions, of course. One Mountain Maidu woman was kidnapped and worked as a slave, but later escaped to recount her experiences. Removal stories that focused on women as soldiers' victims fitted their culture in which men used women or children to punish adversaries. Sometimes, in order to rectify wrongs by proportional compensation, a tribelet might hand over an agreed-upon number of girls to a complainant. Innocence or vulnerability did not exempt female members from attacks by enemy tribelets. In settler culture, deaths of women and children also aroused the strongest reactions. Storytellers still use similar narrative devices to elicit emotional responses from their audiences.

Battle casualties have always included women and children who, at times, were also targets. However, under the conditions of the 1863 removal, the purpose of which was to save lives, what would motivate Starr to order or allow soldiers to kill their Indian charges? In addition, no reports appeared in Tehama and Butte counties' newspapers about California Volunteers who targeted Indian women and children in Northern California at any time. The absence of such coverage is significant because local newspapers were skeptical about the military's effectiveness against Indians and often disparaged soldiers and their superiors. In contrast, as Chapter Five set out, in 1859 the Tehama County *Beacon* reported that the Breckenridge party killed Indian women and children caught in their fire and also a woman who tried to escape captivity. The press covered both settler and soldier abuses of Indians. For example, in a Tehama County tragedy reported during the mid-1860s, settlers killed every Indian in a camp, except for a small boy. When one of the men prevented a cohort from killing the child, the young man argued: "Nits breed lice."[802]

The accusation that soldiers were not just killers but baby killers in Maidu oral histories is of interest, in light of tribal conflict practices that Leland Scott described. For example, he told author Robert Rathbun about a Mountain Maidu who, in retaliation for the murder of his children by a rival tribelet member, tossed the killer's small children into a campfire. Such revenge also appeared in Thankful Lewis's report that her captors fingered scraps dangling from her dress as they told her they planned to set her on fire. Scott also described other incidents in which his people used violence against children to avenge the crimes of their parents or their parents' people. According to Marie Potts, one reason peaceful Indians were so fearful of Mill Creeks was their reputation for killing babies, citing the example of a peaceful Maidu man who returned from hunting to find that Mill Creeks had killed his wife and infant.[803]

Oral histories also accused soldiers of bashing out the brains of babies on boulders or against trees, but this allegation invites further examination. Soldiers' mainstay weapon was guns, but Maidu relied on weapons of wood and rock. Indians at Nome Lackee Reservation beat an employee using a tree branch with heavy knots[804] and tribal men carved rocks into knife blades, arrows, spear points and the stone heads of clubs.

Rock-wielding Indian raiders terrified miners. While camping along the Sacramento River in 1850, Richard Harrison met a miner whose skull had been fractured by an Indian wielding a rock.[805] In 1862, the men who found Frankie Hickok's remains said the Indians had "beat[en] his head to jelly with stones, crowded one down his throat, and left him dead."[806] After Hi Good was shot dead by an Indian youth seven years after the removal, his friends reported his head was "crushed to jelly by stones."[807]

Rock weapons appear in a Maidu myth in which the figure of Nature "lifted a stone far almost to the sky, and brought it down as if to crush [an Indian] with one tremendous blow. ... He escaped after three stone strikes...."[808] In an example of Maidu skill with stones, a year before the removal, explorer William Brewer was in camp between the Sierra Nevada foothills and the Bidwell ranch when he watched a young Indian kill squirrels with a sling that shot stones the size of eggs. The Maidu also stoned rabbits they caught in nets. As recently as 1965, Concow Maidu Starie Potts recalled that Bald Rock Jim had hit a man in the head with a rock.[809]

In summary, there is no factual evidence contemporary to the removal supporting allegations that Capt. Starr's Company F killed removal Indians. The outcome of the removal, a well-defined "high profile" assignment, was of keen interest to the military and government officials. At the same time Starr was briefing his commanding officer, Lt. Col. Hooker, regarding the removal operation, James Eddy was just across the creek in Bidwell's store, gathering medical supplies for the sick Indians on the Death Trail. After Eddy returned to the Mountain House camp to check on the Indians, he moved up the trail to Round Valley Reservation and learned firsthand about the trail events he had not observed. Despite Eddy's declining health from tuberculosis, he had stood up against settler killings of Indians near Chico and would never have condoned any abuse of removal Indians by either soldiers or settlers. For example, in leading a subsequent small removal party from Butte County to Round Valley, Eddy became aware of a stalker on the lookout to abduct an Indian woman. He repeatedly drove the man away, but when an incident diverted his attention, the man grabbed her and disappeared into the forest. Eddy could not leave the others to chase down the man; in the deposition he filed later about this incident, his disgust is unmistakable.[810]

MALARIA SYMPTOMS DEBILITATED INDIANS AND soldiers alike and the soldiers who gave up their horses to the Indians clearly empathized with them. Upon Company F's return to Chico, almost half the company checked into Camp Bidwell's sick bay. By 1865, when the final company of California Volunteers based at Camp Bidwell was reassigned to Modoc County, "a great many of the men were suffering from 'chills and fever' contracted in the Sacramento Valley." However, after several months in the mountains, a doctor reported "they looked like a different set of men."[811]

As angry as James Short was at the military, he never blamed soldiers for the removal Indians' deaths. His criticisms of Indian Affairs indicate he was unaware that Superintendent Hanson had authorized the removal in order to *protect* the Indians from Butte County settlers. In defending himself and his subordinates, Hooker never tried to lay the blame for any part of the removal failure on misconduct by the Indians, such as rebellions or escape attempts that soldiers might have used to justify punitive actions.

INDIAN STORYTELLERS EVIDENTLY SENSED THEIR listeners would not believe malaria alone could produce the agony and large numbers of deaths the Indians experienced on the removal trail. The disease's symptoms—chill-induced spasms, high fevers, shaking, vomiting, diarrhea, hallucinations and death—were repellent and might raise feelings of revulsion. Instead, to instill levels of fear and disgust commensurate with the removal victims' real suffering, storytellers described the soldiers' supposed use of familiar tribal war tactics against rival combatants and innocents alike. Anthropologist Hill understood this storytelling device because she characterized Bain's lurid removal accounts as among his "Favorite Tales."[812] As her meticulous records attest, she realized the dual importance of documenting facts and cultural impressions.

The fullest account of a removal participant on record was that of Concow headman Tome-ya-nem, who understood both tribal culture and Western fact-based thinking; his facility with English enabled him to communicate with a soldier interviewer from both perspectives.[813] Maidu men like him, chosen by shamans for their "maturity, wealth, ability, generosity," led, but they did not rule.[814] Tome-ya-nem's credibility is considerable because, in interviews, he accurately described violent acts by both Whites and Indians between 1859 and 1863. A man of integrity, he spared not even himself from judgment when he recalled events that culminated in the removal and never so much as hinted that soldiers harmed or killed removal Indians. Instead, he declared, "disease and want"—sickness and starvation—weakened and then killed the removal Indians.[815] He recollected that when they arrived at Round Valley Reservation, "there was nothing to eat, and my people began to fall as thick and fast as the acorns of the fall of the year."[816] In other words, many of the eighty who reached the reservation died there.

Along the way to Round Valley, only about a half-dozen Indians escaped, underscoring the removal Indians' fragile health. Starr's report noted two escapes, one oral interview reported three men escaped and another noted that two starving women escaped.[817] Three Indians who left said settlers helped them en route to their Sierra Nevada rancherias. Soldiers still guarding Bidwell's Indians came upon an Indian eating crackers from a barrel set out to feed livestock. Learning he had fled the removal and was going home to the mountains, a soldier advised him how to proceed without attracting the attention of settlers.[818] Considering the dire consequences of the removal walk, it is hard to believe that even Indians who had voluntarily joined it to escape settlers' death threats would have remained with no guards present, unless they were so physically incapacitated it was impossible.

THE CONTRAST BETWEEN MAIDU AND settler versions of the removal becomes apparent in two versions of one event in July 1863. A subject of Chapter Ten, it has significance here.

In the aftermath of the Mill Creeks's killing of the Lewis boys, Maidu Concows went to merchant Michael Wells in Concow for protection against settler vigilantes, who agreed to hide them in the back room of his store. In the settler version, the men tracked them to Wells' place, prepared to kill them. When their presence was discovered by the settlers, they demanded Wells bring them out. He complied but threatened that, if they killed the Concows, he would demand the sheriff charge them with murder. When the men hesitated, he brought their attention to four Indians who appeared different from the peaceful Concows, possibly men from another tribelet. Wells persuaded the pursuers to let the four run for their lives and spare the rest. The settlers agreed and killed two as they ran. (The two survivors were probably the same men later shot dead at a mob's urging in Chico.)[819]

Accounts by Indian descendants Leland Scott and John Adams Clark, the latter a child of a gold miner and a Concow woman, contrasted with those of the settlers. According to Clark, "A white storekeeper, old Mike Wells, understood what the soldiers were saying: that they were going to machine gun them. Mike Wells begged them not to: he tore his shirt off, pulled his hair, and rolled on the ground and cried. So the soldiers did not kill them."[820] Although different, each version got the important facts right: a vigilante party, the Indians' plight, the killing of the two Indians, and Wells' actions to protect the Indians. The Indians' narrative ignored motive, accuracy and cause, instead emphasizing dramatic actions and effects such as death, pain, misery and humiliation. Whites "know" that Wells, the businessman, did not rip off his shirt, pull his hair or roll around in the dirt and weep to persuade the vigilante party to leave the Indians alone.

Similarly, Thelma Wilson described how soldiers intentionally tortured some of the sick women by tying them on their horses and mules, while the soldiers claimed they did so out of concern for their well-being. While the Indian and soldier accounts clash, together they inform one another and, if the cultural differences they so clearly represent can be appreciated, we are all the beneficiaries.[821]

Aside from the core moral problem of the removal itself, its other compelling failure was its flawed execution. Who was really responsible for the ultimate fate of the Indians? Was it Bidwell because he pushed for the removal, then failed to provide all the wagons he agreed to collect? Or, were other settlers also to blame because they, like Bidwell, demanded the immediate removal of the Indians, but then, at first, refused him the wagons and later, when some of them relented, limited the distance they could travel? Or, was the military most responsible because it did not provide the replacement wagons Starr expected?

TRACES OF TRIBAL BELIEFS CONTINUE to shape contemporary Indian perceptions of these historical events. For example, when Durham residents cut down the Legendary Oak Tree to clear ground for a high school, Valley Maidu, grieving the loss of its variety of acorns, believed the oak had "bled."[822] Such imagery also appeared in Starie Potts' 1965 description of Maidu Shaman Jack Edwards, who could "turn into a bear and put his hand out this way, he was a bear" with fur on his feet and then change back into a man by singing a song.[823]

Whites similarly embellish historical events. In a conversation with the author, a local resident claimed young men from nineteenth-century Chico rode around shooting random Rancho Chico Indians to pass the time, although no evidence supports it. While some boys stoned Chinese in central Chico, the Indian community was centered on Bidwell's ranch and did not casually circulate among Whites in town.[824]

Another such anecdote was recalled by a late twentieth-century researcher who heard from a Round Valley Indian that, in 1863, Fort Wright soldiers dynamited the removal Indians at the Mountain House camp and that older women in the removal inserted sand in young women's vaginas to prevent soldiers' rape attempts. Such apocryphal accusations likely will continue unchallenged, for the most part, because modern people who regret the real abuses of Indians, have neither the information, resources nor training to refute them.[825] Speculation feeds Indian and white imaginations alike, and, in a sense, acknowledges the incontrovertible fact that reprehensible actions took place, although few are driven to learn more.

With the probable exception of the Yahi, the principal cause that cost the lives of tens of thousands of Indians across California was not the war violence that is the subject of this account. The primary reasons for massive Indian deaths were settler-borne diseases and "social homicide," Sherburne Cook's term for settler practices that produced excessive drinking, sexual abuses, and the consequences of extreme poverty in the Indian population.

Finally, in the part of California this study treats, government representatives on state and national levels were largely consistent in word and action. Their intent, however flawed in execution, was to protect peaceful Indians from settlers, as demonstrated by their conduct in the 1851 Indian treaty negotiations and the 1863 Round Valley removal. Chapter Ten and this one have spoken to the Army's and California Volunteers' protection of John Bidwell's Indian workers against angry settlers. The military rarely sought and never confronted Tehama and Butte counties' truly dangerous Indians, whose successful defensive tactic was to avoid conflict by hiding in Deer Creek and Mill Creek canyons. The military's failure to provide relief to peaceful Indians and settlers from the attacks of those Indian warriors broadened settler rage to encompass frustration with bureaucrats and soldiers as well.

Having lost most of their ancestors' songs, dances, stories and skills to time, modern Maidu and other tribes' descendants have large gaps in their knowledge about their historical identity. To compensate for this, they have worked together to salvage and reweave fragments of information into a comprehensive narrative that could restore a fuller sense of their roots. In this light, the removal memory plays a prominent part in Maidu history. Members of local tribes continue to meld the storytellers' mix of facts and interpretations with information gleaned from other non-native sources such as formal schooling and popular culture.

Because the soldiers from Company F did not act as some have charged, but instead handled a difficult mission under impossible conditions, their reputations deserve a measure of exoneration and respect.[826] The course of their future lives suggests unease and perhaps guilt at the tragedy they confronted in the removal. Sergeant Baldwin omitted the removal mission from his military record. While Capt. Starr went on to address Civil War conflicts in the Sacramento Valley and became a superintendent in his prominent family's flour mills, he died a bachelor at the age of 72 during a years-long stay at the Napa State Hospital, a mental institution.[827]

In addition, incomplete or skewed information, such as that in the Hooker report, about multiple aspects of the removal has undercut recognition of the historical importance in American history of the Indian removals in Butte and Tehama counties. Finally, after the dramatic events of 1863, the war between Mill Creeks and settlers erupted again in the eastern sections of those counties. When a scattering of Indian raids culminated in settler deaths on the Frenchtown Road in Butte County mining country during the summer of 1865, a final, brutal confrontation between settlers and Mill Creeks took place in Deer Creek Canyon, the subject of Chapter Twelve.

12

Retribution on Mill Creek

Over the winter of 1863–1864, expanding settler control of the foothills again prevented the Mountain Maidu from moving to their traditional foothill refuges, leaving them to starve in snowbound mountain caves. At the same time, mining damaged spawning beds, decimating the fish stock. In January, Indian men headed for the foothills where they stole miners' provisions and farmers' livestock they butchered before reaching the canyons.

With the September 1863 Indian removal in motion, settler threats against John Bidwell's Indian workforce subsided and, with that, his need for troops. However, Indians were still dying on the trail to Round Valley Reservation when others shot and killed Hugh Harvey, "a sober and industrious" miner near Forbestown. The year 1864 no sooner began than Indian raiders launched an aggressive campaign against settlers, freight drivers and traders along the upper reaches of Humboldt Road. Although still under construction, Chico businessmen were already using it to send goods directly to Nevada and Idaho markets. Oroville, therefore, lost its closely held monopoly on mining trade and tensions tightened between valley and mountain interests.

It is not possible to identify which tribe or tribelets made up the raiding parties. Because their raiding methods were indistinguishable from those of the Mill Creeks, the raiders were referred to by that name, which will be used here. However, the location of the raids so far south of Deer Creek suggests the Mill Creeks were largely made up of Mountain Maidu (formerly Butte Creeks) and some Paiute, whose territory Humboldt Road also crossed. Bidwell's $40,000 federal mail contract for guaranteed, dependable mail deliveries was put at risk by these raids, as well as the funds he put up as security for the money he had persuaded the State Legislature to invest in the road. It soon became clear that the forest-lined road facilitated not only settler travel but also that of hostile Indians who killed so many freight drivers the road shut down soon after it opened.[828]

Although Capt. Augustus Starr and Company F of the California Volunteers remained at Camp Bidwell in Chico, with the prospect of the upcoming raiding season Bidwell and other residents remained convinced that state-funded local volunteers were the only effective and motivated Indian pursuers. Also, those soldiers were stationed so far from the upper Humboldt Road ambushes that they could offer only much delayed responses.

In February, when Starr and his men rode out after Mill Creeks on the move, John Bidwell & Co.'s clerk, Charles Stilson, was skeptical about their prospects: "It is difficult to find the rascals in these mountains."[829] The soldiers followed the trail of the suspicious Indian party as far as Deer Creek, but gave up when their targets moved on toward Mill Creek. As Starr later explained, "The country [is] very rough almost impassible, the men being sore & having but five days rations, returned to Camp Bidwell."[830] Indian descendant Beverly Benner Ogle related the Indians' response when they saw the soldiers turn back. Lined up along the ridge top, "They looked down on the soldiers below. They turned their bare Indian rears toward the soldiers and hollered, 'Shoot my –. Shoot my –,' since they knew the soldiers' muskets couldn't reach them so high above."[831] This was a local variation on a Texas Ranger's disdain for the Army's stand-and-shoot tactics against mounted Plains Indians: "The only way the Indians could ever be in danger from these soldiers, was if their ridiculous appearance and ungainly horsemanship caused the Indians to laugh themselves to death."[832]

On February 26, as Starr and his men chased the Mill Creeks across Deer Creek, other raiders struck along upper Butte Creek in the area of Doe Mill Ridge. Lacking skilled Indian trackers, eastern Butte County's mountain residents formed two pursuit parties supplied with ammunition and food from John Bidwell.[833] B. B. Brown, 41, a lumberman to whom the rancher had loaned his own gun for the job, kept him abreast by dispatches along the way.[834] After a two-day search, neither group had made any contact with the Indians.

Then, in early March, perhaps emboldened by their escape from the pursuers, five armed Mill Creeks plundered a mountain cabin, whose returning owner spotted them from a distance and watched from cover. They also shot at a man on Cohasset Road and another on the road to Dogtown. According to information from Indians and settlers who lived in the area, the raiders included men who had evaded the 1863 removal and "returned Indians" who had escaped Round Valley Reservation. This fits historian Albert Hurtado's finding that California "Indians came to regard reservations as part of their seasonal round and few remained there permanently."[835] At Rancho Chico's mountain camp, Valley Indian vaqueros still considered remaining Mill Creeks dangerous so, at Sandy Young's request, Bidwell sent up a rifle.[836]

In early March, residents east of Chico anticipated such incidents would escalate like those of 1859, 1862 and 1863. Frustrated by the military's inattention to the security needs of mountain and foothill settlers, a committee of Humboldt Road businessmen sent an appeal to Assemblyman A. C. Buffum, a former Magalia postmaster, for state money to back private Indian pursuers. Because Bidwell was in the east, his name does not appear among the signatories, although those of his store partner, George Wood, and other local business associates were included. The state had provided support for the Kibbe volunteer campaign in 1859, but since then its revised policy denied public money for civilian Indian pursuit parties. Buffum, therefore, referred the request for help to Brig. Gen. Wright, who turned the job over to Starr's men at Camp Bidwell.[837] Once again, local residents had failed to forestall the deployment of soldiers.

It is fair to note that, while area residents had more confidence in local trackers than soldiers, in the early 1864 incidents, the Mill Creeks had outwitted both the Butte County volunteers and the military. The February failure of the mountain settlers' two pursuit parties was foreordained because the men were inexperienced trackers up against the Mill Creeks' expert mastery of the terrain and evasion tactics. And the Tehama County men who were qualified had cooled on Indian pursuits in Butte County.

Good and Anderson Go to Work in Butte County

Hi Good and Robert Anderson remained the leading Mountain Indian trackers. As discussed in an earlier chapter, after Bidwell gave his word in 1862 that he would seek state backing for Good's party already underway in the pursuit of Mill Creeks, he instead sought Army protection for his own ranch.[838] This may explain why, in 1863 and early 1864, Good and Anderson declined to join Adj. Gen. Kibbe's campaign against Mill Creeks. However, they continued to track Indians in the mountain canyons on their own. By this time, Good and his neighbors had built a case against Mill Creeks, "the boys in the hills."[839]

In order to quickly respond to ongoing raids along upper Humboldt Road, U.S. Army Major General Irvin McDowell ordered Starr to close Camp Bidwell in the spring of 1864.[840] This would permit his Company F to move to a location better suited to pursue the Mill Creeks. While Humboldt Road was serviceable in good weather, it disappeared under winter snows deep enough to bury buildings. Instead of wagons, horses had to pull sleighs and troops, cut off from their provisions, lived on settlers' donations of flour.

While the Army was shutting down Camp Bidwell, Chico merchants realized Company F's relocation meant their businesses would lose the soldiers' valuable trade.[841] In mid-April, Starr and his men left Camp Bidwell and built Fort Bidwell to protect the road through Modoc County's Surprise Valley. John Bidwell & Co.'s Stilson worried that, without soldiers at hand, new Indian raids on the foothills would incite another round of mob threats against his boss: "The Cavalry Co. is about to leave here so that I would not be surprised to hear of trouble in the course of 3 months." Once again, Bidwell's and others' need for military protection on the new road deprived foothill farmers of any help from soldiers against Mill Creeks in the upcoming raiding season.[842]

James Eddy's Journey Comes to an End

In Chico, on May 20, 1864, news arrived that James Franklin

Eddy, 31, had committed suicide in Red Bluff on May 2. In late 1863, Eddy, who had finally completed the removal of Indians from the trail to Round Valley Reservation, accepted Indian Superintendent Elijah Steele's offer of a staff position there. As Eddy readied himself for winter in the Coast Range, he bought gloves, a coat, a scarf and two rugs at Samuel Galland's general store in Tehama. He had stopped there en route from Chico, where he had picked up reservation supplies at John Bidwell & Co. and completed a job for Bidwell. Because Eddy understood the Indians' dialects and culture better than most Whites, he also rode out with Starr and his men to pick up Mountain Maidu, in accordance with the Wells agreement which stipulated that if settlers picked up Indians, the Volunteers would escort them to the reservation.[843] He recognized some of the Indians as those among the sick he had left waiting for help on the trail to Round Valley.

During the winter at Round Valley, Eddy realized his advancing tuberculosis no longer allowed him to carry on his work with the Indians whom he had lived among, cared about and protected, under the most dire circumstances, since the fall of 1862. He submitted his resignation the third week of April.

As a single man without family in the West, he had no one to look after him and considered a move to warm, dry Mexico. Aware that Bidwell was holding a couple of his pay vouchers in Chico, Eddy set off on his last trip to the Sacramento Valley on April 28. While he had made the trip many times before on his own, this time he was too frail to negotiate the long, steep trail so his friend F. A. Nottingham and several Indians, whose names were not recorded, accompanied their old friend.

As the party made its way down the mountain, Eddy collapsed. Near death, he murmured to Nottingham that he had vowed to commit suicide rather than linger in pain and misery. He admitted to his friend that, while it was time to end his life, he had waited too long to do it without help. He managed to dictate his will to Nottingham, who agreed to send his wages and possessions to his sister in their Massachusetts hometown.

It seems unlikely that Eddy, a modest man who did not savor material success or public recognition, realized how fully his final year and a half had honored his family. His grandfather, John Eddy Sr., had led the Revolutionary War unit from

Gloucester, where he later became a town leader. Eddy's father, John Eddy Jr., who served in the Massachusetts State Legislature, had won regard for his own "charity and willingness to help others."[844] Until the present account, the Eddy family was unaware at what cost or with what exceptional conduct James had reflected his family's Yankee ethic of public service. All they had learned about his fate was the date of his death in California—and even that was wrong.

He rallied a little and the Indians carried him on a litter to Red Bluff because his rapid decline did not permit a stop among his friends in Tehama. On Sunday evening, May 1, the Indians and Nottingham settled him in a room at the Tremont House, a respectable and recently refurbished Main Street hotel. Once the proprietor William McCommon had placed Eddy in a comfortable room, he summoned Dr. William G. Hatch. Recognizing Eddy was dying, the physician sent for medicine to ease his pain. The next morning, Hatch returned to Eddy's room where Nottingham and the Indians were present. When the physician returned in mid-afternoon, Nottingham was there, asking McCommon for cash from Eddy's $187 savings to cover his and the Indians' expenses. With Eddy's consent, McCommon gave $87 in coins to Nottingham, who then left with the Indians. Hatch left once Eddy seemed ready to sleep.

Not long afterward, McCommon, seeking help for someone else, returned to Eddy's room, looking for Hatch. He found Eddy dead, his blood, still spewing from his slashed neck, spraying the walls. Blood soaked the bedding, permeated the contents of Eddy's carryall and seeped into the room's new rug. The hotel keeper ran to summon the police, who notified the coroner, who, in turn, conscripted men off the street to assist. They rushed to the Tremont where, after being declared a coroner's jury, they observed Eddy's body and the room's condition.[845]

After a clerk took depositions from McCommon, Nottingham and Hatch, the jury concluded that Eddy had ended his own life, fulfilling the vow he mentioned to Nottingham. They concluded he had pulled his razor from the case left next to him and slashed his throat from ear to ear, cutting both his carotid artery and his jugular vein. While Eddy had no known medical training, he had acquired considerable physiological knowledge from his work with Dr. Sproul in Chico. Red Bluff's undertaker provided a coffin and a volunteer sat with Eddy's body until the next day's funeral. Accompanied by the men from Round Valley Reservation and a few acquaintances from Tehama, a wagon bore his coffin to the Oak Hill Cemetery in Red Bluff. Any marker once on Eddy's grave has disappeared, as has any record of its location.

Eddy's suicide added yet another layer to the Indian removal tragedy. He died intestate because the will he dictated to Nottingham was declared invalid. His modest means on hand came to less than the combined costs of his death and probate. It was five years after Eddy's death before Congress authorized his final three months' back pay of $150 and $37.14 in reimbursement for his horse rentals from Bidwell during his time as reservation camp supervisor in Chico. For all his responsibilities and sacrifices, Eddy's monthly pay had been less than the starting wage of John Bidwell & Co.'s counter clerk.[846]

The Workman Killings

In June 1864, Bidwell, whose old party, the Union Democrats, had disintegrated two years earlier, was at the Republican Union Party convention in Baltimore, unaware that Mill Creeks had raided a farmhouse near the Pence Ranch in Kimshew Township, territory of that tribelet.

One morning, as Thomas Morgan's wife, 29, collected an armful of wood for her cook stove, she noticed all the cattle had turned their heads toward the distant woods. Following their gazes, she glimpsed in the brush a man's face, his eyes on her. Pretending not to notice, she slowly made her way back into the house and raced upstairs for a better look. She counted seven Indians, one with a rifle, as they emerged from cover and moved in her direction. Mrs. Morgan scooped up her two year old and, with her six year old alongside, they slipped out the back door and ran to a distant house. Had the Indians chosen to overtake her, they would have succeeded. Later, when a party of armed neighbors entered the Morgan home, not far from the Lewis family's empty house, they found it thoroughly ransacked. Although Mrs. Morgan's quick flight or the Indians' restraint averted a personal disaster, it presaged a new round of public crises.[847]

Standoff

In Chico, where Wood, Bidwell's partner and others, anticipating a re-run of 1863, with mobs descending on Chico to punish Bidwell and his Indians, sent an appeal to Brig. Gen. Wright for troops.[848]

In response, Wright dispatched Capt. James Van Voast, a West Point graduate and chief aide to Lt. Col. Drum. After reviewing the situation, Van Voast, like Lt. Col. Ambrose Hooker the previous fall, dismissed the townspeople as "overexcited," their problems rooted in poor farmers' jealousy of Bidwell's and Robert Durham's Indian labor. He asserted Chico's Light Infantry could protect them, although the Army had never previously delegated such critical duties to a local militia unit, whose members were local residents with no qualifying expertise.[849] Van Voast's comment suggests some of Durham's Indian workers had returned to his ranch from Round Valley Reservation. The captain's opinion, similar to Bidwell's view of his opponents' underlying motives, denied any legitimacy to the foothill farmers' claims of endangerment. Van Voast concluded the residents' complaint was a civil matter and that "U.S. soldiers in a town like Chico should be the last and only resort."[850]

Despite the Morgan incident in the foothills, when Bidwell returned he focused on his own immediate priority—security on upper Humboldt Road. He described the raiders there in the same terms he and his neighbors used to describe Mountain Maidu who joined the Mill Creeks in the 1850s: "The [raiders'] number is small, but they are, from the peculiarity of the region, capable of great mischief.... My knowledge of these Indians leads me to believe that no such thing as treaty or pacification is possible.... The rocky and abrupt places they inhabit are such that the very paucity of their number is what renders it difficult to find them. They are never seen but as enemies and never approach habitations but to steal and murder. They are peculiarly relentless in their hostility. The aged and young alike meet with the same fate at their hands."[851]

Drum dispatched Capt. James C. Doughty (whose Civil War-related duty in Chico was a subject of Chapter Seven) and Company I, Second Cavalry, California Volunteers, to Camp Bidwell in June 1864. They continued from there to the headwaters area around Lassen Peak with guides Hi Good and William

Morgan (it's unknown if he was related to Thomas Morgan). Doughty's company and Capt. Starr's from Fort Bidwell were charged to protect everyone—Indians and settlers alike—from Chico to Susanville and into southern Oregon. Within a week of their July 18 return to Camp Bidwell, Doughty and his company made a tour of northeastern Butte County "for the purpose of investigating Indian difficulties."[852]

Locals described the Mill Creeks to Capt. Doughty as about twenty to twenty-five "renegades from all the area [tribes who] are generally on Deer, Mill and Butte Creeks."[853] This further confirms that a coterie of Mountain Maidu were integral to Mill Creek parties. Despite military patrols, in August 1864, the Indians continued to seize and hold upper passages on Humboldt Road, cutting off Bidwell's U.S. mail deliveries. The Indians' raids were so successful that for an entire month—between August 20 and September 21—the only mail that reached the post office at John Bidwell & Co. came by steamers at Chico Landing; however, a severe drought and low water levels limited steamship service. Indians were also on edge because on Butte Creek, in early September, a Kimshew Maidu killed a man from a rival Maidu tribelet who had killed his relative.[854]

While Doughty was scouting the Humboldt Road area, raids north and east of Chico brought him back to Camp Bidwell. When the captain asked Good for help in hunting the perpetrators, he said he was "busy" and declined. With no guide, Doughty limited his men's search, no more than a false display of good intentions toward the foothill farmers, to Butte Meadows, Dogtown Road and the Pence Ranch area. Doughty later acknowledged that his company never confronted any Mill Creeks during those pursuits. As his men moved about, he recalled they were always aware of Indians watching them, but they rarely saw them and if they did, they were either too far away to shoot or they could not distinguish between the peaceful and dangerous ones.[855] As they moved through the area, he and his men spotted smoke signals from small visible fires along the canyon tops. Like the officers who preceded him in Butte County, Doughty and his men could not identify Mill Creeks or even locate them, let alone capture or kill them.

Over the course of late 1864 and early 1865, in incidents

similar to those in 1862 and 1863, Mill Creeks escalated their retaliations against settlers, although the record does not identify any specific provocations. In one case, the arrow-pierced body of a miner surfaced between Dogtown and Nimshew. Then, on March 19, 1865, a few miles north of Chico, Mill Creeks killed farm wife Mary Moore, "Grandma Moore," whose husband William was away, and burned their cabin. Stilson and a large party of family and friends drove together from Chico for her funeral.[856] Doughty's unit made a sweep of the area but stopped short of entering Deer Creek Canyon. They observed parties of Indians working with plants and again were aware of surveillance by other Indians mostly hidden from view by heavy underbrush and boulders on higher ground.

This time, with the death of Mary Moore, Hi Good agreed to assist Capt. Doughty and guided fifteen men from Company I on another sortie in late April in search of the Mill Creek killers. When Doughty, who had taken a different route with a separate contingent, returned to camp, he reported that, despite Good's tracking and advice, neither group had encountered any Indians. Doughty explained: "I was not able to see them; at the same time they could observe every move that I made from their hiding places."[857] Even so, senior officers in their San Francisco headquarters continued to call for arrests of Indian raiders, perpetuating settlers' doubts about their fundamental grasp of the situation. The futility of that search further validated Good's and Anderson's long disdain for the military's effectiveness against Mill Creeks.[858]

Meanwhile, Mill Creek raids again intensified in Tehama County and raiders in Butte County continued their killing along upper Humboldt Road. Bidwell had appealed for more mountain patrols in May, but eight out of ten of the California Volunteers' Second Cavalry companies were already out on sorties in response to Indian problems elsewhere. When Capt. Doughty left Camp Bidwell on May 23, local townspeople took little notice.[859] His company's efforts had provided no help against the Mill Creeks. In fact, only a week before their departure, Mill Creeks broke into the empty Bolliver house in the foothills. At the nearby Silva house, two of the Indians cautioned the elderly couple to stand aside while they looted their house.

Afterward, neighbors pursued the Indian party to a bluff above Deer Creek, where they fought them, killing several. Although Anderson had joined that party, Good declined on the grounds that the Mill Creeks had only committed property crimes. Had there been death, he told Anderson, he would have delayed his pack train departure out of state and joined the pursuers.[860]

ON AUGUST 2, WORD REACHED Chico that three days earlier, Brig. Gen. Wright, his wife and his staff had died on the ship *Brother Jonathan* when it sank in an ocean storm near Crescent City. While Wright had never visited Chico during its crises in 1862 and 1863, the soldiers he dispatched there were a stimulus to the town's economy and protected Bidwell's rancheria workforce against threatened settler attacks.[861]

Also early that week, a nine-man Mill Creek party launched an ambitious campaign.[862] Passing down the ridge that separates the Feather River's North and West branches in mountain mining country about twenty-five miles from Chico, the raiders burned down the vacant Concow Valley cabin of Daniel Sutherland, a close friend of Bidwell's supervisor Sandy Young. (After serving in the 1859 Kibbe campaign, Sutherland continued as an occasional Indian fighter. It is highly probable, based on a history of Mill Creek attacks on Indian fighters' property, that his cabin was not a random target.)

While flames engulfed Sutherland's cabin, the Mill Creeks heard the sounds of an approaching rider and hid behind rocks in Sutherland's front yard. When Joseph Miller came within range, they shot and wounded him. As he and his mule took off at a full gallop, the Indians tossed their guns aside and gave chase. Once Miller reached his home further down the road, they turned back. The ledger he carried in a side pocket of his jacket absorbed the impact of the most critical bullet that hit him.[863]

Their next raid took place northeast of Oroville at the Concow Valley home of gold miner Robert Workman, who was away at a claim and did not learn of the attack on his home for several days. One raider struck Workman's wife with his gun and, when she collapsed, dropped a boulder on her chest. Others had shot Mrs. Workman's sister, Rosanna Smith, who had just arrived from Australia for a visit. They slashed her throat, scalped her and so mutilated her body that it aroused exceptional outrage. Behind the Workmans' place, the Indians also shot dead and scalped the couple's gardener, John Banks, a Scot, who had approached the house in response to the women's screams. After looting the house, the Indians left. Mrs. Workman, who had appeared dead, dragged herself to a neighbor's place. Badly wounded, she lived for two years before succumbing to her injuries. The Hickok, Lewis and Workman place killings became the most consequential Mill Creek raids in Butte County.[864]

Neighbors buried Rosanna Smith and John Banks, then organized a pursuit party that followed the Mill Creeks' tracks from Concow Valley through the foothills toward Chico. When the tracks divided, the party split up into two groups. One followed tracks toward Mud Creek and planned to continue north toward Deer Creek Canyon. Along the way those men encountered farmhand Simeon Moak, who had heard about the raids and advised the pursuers not to continue to Deer Creek: "I told them R. A. Anderson had sent word that if the Indians committed any depredations about here we should come north to Rock Creek [where Anderson then lived] and head them off."[865]

The other group, following tracks headed toward Chico, assumed that Valley Indians, including Bidwell's Mechoopda workers, had participated in the raids. When they reached the foothills, they happened upon Anderson as he drove a wagonload of flour bags from the Butte Mill. The advice he gave them drew on his and Good's experience tracking Mill Creeks in 1862 and 1863.

Anderson explained it would not be wise to draw in soldiers because they had a record of deferring to Bidwell's needs and ignoring the settlers'. Anderson and Good (still close friends) concluded Butte County pursuers must track the real Mill Creek perpetrators and not, as in those earlier years, become diverted into threatening Bidwell's Indian workers, even if they believed ranch Indians sometimes participated in raiding parties. When the Concow Valley men became adamant about the importance of evidence that some of these Mill Creeks left tracks headed toward Chico, Anderson disabused them: "The trail you are following is a blind," a shrewd diversion by the Mill Creeks to shift blame for their acts to Bidwell's Valley Indians, their old rivals, even though those Indians played, at most, a minor or peripheral role in earlier years.[866] Anderson impressed on the party that they "would surely breed trouble for themselves if they bothered Bidwell's Indians."[867] Anderson explained that if angry settlers showed up in Chico again to punish Valley Indians for Mill Creek raids, Bidwell would summon soldiers to guard his ranch workers.

Furthermore, Anderson emphasized, as the men headed toward Rancho Chico, they were losing valuable time because the guilty Mill Creeks were escaping into the canyon. The other settler group had not traveled far and was brought back. Anderson sent the reunited group to the Rock Creek home of his father-in-law, Missourian James Gore. Anderson gave them a bag of flour with instructions that, after a night's rest at Gore's place, they should continue to Hi Good's farm on Deer Creek where he would meet them.[868]

Anderson and Good had declined to participate in Butte County pursuits in 1863 and 1864, but now, in 1865, they were both willing to accept lead roles. In 1864, Anderson, 25 and a family man, had moved from Tehama County to his new Mud Creek farm near Rock Creek, less than ten miles north of Chico. This meant that Indian clashes in northern Butte County, such as Mary Moore's murder near his place that March, were now a matter of personal consequence. As mentioned earlier, Good joined pursuits when settlers had been killed; perhaps in this case he wanted to support Anderson. He also may have wanted to reclaim his reputation as an experienced and successful Indian tracker in light of his failure to find the Mill Creeks who had killed Moore that year.

They diverted the settlers' focus away from the few random "wannabe" Mill Creeks among Valley Indians and toward the dangerous Mill Creeks still terrifying and killing settlers and peaceful Indians: "renegades ... numbering about twenty or twenty-five warriors ... [with] a roving disposition."[869] Their studied approach this time demonstrates that Good and Anderson were no longer the "loose cannons" local history writers later derided.

Their plan worked. While the reunited party headed to the Gore place on Rock Creek, Anderson headed for Chico, where

Standoff

he met with Bidwell. Actions then and later infer that Anderson reassured him a disciplined private pursuit party would handle the pursuit and no settler mobs would be attacking his ranch Indians. Bidwell, relieved and grateful for advance notice of their stratagem, sent forty pounds each of crackers and bacon with Anderson. Anderson recruited experienced Butte County pursuers such as foothill farmers Billy Boness, Hardy Thomasson and Dan Sutherland, whom he likely found at work in his Second Street wagon shop. With Sutherland's Frenchtown Road cabin in ashes, he had a vested interest in the hunt.[870]

The settlers were waiting for Anderson at Good's place when he arrived. Good distributed Bidwell's provisions and Good butchered a ewe to feed the sixteen men. At dawn, heeding the two leaders' overriding instruction to make no motion or noise that would reveal their presence to the Indians, Good and Anderson moved out ahead as trackers while the rest crept along the canyon behind them. The two leaders' veteran Tehama County partners and perhaps other veterans supervised the other men who packed the provisions and handled camp duty.

One of the original Concow Valley pursuers described the terrain the men encountered as "the roughest country that ever a white man traveled over, the whole of it being what geologists call 'water made cement.' All the various water channels have formed channels through the different strata of sand and gravel, the bluffs on either side being perpendicular and impassable, except for a few 'passes' known to Capt. Good."[871]

On Sunday, August 13, their search ended about thirty-five miles east of the village of Tehama at a remote site called Three Knolls, where Good and Anderson spotted a Mill Creek camp of about sixty Indians. There, according to a member of the party, the trackers signaled the men behind them to attack. The pursuit party suffered no mortalities and killed nine Indian men, later estimating that survivors fled with "a great number of wounded." Among the dead, Anderson recognized Valley Indian Billy Sills, whom he had known as a recent shepherd in the foothills. Then called a "half-breed," Sills grew up on the former ranch of pioneer Tehama County settler Peter Lassen, which his father Dan Sills, a California resident since 1832, had acquired. Aware that rogue Valley Indians occasionally joined the Mill Creeks,

Anderson evinced no surprise on seeing him.[872]

In later remarks, Anderson offered an example of his and Good's political (but not humane) sensibility. While the Concow Valley men grossly mutilated the Indian corpses, including those of women and children, the veteran pursuers declined to participate but stood back out of deference to the men's desire to avenge the Workman place deaths. In recalling this, Anderson inferred the veterans were not comfortable with the others' behavior and that he, Good and their regular partners ordinarily killed and scalped only adult or nearly adult males.

Anderson also commented that Good usually left the Indian women behind and took orphans to the valley. At Three Knolls, Good made prisoners of a small child and its mother whom, according to Moak, he intended to deliver to Bidwell's rancheria. However, when the woman refused to go with them, one of the men killed her, so they took the child. In 1862, when Good wrote the governor for instructions about where to take captives, the governor did not respond. After that, Good and Anderson relied on their own judgment regarding the treatment of Indians they captured. For example, Anderson believed that they should move children and women out of the canyons because the latter were sought-after quarries of rival Indian raiding parties. Good disagreed and for the most part, prevailed. Evidence that Good sold Indian children is rare, but it was a common practice at the time for farmers to add orphaned children of any race to the family labor force. In practice, Good and Anderson considered it unavoidable that Indian women and children were occasional collateral victims of crossfire, including when they were used as shields by Indian men under fire.[873]

After the Three Knolls battle, Simeon Moak wrote his family that, as the Concow Valley men rummaged among the corpses for battlefield trophies—body parts or stolen bootie from the Workmans' and others' cabins—the cry of an Indian man from the canyon wall froze them all: "You god dam American sons of bitches!"[874]

As Hardy Thomasson and Moak headed for Chico ahead of the returning pursuit party, they stopped near Pine Creek for breakfast at the Oak Grove Hotel and stagecoach station. The restaurant was run by Frank and Elvira Hickok, whose three children had been killed by Mill Creeks in 1862. Despite having been briefed by the men about their successful pursuit, Hickok gave them no break in their bill. When they delivered news of the Three Knolls rout to Rancho Chico, Bidwell dispatched a pair of four-horse teams and two coaches to bring in the rest of the men "as fast as possible" when they reached Mud Creek.[875] Bidwell had Ira Weatherbee, owner of the Chico Hotel, put them up and provide them "the best meal the market afforded and charge it to him."[876]

Bidwell's generosity toward the men not only rewarded them, but enhanced his own reputation in the settler community. Having enjoyed their fill and a brief taste of celebrity, the Concow Valley honorees accepted Bidwell's offer of transportation to Pence's hotel, from which they "footed it" to their homes. They felt they had earned Bidwell's generosity. For Bidwell's part, it was imperative to send them home quickly and in his debt. With his large rancheria of Valley Indians nearby, grateful as he was for the men's success, he did not want armed, novice Indian fighters around town with time on their hands and liquor in their bellies.

In February 1866, white men killed four Indians as they speared fish near Oroville. The killers later claimed, with no evidence, that the Indians were involved in the Workman place killings. A month later, a large party of Mill Creeks attacked Valley Indians working for Bidwell on upper Big Meadows grazing grounds. His Indian workers drove off the assailants, but John Bueno, a well-known Valley Maidu from the rancheria at Chico, died from arrow wounds. In the flurry of fighting, a Mill Creek dropped booty from a previous raid—a book of poetry by Oliver Wendell Holmes.[877]

Collapse of the Mill Creeks

While settlers called the Mill Creeks' attacks criminal, the objectives on each side of the fight were similar: to use any means possible to punish and drive out land grabbers. While the Mill Creeks exacted a painful price from both settlers and peaceful Indians, they paid the highest price. In clashes with Good, Anderson and their allies, Mill Creek raiders lost their lives in far greater numbers than the settlers. After the post-Civil War period, a continuous flow of new arrivals from the eastern states spread throughout the valley and the Sierra Nevada.

Since 1858, Indian fighters had relied on safe havens in the remote Deer Creek and Mill Creek canyons. The canyons were so deep and formidable they provided hiding places where, after clashes with adversaries such as Gore, Anderson, Good, "Bully" Bowman, Obe Field and Sutherland, the Indians could regroup and replenish their ranks with renegades, Mountain Maidu, returnees from Round Valley Reservation and occasional Valley Indian volunteer recruits.[878]

However, the August 1865 attack at Three Knolls, in which Good's and Anderson's pursuit party had moved, undetected, into Deer Creek Canyon, made it clear the surviving Indians could no longer hide in the two canyons from which they had mounted their raids. By 1866, their population was so decimated they could no longer sustain their old way of life. A few clashes continued in Tehama County, but the contest in Butte County ended with "the new people" the victors.

Over the next decades, settlers, including Sutherland, after whom a trail along Sulpher Creek was named, moved deep into Mill Creek and Deer Creek canyons, where they built cabins and raised families. And somehow, the settlers and remaining Indians who lived in nearby caves managed to live parallel lives in peace.[879] Some Indian men left the canyons periodically to hunt and fish. According to Vera Clark McKeen, whose Concow Maidu family set up summer camps under bridges where they enjoyed fishing with spears in the early twentieth century, they once found someone had moved and presumably fished with their spear, and then put it back in a place different from where they always left it.[880] The family believed the user was one of the "hidden" Indians such as Ishi.

Other Indians left the canyons and worked on settler farms. Although hungry Indians continued to steal provisions in small raids on settlers' canyon cabins, the ensuing retaliations never again reached the level of a war.[881]

For the Indians' part, with no treaty rights and no territories left, it was all that successive generations could do to survive and their imprint on the land faded in the Butte County foothills. In a later history of Kimshew Township in that tribelet's former Maidu territory, the author's sole inference that Indians were ever there was that the name "Kimshew" meant "by a stream."[882]

Although the Mechoopdas adapted to Rancho Chico's addition of people from other tribes over the years, historic rivalries were slow to disappear. During the later mid-nineteenth century, when the son of a Mechoopda headman was accosted by a man from a rival tribelet who came onto Bidwell's ranch, the Mechoopda killed the intruder and used one of Bidwell's horses to drag the corpse away from the ranch. When Bidwell learned about the encounter, he followed traces of blood north to Lindo Channel, about a mile away, where he found the body. The leader's son was arrested, tried and sent to San Quentin. His grieving father became moody, and, although formerly a leader, isolated himself from community life on the ranch. Tribesmen shared his sorrow, knowing his son had been wrongly punished for defending his people according to tribal tradition.[883]

In later decades, Whites conceded the Indian wars on the Butte County front began with white abuses and recognized that both sides suffered tragic losses. Anthropologists' studies of Maidu there have preserved tribal oral histories that foster their descendants' interest in their forebears' roles during the upheaval. Settler descendants became well known for their family accounts of Indian survivors who hid along Mill and Deer creeks in Tehama County. Richard Burrill recorded their memoirs and conducted interviews that constitute an important legacy.

As the twentieth century advanced, the old battles between settlers and Indians took on a romantic caste in books and western movies. In the 1950s, television dramas simplified the conflicts into "good versus bad": settlers became the heroes and Indians, the villains. In the 1960s, a period that questioned conventional thinking and raised the issue of discrimination, the tables turned and Indians became noble defenders and settlers wicked aggressors.

In each era, people picked sides and cherry-picked data to prove they were right. And so urban legends and mythical, wrong-headed thinking clouded and compromised the public's understanding of the fuller, more complex and interesting record of both settlers' and Indians' roles in the actual history of the Indian-settler wars in Northern California. The present attempt to weave together the strands of each side's story is necessarily incomplete and certainly imperfect. But, it is hoped that the objective—to promote understanding of the roles of the key players and, most important, why individuals, Indians and settlers alike, acted the way they did—was achieved. The result is more complex and credible, while no less dramatic or tragic, than the hoary renditions that have long gripped public understanding.

Bibliography

Documents

Bancroft Library, University of California, Berkeley
John Bidwell Collection
A. L. Kroeber Papers
O. C. Wozencraft Statement
California State Archives, Sacramento
California Indian Wars Files
California Military Collection
Governor Leland Stanford's Administrative Archive, 1860+
Governor John B. Weller's Administrative Archive, 1850+
California State Library, Sacramento: The California Collection
Annie E. K. Bidwell Collection
John Bidwell Collection
George McKinstry Collection
Warren Sexton Collection
California State University, Chico Meriam Library, Special Collections
John Nopel Collection
John Bidwell Collection
Butte County, California Tax Roll Report, 1860
Charles Lewis Stilson Papers
Dorothy Hill Collection, Indian Papers, "Indian-White Relations of Northern California, 1849–1920."
Henry E. Huntington Library, San Marino
Richard C. Harrison, Diary and Receipt Book, 1850–1853
Ananias Rogers Pond, Diary, 1849
Library of Congress
Abraham Lincoln Papers, Correspondence
National Archives
Office of Indian Affairs, Letters Received
Records of the California Superintendency, Letters Received
U.S. Army, Letters Received

Unpublished Sources

Azbill, Henry. "Some Aspects of Maidu Culture on John Bidwell's Rancho del Arroyo Chico." Interview by Dorothy Hill, 1969. Dorothy Hill Collection, Special Collections, Meriam Library, California State University, Chico.

Bain, Bud. Interview by Dorothy Hill, 1969. Dorothy Hill Collection, Special Collections, Meriam Library, California State University, Chico.

Bidwell, John. "Dictation." John Bidwell Collection, Bancroft Library, University of California, Berkeley.
— — —. Scrapbook. John Bidwell Collection, Special Collections, Meriam Library, California State University, Chico.
Campbell, Sue and Janice Mattice. "Maidu Women." Public talk, 11 March 2001. Chico Heritage Association.
Conway, William [probable author]. *Oral History of Rancho Chico Indians*. Recorded by Julia Pingrey. John Nopel Collection. Courtesy of David Nopel.
Hendrix, Louise Butts. Interview by Marilyn Sevier, 1985. Dorothy Hill Collection, Special Collections, Meriam Library, California State University, Chico.
Hill, Dorothy. "The Durham Oak." Dorothy Hill Collection.
Johnson, Jerald Jay. "Ishi's Ancestors." Draft of paper delivered to unnamed group, 23 September 1994. Anthropology Library, California State University, Chico.
Lyon, Darwin B. Interview, 15 August 1915. Frame 527, reel 199, Ethnological Documents Collection, University of California, Berkeley.
Meriam, C. Hart. Papers Relating to Work with California Indians, 1850–1974. Indian Stocks and Tribes, BNEC 1556: 118. University of California, Bancroft Library.
Potts, Starie. Interview by Dorothy Hill, 1 July 1965. Dorothy Hill Collection, Special Collections, Chico Meriam Library, California State University.
Royce, Charles C. "In Memoriam: John Bidwell." Scrapbook, 1905. John Bidwell Collection, The California Collection, California State Library, Sacramento.
Scott, Leland. Interviews by Robert Rathbun, n.d. Dorothy Hill Collection, Special Collections, Meriam Library, California State University, Chico.
Scott, Roy. "A Maidu Descendent Relates His Family History." Interview by Dorothy Hill, n.d. Dorothy Hill Collection, Special Collections, Meriam Library, California State University, Chico.
Speegle, Claude. "The Thirteen Pages." 1997 transcription by Richard Burrill of notes from Claude Speegle, Homer Speegle's son, c. 1969.
Speegle, Homer Mead. "The Eight Pages." 1997 transcription by Richard Burrill of notes from Homer Speegle c. 1969.
Speegle, Jessie. Speegle memoir (untitled), n.d. John Nopel Collection.
Stilson, *Charles Lewis. Diaries, 1861–1865*. Special Collections, Meriam Library, California State University, Chico.
Sturtevant, Leila Sutherland. "Brief History of the John Sutherland Sr. Family." Aptos, CA: property of Judith Sutherland Pahnke, 1925.
Sutherland, Lewis D. "Notes on the Sutherland Family." Portland, OR: property of Barbara Scot, n.d.
Sutherland, Thomas. "History of the Sutherland Family." Private papers of Eloise Sutherland Helgens, provided to the author by Barbara Scot, n.d.
Wilson, Thelma. "A Mechoopda Descendent Relates Her Family's History." Association for Northern California Records and Research, Oral History Program, 1972. Northeastern California Project, Special Collections, Meriam Library, California State University, Chico.
Wozencraft, Oliver. *Statement of Dr. Oliver Wozencraft*. Bancroft Library, University of California, Berkeley.
Young, Herb. Interview by Dorothy Hill, 1968. Dorothy Hill Collection, Special Collections, Meriam Library, California State University, Chico.

Published Primary Sources

Anderson, Robert A. *Fighting the Mill Creeks: Being a Personal Account of Campaigns Against the Indians of the Northern Sierras*. Chico: Chico Record Press, 1909.

Bibliography

Bidwell, Annie E. K. *The Rancho Chico Indians*. Edited by Dorothy Hill. Chico: Bidwell Mansion Cooperating Association, 1980.
— — —. "The Mechoopda." *Overland Monthly* 27 (January–June 1896).
Bidwell Diaries. Vol. 1. John Bidwell transcription on CD-ROM. Chico: Heidelberg Graphics, 2001.
Bidwell, John. "Address of John Bidwell to the Members of the Society of California Pioneers, November 1, 1897." Edited by Henry L. Byrne. *Quarterly of the Society of California Pioneers* 3 (March 1926).
— — —. *In California Before the Gold Rush*. Los Angeles: Ritchie Press, 1948.
— — —. *The Diaries of John Bidwell*. Chico: Bidwell Mansion State Park Supporting Association, 2001.
Bleyhl, Norris. *Indian-White Relations in Northern California, 1849–1920*. Regional Programs, California State University, Chico. Chico: n.p., 1978.
Brewer, William H. *Up and Down California in 1860–1864: The Journal of William H. Brewer*. Edited by Francis P. Farquhar. Berkeley: University of California Press, 1974.
Briggs, Carl and Clyde Francis Trudell. *Quarterdeck and Saddlehorn: The Story of Edward F. Beale, 1822–1893*. Glendale, CA: The Arthur Clark Co., 1993.
Carson, Arenia Thankful [Lewis]. *Captured by the Mill Creek Indians: A True Story of the Capture of the Sam Lewis Children in the Year 1863*. Chico: A. Thankful Carson, 1915.
Compton, Henrietta Packer. *Mary Murdock Compton*. Chico: privately printed, 1953.
Crowder, D. F. "The Eventful Yesterdays: The Story of Early Chico." *Chico Enterprise*, 28 December 1917 to 28 January 1918.
Derby, George. "The Topographical Reports of Lt. George H. Derby." *Quarterly of the California Historical Society* 11, no. 2 (June 1932).
"Ethnographic Notes on Central California Indian Tribes." *University of California Archaeological Survey* 68, pt. III. (Completed by Robert F. Heizer, December 1967.)
Ferguson, Charles. *The Experiences of a Forty-Niner During Thirty-Four Years' Residence in California and Australia*. Cleveland: Williams, 1888.
Goni, Mary Compton. *Mary Remembers*. Chico: privately printed, 1990.
Josephson, Katie. "Katie Josephson's Mining Story." *Our History*, ed. Eric Josephson. www.maidu.com.
Kappler, Charles J., ed. and compiler. *Indian Affairs: Laws and Treaties*. Vol. 2. Washington, D.C.: Government Printing Office, 1904.
Keller, John E., ed. *Anna Morrison Read*. Lafayette, CA: privately printed, 1979.
Kerr, Thomas. "An Irishman in the Gold Rush, the Journal of Thomas Kerr." *California State Historical Society Quarterly* 8, nos. 1, 3 (1902).
Kibbe, William C. "Adjutant General Kibbe's Report." *Ishi the Last Yahi: A Documentary History*, ed. Robert F. Heizer and Theodora Kroeber. Berkeley: University of California Press, 1979.
— — —. *The Volunteer: Containing Exercises and Movements of Infantry, Light Infantry, Rifle Men and Cavalry, as a Drill Manual for the Californian Militia*. Sacramento: B. B. Redding State Printer, 1855.
Lott, Charles F. "As It Was in the Days of the 49'ers." [Butte County Historical Society] *Diggins* 43, no. 2 (Summer 1999).
Mahan, Bruce. "The Scotch Grove Trail." [Iowa State Historical Society] *The Palimpsest* (November 1923).
Marsh, John. "Unpublished Letters." *Overland Monthly* (February 1890).
McDowell, Jim. "Magalia: A Town Nearly Forgotten." [Butte County Historical Society] *Diggins* 56, no. 3 (Fall 2012).
McIlhany, Edward W. "Recollections of a 49'er." Annotated and researched by Scott J. Lawson. *California [Dogtown] Territorial Quarterly* ((Fall 2006).
Moak, Simeon. *The Last of the Mill Creeks and Early Life in Northern California*. Chico:

privately printed, 1923.
— — — and Jacob Moak. "Moaks Write Home." [*Paradise Post*] *Dogtown Nugget*, 20–23 April 1995, 8–11.
Official Correspondence Between the Governor of California, the U.S. Indian Agents for California, and the Commander of U.S. Troops for California in Relation to Indian Difficulties in the Northern Part of the State. Sacramento: E. Casserly, 1852.
Parker, William Tell. "Notes by the Bay, 1850–51, Being a Diary of His Gold Rush Experiences." *Recollections of a '49er*, ed. Scott J. Lawson. *California* [Dogtown] *Territorial Quarterly* 67 (Fall 2006).
Powell, J. W. "Indian Linguistic Families North of Mexico." *Seventh Annual Report of the Bureau of Ethnology to the Secretary of the Smithsonian Institution, 1885–1886*. Washington, D.C.: Government Printing Office, 1891.
Robinson, John W. "Preserving the West for the Union, The California Volunteers, 1861–1866." *California* [Dogtown] *Territorial Quarterly* (Spring 2013): 8.
Shover, Michele and Vera Clark McKeen. *A Maidu Matron's Twentieth Century Life* (Chico: privately printed, 1998).
Sinclair, Delia Sutherland. *Red River Settlers: Incidents*. Aptos, CA: n.p., n.d. Courtesy of Judith Sutherland Pahnke.
Sutherland, Josephine, Esther Sinclair, and Mrs. Donald O. Sinclair. *Scotch Grove Pioneers*. Monticello, IA: Monticello Express, 1937.
Tassin, A. G. "The Chronicles of Fort Wright: The Concows." *Overland Monthly* 1–2 (July-August 1887).
Wikipedia. Nome Cult Trail. https://en.wikipedia.org//Nome_Cult_Trail

Government Documents

Bureau of Ethnology of the Smithsonian Institution, 1885–1886. Government Publishing Office, 1891.
California. Butte County. County Center. Records Office. Tax Records. Oroville, California.
California. California Superintendency. Office of Indian Affairs. 1849–1880. Roll 39, 1863–1864. National Archives.
California. Legislature. *Journal of Third Session of the Legislature of the State of California*. San Francisco: G. K. Fitch, 1852.
California. Official Correspondence between the Governor of California, the United States Indian Agents for California, and the Commander of U.S. Troops, 1852. California State Archives.
California. *Outline History of the California National Guard*. Vol. 2. Military Collection. California State Archives.
California. Petition to the Commander of the U.S. Force in New Helvetia from Mill Creek, 28 February 1847. Huntington Library.
California. Petition to Governor Weller from Tehama County, 1859. Indian War Files. Military Collection, California State Archives.
California. Petition to Leland Stanford from Butte County, 1862. Indian War Files. Military Collection. California State Archives.
California. Petition, Citizens of Butte and Tehama Counties to the Governor, July 1863. Military Records, California State Archives.
California. Pit River Expedition. California Indian War Files. California State Archives.
California. Report of Adjutant General William C. Kibbe to the California State Legislature, 15 December 1862. California State Archives.
California. Returns from Military Posts. Camp Bidwell Post Returns. Chico, Butte County, California, 1800–1916. Microfilm 617. National Archives.

California. Returns from Military Posts. Fort Wright Post Returns, Mendocino County, California. December 1862–December 1869. Microfilm 617. National Archives.

California. Senate. "Report of the Special Committee of the California State Senate to Inquire into the Treaties Made by the U.S. Commissioners in California." *California State Senate Journal*, 1852.

California. Records of the California Superintendency. Correspondence of Agents to Superintendent, 1863–1873. Office of Indian Affairs/Round Valley Agency. National Archives.

California. Tehama County. County Center. Records Department. Coroner's and Probate Records. National Archives.

Iowa. Jones County. Office of the County Clerk. Probate of Estate of Charles G. Moses, 1860.

"List of Ordinances Issued to Organized Militia." *Annual Report of The Adjutant-General of California in 1862*. Sacramento: State Printer, 1863.

Massachusetts. Town of Dudley. Records, 1732–1754. Pawtucket, RI: Adam Sutcliffe, 1893.

United States. Army. Records of U.S. Army. Continental Command Record Group 393.9. Division and Department of the Pacific. Letters Received May 1850. National Archives.

United States. Army. *Statistical Report on the Sickness and Mortality of the Army of the United States, The Records of the Surgeon General's Office, 1839–1855*. Washington, D.C.: A.O.P. Nicholson, Printer, 1856. [Courtesy of The Citadel: Military College of South Carolina.]

United States. Congress. "Resolution of the Legislature of California." 34th Cong., 1st sess. House Miscellaneous Document 87, vol. 2, 7 April 1856.

United States. Congress. "Schedule of Indian Land Cessions." Vol. 18, pt. 2 (1896–1897). *Annual Report of the Bureau of Indian Ethnology to the Secretary of the Smithsonian Institution*. Washington D.C.: Government Printing Office, 1899.

United States. Congress. *Annual Report of the Commissioner of Indian Affairs, 1850*. 31st Cong., 2d sess., Senate Executive Document 1, vol. 1, pts. 1–2, December 1850, ser. set 587, 35–175.

United States. Congress. *Annual Report of the Commissioner of Indian Affairs, 1867*. 40th Cong, 2d sess., House Executive Document 1, 15 November 1867, serial set 1326, 1–397.

United States. Congress. *Annual Report of the Commissioner of Indian Affairs, 1868*. 40th Cong., 2d sess. House Executive Document 200, vol. 15, 4 March 1868, serial set 1341.

United States. Congress. *Samuel Norris v. U.S.* (Washington, D.C.: 1860.) John Bidwell's deposition, consisting of documents submitted to the U.S. Congress by Samuel H. Huntington, Chief Clerk, Court of Claims. Issued as U.S. House of Representatives Report C.C., no. 257, 36th Cong., 2d sess., December 18, 1860. In portfolio.

United States. Congress. *Congressional Globe*. 32d Cong., 1st sess., 26 March 1872, 890.

United States. Congress. "Estimate of Appropriation for Indian Service in California." *Congressional Globe*. 32d Cong., 1st sess., vol. 24, pt. 2, 26 March 1852.

United States. Congress. "Estimate of Appropriation for Indian Service in California." 40th Cong., 2d sess., House Executive Document 200, vol. 15, 4 March 1868, serial set 1341.

United States. Congress. "Message on California and New Mexico." Col. R. B. Mason to Lt. John A. Anderson. 31st Cong., 1st sess., Senate Executive Document 18, vol. 1, 24 January 1850, serial sets 557, 658.

United States. Congress. 32d Cong., 2d sess. Senate Executive Document 57, vol. 7, March 3, 1853, serial set no. 665.

United States. Congress. 34th Cong., 1st sess. House Executive Document 118, vol. 12, 8 July 1856.
United States. Congress. *Congressional Globe*. 36th Cong., 1st sess., 2365–2369, Senate Debate, 26 May 1860.
United States, Department of the Interior. Civil War Bounty Land Warrant Files, Daniel Sutherland. Land Warrant File 1348-133. Document of naturalization.
United States. Department of the Interior. Office of Indian Affairs. Letters Received, 1849–1852. California. Microfilm 234. National Archives.
United States. Department of the Interior. Office of Indian Affairs. Letters Sent, 1849–1903. Microfilm 606. National Archives.
United States. Department of the Interior. Office of Indian Affairs. Letters Received, 1862–1863. Microfilm 39. National Archives.
United States. Department of the Interior. Office of Indian Affairs. *Records of the Round Valley Reservation, 1859–1930*. Letters and Invoice Book. National Archives.
United States. Department of the Interior. R. T. Lincoln Collection. National Archives.
United States. Department of War. Office of the Adjutant General. *Martial Law in Round Valley, the Evidence Brought Out by a Court of Investigation Ordered by Brig. Gen. G. Wright, 1863*. National Archives.
United States. Department of War. Office of the Adjutant General. *Martial Law in Round Valley, Mendocino County, CA*. Ukiah City, CA: Herald Office Printers, 1863. National Archives.
United States. Department of War. *The War of the Rebellion: A Compilation of the Official Records of the Union and Confederate Armies*. Series 1, vol. 50, part II. Washington, D.C.: Government Printing Office, 1897.
United States. Federal Census, 1852. CA. Klamath County.
United States. Federal Census, 1860. CA. Butte County.
United States. Senate. 34th Cong., 1st sess. Miscellaneous Document 67, vol. 1, 19 June 1856.
United States. Senate. *Report of G. W. Barbour, Indian Commissioner for Northern California*. Miscellaneous Documents, no. 688, 33d Cong., spec. sess. Reports and Executive Data.
United States. Senate. Laws. *Indian Affairs Laws and Treaties*. Vol. 4. 70th Cong., 1st sess., Senate document 53, serial set 10458.
United States. Senate Resolution, March 3, 1859. "Depredations Committed upon Citizens of Butte County by Indians, 1852. Petition by John Bidwell."

Newspapers

Butte Democrat (Oroville)
Butte Record (Oroville)
Butte Union Record (Oroville)
California Alta (San Francisco)
Cascade Union (Klamath County)
Chico Chronicle Record
Chico Courant
Chico Enterprise
Chico Enterprise-Record
Chico Index
Chico Morning Chronicle
Chico News And Review
Chico Record
Del Norte Record (Humboldt, formerly Klamath, County)

Dogtown Nugget (Paradise Post publication)
Amador Ledger Dispatch
Marysville Express
Marysville Herald
Marysville Record
Niles Register
Northern Advocate (Humboldt County)
Northern Enterprise (Chico)
Oroville Daily Record
Oroville Mercury
Oroville Union Record
Quincy Union
Plumas National Bulletin
Red Bluff Beacon
Red Bluff Tri-Weekly Independent
Sacramento Bee
Sacramento Union
San Francisco Alta
San Francisco Daily Evening Bulletin
San Francisco Express
San Francisco Herald
Santa Rosa Democrat
Shasta Courier
Shasta Herald
Tehama County Times
Union Record (Oroville)
Yreka Union

Selected Secondary Sources

Allen, Susan. "The Nome Lackee Indian Reservation." [Colusi County CA Historical Society] *Wagon Wheels* 17 (February 1967).
Almquist, Alan F. *The Other Californians: Prejudice and Discrimination under Spain, Mexico, and the United States to 1920.* Berkeley: University of California Press, 1977.
Ambrose, Stephen E. *Undaunted Courage: Meriwether Lewis, Thomas Jefferson, and the Opening of the American West.* New York: Touchstone, 1996.
Anderson, Bill. "The Settlement of Northern California, Part 3." *California* [Dogtown] *Territorial Quarterly* 12 (Winter 1992).
Apperson, Eva Marie. *We Knew Ishi.* Red Bluff, CA: Walker Lithograph, 1971.
Alt, David D. and Donald W. Hyndman. *Maps in Roadside Geology of Northern California.* Missoula, MT: Mountain Press Publishing Co., 1975.
Azbill, Henry. "Bahapki." *The Indian Historian* 4, no. 1 (1971).
— — —. "Maidu Indians: A Historical Note." *The Indian Historian* 4, no. 1 (1971).
Bancroft, Hubert Howe. *The Works: History of California.* Vols. 7, 18, 24. San Francisco: The History Company, 1890.
Barbour, George W. Edited by Alban W. Hooper. "The Journal of George W. Barbour: May 1 to October 4, 1851." Pt. 2. *Southwestern Historical Quarterly* 40 (January 1937).
Baumgardner III, Frank H. *Killing for Land in Early California: Indian Blood at Round Valley, 1856–1890.* New York: Algora Publishing, 2006.
Becker, Nick. "Manoah Pence of Pence's Ranch." *California* [Dogtown] *Territorial Quarterly* (Winter 1991).
Bleyhl, Norris A. *Three Military Posts in Northeastern California, 1849–1863.* Chico:

279

Association for Northern California Records and Research, 1984.
———. "Indian-White Relationships in Northern California, 1840–1820." Bleyhl Collection, Special Collections, California State University, Chico.
Blythe, John. "Every Map Tells a Story." North Carolina Miscellany. www.lib.unc.edu/blogs/nem/index.php/2010/07/30/every-map-tells-a-story/.
Bosquet, Tim. "Wiping Out the Redskins: A Look at Chico's Role in the Idaho Indian Wars." *Chico News and Review* 12 (January 1995): 16–19.
Boyle, Florence Danforth. *Old Days of Butte*. Chico: Association of Northern California Historical Research, 2006.
Burchfield, Christopher. "The Golden State's First Senator and the Perils of Patronage." *California* [Dogtown] *Territorial Quarterly* (Spring 2011).
Burrill, Richard. *Ishi Rediscovered*. Sacramento: Anthro, 2001.
———. *Butte Creek Canyon*. Chico: Colman Museum, n.d.
———. "Hi Good's Cabin Report." Chap. 2. www.ishifacts.com/hisgood.asp.
Butler, Velma. "One Hundred Years of the Nimshew Ridge." *Tales of the Paradise Ridge* 6, no. 2 (1965).
"California and the Civil War: 2nd Regiment of Cavalry, California Volunteers." www.militarymuseum.org/2dCavVC.html.
"California's Native People: The Central Region: Sociopolitical Organization." Washington, D.C.: Smithsonian Institution, 1978. www.cabrillo.edu/~crsmith/anth6_central_politics.html.
Carranco, Lynwood and Estle Beard. *Genocide and Vendetta: The Round Valley Wars of Northern California*. Norman: University of Oklahoma Press, 1981.
Carter, Henry Rose. "Report: Place of Origin of Malaria: America?" Miscellaneous, Phillip S. Hench/Walter Reed Yellow Fever Collection.
Castillo, Edward D. "The Impact of Euro-American Exploration and Settlement." *Handbook of North American Indians: California*, vol. 8, ed. Robert F. Heizer. Washington, D.C.: Smithsonian Institution, 1978.
Chalmers, J. W. *Red River Adventure*. Toronto: Macmillan, 1956.
Chandler, Robert. "The Failure of Reform: White Attitudes and Indian Response in California During the Civil War Era." *The Pacific Historian* 24 (Spring 1980).
———. "Success to Civil War Tragedy: The Greathouse Brothers and Slicer's Express." *Western Express* 46 (March 1996).
Chase, Don M. *People of the Valley: The Concow Maidu*. Sebastopol, CA: Don M. Chase, 1973.
Christensen, Scott R. *Sagwitch: Shoshone Chieftain, Mormon Elder, 1822–1887*. Logan: Utah State University Press, 1999.
Clark, K. W. "The Yana and Yahi Indians of Butte County." [Butte County Historical Society] *Diggins* 3, no. 3 (1959).
Clough, F. S. *The House at 5th and Salem*. Chico: Stansbury House Preservation Association, 1978.
Collsley-Batt, Jill. *The Last of the California Rangers: The Capture of Joaquin Murieta*. New York: Funk & Wagnalls, 1928.
Conners, Pamela A. *The Chico to Round Valley Trail of Tears*. Willows, CA: Mendocino National Forest Service, 1993.
Cook, Sherburne F. "The American Invasion, 1848–1870." *Ibero-America* 23 (1945).
———. "The Method and Extent of Dietary Adaptation Among California and Nevada Indians." *Ibero-Americana* 35 (1945).
———. *The Epidemic of 1830–1833 in California and Oregon*. Vol. 43, *University of California Publications in American Archaeology and Ethnology*. Berkeley: University of California Press, 1955.

———. *The Population of the California Indians, 1769–1970*. Berkeley: University of California Press, 1976.
———. *The Conflict Between the California Indian and White Civilization*. Los Angeles: University of California Press, 1976.
———. *Colonial Expedition to the Interior of California, Central Valley, 1800–1820*. Oxford: Benediction Classics, 2012.
Crouter, Richard and Andrew F. Rolle. "Edward Fitzgerald Beale and the Indian Peace Commissioners in California, 1851–1854." *Historical Society of Southern California Quarterly* 42, no. 2 (June 1960).
Currie, Anne H. "The Bidwell Rancheria." *California Historical Society Quarterly* 36 (December 1957): 313–25.
Curtin, Jeremiah. "The Yana (1864)." *Ishi the Last Yahi: A Documentary History*, ed. Robert F. Heizer and Theodora Kroeber. Berkeley: University of California Press, 1979.
Curtis, Edward S. *The North American Indian: The Maidu*. Vol. 14. Seattle: E. S. Curtis, 1924.
Dana, Julian. *The Sacramento River of Gold*. New York: Farrar and Rhinehart, 1939.
Davis, Hugh Graham and Ted Robert Gurr, eds. *History of Violence in America*. New York: Praeger, 1970.
Davis, James T. *Trade Routes and Economic Exchange Among the Indians of California*. Ramona, CA: Ballena Press, 1974.
Davis, Winfield J. *History of Political Conventions in California, 1849–1862*. Sacramento: California State Library, 1892.
Decker, Jody. "Depopulation of the Northern Plains Natives." *Social Science and Medicine* 33 (1991).
Dixon, Roland B. "The Northern Maidu." *Bulletin of the American Museum of Natural History* 16, no. 3 (May 1905).
The Eddys in America: A Genealogy. Boston: privately printed, 1930.
Ellison, William Herbert. "The Federal Indian Policy in California, 1846–1860." *The Mississippi Valley Historical Review* 9 (June 1922).
———. "Rejection of California Indian Treaties." *The Grizzly Bear* (May-July 1925).
Engelhardt, Zephyrin. *San Luis Rey Mission*. San Francisco: James Barry, 1921.
Faust, Ernest Carroll. The History of Malaria in the United States. n.d. www.jstor.org/discover/10.2307/27826354?sid=21106308042253&uid=4&uid=3739560&uid=2&uid=3739256
Florcken, Herbert. "Law and Order View of the Vigilance Committee in 1856." Part 2. *California Historical Society Quarterly* 15 (1936).
Foreman, Amanda. *A World on Fire: Britain's Crucial Role in the American Civil War*. New York: Random House, 2010.
Furnell, Henrietta Catherine. *From the Prairie to the Pacific*. Edited by Mai Lumen Hill. Chico: Association of Northern California Records and Research, 2005.
Gates, Paul W. *California Ranchos and Farms*. Madison: State Historical Society of Wisconsin, 1967.
Gilfillan, J. A. "A Trip Through the Red River Valley in 1864." *North Dakota Historical Quarterly* 1, no. 4 (July 1927).
Gillis, Michael J. "John Bidwell and John Muir: The Forgotten Friendship." *California [Dogtown] Territorial Quarterly*, no. 21 (Spring 1995).
———. "John Bidwell and the Indians of Chico Rancheria: Was He Their Protector—or Their Enslaver?" *Chico News and Review*, 23 February 1995.
——— and Michael F. Magliari. *John Bidwell and California: The Life and Writings of a Pioneer, 1841–1900*. Spokane: Arthur H. Clark, 2003.
Graham, Hugh Davis and Ted Robert Gurr. eds. *History of Violence in America*. New York: Praeger, 1970.

Gray, Harold Farnsworth and Russell E. Fontaine. "A History of Malaria in California." Proceedings and papers of the 25th annual conference of the California Mosquito Control Association, 30 June 1957.

Guinn, James Miller. *A History of the State of California and Biographical Records of the Sacramento Valley*. Chicago: A. M. Chapman Publishing, 1906.

Gwynne, S. C. *Empire of the Summer Moon*. New York: Scribner, 2010.

Heizer, Robert F., ed. *The Eighteen Unratified Treaties of 1851–1852 Between the California Indians and the United States Government*. Edited by Robert F. Heizer. Berkeley: Archaeological Research Facility, Department of Anthropology, University of California, 1972.

———. *Reprints of Various Papers on California Archaeology, Ethnology and Indian History*. Berkeley: Archaeological Research Facility, Department of Anthropology, University of California, 1973.

———. *The Destruction of the California Indians: A Collection of Documents from the Period 1847 to 1865*. Santa Barbara: Peregrine Smith, 1974.

———, ed. *Handbook of North American Indians: California*. Vol. 8. Washington, D.C.: Smithsonian Institution, 1978.

——— and Alan F. Almquist, eds. *The Other Californians: Prejudice and Discrimination under Spain, Mexico, and the United States to 1920*. Berkeley: University of California Press, 1977.

——— and Theodora Kroeber, eds. *Ishi the Last Yahi: A Documentary History*. Berkeley: University of California Press, 1979.

——— and M. A. Whipple, eds. *The California Indians: A Source Book*. Berkeley: University of California Press, 1951.

Hill, Dorothy J. *Collection of Maidu Indian Folklore of Northern California*. Durham: Northern California Indian Association, n.d.

———. *The Indians of Chico Rancheria*. Sacramento: State of California Department of Parks, 1978.

Hittel, Theodore H. *History of California*. Vol. 4. San Francisco: N. J. Stone, 1898.

Hoopes, Chad L. *What Makes a Man*. Fresno, CA: Fresno Valley Publishers, 1973.

———. "Redick McKee and the Humboldt Bay Region, 1851–1852." *California Historical Quarterly* 49, no. 3 (September 1970).

Hunt, Aurora. *The Army of the Pacific: Its Operations in California, 1860–1866*. Glendale, CA: Arthur C. Clark Co., 1951.

Hunt, Rockwell. *John Bidwell: Prince of California Pioneers*. Caldwell, ID: Caxton Printers, 1942.

Hurst, Robert C. *Indians: Stories Based Upon Legends and History of the Deer Creek and Mill Creek Tribes in Northern California*. Richardson Springs, CA: Richardson Mineral Springs, n.d.

Hurtado, Albert L. *Indian Survival on the California Frontier*. New Haven: Yale University Press, 1988.

———. *John Sutter: A Life on the California Frontier*. Norman: University of Oklahoma Press, 2006.

Hutchinson, W. H. *Tales from "Old Hutch."* Chico: Association for Northern California Records and Research, 1990.

———. *When Chico Stole the College*. Chico: Quadco Printing, 1992.

"Indians of the Concow Valley, Yankee Hill and Cherokee." Parts 1 and 2. [Yankee Hill Historical Society] *Yankee Hill Dispatch* 4 (October 2011).

"Indian Youth Speak." [California State University, Chico] *Inside Chico State* 42, no. 8 (25 November 2012).

"Ishi May Not Have Been All Yahi, UC Expert Says Tribe's Legendary Last Survivor of Mixed Ancestry." SFGate.com/ArticleCollections.

Jacobs, Margaret D. "Resistance to Rescue: The Indians of Bahapki and Mrs. Annie E. K. Bidwell." *Writing on the Range: Race, Class and Culture in the Women's West*, ed. Elizabeth Jameson and Susan Armitage. Norman: University of Oklahoma Press, 1997.

Johnson, Beulah. "Old Station." *The Covered Wagon*. Riverdale, CA: Riverdale Press, Shasta County Historical Society, 1974.

―――. "The Yahi and the Southern Yana: An Example of Conservation, Genetic Isolation, and an Impoverished Resource Base." *Proceedings of the Society for California Archaeology* 16 (2003).

Johnson, Kenneth M. *The Indians of California*. Los Angeles: Dawson's Book Shop, 1996.

Johnston-Dodds, Kimberly. *Early California Laws and Policies Related to California Indians*. Sacramento: California Research Bureau, 2002.

Jones, Burle L. "Relics of a Lost Tribe." *Overland Monthly* 55, no. 5 (1910).

Jones, David S. "Virgin Soils Revisited." *William and Mary Quarterly* (October 2003). www.historycooperative.org/journals/wm/60.4/ jones.html.

Josephy, Alvin. *The Civil War in the American West*. New York: Alfred Knopf, 1992.

Katz, Bob. "General George Crook." www.desertusa.com/mag99/may1/paper/ctc.

Kelsey, Harry. "The California Indian Treaty Myth." *Southern California Quarterly* 55 (Fall 1973).

Kenny, Robert W. *History and Proposed Settlement Claims of California Indians*. Sacramento: State Printing Office, n.d.

Kerr, Thomas. "An Irishman in the Gold Rush: The Journal of Thomas Kerr." *California Historical Society Quarterly* 8, nos. 1–3 (1929).

Keyes, Erasmus Darwin. *From West Point to California*. Oakland, CA: Biobooks, 1950.

Kibby, Leo. "California, the Civil War, and the Indian Problem: An Account of California's Participation in the Great Conflict. Part II." *The Journal of the West* 4 (1913).

Klement, Frank L. *Dark Lanterns: Secret Political Societies, Conspiracies, and Treason in the Civil War*. Baton Rouge: Louisiana State University Press, 1984.

Kroeber, Alfred L. "Elements of Culture in Native Californians." *The California Indians: A Source Book*, ed. Robert F. Heizer and M. A. Whipple. Berkeley: University of California Press, 1971.

―――. "The Elusive Mill Creeks." *Ishi the Last Yahi: A Documentary History*, ed. Robert F. Heizer and Theodora Kroeber. Berkeley: University of California Press, 1979.

―――. *Handbook of the Indians of California*. New York: Dover Publications, 1925.

Kroeber, Theodora. *Ishi in Two Worlds: A Biography of the Last Wild Indian in North America*. Berkeley: University of California Press, 1976.

―――. *Ishi, the Last of His Tribe*. New York: Bantam, 1974.

Kunitz, Stephen. *Disease and Social Diversity: The European Impact on the Health of Non-Europeans*. Oxford: Oxford University Press, 1994.

Kurtz, Patricia L. *A History of Indian Valley, Plumas County*. Quincy, CA: privately printed, 2010.

Laney, Anita. "Marysville's Methodist Episcopal Church: The Critical Years, 1850–1864." *Sutter County Historical Society News Bulletin* 13, no. 4, (1974).

Laris, Michael. "London Mosquitoes Show Malaria." *Washington Post*, 28 September 2002.

Lewis, E. J. *History of Tehama County, California*. San Francisco: Elliott and Moore, 1880.

Lingenfelter, Ruth. *Leaves of the Past: An Index of Tehama County Pioneers*. Red Bluff, CA: privately printed, 1980.

Lodge, R. C. *Manitoba Essays*. Toronto: Macmillan, 1937.

Lyman, Henry. *The Practical Home Physician: History, Cause, Means of Prevention and Symptoms of All Diseases*. Chicago: George Cline, 1889.

Magliari, Michael F. "Free State Slavery: Bound Indian Labor and Slave Trafficking in California's Sacramento Valley, 1850–1864." *Pacific Historical Review* 81, no. 2 (May 2012).

"Maidu Indians on the Dogtown Ridge." *California* [Dogtown] *Territorial Quarterly* 12 (Fall 1990).

Martial Law in Round Valley, Mendocino, California, the Causes which Led to that Measure, the Evidence, as Brought Out by a Court of Investigation Ordered by Brig. Gen. G. Wright, Commanding U.S. Forces on the Pacific. Ukiah City, CA: Herald Office Printers, 1863.

Mansfield, George C. *History of Butte County, California*. 2nd ed. Berkeley: Howell-North Books, 1973. First published 1918.

Mark, Andy. "1859 Butte Creek White Settler-Indian Conflicts." [Butte County Historical Society] *Diggins* 54, no. 1 (Summer 2010).

Martin, Charles. "The Battle of Eagle Peak: 1862." [Colusi Historical Society] *Wagon Wheels* 50, no. 2 (Fall 2000).

Martin, Oscar F. "Pioneer Sketches—I. The Old Lassen Trail." *Overland Monthly* 25 (July 1888).

Matthews, Chris. "You've Got Malaria." *San Francisco Chronicle*, 18 August 2002.

McCullough, David. "Book Talk." 2011 National Book Festival. CSPAN-2, 25 November 2011.

McDonald, Lois Halliday. *Annie Kennedy Bidwell: An Intimate History of Chico*. Chico: Stansbury Publishing, 2004.

McGie, Joseph. "Fremont Pays a Visit to Butte County." [Butte County Historical Society] *Diggins* 2, no. 1 (1959).

———. "Notes on Butte County Indians." [Butte County Historical Society] *Diggins* 1, no. 1 (1957).

McLeod, Laura J. "Assessment of Fitness to Work: Malaria Risk." www.med.ucalgary.ca/oemweb/malaria.htm.

McMurtry, Larry. "Texas: The Death of the Natives." *New York Review of Books* 53, no. 14 (September 3, 2006).

Melendy, Howard. "Orleans Bar." *California Historical Society Quarterly* 39 (March 1960).

Mendelsohn, Daniel. *The Lost: A Search for Six of Six Million*. New York: Harper Collins, 2006.

Merrill, Asa Fairfield. *Fairfield's Pioneer History of Lassen County to 1870*. San Francisco: H. S. Crocker Co., 1916.

Miller, Joaquin. *Unwritten History: Life Amongst the Modocs*. Hartford: American Publishing Co., 1874.

Miller, Mabel L. "They Called Them Diggers." *Appleton's Popular Science Monthly* 50 (1897).

Nathan, Elroy. "Cohasset Ridge." [Butte County Historical Society] *Diggins* 17 (Spring 1973).

National Institute of Allergy and Infectious Diseases. "Human Immune Resistance to Malaria in Endemic Areas." *NIH Guide* 26, no. 26 (August 15, 1997). RFA AI-97-002. Grants.nih.gov/grants/guide/rfa-files/RFA-AI-97-002.html.

Nopel, John. "The Yana and Yahi Indians of Butte County." [Butte County Historical Society] *Diggins* 3 (Fall 1959).

"Northeastern Maidus." *Plumas County Historical Society Publications* 34 (1969).

Ogle, Beverly Benner. *Spirits of Black Rock*. Paynes Creek, CA: privately printed, 2003.

Osborne, A. J. J. *Granville Doll and the Formative Years of Red Bluff*. Chico: Association for Northern California Historical Research, 1985.

Pancoast, Charles E. *A Quaker Forty-Niner: The Adventures of Charles Edward Pancoast on the American Frontier*. Edited by Anna Paschall Hannum. Philadelphia: University of Pennsylvania Press, 1930.

Parry, C. C. "Rancho Chico." *Overland Monthly* 11 (June 1888).
Pettit, George. *Primitive Education in North America*. Vol. 43, *University of California Publications in American Archaeology and Ethnology, 1946–1956*. Berkeley: University of California Press, 1956.
Phillips, George Harwood. *Indians and Indian Agents: The Origins of the Reservation System in California, 1849–1852*. Norman: University of Oklahoma Press, 1997.
Potts, Marie. *The Northern Maidu*. Happy Camp, CA: Naturgraph, 1977.
Powers, Stephen. "California Indian Characteristics." *Overland Monthly* 14, no. 4 (April 1875).
———. *Tribes of California*. Washington, D.C.: Government Printing Office, 1877.
Quinn, Arthur. *The Rivals: William Gwin, David Broderick, and the Birth of California*. New York: Crown, 1994.
Raphael, Ray and Freeman House. *Humboldt History: Two Peoples, One Place*. Vol. 1. Eureka, CA: Humboldt County Historical Society, 2007.
Rasmussen, Louis J. *California Wagon Lists*. Vol. 1. Colma, CA: San Francisco Historic Records, 1994.
Rathbun, Robert [Coyote Man]. *Coyote Man, The Destruction of the People*. Berkeley: Brother William Press, 1973.
——— and Brother William. *Get the Buzzon or a New World Immigrant's Guide to Dope, Herbs, Indians and Magic Meeting Places*. Berkley: Brother William Press, 1972.
Rawls, James J. "Gold Diggers: Indian Miners in the California Gold Rush." *California Historical Society Quarterly* 55 (1976).
Reed, Anna Morrison. "A Pioneer Mother Who Built Her Own Monument." [Butte County Historical Society] *Diggins* 19 (Winter 1950).
Richards, Leonard L. *The California Gold Rush and the Coming of the Civil War*. New York: Knopf, 2007.
Riddell, Francis A. "Maidu and Koncow." *Handbook of North American Indians: California*, vol. 8, ed. Robert Heizer. Washington, D.C.: Smithsonian Institution, 1978.
Rodman, Paul M. *California Gold: The Beginning of Mining in the Far West, 1846–1890*. Berkeley: University of California Press, 1966.
Ross, Alexander. *The Red River Settlement*. Minneapolis: Ross and Haines, 1957.
Royce, Charles C. *Incidents in the Life of General John Bidwell*. Chico: privately printed, 1906.
———. "Indian Land Cessions in the U.S." *Annual Report of the Bureau of American Ethnology to the Secretary of the Smithsonian Institution*, vol. 18, pt. 2. Washington, D.C.: U.S. Printer's Office, 1895.
Sauber, H. H. "Hi Good and the Mill Creeks." *Overland Monthly* 30 (July-December 1897).
Schlicke, Carl P. *General George Wright: Guardian of the Pacific Coast*. Norman: University of Oklahoma Press, 1988.
Schoonover, Steve. "Who Were the Victims of the Three Knolls?" *California* [Dogtown] *Territorial Quarterly* 16 (Winter 1993).
———. "Putting Ishi's Villages on the Map." *California* [Dogtown] *Territorial Quarterly* 13 (Spring 1993).
———. "The Three Knolls Massacre." *California* [Dogtown] *Territorial Quarterly* 15 (Fall 1993).
———. "Kibbe's Campaign." *California* [Dogtown] *Territorial Quarterly* 20 (Winter 1994).
———. "Captured by the Mill Creek Indians by Mrs. A. Thankful Carson." *California* [Dogtown] *Territorial Quarterly* 22 (Summer 1995).
———. *Before Ishi: The Life and Death of the Yahi*. NorCal Blogs (7 November 2007–17 March 2011).
Schulz, Paul E. *Indians of Lassen Volcanic National Park and Vicinity*. Mineral, CA: Loomis

Museum Association, 1954.
Secrest, William B. *When the Great Spirit Died: The Destruction of the California Indians, 1850–1860*. Sanger, CA: Quill Driver Press/Word Dancer Press, 2003.
Shackley, M. Steven. "Ishi Was Not Necessarily the Last Full-Blooded Yahi." [Archaeological Research Facility, Department of Anthropology, University of California, Berkeley] *Newsletter* 3, no. 2 (Spring, 1973).
Shah, Sonia. *The Fever: How Malaria Has Ruled Mankind for 500,000 Years*. New York: Farrar, Strauss and Giroux, 2011.
Sharp, Irene L. *Sorenson Hill*. Paradise, CA: privately printed, 1972.
Sheridan, P. H. *The Personal Memoirs of P. H. Sheridan*. New York: Charles L. Webster, 1888.
Shipley, William. *The Maidu Indian Myths and Stories of Hanc'ibyjim*. Berkeley: California Heyday Books, 1991.
Shinn, Charles Howard. "The Story of a Great California Estate: Rancho Arroyo Chico, the Home of the Late General John Bidwell." *Country Life in America* 1, no. 3 (January 1902).
Shover, Michele. "The Doctor, the Lawyer, and the Political Chief." *The University Journal*, spec. ed. Chico: California State University, 1982.
— — —. *Blacks in Chico, 1860–1935: Climbing the Slippery Slope*. Chico: Association for Northern California Records and Research, 1991.
— — —. "John Bidwell: A Reconsideration." *Ripples of Chico Creek*. Chico: Penwomen, 1992.
— — —. "Fighting Back: The Chinese Influence on Chico Law and Politics." *Exploring Chico's Past*. Xlibris Books, 2005. Also in *California History* (San Francisco: California State Historical Society, 1995).
— — —. "John Bidwell: Reluctant Indian Fighter, 1852–1856." *California* [Dogtown] *Territorial Quarterly* (December 1998).
— — —. *Vera Clark McKeen of Yankee Hill: Memoir of a Maidu Matriarch*. Chico, CA: privately printed, 1998.
— — —. "The Politics of the 1859 Kibbe Campaign: Northern California Indian-Settler Conflicts of the 1850s." *California* [Dogtown] *Territorial Quarterly* 38 (August 1999).
— — —. "John Bidwell and the Rancho Chico Indian Treaty of 1852." *California* [Dogtown] *Territorial Quarterly* (August 2000).
— — —. "Chico's Confederate Sympathizers v. John Bidwell: Indian War Politics, 1860–1865." *California* [Dogtown] *Territorial Quarterly* (September 2001).
— — —. "John Bidwell's Role in the 1863 Indian Removal from Chico, Part 1." *California* [Dogtown] *Territorial Quarterly* (Spring 2002).
— — —. "John Bidwell's Role in the 1863 Indian Removal from Chico, and Through 1866, Part 2." *California* [Dogtown] *Territorial Quarterly* (Summer 2002).
— — —. "The Round Valley Removal of 1863: A Reconsideration, Part 1." *California* [Dogtown] *Territorial Quarterly* (Winter 2003).
— — —. "The Round Valley Removal of 1863: A Reconsideration, Part 2." *California* [Dogtown] *Territorial Quarterly* (Spring 2004).
— — —. "The Sutherland Boys' Excellent Adventure in Butte County of the 1850s and After." [Butte County Historical Society] *Diggins* (Fall 2004).
— — —. "Bidwell's Earlier Mansion in the First Chico Village." [Butte County Historical Society] *Diggins* (Winter, 2012).
— — — and Thomas Fleming. *Black Life in the Sacramento Valley, 1850–1934*. San Francisco: Max Millard, 1998.
Simmons, William L. "Indian People of California." *Contested Eden: California Before the Gold Rush*, ed. Ramon Guttierez and Richard J. Orsi. San Francisco: California Historical Society and Berkeley: University of California Press, 1998.

Simon, John Y. "Abraham Lincoln and Ann Rutledge." *Journals of the Abraham Lincoln Association* 11, no. 1 (1990).
Smith, Dottie. *The History of the Indians of Shasta County.* Redding, CA: CT Publishing Co., 1995.
Speegle, Mel. "A Trip to Ishi's Cave." *California [Dogtown] Territorial Quarterly* 12 (Winter 1992).
Spencer, D. L. "Notes on the Maidu Indians of Butte County." *Reprints of Various Papers on California Archaeology, Ethnology and Indian History*, ed. Robert F. Heizer. Berkeley: Archaeological Research Facility, Department of Anthropology, University of California, 1973.
Starn, Orin. *Ishi's Brain: In Search of America's Last "Wild" Indian.* New York: W. W. Norton, 2004.
Starr, W. A. "Abraham Dubois Starr." *California Historical Society Quarterly* 27 (September 1948).
Stillman, J. D. B. "Seeking the Golden Fleece." *Overland Monthly* 11 (1873).
"A Story of Robert Allen Anderson." [Butte County Historical Society] *Diggins* 13 (Spring 1969).
Strobridge, William F. *Regulars in the Redwoods: The U.S. Army in Northern California, 1852–1861.* Spokane: Arthur H. Clark, 1994.
Stuart, Granville. *Forty Years on the Frontier.* Edited by Paul C. Phillips. Lincoln: University of Nebraska Press, 1977.
Tailings of Butte Creek Canyon, 1833–1871. Paradise, CA: Centerville Recreation and Historical Association, 1972.
Tehama County Illustrations. San Francisco: Elliott and Moore, 1880.
Thompson, Gerald. *Edward F. Beale and the American West.* Albuquerque: University of New Mexico Press, 1983.
Tishkoff, Sarah. "The Archeology and Genetics of Malaria Resistance." *Daily University Science News* (30 December 2004). unisci.com/stories/20012/0626011.htm.
"The Topographical Reports of Lieutenant George H. Derby." *Quarterly of the California Historical Society* 11, no. 2 (June 1932).
Treco, Donald G. "Captain Augustus Starr." *California [Dogtown] Territorial Quarterly* (Summer 2007).
Ulrich, Laurel Thatcher. *A Midwife's Tale.* New York: Vintage, 1991.
Walsh, Madge Richardson, ed. *The Journal of Pierson Barton Reading. Overland to California.* Chico: Association of Northern California Historical Research, 2008.
Waterman, T. T. "Ishi the Last Yahi." *The Californian Indians: A Source Book*, ed. Robert F. Heizer and M. A. Whipple. Berkeley: University of California Press, 1951.
–––. "The Last Wild Tribe in California." *Reprints of Various Papers on California Archaeology, Ethnology and Indian History*, ed. Robert F. Heizer. Berkeley: Archaeological Research Facility, Department of Anthropology, University of California, 1973. First published by *Popular Science Monthly*, March 1915.
Wells, Harry L. and W. L. Chambers. *History of Butte County, California.* Berkeley: Howell-North Books, 1873.
Wheat, Carl E., ed. "California's Bantam Cock: The Journals of Charles DeLong, 1854–1863." *California Historical Society Quarterly* 9 (Winter 1930).
White, Loring. *Frontier Patrol: The Army and the Indians in Northeastern California, 1861.* Chico: Association for Northern California Records and Research, 1974.
Whiting, John. *Review of The Life and Time of I. F. Stone by D. D. Guttenplan.* www.kpfahistoryinfo/pa/i-f-stone.html.
Wilson, Emma. "John Bidwell." *Here is My Land.* Chico: National League of American Penwomen, Butte County Branch, 1940.

Theses And Unpublished Papers

Bauer, William J. "Agricultural Labor, Race, and Indian Policy on the Round Valley Reservation, 1850–1941." PhD diss., University of Oklahoma, 2003.

Bowman, J. B. *Index of the Spanish-Mexican Private Land Grant Record and Cases in California.* Unpublished Manuscript. Bancroft Library, University of California, Berkeley.

Bowman, Paul. "Maidu Indians on the Dogtown Ridge." *California* [Dogtown] *Territorial Quarterly* 17 (Spring 1994): 12.

Eccleston, Robert. *Diary*, 29 July 1853. University of California, Berkeley, Bancroft Library.

Gabriel, Kathleen. "James Lawrence Keefer, 1820–1901: An Ethnology of a Butte County Pioneer." Master's thesis, California State University, Chico, 1981.

Hislop, Donald Lindsay. "The Nome Lackee Indian Reservation, 1854–1870." Master's thesis, California State University, Chico, 1975.

Howard, Jeannie. Term paper for Mr. Eggers, Red Bluff High School, 27 May 1966. Tehama County Library, Red Bluff, CA.

Hurtado, Albert L. "Ranchos, Gold Mines and Rancheros: A Socioeconomic History of Indians and Whites in Northern California, 1821–1860." PhD diss., University of California, Berkeley, 1981.

Johnston-Dodds, Kimberly. "Bearing Archival Witness To Euro-American Violence Against California Indians, 1847–1866: Decolonizing Northern California Indian Historiography." MPA thesis, Indiana University School of Environmental and Public Affairs, 1999.

Lee, Bertha. Scrapbook. Courtesy of Mary Hanson, Chico, California.

Lyon, Darwin B. Interview, 15 August 1915, Frame 527, reel 199, Ethnological Documents Collection, University of California, Berkeley.

Trussell, Margaret E. "Land Choices by Pioneer Farmers: Western Butte County Through 1877." PhD diss., University of Oregon, 1969.

Wilson, Darryl Babe. "Remove Them Beyond the West: California Gold." PhD diss., University of Arizona, 1997.

Acknowledgments

Archives of government documents, correspondence, diaries and newspapers have made it possible to reconstitute the ideas and practices that shaped northeastern central California's Indian and settler relations in the mid-nineteenth century. For thirty years, former department head Bill Jones, Pam Bush and the late Mary Ellen Bailey guided me through Special Collections, the archives of California State University (hereafter, CSU), Chico's Meriam Library. Their resources include the work product of their late colleague Norris Bleyhl, whose Indian data collection represents scholarship of value to every generation. Present department head George Thompson came through with a successful map search and copied evocative photos. I am particularly grateful to Juliann Clarke who, in her years as the head of Periodicals, eased my access to microfilms. JoAnn Bradley of Interlibrary Loans secured obscure materials from far-flung places. The staff of the California State Library and the State Archives have trundled trolley upon trolley of files and ledgers for me to consider in their commodious and well-lighted rooms. The National Archives in Washington, D.C. and San Bruno came up with Nome Cult Reservation information, as well as land and military records I had not expected to find. Peter Blodgett of the Huntington Library in San Marino led me to gold miner diaries from Butte and Tehama counties.

My colleagues in the Department of Political Science at CSU, Chico never discouraged my turn to political history. Robert Stanley, a legal historian whose Butte Hall office was across from mine, advised me on the earliest version of the treaty negotiation chapters. When anthropologist Dorothy Hill previewed a draft of Chapters One and Two, she told me, "I think you've got it." This validated my sense the rest of the story also must be worth a look. Professor Orin Starn of Duke University, author of *Ishi's Brain,* offered advice on several chapters and encouraged my critique of Theodora Kroeber on the 1859 conflicts. Eric Josephson, a Concow Maidu, helped me with tribal language and identities. Researcher Paul Bowman identified the until-then obscure location of a conflict between rancher John Bidwell and his Indian pursuit party, a subject of Chapter Three. I am in debt to DaVe Veith and David Nopel for a copy of an Indian oral history document from the late John Nopel's archive. David York enhanced old photos. Professor of history Michael Magliari's contribution was his discovery of Bidwell's 1859 legal deposition. Because the analysis here differs from Magliari's, readers of this account would do well to consider his version, in his Indian chapter of *John Bidwell and California: The Life and Writings of a Pioneer, 1841–1900.*

While my findings challenge conventional versions, the late anthropologist Dorothy Hill and the late Ted Meriam, a university trustee, from Chico, were emphatic: each wanted the "real story." After Ted moved near campus in his last years, he walked over to my office several times to comment on one or another of the *California Territorial* articles from which this fuller account evolved. He suggested topics and helped me with "stumpers." The late Larry V. Richardson, whose roots in the area went deep, exchanged letters with me during the initial research years. He provided memories and documents on people, conditions and locations. I gave his correspondence to the Special Collections archive. The late Dr. John Copeland drew on John Bidwell & Co.'s ledger to explain uses for medications Indian subagent James Eddy purchased to treat sick Indians.

Eddy's experiences in Tehama County reached me through research by Ben Hughes, Gene Serr and Mary Lee Grimes. Genealogist Mary Catherine Grobis of Fort Wayne, Indiana, traced the Eddy family's roots. I am in debt to CSU, Chico anthropologists Mark Kowta and Antoinette Martinez, who each waded through a lengthy draft and helped me fine-tune my analysis. Richard Burrill's published data files provided useful details on the Yahi tribe and settlers. Of course, none of these generous contributors is responsible for my errors or oversights.

The *California Territorial Quarterly's* Bill Anderson, who

Acknowledgements

published the early manuscripts as articles, sent each one to historians Robert Chandler and George Stammerjohann, who put me through successive drills and cheered me on. David Freeman's tracking of the 1863 Indian removal was helpful and evocative. Steve Schoonover, author of articles and an invaluable e-book on the Yahi, extricated me from an early research crisis "just in time." By independent avenues of research, he and I have reached common conclusions that classic works on Ishi misconstrued Yahi culture and distorted their role in the 1859 raids on Tehama County farms.

Copy editor Linda Moore provided the initial technical organization that gave the manuscript a cohesive format. Gary Kupp, a veteran *Enterprise Record* copy editor, smoothed the narrative. Rachel Arteaga assembled the illustrations and advised on the legal rules. Copy editor Anne Russell worked with me for three years to fine-tune the manuscript on every level.

Professor emeritus of history G. D. "Don" Lillibridge, my late husband, offered encouragement and professional advice. Educator and friend Ramona Flynn has supported me in my personal and professional life for forty years. Without capable helpers at my home and office, I could not have concentrated on this work. They include Liz Handy, Monica Garcia, Melissa Garcia, Dan Turner, Martin Ayala, Melissa Land and others.

While this subject has consumed decades, another one could not produce a perfect account. Information not available today will tweak the analysis tomorrow. As an example of how data can change, as late as 2010, Steve Schoonover discovered a nineteenth-century scrapbook item with a Yahi account from an 1860s newspaper that is missing from archival microfilms. What else lingers in an attic or a court file? In addition, while this account reflects the ideas and actions on record, from full reports to scraps of memory over generations, some sources may mislead, some are ambiguous, some are thin and some contradict others. In other words, in every author's account of this subject, judgment calls are unavoidable. However, extensive data (often in fragments) have made it possible to compare multiple accounts in the context of other relevant evidence. As a result, descriptions of events have taken into account the alternatives and represent what I conclude most likely happened. As this leaves my custody, what matters is that it is as right as I can make it. Most important, the more consequential the issues addressed here, the greater my confidence.

Finally, with regard to information and photographs, I have made an effort to attribute sources and ownership throughout. While the number of footnotes appears excessive, each one represents payment on my debt to those who made or preserved the records. I will be happy to correct errors and omissions in any later printing or edition.

Appendix A

Treaty At Rancho Chico, 1851

A treaty of peace and friendship, made and concluded near Bidwell's ranch, on Chico creek, between the United States Indian agent, O.M. Wozencraft, of the one part, and the chiefs, captains, and headmen of the following tribes, viz: mi-chop-da, Ho-lo-lu-pi, To-to, Su-nus, Che-no, Bat-si, Yut-duc, and Sim-sa-wa tribes, of the other part.[884]

ARTICLE 1. The several tribes or bands above mentioned do acknowledge the United States to be the sole and absolute sovereign of all the soil and territory ceded to them by a treaty of peace made between them and the republic of Mexico.

ART. 2. The said tribes or bands acknowledge themselves, jointly and severally, under the exclusive jurisdiction, authority, and protection of the United States, and hereby bind themselves hereafter to refrain from the commission of all acts of hostility and aggression towards the government or citizens thereof, and to live on terms of peace and friendship among themselves and with all other Indian tribes, which are now or may come under the protection of the United States; and furthermore, bind themselves to conform to, and be governed by, the laws and regulations of the Indian bureau, made and provided therefore by the Congress of the United States.

ART. 3. To promote the settlement and improvement of said tribes or bands, it is hereby stipulated and agreed that the following district of country, in the State of California, shall be, and is hereby, set apart forever for the sole use and occupancy of the aforesaid tribes and bands, to wit: commencing at a point on Feather River two miles above the town of Hamilton, and extending thence northwesterly to the northeast corner of Neal's grant; thence northwesterly along the boundaries of Neal's, Hensley's and Bidwell's grant, to the northeast corner of the last-named grant; thence northeasterly, six miles; thence southeasterly, parallel with a line extending from the beginning point to the northeast corner of Bidwell's grant to Feather River; and thence down said river to the place of the beginning. *Provided*, That there is reserved to the government of the United States, the right of way over any portion of said territory, and the right to establish and maintain any military post or posts, public building, schoolhouses, houses for agents, teachers, and such others as they may deem necessary for their use or the protection of the Indians. The said tribes or bands, and each of them, hereby engage that they will never claim any other lands within the boundaries of the United States, nor ever disturb the people of the United States in the free use and enjoyment thereof.

ART. 4. To aid the said tribes or bands in their subsistence while removing to and making their settlement upon the said reservation, the United States, in addition to the few presents made them at this council, will furnish them, free of charge, with two hundred head beef cattle, (200) to average in weight five hundred pounds, (500 lbs) seventy-five sacks flour, on hundred pounds (100 lbs.) each, within the term of two years from the date of this treaty.

ART. 5. As early as convenient after the ratification of this treaty by the President and Senate, in consideration of the premises, and with a sincere desire to encourage said tribes in acquiring the arts and habits of civilized life, the United States will also furnish them with the following articles, to be divided among them by the agent, according to their respective needs and wants, during each of the two years succeeding the said ratification, viz: one pair strong pantaloons and one red flannel shirt for each man and boy; one linsey gown for each woman and girl; 2,000 yards calico and 500 yards brown sheeting; 20 pounds Scotch thread and 1,000 needles; 6 dozen thimbles and 2 dozen pairs scissors; 1 2½-point Machinaw blanket for each man and woman over fifteen (15) years of age; 1,000 pounds iron; 100 pounds steel. And in like manner, in the first year, for the *permanent use* of said tribes, and as their joint property, viz: 25 brood mares and one stallion; 100 milch cows and six bulls; four yoke work cattle, with yokes and chains; six work mules or horses; 12 ploughs, assorted sizes; 75 garden or corn hoes; 25 spades; four grindstones.

The stock enumerated above, and the product thereof, and no part or portion thereof, shall be killed, exchanged, sold, or otherwise parted with, without the consent and direction of the agent.

ART. 6. The United States will also employ and settle among said tribes, at or near their towns or settlement, on practical farmer, who shall superintend all agricultural operations, with two assistants, men of practical knowledge and industrious habits, one carpenter, one wheelwright, one blacksmith, one principal schoolteacher, and as many assistant teachers as the President may deem proper, to instruct said tribes in reading, writing, &c., and in the domestic arts upon the manual labor system; all the above-named workmen and teachers to be maintained and paid by the United States for the period of five years, (5) and as long thereafter as the President shall deem advisable.

The United States will also erect suitable schoolhouses, shops, and dwellings for the accommodation of the schoolteachers and mechanics above specified, and for the protection of the public property.

In testimony whereof, the parties have hereunto signed their names and affixed their seals this first day of August, in the year of our Lord one thousand eight hundred and fifty-one.

For and in behalf of the Mi-chop-da,
    LUCK-Y-AN

For and in behalf of the Es-kuin
    MO-LA-YO

For and in behalf of the Ho-lo-lu-pi
    WIS-NUCK

For and in behalf of the To-to

WE-NO KE

For and in behalf of the Su-mus
WA-TEL-LI

For and in behalf of the Che-no
YO-LO-SA

For and in behalf of the Bat-si
YOU-NI-CHI-NO

For and in behalf of the Yut-duc
SO-MIE-LA

For and in behalf of the Sim-sa-wa
PO-MO-KO

Signed, sealed, delivered, after being fully explained, in presence of—

E. H. FITZGERALD,
Brevet Major and Captain First Dragoons.

GEO. STONEMAN,
Lieutenant First Dragoons.

J. BIDWELL.

E. S. LOVELL,
Secretary United States Indian Agency.

Appendix B

Letter from John Bidwell to Joseph McCorkle

Chico 20 December 1851

Dear Mac

I ought to have written to you much earlier,—and indeed it was my intention to have done so—and I have no excuse to plead—but a kind of submission to procrastination, which is the thief of time.

Our own circumstances in California are as you well know by a small experience and observation in very many respects peculiar. There are bands and tribes of Indians on the whole frontiers of the Atlantic States—But here we have not only Indians on our frontiers, but all among us, around us, with us—hardly a farm house—a kitchen without them. And where is the line to be drawn between those who are domesticated and the frontier savages? Nowhere—it cannot be found. Our white population permeates the whole entire State and Indians are with them everywhere. The farmer no sooner settles down than he is surrounded by them with their families; and children will leave the villages alone to cling around his house; and if he be a humane man and treat them always consistently they naturally and voluntarily domesticate themselves. They look up to the white man with a filial obedience to his commands, and expect from him a kind of parental protection. When he wants them to work he tells them to go into his fields—when they want food they invariably come to him—also clothing and whatever their necessities require. And it would be cruel indeed to force these harmless creatures from the places of their ancient habitations. The system pursued by the UStates Govt. towards Indian tribes on the Atlantic side may be adapted to circumstances there—but they must learn that all Indians as well as all frontier territory are not alike—and that the same system will by no means apply here. The nature of our state is such that the Indians cannot be all collected together on one body of land reserved for them—because the valleys are already covered with a white population that cannot be disturbed—the large ones are shingled over with Spanish grants. And these timid and defenseless beings cannot be thrown into the rugged and barren mountains with only here and there a little valley of a few acres, affording not a hundredth part of the grass required for the animals of the miners who traverse and occupy ever nook, glen, corner, and ravine of our almost boundless mountain regions.

The Indian Commissioners have seen so far—that they could not all be placed upon one reserve—and the only thing that surprises me is that men who should have been selected for their practical knowledge of Indian affairs in this country—could see no further—When you begin to lay plans, for removing the entire Indian population to any one body of country the impractability, the injustice to the Indians, the expense, and the impossibility of executing such a law all become too apparent, and forbid it as cruel and impolitic. If you vary the plan,—and make a number of reserves instead of one, the same objections exist with undiminished force, until you increase the number of reserves to as many as there are Indian villages in the State—then you have it exactly right—that is—let the Indians alone—make laws to protect them against the brutal treatment which is so often inflicted upon them—Let them cultivate a garden and have a reasonable quantity of land for pasture just where they live, and work in their vicinity to obtain food and clothing do for whom and where they please—They are sure to cling around and shelter themselves under the protection of him who treats them best. The UStates can enact laws for their protection and appoint an Indian agent to be constantly employed, and always on hand, to be present at the trial and punishment of Indians, when they have been accused of crime, and see that they have justice done them—that punishments are not inflicted in a cruel manner.—Make it a provision of the law that the Ind Agent be notified on all such occasions—In this manner chastisements would have a salutary effect. The Indians would see the reason & justice of it—make the shooting of Indians, which has heretofore been as common as the shooting of wolves, a heavy penalty—and teach the malicious and brutal vagabonds who have shot thousands of these innocent creatures because a horse happened to be missing, or some imaginary offence was committed, thereby destroying all the confidence the poor Indians had reposed in the white man, and thereby exposing the industrious and well disposed miner to dangers and death. If the UStates cannot be persuaded to enact a law to protect and govern the Indians where they now are even in our midst, they should permit our State Govt. to do it, under such restrictions as they may deem wise. In making small reservations of a few acres in the localities of their villages, or adjacent to them, no injustice could be done to anyone, whether he be owner of Mexican or Spanish Grants or not; for every such title contains a provision of their villages. I have to regret that such a provision was not engrafted in the law passed by the last Congress for the settlement of land claims in California. But it is not too late now. I for one intend to donate lands for the Indians in this neighborhood whether Congress makes such provision or not.

You will believe me candid when I tell you that I have no other object in setting forth these views than the real good of the Indians as well as that of the white population. I am a permanent settler—and anything that disturbs the Indians in the neighborhood affects me, more or less—so it is with every citizen all over the State. I do solemnly declare that the action of the Indian Commissioners here in California is an outrage upon the citizens of the State both the old settlers and the new comers, an abuse and an idle perversion of the spirit of the law under which they are acting, a great expense to the Govt. and has and will be productive of no benefit to the Indians, on the contrary its tendency is to injure and degrade them, and to render them pilfering vagabonds—

The Commissioners have been feeding the Indians during the summer on the beef of the Govt. at a time when they need no such assistance—and the very means too which the law promises them to enable them to move to the reserves made for them; and begin to cultivate for themselves—and this too before the Treaties made have been ratified, by the President & Senate, or even an attempt to set them farming.

I must close now for want of time, but I shall address you on various subjects; and shall be very happy to see you have the honor of bringing about many measures that will be for the benefit of the country. I have written this very confusedly and it is now late in the evening.

   I am very truly Yours

   J Bidwell

P.S. Don't fail to send the documents etc. I have not time to write to do it. Gwinn—Please show him this letter if you deem proper.[885]

Appendix C

A Note on Confusion in Accounts

Mixed-up memories challenge analysis and that was the case here in several instances. A case in point is John Bidwell's memoir from the early 1890s, in which he confused the sequence of events in 1862 and 1863. Speaking about 1862, he declared, "The soldiers came here to keep the rebels in check." However, when he spoke of the threat from the foothill farmers (which came up at the 1862 meeting over his store during which the South was the divisive issue), he sought troops, but the military sent no troops to Chico that year. Speaking about 1863, Bidwell said, "Finally I got sick of [local Southerners' harassment]. Brig. Gen. Wright sent two companies of troops up ... and they remained with us until the end of the war."[886] There is no evidence that problems with Southern rebels led to their dispatch to Chico that year. Instead, California Volunteers set up camp near Bidwell's home to protect his Indian workforce from the threats of foothill settlers angry about having no protection against Indian raids.

A possible reason for the confusions is that Indian and Civil war tensions consumed both years. In 1863, Mill Creek raids on outlying Butte County farms were so overwhelming to Northerners and Southerners alike that they took precedence over their Civil War divisions. According to Virginia native John Guill, "everything [about the war] was forgotten save the protection of our wives and little ones from the raids of the Indians."[887]

Like Bidwell, at least one local Southerner also confused events during the same two years. In 1886, farmer John Guill agreed that, in 1862, supporters of the South had labeled Bidwell an Indian slaver. However, when Guill went on to link this with the arrival of troops at Chico to "keep down copperheads" (antiwar Democrats), he got the year wrong.

Standoff

The Bidwell and Guill confusions about when and why soldiers camped at Chico became established as "fact" in the town history that the *Enterprise* published in 1918 as a memoir by Frank Crowder, with contributions from earlier *Butte Record* publisher George Crosette. Both mixed up events in 1862 and 1863, concluding that "the troops were sent here primarily on account of anti-Union sentiment."[888] Frank Crowder was an excellent source because he had observed the Southerners' anger at Bidwell in the 1862 meeting after Hi Good's search party brought in Frankie Hickok's body. Despite his firsthand presence, he was in error decades later about when and why soldiers arrived at Chico. Such confusion is not significant in and of itself, however, in an account such as this one, which intends to sort out the history of a major conflict, details have consequences.

Appendix D

The Kroeber Version

This account presents an alternative view to that of Theodora Kroeber, whose publications on the role of the Yahi's Mill Creeks as the sole raiders on the Sacramento Valley appeared in her mid-twentieth-century publications, *Ishi in Two Worlds* and *Ishi the Last Yahi*,[889] which brought international attention to these local settler-Indian clashes. Even a member of France's version of the Supreme Court made a side trip to visit Ishi's canyon cave. Sometimes called the "last wild Indian," Ishi, probably born in the mid-1850s and one of the last members of the Yahi tribe, appeared in Oroville in 1911, driven out of hiding by starvation. After he was captured, University of California, Berkeley anthropologists Alfred Kroeber (Theodora's husband) and his colleague T. T. Waterman brought him to their campus laboratory where they conducted research and documented extensive interviews with him. He lived at the lab until his death in 1916.[890] T. Kroeber's analysis relied on her husband Alfred Kroeber's and Waterman's findings.

In part, because Ishi asserted to Waterman that his people considered every other tribe their enemy, Waterman and the Kroebers deduced that the Yahi would never have entered into alliances with other Indians or permitted them access to their territory.[891] Therefore, the Kroebers and Waterman concluded that the Yahi were solely responsible for the Sacramento Valley raids out of Deer Creek and Mill Creek canyons in Tehama County through the 1850s and in Butte County in the early 1860s. While Ishi's impressions about his people's attitudes half a century earlier are invaluable, they are counterbalanced by the recorded observations of other observers in the 1850s and 1860s.[892] While the Yahi, like all or most of the Mountain tribes, always had rivals, it does not follow that they alone carried out the ambitious 1859 valley raids. It appears that T. Kroeber and Waterman overlooked significant evidence from 1859 that Mountain Maidu and renegade Indians—under pressure from the invasion of settlers, and miners in particular—had moved into the Yahi's canyons in their search for a safe haven and a new raiding base.

A. Kroeber's theory was that settlers drove the Yahi Mill Creeks off their land "before the year elapsed after the first gold rush"[893] in the later 1840s and that the Mill Creeks launched a defense, but suffered early defeats. In response, he said, "they only hardened their undying spirit of tenacity and love of independence and began a series of vigorous reprisals and for nearly ten years they maintained an unflagging warfare destructive mainly to themselves, but nevertheless an unparalleled stubbornness, with the settlers of Tehama and Butte counties."[894]

Early miners and farmers had no interest in the Yahi's winter canyons that contained no gold and were unsuited to farming. From the late 1840s through the mid-1850s, Yahi raided rival tribes and foothill farms for provisions unavailable in their rugged canyon territory. However, the Tehama County raids the Kroebers focused on were those in the late 1850s. Because the raiders, like earlier ones, escaped into Yahi territory, A. Kroeber deduced that those too must have been only Yahi.

Waterman and the Kroebers overlooked evidence that by 1859, Butte Creeks (Mountain Maidu warriors) and renegade Indians around Lassen Peak participated in operations out of Deer Creek Canyon, no longer the purview of only the Yahi. Chapters Four and Five established that, in 1857, Mountain Maidu and others persuaded or forced the Yahi to share Deer Creek and Mill Creek canyons.

T. Kroeber did not address valley settlers' allegations that Yahi were not solely responsible for the raids. For example, she overlooked evidence (the basis of Chapter Five) that miners in the Sierra Nevada acted as provocateurs who attempted to protect an informal "truce" with the impoverished Mountain Maidu by convincing their Butte Creek raiders to plunder Tehama County farms instead of mining camps. By 1859, settlers there concluded that Indian raiders from Deer Creek canyon now included Butte Creeks. Settler pursuers confirmed these suspicions when a party of violent Mill Creeks they were following turned away from Deer Creek and into Butte County's Mountain Maidu territory. T. Kroeber's analysis dismissed such first person accounts by pursuers, ranchers, mill owners and farmers.

What motive would have led such sources, independent of one another, to discount the Yahi's role and inflate those of other tribes? The observations by these Whites were consistent about Indian raiders' identities, motives and locations. After all, as pursuers moved through the canyons, outnumbered by Indians, their lives depended on their close attention to detail. Their information about Maidu participation in Deer Creek Canyon-based raids influenced Adj. Gen. Kibbe's 1859 campaign for the Mountain Indian removal and shaped the understanding of the press and community leaders in Tehama and Butte counties. Anthropologists Jerald Jay Johnson and Orin Starn have acknowledged the likelihood of multi-tribal raiding parties from the Yahi's canyons on the valley.[895] More recently, Steve Schoonover, an independent researcher with a Yahi focus, has added weight to the premise that the Yahi were not the only participants in Mill Creek raids. While some Yahi likely participated in the 1859 raids, that single tribe lacked the numbers, resources and reach the Kroebers and Waterman later ascribed to them.[896]

While the Kroebers and Waterman based their analysis on the Yahi's isolation, aggression, and, primarily it seems, on Ishi's remark about his people's hatred of all other tribes, cross-tribal rivalry for space and resources embroiled all the area tribes, including the Yahi. While Yahi collaboration with other tribes was limited, there was at least one precedent for their 1859 collaboration. An 1847 petition by Tehama County settlers mentioned rival Yahi and Valley Indians collaborating in raids. According to the settlers, "the Indians of the valley are uniting with those of the mountains which will make their number much greater than it has before."[897]

During that early settlement period, white residents east of the Sacramento River adopted informal Indian nomenclature: they identified Indian groups by their location. Scholars and descendants passed on those geography-based identities into twentieth-century publications which even today—like here—speak of tribelets such as Hat Creeks, Butte Creeks and Mill

Creeks., Although anthropologists soon added formal tribal identities "Yana Yahi" or "Yahi of the Yana" tribe for occupants of Deer Creek and Mill Creek canyons, the terms "Mill Creeks" and "Deer Creeks" were so entrenched in the nineteenth century that the Kroebers and others with incomplete historical understanding continued to use them for any Indians who used those canyons. The anthropologists' thinking, therefore, remained that, since Mill Creek and Deer Creek canyons had for a long time been the territory of the Yahi and their Mill Creek warriors, those who raided out of there in 1859, must still have been solely Yahi.

Waterman, aware of Indian attacks on miners south of Deer Creek Ridge, concluded that Yahi territory extended in that direction as far as Butte Creek. However, those areas were not Yahi territory: they were territory of the countless tribelets that made up what anthropologists would soon call Mountain Maidu, who were not only enemies of the Yahi but also clashed among themselves and with Valley Maidu. Like Waterman, T. Kroeber addressed the Yahi attacks south of Deer Creek Ridge. Unlike Waterman, she recognized that was the territory of Maidu "Tigers," which she surmised was an alternative name for Yahi. To the contrary, according to John Bidwell and his mountain employees in the 1850s, the Tigers, possibly Kimshews or Picas, were actually Mountain Maidu.[898]

T. Kroeber reasoned that the Yahi could readily attack Mountain Maidu further south "because they lived peaceably and accessibly along Concow Creek and the Feather River."[899] In this, she relied on Alfred Kroeber's erroneous assertion that the Yahi "were ... more warlike that their neighbors [the Maidu], who partook of the sluggish and apathetic character so marked among the Indians of California who were, therefore, ill able to withstand the sudden and fierce attacks of the unique but dreaded [Yahi] mountaineers."[900] Lost to both Kroebers and Waterman was the stark distinction between Mountain Maidu, a fearless and aggressive warrior culture, and the markedly more peaceful, although intensely vigilant, Valley Maidu.

The Kroebers and Waterman challenged the observation of researcher Jeremiah Curtin in the 1890s: "Certain Indians lived, or rather lurked around Mill Creek, in wild places east of [the village of] Tehama and north of Chico. These Mill Creek Indians were fugitives, outlaws from various tribes, among others [Yahi] from the Yanas."[901] They disparaged Curtin's sources—turn-of-the-century Whites residing in and around Deer Creek Canyon. One was probably Homer Speegle, who recalled the Mill Creeks were "made up mostly of outlaws from every tribe within a hundred miles, which accounted for them being the only vicious Indians my people [the Speegles] ever knew."[902]

While Waterman acknowledged Curtin's position that "it has always been supposed that remnants of several tribes made up Mill Creek renegades," he held to his own belief that the Yahi raided alone, as did T. Kroeber, who stated that "it seems very unlikely that there was more than one tribe involved."[903] Despite ample evidence to the contrary, T. Kroeber, her mentors and followers long clung to the notion that the Yahi's Mill Creek fighters were a pure and unique group whose violent campaign was an understandable and valiant, though tragic, response to displacement, isolation and desperation.

T. Kroeber considered Mill Creek attacks retribution for Whites' seizure of Yahi territory. However, miners never set up camps in Deer Creek and Mill Creek canyons, instead seizing gold-bearing creeks in Maidu territories. Miners, farmers and peaceful Maidu (Mountain and Valley) were so terrified of canyon-based raiders they would not enter the canyons. T. Kroeber also suggested settlers' descendants who talked with Curtin or published memoirs exaggerated the danger Yahi presented and painted the tribesmen as "evil" in order to vindicate the moral standing of the settlers she called "vigilantes," who made up Indian pursuit parties. T. Kroeber did not accept that settlers' Indian pursuits were often legitimately defensive responses, but instead inferred all pursuers were deranged individuals. As one consequence, by the later twentieth-century, members of pursuit parties, respected in their day as the only effective defenders of settlers, were equated with thugs. While relentless in their pursuit and violence against Indians they considered even potentially dangerous, it does not appear they were deranged.

The situation was more complicated than T. Kroeber presented. When Curtin conducted his interviews, pursuers, such as Frank Crowder, Robert Anderson, Daniel Sutherland and Pleasant Guynn, were still alive to provide first-person accounts. As old men, Crowder and Anderson expressed sympathy for the Mill Creeks and expressed some remorse for their roles. As Anderson stated, "The first act of injustice, the first spilling of blood, must be laid at the white man's door."[904] At the same time, settler descendants remained respectful of the former pursuers as their community's only defense against violent Indians.

In the twentieth century, after T. Kroeber's books became popular, all Indian pursuers of old in Butte and Tehama counties were reviled. While some fitted that description at times, the generalization collapses when set in the full context of that time. While she set out ample grounds for some Indian violence, she neglected to recognize the gravity of losses some settlers experienced or feared that drove them to extreme measures to protect themselves. And, regardless of some warriors' acts, all Indians became venerated victims. In the twenty-first century, a fresh review of the historical record has enabled the discovery of a more complex array of individuals and groups reflecting a broad range of strategies, tactics and moral understandings.

In the end, T. T. Waterman and Alfred and Theodora Kroeber were correct that Mill Creeks raided the Sacramento Valley in 1859, but all three were incorrect when they insisted that from this time into the mid-1860s Mill Creeks were still only Yahi.

Appendix E
Iowa's Sutherland Boys in Butte County Mining Camps, Town Jobs and Indian Pursuits

Author's note: This essay appeared in the fall 2004 *Diggins*, a publication of the Butte County Historical Society. The version here reflects refinements based on later data.

Preface

For close to 35 years, as I worked at reconstructing aspects of Butte County's past, I considered it an advantage to be an outsider. However, nineteen years after I moved to Chico, I discovered that members of my own family were among the earliest visitors and residents in areas I had made the focus of my work.

I first found out about my historical connection in July 1987 in Monticello, Iowa. As I began to leave the Masonic memorial service for my father, Myric Shover, a woman introduced herself as Judith Sutherland Pahnke, a distant cousin and a California resident. She explained briefly then, and more fully a few days later, that we both descended from John and Margaret Sutherland, our generation's great-great-grandparents. I was already aware that my grandmother, Olive Shover, had been proud of her father's family, the Sutherlands, because they were among the founders of Scotch Grove, a tiny farm village in Iowa Territory. My sister, Connie, decorates Sutherland graves at the cemetery there each Memorial Day.

Judith explained she had spotted my Chico residence in my father's obituary. She told me that four sons of John and Margaret Sutherland had participated in the California Gold Rush. Their only sister was my ancestor Catherine Sutherland Moses — the brothers were my grandmother's great-uncles. Judith told me that two of the young men, Roderick and Daniel, had stayed in Butte County and are buried in the Chico Cemetery. Startled and intrigued, I assured her that I would watch for information about them.

Deep in my research on the Chico Chinese at that time, I copied Sutherland items I spotted in newspapers or letters for Judith and myself. As I explained in the preface, I eventually identified issues concerning Indian-settler relations that intrigued me. After about ten years of research, I prepared an article series for the California Territorial Quarterly.

By mid-2003, I had come upon enough information about Daniel Sutherland and his brothers that a reasonably full picture of their years in Butte County emerged. His brother Roderick's work as a supplier to miners ended with his death in 1861. Along the way, I also followed two other brothers who moved among the gold camps with stops in Chico. Sources also told of the Sutherlands' encounters with Indians, other settlers and game. Typical of family histories, I cannot guarantee the accuracy of mine. Therefore, I have used the information that makes sense in terms of the place and times, according to other contemporary accounts, and have omitted parts that failed this test.

As bachelors, the Sutherland men were examples of the most common type of California settler in the decade after 1849. John, David, Daniel and Roderick arrived in Butte County already steeled by their upbringing in two other frontiers. They moved through the Sierra Nevada, the Cascades and the Coast Range with ease, making stops in small hamlets and choosing Chico as their base when winters shut down gold mining. Of particular interest to modern readers is Daniel's participation in settler pursuit parties, a controversial issue that raised doubts about the character of Indian fighters. This narrative sets out the Sutherlands' Indian experiences before their California years and then focuses on Daniel's experiences in Indian fighting, gold mining and local frontier life in California.

Information was gleaned from Butte County's press, government records, memoirs and letters. Also valuable were Sutherland family genealogical reports and memories that John and David Sutherland's children recorded in family scrapbooks.

Reared on Two Frontiers: British Canada and Iowa Territory

Daniel Sutherland, a son of the Ontario frontier and Iowa Territory, became a Butte County sharpshooter whose name surfaced in accounts of settler conflicts with Indians. For example, Adj. General William Kibbe's 1859 campaign to remove Mountain Indians from Butte and Tehama counties listed Sutherland as a militia volunteer. In 1865, he was a member of the pursuit party assembled by Indian fighters Robert Anderson and Harmon "Hi" Good, which avenged the Workman place murders (see Chapter Twelve). While Anderson mentioned Daniel's role, Simeon Moak added more detail. After the Civil War, Sandy Young, John Bidwell's chief vaquero who later killed Good's murderer, became Daniel's gold mining partner and close friend.

It is not hard to understand why such men would regard Daniel as one of their own. In contrast to the lawyers, shopkeepers, doctors and farmers who quickly traded gold mining for their old professions and trades, he thrived in the California wilderness and sought it out for the rest of his life. While Daniel at times made his living as a wainwright in and around Chico, he always kept a place deep in the woods. Since Daniel was the only brother who lived out his life in Butte County, he is the primary subject here.

The "British Canada" Frontier

The Sutherland family became residents of Fort Garry in what their son Daniel called "British Canada," well before Winnipeg grew around it. The future California sojourner's father was John Sutherland, a Highlander Scot employee of Thomas Douglas, the Scottish Earl of Selkirk. Lord Selkirk headed the Hudson's Bay Company, for which he purchased what was later the province of Manitoba and northern sections of the later states of Minnesota and North Dakota. Lord Selkirk's workers in that heavily French area of Canada principally included burly Scottish clansmen, whom the Duke of Sutherland—no modern relation to our humble subjects—had forced off their ancient lands around the village of Kildonan. In 1812, Lord Selkirk moved John Sutherland and many other Kildonan men to Canada.

The following year, when John worked as a trapper in the great Canadian forests, Lord Selkirk sent a second ship to bring his men's families to join them. John's father—also named John—died of cholera just as the ship arrived at Fort Churchill, Manitoba, on Hudson's Bay. John's mother, Katherine Grant Sutherland, and other family members portaged and canoed for a grueling eight hundreds from the coast to Fort Garry, Ontario, where they reunited with Katherine's son John.

When Daniel was born in 1827, he was the middle son of John Sutherland Jr. and his wife, Margaret Macbeth Sutherland. They lived in a community of about two thousand people whose farmsteads lined the banks of the Red and Assiniboine rivers. Because 80 percent of this population were Indians, some native to British-held areas and a large number French-Indian, the four Sutherland boys grew up among Indians. The Sutherlands and other colonists survived a particularly severe Canadian winter by their temporary move to Pembina, near the border with the United States. Indians there shared food with them through the worst of the season. The boys developed sturdy physiques from swimming, skating and boxing with Crees and Chippewas, tribes friendly and helpful to the Selkirk settlers. However, Bois-Brûlés, Indian descendants of French trappers and an offshoot of the Dakotas, were employed by the rival North West Company to destroy the Hudson's Bay Company and were responsible for many deaths within the Selkirk community.

In the Hudson's Bay clashes with the North West Company, the Sutherland family displayed a staunch loyalty to Selkirk. When North West agent Cuthbert Grant, an educated Indian, pressed Daniel's grandmother, Katherine Sutherland, to move her family to another province, she snapped: "As for me and mine, we will keep faith. We have eaten Selkirk's bread, we dwell on lands he bought. We stay here as long as he wishes and if we perish, we perish."[905] In 1816, when Grant led the Bois-Brûlés against the Selkirk colony, which left many residents homeless, he offered the Sutherlands food. Again, the widow lashed out at him: "I cannot curse you, Cuthbert Grant, for I am a Christian woman, and if you came to me hungry I would feed you, for so Christ bade us do to our enemies. But he never commanded that we should take food from our enemies—so I throw your charity in your face."[906]

When Lord Selkirk left for England after an 1817 visit, his departure "was marked by a feast, at which the Indians wore their brightest blankets ... the officers their swords and plumes." Highlanders present in proud array were "McKays and Sutherlands and Farquharsons in their green kilts, Mathesons and McLeans in their red tartans swinging to the skirl of the pipes."[907]

Natural crises such as drought, a one hundred-year flood and grasshopper plagues regularly tested the Sutherlands and their neighbors. Along the way, the Indians taught them how to use local flora and fauna and hunt buffalo to carry them through long, harsh winters. By the 1820s, the Sutherland men were "good hunters; they could kill the buffalo; walk on snowshoes; had trains of dogs trimmed with ribbons, bells and feathers, in true Indian style and in other respects were making rapid steps in the arts of savage life."[908]

Assimilating skills and attitudes the sons would later apply in California, the Sutherlands held a generally positive view of Indians. At Fort Garry, "the Scotch were convinced, that when not influenced or roused by bad counsel, or urged on to mischief by designing men, [the Indians'] natural disposition ... is humble, benevolent, kind and sociable."[909]

The lessons of the Sutherlands' own experiences in Scotland probably influenced how the family treated Indians. In the parents' own lifetimes, the Scottish nobility had appropriated their land, so how could they not recognize the moral injustice of appropriating Indian land? When the sons' grandfather and others made respectful entreaties to remain on their ancient Scottish holdings, the Duke of Sutherland's representative replied: "You are an insolent lot for all your meekness of mouth. I will have no more dallyings with you. Tell your people to clear themselves, their children, and their chattels from my holdings and at once."[910]

At Fort Garry, the colonists lived off the land, five hundred miles from the nearest market, and depended on a bartering system. Two decades after the Sutherlands left for Iowa, Fort

Garry was still "a spot ... which travelers do not visit and from which civilization seems in a measure shut out.... No railroads or steamers, or telegraph wires, or lines of stages make their way thither: to reach it, or once there to escape from it, is an exploit of which one may almost boast.... Almost every man is his own carpenter, house builder, wheelwright, blacksmith and all are either small farmers or hunters."[911] Despite the hardships, the families developed farms and sent their children to school. John's and Margaret's sons, John and Daniel, have left letters in which each set down his thoughts clearly in well phrased sentences.

Iowa Bound

In 1835, at Fort Garry, John Sutherland Sr. took interest in reports about the Blackhawk Purchase west of the Mississippi River. Farming prospects looked good there and the weather was said to be milder than in Ontario. The Sac and Fox Indians' treaties with the American government had opened the area to settlement. In 1837, the family and their friends decided to leave the Selkirk settlement for western Wisconsin Territory—soon to be Iowa Territory. John Sr. was a church elder and a leader of the Selkirk dissidents who wanted to establish a Presbyterian-based community free of Anglican dominance.

The journey took place when John Jr. was 19 and Daniel 9— old enough to remember the open stretches of the Red River Trail. With help from Chippewas, but wary of the Sioux, the Selkirk party plodded south into North Dakota and crossed Minnesota to the Mississippi River. Like other members of the company, the Sutherlands walked alongside oxen-drawn wagons like those of Canada's French immigrants. Daniel, later a Chico wagon builder, and his brothers rarely rode in the heavy, square boxes with deep sides between two huge wooden wheels, which were easy to repair or replace along the way.[912] As the wagon train rumbled across the prairie, the wheels' penetrating screech could be heard far away.

During the journey, John and David were old enough to share the watch for North Dakota Sioux, who objected to settler encroachment. Although the Indians relaxed once the travelers explained their plan to continue south, they still stole the party's cattle. When the party's leaders met with the Sioux headmen, the Indians insisted that "the White Father" in Minnesota would reimburse their party for the thefts. Although the Selkirk party was skeptical, the Indians' information proved correct.[913]

Following the Mississippi south, the Selkirk party turned inland at Dubuque in western Wisconsin Territory and continued about fifty miles inland to what would become Jones County, Iowa. With winter's approach, the new arrivals reached the present site of Scotch Grove, a farm village. They built an expansive log building for all the families as they waited for spring. As in Canada, game was so abundant that it seemed inexhaustible. John Sr. spoke of killing three deer before breakfast, while his wife told of finding thirty or more prairie chickens in her trap. Their son Adam would recall seeing herds of thirty to forty deer and elk on their farm. Reflecting this wealth of food, in California, Daniel and his brothers would regard game as alternately a meal or target practice.

Years of hard labor proved necessary before fully functioning farms could support large families in Iowa, which became a territory the year after the Sutherlands arrived. Therefore, for a decade or so, John Sr. and his older sons periodically left for Illinois, where they reaped wheat and worked in the Galena lead mines. While they were away, in about 1840, when Daniel and Roderick were still boys, their mother, Margaret, had to manage her family and the farm's operations on her own. One day, as she hung cuts of meat to dry outside their log house, she noticed the approach of a ragged group of Indians whom the American treaty had impoverished in bountiful Iowa. While most settlers there dismissed the Indians as pests and thieves, Margaret's experiences in Canada had made her sympathetic to their plight. When she saw the starving Indians' eyes fixed on the meat, she gave them all of it.[914]

As pay for one of their jobs in Illinois, John Sr. and his sons acquired a herd of pigs they managed to drive along a timber-lined trail for sixty miles from the Mississippi River to Scotch Grove, where they released them into the woods, after which men hunted generations of wild hogs for years.[915] Such grueling effort and resourcefulness gradually enabled John Sr. to buy land. With this, he made another commitment. He travelled to the Jones County district court in the hamlet the Scots named Edinburgh. There, he waived his allegiance to Queen Victoria in order to become a naturalized American citizen. The Sutherlands still lived and spoke like Scots, but now they were Americans.[916]

Tough and Scrappy

From Illinois, eldest son John Jr. and David caught ships down the Mississippi River, traveling as far as Louisiana, working any jobs they could find. One night, when John fell overboard, he managed to swim a mile or more across the giant river toward the glimmer of a candle on shore. From their ship, docked at river wharfs, they could hear men's challenges to fight and happily joined in the slugfests whenever possible. Some of their experiences were unique. One of the more "Bunyanesque" of these took place while John Jr. worked at a Louisiana sugar mill. His employer shot an alligator but it continued charging his terrified workers, so John grabbed a long board and rammed it through its wide-open jaws and down its throat. Before John let go of the board, the alligator shook its head hard, throwing John, who was six feet tall and weighed more than two hundred pounds, "end over end." According to the family, John, although shaken, sprung up, grabbed a rifle and shot the alligator dead. David and John were still travelling for work when their younger siblings were in their mid-to-late teens. Daniel, once in his early twenties, was old enough to share some of these journeys. Daniel and Roderick certainly modeled themselves on their older brothers.[917]

California Calls

Iowans dreamed of owning land and building farms, however, affordable land had become expensive by 1849. Therefore, the Sutherland sons and their neighbors were excited when word of the California Gold Rush reached the plains. Travel to California presented no problem for the hardy lot. John Jr., 31, and Roderick, 20, were the first to go.[918] With their friends William McIntire and Martin Dreibelbis, they built their own "prairie schooner," and drove it away from Scotch Grove behind eighteen yoked oxen. They completed their outfitting in Omaha, Nebraska, where they joined fifty wagons of the Wisconsin and Iowa Union Company that left Council Bluffs, Iowa, on May 23, 1849. The Sutherlands later discovered that the heavily traveled trail they used became the route for the Union Pacific and Southern Pacific railroads. Although Roderick became ill and some died along the trail already marked by graves, the wagon train encountered no hostile Indians. More worrisome was the possibility of stampedes by vast buffalo herds, one of which covered six square miles. David later remembered nailing small trees to the undersides of the wagons, creating rafts they floated across the Platte and other rivers.[919]

A New Life in California

John Jr. and Roderick reached the Feather River in early fall 1849 and immediately set to mining. They sent home glowing reports of gold mining in the Sierra Nevada, enticing their brothers David, 26, and Daniel, 23, to leave for California with their neighbor Lewis Dreibelbis in April 1850. At least until they reached Laramie, Wyoming, their wagon train traveled along a trail that Dreibelbis described to his wife, Mary, as "a road like your dooryard."[920]

David cooked and Lewis handled the reins. In Wyoming, they saw thousands of buffaloes—stupid, but dangerous, according to the men. In their unpredictable stampedes, they stopped for nothing, even trampling one another. When the company spotted a herd headed their way at 10 p.m., men shot four to turn them. A group from that herd sank into mire, becoming totally helpless. While Daniel shot one, Lewis could not bring himself to do the same, leaving them alive to die in the mire. Men would ride out from the train to shoot buffaloes just to break the boredom. Some, according to Lewis, would cut out one slab of flesh for meat and leave the rest. He also described how Daniel, bored, would head out from the party to take shots at the big, lumbering beasts. Decades later, the Sutherland family in Iowa would remember "Uncle Dan" as "a fine rifleman and a great hunter."[921] The two brothers arrived in California and were soon mining with their two older brothers.

When snows shut down the mining camps, the brothers looked for work in the milder Sacramento Valley. Ranch owners were always shorthanded because the low wages they offered did not appeal to the thousands of miners, like the Sutherlands, who dreamed of striking it rich in the gold mines.

Like other early arrivals, the Sutherlands' gold mining efforts were successful: all four made more than $25,000 (whether each or together is not clear) during the first year. David found a single gold nugget worth $375, then a handsome sum. As thrifty men, the cost of living in the camps was a chief concern. After they had to pay $1 for one egg, David and Roderick started a business using burros to carry provisions to the mining camps. Then, according to David's daughter, Leila Sutherland, "A man offered to stake my father who was a blacksmith for material to make miners picks if he would make them and divide the proceeds equally."[922] Since David was living in Chico Township by 1852, that man was likely John Bidwell, a miner himself and vendor to miners. (At least no records of other local men who traded on such a scale have come to this researcher's attention.) David made eighteen to twenty pickaxes a day, which sold for $16 apiece. Previous to this, a Sacramento vendor sold Bidwell the pickaxes.[923]

On Sept. 3, 1851, David, Roderick and a Scotch Grove companion rode to Duncan Neil's ranch south of Rancho Chico. There, they joined twenty-eight voters who gave the Whig candidate, Pierson B. Reading, their unanimous vote for governor of California. Talk that day was about the federal Indian treaty meeting just concluded at Bidwell's place up the Oroville-Shasta trail. Their candidate lost the election, but the Sutherlands kept remarkable company that day. Although a sparsely populated precinct, the voters at Neil's place included ranchers Bidwell, Peter Lassen and Justice of the Peace Thomas Wright. Recording their votes was Amos Frye, Bidwell's clerk, who would be killed in a battle between Mountain Maidu and Bidwell's rancho workers—Whites and Mechoopdas—the following July 2.[924]

In 1852, while their eldest brother, John, mined in Klamath County, David and Roderick were at a Feather River mining site when they suddenly recognized Mexican bandit Joaquin Murieta.[925] Their recollection is consistent with the memories of

Butte County judge Charles Lott and others who recalled that Murieta and his companions stole from and murdered area miners in the vicinity of Long's Bar and Bidwell's Bar. While later local historians doubted such reports, David's sighting was first-hand. According to his son Thomas, "Father and Uncle Roderick were digging a test hole when they saw the bandit approaching. Knowing of his revengeful spirit toward all miners, they got their rifles ready. Murieta saw them and rode on. When he had gone about 11 yards up the trail, they heard a yell. He had lassoed a negro and was dragging him behind his galloping horse. They fired two shots after him but he escaped, leaving behind him the battered body of the dead Negro."[926]

In-between mining, David worked as a blacksmith at Bidwell's Rancho Chico. Roderick, plagued by the illness he contracted on the journey to California and unable to endure the arduous labor and frigid creek water that were integral to mining, decided to become a farmer.[927] With the miners' needs in mind, he began to raise sheep and developed a row crop farm north of Mud Creek in Rock Creek Township in the early 1850s. Sheep raising had been important to the communities his family and friends built in Canada and then in Iowa, where some were still raising sheep and cattle.

While David most often told his family about the Feather River, the brothers' center of operations, he and Roderick also followed eldest brother John Jr. to the Salmon River in the rugged inner canyons of Klamath (later Humboldt) County. There, David packed in merchandise to sell to miners. He gave up on Klamath County, however, although Daniel would later give it a try.[928] Of the brothers, John travelled the most. After a spell in the Klamath River area in 1852, he worked his way north to Oregon's Columbia River.[929]

On a Sierra Nevada mining excursion, its location unidentified in family stories, David found himself in a situation where relations between miners and Indians were troubled. He happened upon a frightened lone Indian boy who had a fresh snake bite. He calmed the boy with a generous portion of whiskey. Then, he made a cut over the bite and sucked out the poison (a method now known not to work). The boy remained in David's camp until he recovered and returned to his people. To David's

Standoff

surprise, the young fellow reappeared one night. Acting on his people's ethic of reciprocation in kind for good (and bad) acts, the boy warned David of his elders' plan to ambush the camp.[930] Forewarned, David and his companions attacked first.

In another incident, Indians launched a surprise raid on John and other miners. Running just ahead of their assailants' arrows, the men barricaded themselves in a log building, where they stayed until the approach of an army unit frightened off the Indians. Later, the family recalled that the soldiers' officer was William T. Sherman, who became a Union army general. However, the family may have confused the future General Sherman with P. H. Sheridan, the lieutenant, then stationed at Fort Reading, who also became a general. Sheridan's memoir mentioned a sortie to Mount Lassen right after his 1855 arrival when the Pit River Indians "were very hostile."[931] However, Sheridan did not mention an incident when his approach frightened off Indians and freed miners from their cabin-fort. (The name confusion is characteristic of the Sutherland boys' ancillary descendants, one of whom named a baby William Bradford Moses after William Bradford when their actual ancestor was William Brewster.)

In the winter of 1855–1856, John, David and Daniel built sluice boxes they sold to Butte County miners. John would recall the exacting work of using their 8" augur to drill a hole straight through each thick log. Although this was lucrative work, it held no long-term attraction for any of them.[932]

When spring arrived, John and David each still had about $2,00 and decided to go home and buy Iowa farms. This time, they could afford ship passages from San Francisco to Panama, where they crossed the isthmus on foot., Then they sailed to New York where they boarded a train for Iowa. Although they arrived at Scotch Grove ready to settle down, they learned others had bought up the land they wanted. David, pondering a return to Butte County, sent an inquiry to Daniel, at the mouth of the Salmon River in Klamath, about purchasing Roderick's Chico farm for $1,000. Roderick agreed, but suggested David not send his money to California "as he had no particular use for it."[933] When David found both the right farm and a wife in Iowa, he changed his mind and commenced to rear a large family near Scotch Grove.

John did not find the Iowa farm he wanted so helped his sister Kate's husband, Charles Moses, build a large barn. When Moses suddenly died in 1860, John stayed on to help Kate, now a young widow with three children, manage her farm and pay off the family's debts. When the Civil War began he enlisted in the Iowa Volunteer Infantry and headed for battles in Arkansas.[934]

Meanwhile, in Butte County during the second half of the 1850s, Roderick worked on his Mud Creek farm, from which his partner ran supply trains to the mining camps. Daniel had developed a good reputation for his wagon building, but mining remained his first priority. Just as he had done on the long wagon train days en route to California, Daniel passed the time shooting his pistol at animals who wandered into view; one evening after dinner, he killed three foxes. In December 1856, from Orleans Bar on the Salmon River, he wrote David a lonely sounding letter, complaining about Klamath County's harsh winters and gossiping about miners and vendors they both knew. Such conditions made Iowa farming more appealing. Earlier that year, after David wrote Daniel about the prosperity that he and John found when they returned home to "the Grove," Daniel was tempted to leave. However, in subsequent letters, David wrote him that he was becoming discouraged about financial strains, so Daniel decided to stay in California "a while longer."[935]

Daniel Enlists in Adj. General Kibbe's River Expedition

By the end of the 1850s, Daniel had moved to Chico Township, where he shared winter quarters with miner John Latham, an Ohio man.[936] This was a time when Indian and settler hostilities ranged from eastern Tehama County through northeastern Butte County. The violence reached such proportions that, in 1859, settlers demanded that Governor Weller back a party of local Indian fighters. Unwilling to trust private pursuers, he dispatched Kibbe, commanding officer of the State Militia to Tehama County. There, Kibbe launched a campaign to collect the area's Mountain Indians for removal to reservations.[937]

Kibbe selected local men familiar with the remote canyons'

Standoff

terrain and experienced in conflicts with violent Indians. Kibbe signed up several men, including Daniel Sutherland, who had recently participated in another pursuit party. Kibbe assigned Daniel to the company of Capt. William Burns, a tall, blue-eyed "California Ranger" with many "shot marks" on his body, who had been Murieta's partner in monte games.[938]

More typical than the unit's assaults was their experience in Hat Creek country. According to one of Daniel's compatriots, "One of the darkest nights ... found us on the summit of one of the highest mountains in that region. The rain came down in torrents so intense that we were obliged to hold on to the trees under which we crouched for shelter to prevent being carried off by the sudden gusts of the tornado which then existed; our sole anxiety being wrapt in the one great object of keeping our arms dry, and by doing so secure our safety in the contemplated conflict with the enemy. Having only one blanket each, yet we could not restrain the cravings of nature—morpheus enfolded us damply in his embraces, and spread such lucid imaginings in my half slumbering brain that my only great reluctance in awaking was why fate did not allow me still to slumber on.... In the morning we held a consultation and resolved to find the Indians, return home, or starve. Being out of provisions, and forty miles from headquarters ... we anticipat[ed] our success to regale luxuriantly upon a hearty meal of acorns. [Eventually we found] in a sequestered nook to our great joy the rancheria we were in quest of. We were twenty-six in number and forming a circle, we advanced so carefully that the Indians were not aware of our approach until within fifty feet of their wigwams. A rush to the doors—a piercing shriek from some of the squaws—papooses screaming, while the bucks lay passive on the floor, were all that I observed, and in two minutes they were all our prisoners. Not one was hurt, but all were frightened, and satisfying ourselves of our success we pitched into the acorns. The Indians were sixty in number, male and female, and in less than an hour we were all en route for head quarters, where we arrived two days after, much debilitated."[939]

Most engaging to the unit's men was the game they hunted along their way: bears, antelopes and "panthers" (probably mountain lions). According to Sutherland family lore, Daniel was a dedicated bear stalker. His nephew, who was enthralled by the figure of his uncle on the frontier, elevated Daniel to family mythology with the claim that he killed more bears than any white man or Indian in California. While that is a claim no one could validate, a fellow member of Burns' unit recalled that, as far as talk about extermination was concerned, game "suffered more extensively than the Indians."[940] Burns' men killed so many animals that the member who wrote about it was somewhat defensive. He argued vaguely that the hunters somehow "saved the State expense" and acknowledged that it was "a source of luxury to all who participated."[941]

Newspaper coverage and the state's pay records confirm that Capt. Burns' Chico volunteers were in the field for a considerable length of time. According to the state's voucher, made out to "D. Sunderland & Co.," the volunteers received $670.63 for their pay and expenses.[942]

The misspelling of Daniel's name on the 1859 pay voucher brings up another aspect of his experience in Butte County. Reared among first-generation Scottish immigrants, he evidently spoke with a characteristic burr that confused listeners. Through the 1850s, the family commonly spelled their last name as Southerland. However, in early Butte County records, Daniel also appeared as Sutherlin, Southern, and, as above, Sunderland. The latter version probably confused his last name with that of another Chico member of the 1859 Indian collection party, Hank Sunderlin. Daniel's first name also varied. The Scotts pronounce Daniel as Duh *neal'*, with the accent on the last syllable. That was why some called him Neil, including the 1860 census taker and pursuit party companions Simeon Moak and his brother Jake. As late as 1881, Daniel appeared on a legal record as Southerland. However, by the mid-1860s, the Sutherland spelling had prevailed, and, after so many years away from his people had anglicized Daniel's speech, Neil had become the Americanized Daniel. After 1866, he most often appeared on records as "Dan Sutherland."[943]

Roderick, the Chico Township Farmer

Because Daniel's brother Roderick lived north of Chico on

Mud Creek, he traded at James Keefer's store. However, on occasional trips to Chico, he stopped at John Bidwell & Co. where, in 1860, he bought a blacksnake whip at one stop and, on another, a cinch or strap for his saddle. Presumably, he and Daniel visited back and forth. Roderick was not alone on his farm. Peter Moulder, who had no financial investment in the farm, also stayed there, and may have been the partner who conducted Roderick's pack trains to the mines. Farmhand Lloyd Clerds also lived at Roderick's place. Roderick built up his operation through the mid-to-late 1850s, so that by 1860, its tax value was $1,000. His personal property—probably livestock—was worth about $2,400.[944]

Despite his entrepreneurial spirit and achievements, Roderick's health continued to falter. He died on March 9, 1861, at the age of 32. Daniel's last service to his younger brother—his only remaining family member in California—was to provide a simple but handsome Vermont marble tombstone on which Roderick's name and death date appear in the Chico Cemetery. Daniel also bought the plot next to Roderick for himself. As Daniel wound up his brother's affairs, he sold Roderick's herds and sent their father the proceeds in one hundred dollar bills. Old John Sr., still a pillar of Scotch Grove as an elder in the Presbyterian Church, referred to this cash as "my money, with the one and the two 0's."[945] The family did not forget Roderick. His younger brother Robert named his son Roderick. This namesake would serve two terms in the United States Congress from the Fifth District of Nebraska.

Daniel and the Civil War as the Settler-Indian War Continued

In 1862, a Mill Creek party killed three of the Hickok children in retaliation for the lynching of five Indian men by miners on Butte Creek (who had retaliated for Indian offenses against miners). Daniel signed a petition seeking state funds for a party of pursuit volunteers under the direction of experienced tracker Hi Good. Bidwell carried this petition to the governor; however, word reached Chico, while the pursuit party was camped in the

Appendicies

mountains, that the state would not help. Although there is no evidence who made up most of this party, Daniel's signature on the petition and his experience in Kibbe's campaign suggest he participated.[946]

Daniel's name does not appear as a pursuit party member between 1860 and 1864 in the few surviving, fragmented accounts. Through the 1860s, he worked as a Chico wheelwright and wagon builder. According to his family, he was a master builder of "overshot" wheels. When a branch of the Odd Fellows organization started up in Chico in June 1863, Daniel was a founding member and became an officer.[947]

Although the Civil War was under way, Daniel, like most California men, did not join the Army. However, both of his younger brothers, Thomas and Morrison, fought at Pea Ridge, Arkansas, where the former died from an exploding shell. Morrison died a few years later from his wounds. Another brother, Adam, a teacher who had been one of the first white children born in Dakota Territory as the family traveled to Iowa, served as a nurse and regimental clerk with the Ninth Iowa Volunteer Infantry.

John Jr., the former Butte County gold miner, began the war with his younger brothers' unit. He, was wounded at Pea Ridge, Arkansas, where half his company was killed. As part of Gen. Sherman's army, John and Adam crossed into the South where John received a battlefield promotion from sergeant to first lieutenant. He managed to get off a letter to David, at home in "the Grove," just before he was shot in the back by friendly fire during the attack at Lookout Mountain on Nov. 24, 1863. After the Gold Rush and the war, John lost his appetite for adventure. Like David in the 1850s, he returned to Scotch Grove, where he bought a farm on which he and his new wife reared a large family and he succeeded his father as a Presbyterian Church trustee.[948]

In support of the Union cause to which his brothers had given so much, Daniel joined the Chico Light Infantry on Nov. 28, 1863. Although these militias had no official duties, Charlie Stilson's diary suggests that participation in the Chico unit provided special satisfaction to village men like himself and Daniel, whose brothers suffered and died in battles. Although the militia only drilled and paraded, Stilson's diary verifies that Union supporters found its activities a satisfying irritant to northern Butte County's Southerners. Although 36, Daniel was still a private when the Chico militia turned in its equipment and uniforms in 1866.[949] Fellow militia members would show up later in Daniel's life.

The Workman Place Murders

Although Daniel had a place in Chico where he worked in the wheel and wagon trades, he also kept a cabin in eastern Butte County, about sixteen miles from Oroville near Nelson Bar Hill, a mining location between the west branch and north fork of the Feather River. (The area is now under Lake Oroville.) Residents then considered this part of Concow Valley. During August 1865, Daniel was away from his cabin when a band of about nine Indians from various tribes traveled south along a ridge to where Sutherland and his neighbors resided. Moving down the Frenchtown Road, they carried out one of the most infamous raids in Butte County's history. After robbing the Wannemaker house, they ransacked Daniel's cabin and then burned it to the ground. Daniel was fortunate that day because, as good a shot as he was, he would have found it difficult to defend himself against such a large party. The Mill Creeks continued along the road until they arrived at the house of another miner, Robert Workman, where they killed his sister-in-law and the gardener and gravely wounded Workman's wife, whom they left for dead.[950]

There is no way to know why the Mill Creeks took that particular path that day. Because he had joined Indian pursuit parties, Daniel believed they had come for him. According to an account based on an interview with him, it was unusual for Mill Creeks to seek out settlers that far south of their Deer Creek base camps. Using arson, theft and murder, they had already targeted Sutherland's associates Good, Anderson and others in pursuit parties who had killed Indians, stolen tools and destroyed their camps. The Indians' pattern of retribution was mentioned by a surveyor who worked in the Sulphur Creek area where Daniel would later have a cabin: "It is a remarkable thing, that the white men who hunted the Mill Creek Indians, between the years 1854 and 1865, have always had their camps robbed in after years."[951]

In the case of Daniel, the Indians could not have missed him in their encounters. As men of small stature, they surely noted his size: he was one of Chico's "solid" men at two hundred pounds and 6' 1" tall.[952] If they considered him threatening enough to seek out that day, it would suggest he participated in more Indian pursuit parties than those found in the fragmentary records. It is conceivable that the Workman household killings were a tragic side effect of his role as Indian pursuer.

Although Daniel may have joined the initial Concow Valley party of miners and farmers who set out after the Mill Creeks, it is more probable he did not because Simeon Moak, who knew him, described those men as inexperienced in Indian searches. However, when the pursuit party reorganized for a second search under Good and Anderson, Daniel's participation is supported in Anderson's 1866 interview: "Mr. Southern and a party from our township took part in the pursuit."[953]

As promised, Good and Anderson picked up the Mill Creeks' path and Sutherland, the Moaks, the Concow Valley men and others in the party surprised the Indians in their canyon camp at a site called Three Knolls. According to Anderson decades later, the party killed five or six Indians (nine according to another party member) and gravely wounded as many. In contrast, according to Daniel, in 1866, they killed twelve to sixteen Indians, but omitted mention of Anderson's recollection of what happened next: the veteran Indian fighters stood back and allowed the Concow Valley novices to mutilate the dead Indians. Because Anderson mentioned Daniel as a veteran, it is probable he did not participate.[954]

The Harsh Aftermath of the Workman Affair

Daniel rebuilt his cabin on the same site, despite the continued threat of Mill Creeks. He was there during July 1866, a peak month for Indian raids and mining because the weather was dry and the creeks were low. A series of minor Indian incidents already had signaled to farmers and miners that the usual seasonal clashes would begin soon.

Such was the situation on July 14, a Saturday evening. Daniel had gone to his bedroom when his dog began to bark about 9 p.m. and would not stop. Both Indians and settlers in the region kept dogs for security. Settlers relied on their bark, while Indians trained their dogs to sniff warnings of danger. Mrs. Dowley, possibly a guest or housekeeper, was also present. Apparently they did not share a bedroom because Mrs. Dowley responded to the barking by peeking outside from another room to see what was troubling the dog.

As Mrs. Dowley peered outside, Daniel remained in his room, loading his weapons. Because automatic weapons did not exist, rapid firing meant shooting off one weapon after another.[955] When he heard steps approach his bedroom door, he called out and, hearing no response, fired three shots through the door. Daniel had shot Mrs. Dowley! One of Daniel's right-handed shots passed from left to right through her body, nicking the petite woman's windpipe and hitting her collarbone as it continued down along her right breast where it lodged. The pattern indicates that the ball had hit her in profile as she was walking past Daniel's door. Daniel set off for Cherokee Flat and brought back Dr. Davis, who could not find the ball. Mrs. Dowley, who evidently survived, had had the extremely bad luck to be shot by one of the area's best marksmen.[956] And, it turned out, there had been no Indians at his house that night. The previous February at Chico, Daniel had placed second to a soldier in the target shooting contest that the Chico Light Infantry sponsored at the previous location of Camp Bidwell.[957] Because Daniel had shot Mrs. Dowley by accident, the sheriff filed no charges.

Daniel's Move to Chico and Deer Creek

After his shooting fiasco, Daniel gave up his Feather River cabin and moved closer to Chico. In early 1868 he entered business with Israel Hull, a fellow member of the Chico Light Infantry. In March, they purchased J. R. Woollen's livery, a large building on East Broadway at Second Street, which they turned into a wagon shop. They leased an adjoining building to painters who finished their wagon jobs. In operation by mid-April, their building rapidly filled with work, which impressed the editor of the *Chico Courant* in his office across the street. Hull and Sutherland, he said, had "wagons in all stages of completion. There is a huge amount of business done at the mechanics shops."[958]

Although Daniel gave up his Feather River cabin, he remained a frontiersman at heart, and, incredibly, bought land in the heart of Indian country. He and William Whiteline purchased canyon property where Sulphur Creek empties into Deer Creek. Daniel's cabin lay between what Ishi referred to as Grizzly Bear's Hiding Place and his people's Upper Camp. Sutherland's property was once again surrounded by potentially violent Indians who had access to it whenever Daniel and his partner were away. Despite this seemingly impossible situation, Daniel, his partner and the last of the Mill Creeks somehow made their peace.[959]

At the cabin, Daniel and his partner planted an orchard and kept a garden at the canyon's base. While Daniel's wagon work kept him away a lot, he was good friends with his Deer Creek neighbors who knew his property as "Dan's place"—a name still familiar in that area. In 2003, one of his neighbors' descendants, Walter Rose, remembered references to Daniel Sutherland as one of the Speegle and Apperson families' circle.

Meanwhile, Hull and Sutherland benefited from Chico's recently completed Humboldt Road to the Idaho gold mines since wagons were essential to carry the heavy freight. Daniel took out a loan in 1869 to expand his wagon business. Luckily, he paid off the loan the following year before direct railroad service to Idaho destroyed the Humboldt Road trade.[960] Hull and Sutherland had also built up a clientele of local farmers. In 1870 they built a "tree lifter" for Bidwell, who noted in his diary how he savored leaving a tree suspended from it when he headed home for supper.[961]

Although his Chico trade slowed in the early 1870s, in 1871, Daniel was awarded a federal land warrant for his service in "Captain Young's Company, California Volunteers, California Indian Wars."[962] (It is possible Captain Young was Bidwell's chief vaquero, Sandy Young.) While this suggests he went on from service in Kibbe's unit to join another state militia unit, no other information was found that explains his qualification for the warrant. He wanted to acquire land in the vicinity of Roderick's Mud Creek place, where he lived as a squatter while working in Chico. Depositions from neighbors about his residence there and improvements to the property led to federal approval of Daniel's land warrant in 1872.

If "Captain Young" was Sandy Young, he was a man well regarded by Chico settlers and Valley Indians. In the early 1860s, Young left the employ of the Neil ranch south of Bidwell's ranch because of the owner's cruel treatment of Indian ranch hands. Young then became Bidwell's chief vaquero and supervised the Indian cowboys in Rancho Chico's cattle operations at Butte Meadows.[963] He trained ranch Indians to work with livestock, lived closely with them and earned their trust. By 1871, after years in the rough frontier, Young, like Daniel, was ready for life in town. Young continued to work in Bidwell's livestock operations at the ranch, acquired land from Bidwell and became his managing partner in a Second Street butcher shop near Hull and Sutherland.[964] Young and Daniel were now downtown businessmen.

Starting Over—Again

Life was good for Daniel in 1872. He had a decent stash of gold dust, a good horse, a substantial wagon, a fancy gun and was buying farmland. Then, in 1873, disaster struck. Sandy Young's butcher shop and Sutherland's wagon shop burned down, along with the whole block from Main to Broadway, between Second and Third streets and beyond. As Bidwell described it: "Fire tremendous in Chico! It broke out in Shearer's stable, destroying one and a half blocks in the town."[965] After this loss, Daniel returned to gold mining in Klamath County. Needing money, he sold the land he had just acquired a year earlier at Mud Creek and bought a solid gold pocket watch, the mark of a successful Chico man. He was able to keep his place approximately where Sulphur and Deer creeks meet.[966]

Daniel's mining preparations took about a year. In September 1874, he entered into a mining partnership with William Silsby, a Chico man with whom he had drilled in the wartime militia. Together they bought the Big Bar Placer Mine on the north side of the Klamath River, eight miles below Orleans Bar. Sandy Young, ready for a change, accompanied Sutherland and

Silsby to Klamath County to see the mine. Although busy with his new enterprise, Daniel did not forget Chico. Two years later, he included a note to the editor with his *Chico Enterprise* subscription renewal, informing his friends that "everything is going nicely, gold dust is plenty, and in fact the only thing they have got up here."[967] Morale remained high the next year when Daniel again wrote the editor that even a "simple pan of dirt" contained "large paying amounts."[968] By the next year, Sutherland, Young and Silsby, now partners, had built two flumes and laid one thousand feet of iron pipes to redirect creek water around their digs.

Sandy Young's Death

In 1880, dissatisfaction grew among the partners. Young sold his share in the mine and settled down on the Sandy Young Ranch in the mountains of Klamath County. In late June, on a visit to his old friend, Daniel stopped in at the ranch house where Young's companion, Mrs. Sewell, told him Sandy had left to work on his mining claim a week earlier and had not returned. When Daniel reached his cabin, Sandy was not there, but he found his friend's personal effects, including his gold watch, undisturbed. Sandy's dog was there and would not leave the top of a creek bank along the Klamath River. Daniel left for help and returned with more men to search. Noting the dog's insistent returns to peer over that same creek bank, they suspected foul play but never found Sandy's body. A storekeeper reported Young had earlier asked him not to give out information about him to any stranger. Suspicion initially fell on Mrs. Sewell, who had left her husband, a Butte County miner, and moved to Klamath County to live with him. Without grounds to charge the woman, authorities arrested a local man, but soon released him for lack of evidence.

Back in Butte County, the idea took root that Young was the victim of Indians avenging his killing of Nimshew headman Ned, who had once lived in Sandy's home and killed his close friend, Hi Good, in 1871. However, in 1888, Hi Sewell made a deathbed confession in Magalia: he killed Young for stealing his wife. Sewell said he traveled to Klamath County in secret and waited in the thick forest on Young's claim. When Young came along, he killed him and threw his body into the Klamath River. The dog's sentinel at that spot matched Sewell's account.

The disappearance of Young's body took such a hold in Butte County that over a century after Young died, a writer gave credence to a rumor of a Young sighting as sufficiently credible "evidence" sufficient to challenge Sewell's deathbed confession and other supportive evidence.[969]

Daniel Sutherland Returns to Butte County

By 1883, Daniel, 56, had returned to northern Butte County, where he reregistered in its *Great Record*, the voter registry, as a Republican. Having put mining behind him, he resumed his trade as a wagon maker.[970]

During this period, Daniel also worked for a rancher near Rock Creek and took up part-time residence again at his Deer Creek cabin across the Tehama County border. The path to it, along Deer Creek, became known as the Dan Sutherland Trail. (While it appears in mid-twentieth century maps, it has not been maintained and has largely disappeared.) He found companionship there at the Speegle family's farm and the Apperson Camp.[971]

As in the early 1870s, Sutherland, the Speegles and the Appersons lived close to the survivors of the Yahi and other tribes, who isolated themselves from Whites. By the 1880s, when settlers were away, these hungry Indians stole food and small items from nearby cabins and gardens. Because Apperson and Speegle descendants have spoken about their families' awareness of these reclusive Indians, Daniel must also have been aware of them, but no evidence speaks to clashes with them.[972] Life there seems to have suited him because he stayed on for the next ten years.

During that time, Daniel also worked and visited in Chico, where he rejoined the Odd Fellows. This proved a wise move for the aging frontiersman who had no family to care for him nor any government assistance. When his health deteriorated, he took up residence in the order's spacious and beautiful home for the aged. In the early twentieth century, the Odd Fellows had acquired Oroville's Bella Vista Hotel, which was built in 1888 as a resort and overlooked a palm tree-lined circular drive. Daniel was living there in 1909 when Robert Anderson recalled his participation in the clash with miners at Forks of Butte.[973]

Daniel found unaccustomed comfort and services in the Odd Fellows home until his death on February 28, 1911, at the age of 83. Lung congestion, a stroke and other maladies had stripped thirty from the two hundred pounds that made Daniel one of Chico's bigger men in the 1860s. In the pioneer section of the Chico Cemetery, his remains rest next to the plot he purchased for his brother Roderick in 1861.

Author's note: Having lived in Chico for almost fifty years, far from members of my Iowa family, who reside up the road from Scotch Grove, I still find it remarkable that two of my grandmother's great-uncles chose to live in Chico, a place our family knew nothing about before I took a teaching position there. My only material link to Daniel, Roderick and their brothers is a small mine-cut diamond their nephew Charles gave my great-grandmother Josie, whose daughter, my grandmother, gave to me when I finished my PhD in 1968 at Tulane at New Orleans—near where the young Sutherland men once worked. Her great-uncles Daniel and Roderick remain in Chico Cemetery under granite stones provided for each after the one Daniel bought was shattered by vandals. In the shifting shadows of archives, their traces surface and recede in the company of their friends and the Mill Creeks, adversaries who became his neighbors.

Abbreviations

ABCSL—Annie E. K. Bidwell Collection, The California Collection, California State Library, Sacramento

ABSCML—Annie Kennedy Bidwell Collections, Special Collections, Meriam Library, California State University, Chico

Bancroft Library—University of California, Berkeley

Barbour Report—United States. Senate, *Report of G. W. Barbour, Indian Commissioner for Northern California*, Miscellaneous Documents, no. 688, 33^d Cong., spec. sess., Reports and Executive Data

Bidwell Deposition—United States. Congress. *Samuel Norris v. U.S.* Washington, D.C.: 1860. Cf. John Bidwell's deposition, A report, consisting of documents submitted to the U.S. Congress by Samuel H. Huntington, Chief Clerk, Court of Claims, issued as U.S. House of Representatives Report C.C., no. 257, 36th Cong., 2^d sess., December 18, 1860, In portfolio.

Bleyhl Collection—Bleyhl Collection, Indian-White Relationships in Northern California, 1820–1920, Special Collections, Meriam Library, California State University, Chico

CSA—California State Archives, Sacramento

CSL—California State Library

CSLS—California State Library, Sacramento: The California Collection

CSUC—California State University, Chico

CSUC Special Collections—Special Collections, Meriam Library, California State University, Chico

Hill Collection—Dorothy Hill Collection, Indian Papers, Indian-White Relations of Northern California, 1849–1920, Special Collections, Meriam Library, California State University, Chico

Indian Affairs Annual Report, 1850—United States. Congress, Report of Capt. Hannibal Day, *Annual Report of the Commissioner of Indian Affairs, 1850*, 31st Cong., 2^d sess., Senate Executive Document 1, vol. 1, pts. 1–2, December 1850, ser. set 587, 35–175

Indian Affairs Annual Report, 1867—United States. Congress, *Annual*

Report of the Commissioner of Indian Affairs, 1867, 40th Cong, 2[d] sess., House Executive Document 1, 15 November 1867, serial set 1326, 1-397

Indian Affairs Annual Report, 1868—United States, Congress, *Annual Report of the Commissioner of Indian Affairs, 1868*, 40th Cong., 2[d] sess. House Executive Document 200, vol. 15, 4 March 1868, serial set 1341

Indian Affairs, NAM—Microfilms 39 and 234, Letters sent and received, 1849–1852, Office of Indian Affairs, National Archives

JBCSL—John Bidwell Collection, The California Collection, California State Library, Sacramento

JBSCML—John Bidwell Collection, Special Collections, Meriam Library, California State University, Chico

SCML—Special Collections, Meriam Library, California State University, Chico

SED—U.S. Senate Executive Document

U.S. Army, NAM—Letters Received, U.S. Army, National Archives

Endnotes

Preface

1. Dorothy J. Hill, *The Indians of Chico Rancheria* (Sacramento: State of California Department of Parks, 1978). Researchers Hill and Robert Rathbun collaborated with anthropologist Francis Riddell in documenting Maidu culture and recording the far flung tribe's oral histories.
2. C. C. Parry, "Rancho Chico," *Overland Monthly* 40 (June 1888): 576.
3. Quoted by John Whiting. Review of D. D. Guttenplan's *The Life and Times of I. F. Stone*, www.kpfahistoryinfo/pa/i-f-stone.html.
4. Albert L. Hurtado. *Indian Survival on the California Frontier* (New Haven: Yale University Press, 1988).
5. David McCullough, "Book Talk," 2011 National Book Festival, CSPAN-2, Book TV (November 25, 2011).

Introduction to the People and Places

6. Examples of extreme and irrational killings are represented by Tehama village's Bill Farr, who shot and killed many Indians just "to see them fall." *San Francisco Daily Evening Bulletin*, 7 January 1859; *Butte Record*, 26 January 1859. Examples of angry outbursts were more common, such as that of Plumas County miner George Rose, who shot an Indian over job performance. Afraid his act might provoke Indian avengers, Rose's partners "tried" and hanged him. Patricia L. Kurtz, *A History of Indian Valley, Plumas County*, (Quincy, CA: privately published, 2010), Bleyhl Collection. Another type of malefactor was William Macon, who killed several Indian rivals for an Indian woman. Cf. *Butte Record*, 31 December 1852 and 26 January 1854. Other examples of moral corruption included liquor sales to Indian men and women who appeared drunk on village streets. Officials made sporadic prosecutions of non-Whites, such as a Chinese seller. *Butte Record*, 1, 29 March 1856.
7. Tribelets: "... an independent and sovereign nation that embraced a defined and bounded territory, exercising control over the natural resources contained therein," from "California's Native People, The Central Region: Sociopolitical Organization" (Washington, D.C.: Smithsonian Institution, 1978), http://www.cabrillo.edu/~crsmith/anth6_central_politics.html. This definition is inexact in its application to the area studied here in that the Mountain Maidu tribelets' rancherias were in defined territory, but their control of them was incomplete.
8. Ray Raphael and Freeman House recognized this as the situation in Humboldt County as well. Ray Raphael and Freeman House, *Humboldt History: Two Peoples, One Place*, vol. 1 (Eureka, CA: Humboldt County Historical Association, 2007), 109–10. By contrast to Humboldt County, where organized killings of Indians

in prodigious numbers seemed practically continuous by the late 1850s, Indian mortality in northern Butte County by settlers was substantial, but sporadic, concentrating in late spring through the fall.

9   Francis A. Riddell, "Maidu and Koncow," vol. 8, *Handbook of North American Indians: California*, ed. Robert Heizer (Washington, D.C.: Smithsonian Institution, 1978); Louise Butts Hendrix, interview by Marilyn Sevier, 1985, Dorothy Hill Collection, Indian Papers, SCML; Norris Bleyhl, "Indian-White Relations of Northern California, 1849–1920" (Chico: 1978); *Butte Record*, 14 April 1859.

10 Captain Adam Johnston to the Indian Bureau from Rancho Chico, 6 July 1850, Letters Received, 1859–1952, NAM. Johnson, at a few points, merges observations of Mountain and Valley Maidu, both of which he considered at risk to settlers; however, the appropriate distinctions emerge in a closer reading.

11 Annie Bidwell, *The Rancho Chico Indians*, edited by Dorothy Hill (Chico: Bidwell Mansion Cooperating Association, 1980), 61.

12 *Butte Record*, 14 April 1859. In their Penutian language, the word "Maidu" means "the people." Sherburne F. Cook, "The Conflict Between the California Indians and White Civilization," *The California Indians: A Source Book*, ed. Robert F. Heizer and M. A. Whipple (Berkeley: University of California Press, 1971), 163.

13 E. J. Lewis, *History of Tehama County, California* (San Francisco: Elliott and Moore, 1880), 43–50; Cook, *Conflict*, 243. This percentage is from extensive work by Cook, who includes what he calls "social homicide" or deaths caused by stress linked to immersion in a hostile, outside culture that would not have appeared in a peaceful, ordered society. Examples are Indian deaths linked to alcohol-related clashes, fights over sex, and lynchings of Indians. While he also includes tribal warfare and Indian killings by other Indians, that was not an appropriate factor to include as new because traditional tribal culture was contentious and clashes were common to tribelet experience.

14 Hill, chapter one; Kenneth M. Johnson, *The Indians of California* (Los Angeles: Dawson's Book Shop, 1996); also in Robert F. Heizer, *Handbook of North American Indians: California*, vol. 8 (Washington, D.C.: Smithsonian Institution, 1978), 12. In May 2011, professor of anthropology Mark Kohta reminded the author of Valley Indians' elaborate costuming and ceremonies. Hill wrote about this and collected examples of the costumes. Coyote Man [Robert Rathbun] and Brother William, *Get the Buzzon or the New World Immigrant's Guide to Dope, Herbs, Indians and Magic Meeting Places* (Berkley: Brother William Press, 1972).

15 Sue Campbell and Jamie Mattice, "Maidu Women," public talk, 11 March 2001, Chico Heritage Association; Loring White, *Frontier Patrol: The Army and Indians in Northeastern California, 1861* (Chico: Association for Northern California Records and Research, 1974), 13–14; John Bidwell, "Dictation," 21, John Bidwell Collection, Bancroft Library; author's discussion with professor of anthropology Frank Bayham, CSUC, September 1997; John Bidwell to George McKinstry, 30 September 1848, George McKinstry Collection, CSLS.

16 *Indian Affairs Annual Report, 1850*, 91–93. Capt. Hannibal Day, a Vermont native, was a West Point graduate. Thanks to Robert Chandler for information about Day. Stephen Powers, "California Indian Characteristics," *Overland Monthly* 14, no. 4 (April 1875): 302; A. L. Kroeber, "Elements of Culture in Native California," *The California Indians: A Source Book*, ed. Robert F. Heizer and M. A. Whipple (Berkeley: University of California Press, 1971), 25.

17 Dixon. Dixon's work, like that of Kroeber and Cook, is a major source here. Of course, the Foothill or Hill Maidu, as Cook referred to them, shared characteristics of the Mountain and Valley peoples on either side of them. In order to gain seasonal access to their milder foothill climate, the Mountain Maidu negotiated permission

or intimidated the foothill people. While the Valley Maidu precluded any rivals' extended access to their warmer sites and fertile lands, the proximity of the smaller number of Foothill Indians to fierce Mountain tribelets meant they had to relent. Over time, members of the Foothill Maidu became closer to Mountain Maidu as antagonists to Valley Indians and settlers alike. For purposes of simplicity, Foothill Maidu will be treated here, as in the nineteenth century, like one group with Mountain Indians. Note: Cook refers to "Hill Maidu," but, for the most part, elided that designation, merging it into the conventional "Mountain Maidu" term used here. Sherburne F. Cook, *The Population of the California Indians, 1769–1970* (Berkeley: University of California Press, 1976).

18 Steve Schoonover, *Before Ishi: The Life and Death of the Yahi*, NorCal Blogs (7 November 2007–17 March 2011). Jerald Jay Johnson, "Ishi's Ancestors," draft of paper delivered to unnamed group, 23 September 1994, Anthropology Library, CSUC, 1–2. Alfred Kroeber erred in "The Elusive Mill Creeks" when he said that it was gold miners who drove the Yahi into the canyons. It was to gold miners he attributed the Yahi's "unflagging warfare, destructive stubbornness with the settlers of Tehama and Butte counties." There was no gold in their canyons to attract miners. Alfred L. Kroeber, "The Elusive Mill Creeks," *Ishi the Last Yahi*, ed. Robert F. Heizer and Theodora Kroeber (Berkeley: University of California Press, 1979), 81.

19 Cook made the only attempt at a count that came to the author's attention for this, the present study. Cf. Cook, *Conflict*.

20 George Mansfield, *History of Butte County* (Berkeley: Howell-North, 1973), Indian section; *Oroville Daily Record*, 2 July 1907. Such holes could be sixty feet deep. *Butte Record*, 12 April 1862. On occasion, the acts of white murderers were mistakenly attributed to Indians. However, settlers learned how to distinguish between Indian and settler criminal or war methods.

21 Cook, *Conflict*, 3; *Red Bluff Beacon*, 25 May 1859. This rural editor used sarcasm to describe an urban counterpart who objected to country residents' violent retaliations as "the philanthropic editor of the Sacramento Bee, who is entirely out of danger."

22 The Topographical Reports of Lieutenant George H. Derby," *Quarterly of the California Historical Society* 11, no. 2 (June 1932); A. L. Kroeber, "Elements of Culture in Native California," 37. Significant information that follows comes from this and other works by Kroeber. Sherburne F. Cook, *Colonial Expeditions to the Interior of California, Central Valley, 1800–1820* (Oxford: Benediction Classics, 2012).

23 Roland B. Dixon, *Bulletin of the American Museum of Natural History* 16, no. 3 (May 1905).

24 For examples of Mountain Maidu's random killing of settlers in 1850, cf. *San Francisco Alta*, 27 October 1850; *Butte Record*, late June and 8 July 1854.

25 Rathbun and Brother William, *Get the Buzzon*.

26 Cited in Edward Washington McIlhany, "Recollections of a 49'er," annotated and researched by Scott J. Lawson, [Dogtown] *California Territorial Quarterly* (Fall 2006): 26. The editor ventures that these Maidu were from the Enterprise or Estom Yumeka tribelet. The men cited headed for Feather Falls or Concow tribelet territory.

27 Ibid.

28 Rathbun and Brother William, *Get the Buzzon*.

29 Lt. Michael Morgan to Headquarters, U.S. Army, Pacific Division, 1 July 1857, U.S. Army, NAM.

30 Adam Johnston to Orlando Brown, 16 September 1850, NAM, cf. T. T. Waterman, "Ishi the Last Yahi," in *The Californian Indians: A Source Book*, ed. Robert F. Heizer

and M. A. Whipple (Berkeley: University of California Press, 1951); Kroeber, "Elements of Culture," 37; *Tailings of Butte Creek Canyon*, 12.
31 Cook, *Conflict*, 224–25; Hurtado, 29; Alan F. Almquist, *The Other Californians: Prejudice and Discrimination under Spain, Mexico, and the United States to 1920* (Berkeley: University of California Press, 1977), 4; A. L. Kroeber, *Handbook of the Indians of California* (New York: Dover Publications, 1925), 398.
32 Report of Capt. Hannibal Day, *Indian Affairs Annual Report, 1850*, 91–93. Day, a Vermont native, was a West Point graduate. Thanks to Robert Chandler for this information.
33 Jessie Speegle, *Speegle Family Biography* (Chico: private document, n.d.), John Nopel Collection, used with appreciation to the Nopel Family; Dixon.
34 White, *Frontier Patrol*; Report of Capt. Hannibal Day, *Indian Affairs Annual Report, 1850*, 91–93.
35 S. C. Gwynne, *Empire of the Summer Moon* (New York: Scribner, 2010), 254–59. Later references to Cheyenne experience reference this excellent work.
36 Hugh Graham Davis and Ted Robert Gurr, ed., *History of Violence in America* (New York: Praeger, 1970).
37 James Miller Guinn, *A History of the State of California and Biographical Records of the Sacramento Valley* (Chicago: A. M. Chapman Publishing, 1906), 210; Kroeber, "Elements of Culture," 36–37; Powers, "California Indian Characteristics," 302; Oliver Wozencraft to Luke Lea, 14 October 1851, NAM; Dixon; Waterman, "Ishi the Last Yahi," 37; Kroeber, "Elements of Culture," 37; Paul E. Schulz, *Indians of Lassen Volcanic National Park and Vicinity* (Mineral, CA: Loomis Museum Association, 1954), 28; Riddell, 375.
38 *Butte Record*, 16 August 1856; Powers, "California Indian Characteristics," 308; *Barbour Report*; *Alta California*, 27 October 1850; Rathbun and Brother William, *Get the Buzzon*.
39 Cook, *Population*, 6.
40 Captain Adam Johnston to the Indian Bureau from Rancho Chico, 6 July 1850, Letters Received, 1859–1952, NAM.
41 *Chico Courant*, 13, 20, 27 January 1865. During January of that rain-drenched winter, town residents watched as Indians walked up the Oroville-Shasta Road through Chico with their baskets full of ground squirrels. Sherburne Cook mentions their preference for some rodents over larger animals for food. *Marysville Express*, 24 September 1853; *Butte Record*, 23 August 1854, 29 November 1856; *Marysville Appeal*, 1 July 1853. The *Marysville Appeal* covered Butte County events in its early years. For comparisons to the "The Northeastern Maidu," see *Plumas County Historical Society Publication* 34 (1969): 16.
42 Adam Johnston to Orlando Brown, 16 September, 6 July 1850, NAM; *Tailings of Butte Creek Canyon, 1833–1871* (Paradise, CA: Centerville Historical Association, 1972), 12.
43 Powers, "California Indian Characteristics," 302; Adam Johnston to Orlando Brown, 16 September 1850, NAM; Oliver Wozencraft to Luke Lea, 14 October 1851, NAM; Dixon; Oliver Wozencraft at Bidwell's ranch to Office of Indian Affairs, 16 September 1850, NAM.
44 Cook, *Conflict*. Several items in Butte County newspapers mentioned deaths in such battles. Riddell, 380–81.
45 Powers, "California Indian Characteristics"; Kroeber, "Elements of Culture," 25.
46 John Bidwell, "Address of John Bidwell to the Members of the Society of California Pioneers, November 1, 1897," ed. Henry L. Byrne, *Quarterly of the Society of California Pioneers* 3 (March 1926): 9–10. The source explains this practice as the substitute for fencing on ranches. Although Bidwell did not make any direct claim to that

practice on his ranch, neither did he deny its use in his ranch operations. Dorothy Hill inferred this a reference to his experience in Chico then, and this author agrees that its fullness of description directly applied to his situation. Cf. Michael Gillis and Michael Magliari, *John Bidwell and California: The Life and Writings of a Pioneer, 1841–1900* (Spokane: Arthur H. Clark, 2003), 85. Their quote from Bidwell about the use of Indians to monitor borders in the place of "fences" in 1841 appeared in a legal case. On population patterns in the American period, see Cook, *Population*; Rathbun and Brother William, *Get the Buzzon*.

47 Ibid, Powers.
48 Powers, *Tribes of California*; Powers, "California Indian Characteristics," 302; Rathbun and Brother William, *Get the Buzzon*, 66.
49 Guinn, *History of California*, 210; Kroeber, "Elements of Culture," 36–37; Powers, "California Indian Characteristics," 302; Oliver Wozencraft to Luke Lea, 14 October 1851, NAM; Dixon.
50 Powers, *Tribes of California*.
51 Bud Bain, interview by Dorothy Hill, Hill Collection, 32; *Chico Enterprise*, 2 January 1918; Ananias Rogers Pond, Diary, 25 October 1849, courtesy of Peter Blodgett, curator of western historical manuscripts, Henry E. Huntington Library, San Marino.
52 Bidwell, in Gillis and Magliari, 121; James J. Rawls, "Gold Diggers: Indian Miners in the California Gold Rush," *California Historical Society Quarterly* 55 (1976); Granville Stuart, *Forty Years in the Frontier*, ed. Paul C. Phillips (Lincoln: University of Nebraska Press, 1977), 54–55.
53 Peter J. Barnett, who camped one night near John Potter's place, described the man as "primitive," with the example that his adobe house's front yard was carpeted in fresh cattle manure. The site operated as a butcher shop where big slabs of beef hung on lines suspended across the yard to dry. Mansfield, *History of Butte County*, 222. For information on the dispute with Potter heirs, see correspondence between Bidwell and the heirs' lawyer, Charles Lott of Oroville, about their preference to sell to another party right before the sale took place. Courtesy of Butte County Historical Society archives.
54 Powers, "California Indian Characteristics."
55 Bidwell described this in his notes on arrival years in the John Bidwell Collection, CSLS. Rawls, "Gold Diggers," 54–55. He heard rumors that Bidwell took out $100,000 in gold.
56 Robert Chandler to Michele Shover, email, fall 2007.

Chapter One

57 Wozencraft's correspondence mentioned contact with both the Indian Bureau and the Indian Affairs Department. For example, on 1 August 1851, he wrote the Hon. Luke Lea, Commissioner of Indian Affairs, Washington, D.C.: "I am pleased to hear from the Department and at the same time to learn that our labors are not only appreciated but ... met with the approbation of the Indian Bureau." NAM.
58 Ibid; Kenny, *History and Proposed Settlement Claims*; cf. William H. Ellison, "Rejection of California Indian Treaties," *The Grizzly Bear* (May-July 1925): 4–5. The Ellison series presents treaty issues in a broader context than the present account, but its analysis is consistent with this author's conclusions about the generally worthy intent of the Indian commissioners in their work on behalf of both of the treaties and the general justifiability of their claims for reimbursements to creditors and themselves. Ellison considered Adam Johnston's "services in the Indian affairs of California were more important than those of any other person in the period."

Ellison, "The Federal Indian Policy in California, 1846–1860," *The Mississippi Valley Historical Review* 9 (June 1922).
59 Acting Commissioner Loughery to Oliver Wozencraft, 15 October 1850, U.S. SED; *Indian Affairs Annual Report, 1850.*
60 *Alta California*, 26 July 1851.
61 Foothill Maidu are included here as Mountain Maidu for efficiency and because their cultures were more similar to one another than to Valley Maidu. Bidwell, "Dictation." Bidwell dictated this to his wife Annie, whom he married in 1868. No mention of the treaty meeting at Chico appears there or elsewhere in the Bidwell archives, nor in *Incidents in the Life of General John Bidwell* by ranch supervisor and prominent Indian researcher Charles C. Royce (privately published, 1906), who mentioned Bidwell's planting of grapes and fruit trees in 1851. Edward Nelson Blake, who was there, recollected his role in the planting. That Royce included nothing about the treaty negotiations at the ranch where he began to work in the late 1880s is of interest because he was the nationally respected author of three prominent reports which specialized in American Indians. These included Charles C. Royce, "Indian Land Cessions in the U.S.," *Annual Report of the Bureau of American Ethnology to the Secretary of the Smithsonian Institution*, vol. 18, part 2 (Washington, D.C.: U.S. Printer's Office, 1895). It was published when Royce was John Bidwell's manager at Rancho Chico.
62 Hurtado, 138; Stuart, *Forty Years on the Frontier*.
63 Stuart, *Forty Years on the Frontier*, 54; Bidwell, deposition, question 2. According to his papers in those earliest years, Bidwell commonly referred to his place not as "my ranch," but as "my farm." By the mid-1850s, his references increasingly used "ranch." Hurtado, 139; cf. Robert Kenny, *History and Proposed Settlement Claims of California Indians* (Sacramento: State Printing Office, n.d.).
64 Adam Johnston to the Indian Bureau, Department of the Interior, 6 July 1850, NAM; *Indian Affairs Annual Report, 1850*, 91–93. Quotes from Adam Johnston and Capt. Hannibal Day are from these documents. Mansfield, 185; Hill, 18–19; *Niles Register*, 18 April 1849.
65 Richard Crouter and Andrew F. Rolle, "Edward Fitzgerald Beale and the Indian Peace Commissioners in California, 1851–1854," *Historical Society of Southern California Quarterly* 42, no. 2 (June 1960): 107.
66 William Tell Parker, "Notes by the Bay, 1850–1851, Being a Diary of the Gold Rush Experience," *Recollections of a '49er*, ed. Scott J. Lawson, *California* [Dogtown] *Territorial Quarterly* 67 (Fall 2006): 25; cf. Anna Morrison Reed, "A Pioneer Mother Who Built Her Own Monument," [Butte County Historical Society] *Diggins*, 19 (Winter 1950); cf. John E. Keller, ed., *Anna Morrison Read* (Lafayette, CA: privately published, 1979). Theodora Kroeber and her associates erred when they referred to "Picas" as all Indians dangerous to Whites. It was a specific aggressive Maidu tribelet village located close to the south side of Deer Creek canyon, according to John Bidwell and other accounts.
67 Bidwell, deposition, question 9.
68 Oliver Wozencraft to Luke Lea, 14 May 1851, NAM; Powers, "California Indian Characteristics," 308.
69 Adam Johnston to Orlando Brown, 16 Sept. 1850, NAM.
70 Quoted in Gillis and Magliari, 290; Carl Briggs and Clyde Francis Trudell, *Quarterdeck and Saddlehorn: The Story of Edward F. Beale, 1822–1893* (Glendale, CA: The Arthur Clark Co., 1993), 127.
71 *Barbour Report.* Redick McKee was Treaty Commissioner for Northwestern California and George Barbour for roughly the rest of the state.
72 Oliver Wozencraft to Luke Lea, 14 May 1851, SED. After he left the Chico

negotiation, Wozencraft became the legal guardian of an orphaned or abandoned Mountain Indian infant he discovered after he left Bidwell's ranch. She lived with the Wozencrafts until she died as an adult, www.genforum.genealogy.com/wozencraft/messages/186/html.

73   Quoted in Briggs and Trudell, 127.
74   *Indian Affairs Annual Report, 1850*, 91–93.
75   Ibid. Daniel Sutherland, a Butte County gold miner and wheelwright, used to pass the time outside his cabin picking off small game with his "pistols." He later placed second in a Camp Bidwell shooting match and joined in pursuit parties against Mill Creeks. Lewis D. Sutherland, "Notes on the Sutherland Family" (Portland, OR: Properly of Barbara Scot, n.d.); cf. Appendix E; Daniel Sutherland to John Sutherland, 21 December 1856, property of Judith Sutherland Pahnke.
76   Adam Johnston to Orlando Brown, 1 July 1850, NAM; Redick McKee to Governor John Bigler, 15 April 1852, NAM; *Barbour Report*.
77   This section combines information from the Senate Executive Documents of the Office of Indians Affairs archival papers cited above and below. Chippewa, Shawnee, Choctaw and other reservations were already in place by the 1840s. Cf. Royce, "Indian Land Cessions."
78   This information from the time conflicts with a summary record later published that states the proposed treaty set out land for Northwestern Maidu (Mechoopdas) along the Feather River, ceding all right to other land. This makes no sense in light of information about the time from the treaty commissioner's correspondence. It may have meant to refer to the next treaty meeting with the Yubas; however, it names the Mechoopdas and gives the August 1 date when they and other tribelets signed the treaty at Rancho Chico, Chart in Royce, "Indian Land Cessions."
79   Hill, 89; Currie, 315. The latter cited Wozencraft's boundary description from Charles J. Kappler. United States Senate Laws, *Indian Affairs Laws and Treaties*, vol. 4, 70th Cong., 1st sess., Senate document 53, serial set 10458. In his response to deposition question 14, Bidwell represented the choice of poor land as an example of Wozencraft's abuse of his responsibility. He did not explain the reasons why treaty commissioners chose such lands. He also omitted that Wozencraft had protected his property by its exclusion from the Maidu reservation plan; cf. Redick McKee in January 1852; *Barbour Report*, 235.
80   Oliver Wozencraft to Luke Lea, 11 May 1851, SED.
81   Bidwell, deposition, questions 20, 21; Mr. Stout to John Bidwell, 19 March, 9 April 1852, JBSCML.
82   The location is probable, based on the location at the time of the ranch headquarters and the Mechoopda Indian camp southeast across Chico Creek. An Indian elder in the mid-twentieth century said the meeting was on the south bank of Chico Creek across from the later Normal School. However, Bidwell did not own that land then. John Bidwell, in his *Samuel Norris v. U.S* deposition, said he produced three hundred Indians for the meeting. The number of "over two hundred" arrivals from beyond the ranch is a surmise that allows in the account for the Bidwell Ranch's Mechoopdas and other Valley Indians already in place. There is no way to know whether the account included women, but it probably did not. Riddell, 373.
83   The Mechoopdas planted the peach orchard with Alex Barber and Nelson Blake, who supervised and laid out the rows. Edward Nelson Blake to John Bidwell, 26 April 1852, JBSCML; *Northern Enterprise*, 19 February 1875. Apparently the store was completed or underway by this time because ranch supervisor Barber bought an expensive county license to sell goods from his home only from May to November 1850. Records Office, County Auditory, Butte County, CA, License no. 107; Mansfield, 38; Federal Census, 1860, CA, Butte County, Chico Twp.; William

Standoff

Conway [probable author], *Oral History of Rancho Chico Indians*, recorded by Julia Pingrey, John Nopel Collection, courtesy of David Nopel. Some probably camped on the forested site of the flour mill built in 1854 across from Bidwell's headquarters. R. D. Crane to John Bidwell, 26 April 1854, JBCSL; James Callen to John Bidwell, 6 July 1851, JBSCML; Edward Nelson Blake in *Northern Enterprise*, 19 February 1875. Blake remembered the buildings from his arrival on Bidwell's ranch for work in 1851 and 1852. The frame store rose in time for the treaty meeting. On Potter, see "Petition to the Commander of the U.S. Force in New Helvetia from Mill Creek, 28 February 1847." Military Collection, CSA. The descriptions rely on the several 1859 legal depositions that support reimbursement from the federal government to Bidwell for his losses to Indians. Bidwell, deposition.

84 Oliver Wozencraft to John Bidwell, 20 October 1851, NAM.
85 Bidwell, deposition, question 10; Jerald Jay Johnson, "Ishi's Ancestors."
86 Oliver Wozencraft to Luke Lea, 18 July 1851, NAM.
87 Redick McKee to Indian Affairs Superintendent Edward Beale, 22 September 1852, NAM and R. Stuart to John Bidwell, 6 July 1851, JBSCML; cf. Bidwell, deposition.
88 Johnson, *The Indians of California*, 12; Bidwell, "Dictation," 21; John Bidwell to D. R. Seeper, 29 July 1897, JBSCML. Bidwell said only the Mountain Indians, at the time, made bows. Anthropologists have clarified that where they were made depended on the location of the best artisan at the time.
89 This reconstruction is based on Indian historical behavior, culture and Bidwell's actions when he arrived. Hill, 16.
90 Oliver Wozencraft to Luke Lea, 1 August 1851, NAM.
91 O. M. Wozencraft Statement, Bancroft Library.
92 Oliver Wozencraft to Luke Lea, 14 May 1851; *Barbour Report*, 113.
93 John Bidwell to D. R. Seeper, 29 July 1897, JBSCML; A woman named Napani or Napana became the wife of Luc-a-yan's successor Lofonso after, following tradition, he stole her and she made an unsuccessful struggle to escape (which, by custom, would have freed her). Miller, "California Diggers," 208; Speculation persists that a Nopanni, her daughter perhaps, became Bidwell's "wife." By 1865, when Bidwell married Annie Kennedy, the younger woman would have been about 24 years old. No information this author came across, including some from men quick to accuse him, linked John Bidwell to any local women, Indian or White. He did, however, take particular interest in women like Sophronia Maxson, wife of his carpenter, but that was because she made fabulous fruit pies. His diary regularly noted occasional sightings of Sarah Chapman, like his wife, an attractive and very petite woman.
94 Oliver Wozencraft to Luke Lea, 12 July 1851, NAM.
95 A. L. Kroeber, 25–36; Annie H. Currie's interview of Emma Cooper. Anne H. Currie, "The Bidwell Rancheria," *California Historical Society Quarterly* 36 (December 1957): 313–25. This author speculates that Napani was Cooper's source because she was a principal elder when Cooper was young. This helps explain the transmission between two women of simple details or very specific, obvious treaty points about material benefits for Indians, translated between Maidu dialects and English. As an adult, according to Dorothy Hill, Napani was much respected at Rancho Chico. In Bidwell's deposition, he only mentioned his aide, Rafael, as a translator. Emma Cooper will be a subject later in this chapter. Oliver Wozencraft to Luke Lea, 18 May 1851, SED.; Bidwell, deposition, question 17. Antoinette Martinez, professor of anthropology, California State University, Chico (hereafter, CSUC), has pointed out that Wozencraft copied the Russians on the northern California coast who dispersed bright jackets to Indians whose standing as tribal leaders they wanted to elevate. Discussion with author, August 2011.

96 Bidwell, deposition, question 17; Kroeber, "Elements of Culture," 25.
97 Ibid.
98 Oliver Wozencraft to Luke Lea, 7 August 1851, NAM.
99 Harry Kelsey, "The California Indian Treaty Myth," *Southern California Quarterly* 55 (Fall 1973): 231.
100 Currie, 314-15.
101 Ibid.
102 The U.S. government employed Indian languages to communicate from and to battlefields in WWII. This provided a reliable code. While they prepared to use the Maidu language, they made another choice.
103 Interview, Michele Shover with Dorothy Hill, July 1990; Hill, 18.
104 Currie, 314–15.
105 Joaquin Miller, *Unwritten History: Life Amongst the Modocs* (Hartford: American Publishing Co., 1874), 243.
106 Bidwell, deposition, question 17.
107 Ibid., 314–15.
108 Bidwell, "Dictation," 17. The many examples he offered in the memoir include none from the colorful and dramatic treaty negotiations.
109 Unless otherwise indicated, "Bidwell" will identify John Bidwell and his wife will be referred to as Annie Bidwell.
110 Men could cool off in the earthen dance-house, while women and children had to find their own relief; Powers, 299; Quoted in Mansfield, 35; Oliver Wozencraft to Luke Lea, 4 August 1851, NAM.
111 Cook, 72–73, 93; see also p. 25.
112 "Bidwell Harvest in 1855" and "Indians Harvested Grain with Naked Hands," Old Timer Series, *Enterprise Record*, Special Collections, Meriam Library, California State University, Chico (hereafter, SCML); Albert Hurtado (*John Sutter: A Life on the California Frontier* [Norman: University of Oklahoma Press, 2006], 157) cites Bidwell's description of this method at Sutter's place.
113 Conway.
114 Ibid.
115 "Bidwell Harvest in 1855" and "Indians Harvested Grain with Naked Hands," Old Timer Series, *Enterprise Record*, Special Collections, Meriam Library, California State University, Chico (hereafter, SCML); Hurtado (*John Sutter*, 157) cites Bidwell's description of this method at Sutter's place.
116 Powers, 299; Gillis and Magliari, 293. The Shasta Indians were described in like terms: "Indolence is one of their greatest vices. They will work for a white man, if well paid, but never for themselves." The writer quoted did not recognize that they were savvy about the Whites' economic system in which a value was placed on their labor and that they understood that receipt of pay for their labor amounted to work for themselves. "The Shasta and Their Neighbors," Document 2648, from 1873, Bleyhl Collection; Stephen Powers, in Mansfield, 33; The horse runs over wheat stalks to separate wheat from chaff took place in very large circles defined by walls built of "married" local rock. One remains on the Garner ranch in northeastern Butte County.
117 Powers, 299; *Oroville Record*, 25 October 1856. It is appropriate to recognize that, similar to Indian women, many or most rural settler women spent their lives consumed in isolation and ceaseless, often grueling labor; Annie K. Bidwell, Notes, box 32, ABCSL.
118 Conway; Hill.
119 Bidwell, "Address to Society," 9–10. The source explains this practice as the substitute for fencing on ranches. Bidwell never claimed to use that practice on for

his ranch not did he separate his ranch for it when he mentioned it. Dorothy Hill considered this a reference to his experience at Chico and this author agrees that its fullness of description directly applied to his situation; cf. Gillis and Magliari, 85. Their reference from a different source was also to Indians whose watches and field patrols did the job of fences. This referred to a practice he noted in 1841. On population patterns in the American period, see Cook, *Population*.

120 Currie, 314–15. According to Gillis and Magliari, Bidwell's practices were distinguished by his respect for the Indians' culture, so long as their actions did not break laws or imperil the ranch. No observers recorded uses of violent domestic practices or corporal punishment on his ranch. With respect to Mountain Maidu methods, anthropologist A. L. Kroeber offered examples of the tribe's torture of opponents in "Elements of Culture," 35–37. Valley Indians such as the Mechoopdas were always on the defense against capture by Mountain Maidu. The source of the practices Kroeber described were recollections of his Maidu Indian sources whose memories extended as far back as the 1840s. In 1871, Stephen Powers spoke of the Maidu's "dark side" which resulted in revenge, assassination and treachery among the tribelets. He also went on, as mentioned earlier, to emphasize that "There was nothing ever perpetrated by the California Indians which has not been matched by acts of individual frontiersmen" [emphasis in original], 298–99.
121 Bidwell, "Dictation," 21; Oliver Wozencraft to Luke Lea, 14 May 1851, NAM.
122 Currie, 313–25; Conway.
123 Cf. Hurtado, *John Sutter*.
124 Conway.
125 Ibid. The treaty date sometimes appears as August 1.
126 Hill, 8, 20–23. Hill described those who signed the treaty as the whole body who attended. Maidu elder Eric Josephson to author, November 29, 2011. It is not possible to know whether this was the later expressed opinion of Concows who left early with the other Mountain Maidu, or whether some stayed on for the whole meeting and then stood back while the signers endorsed the document.
127 Ibid. Oliver Wozencraft to Luke Lea, 4 August 1851, NAM, cf. Gillis and Magliari, 300. In 1858, as in 1851, Bidwell deposed that, for the most part, Indians on his place fended for themselves.
128 Oliver Wozencraft to Luke Lea, 4 August 1851, NAM; cf. Gillis and Magliari, 300. In 1858, as in 1851, Bidwell deposed that, for the most part, Indians on his place fended for themselves.
129 Ibid. Bidwell's later deposition discounted the Indian trade license as of little interest to him: one he "never acted on as an Indian trader." He inferred that it was the idea of Wozencraft, who explicitly told his supervisor that his usual practice was to deny licenses, but considered Bidwell an exception due to his valuable assistance. Bidwell, deposition, question 21. According to a handwritten letter, whose author is unknown but appears an "old timer," Bidwell had a trading post license for a place on Little Chico Creek in the mid-1840s. Conway mentioned an 1850s "trading store" on the ranch itself and suggested Bidwell stayed on its second floor until his burned down house was replaced by the adobe hotel.
130 E. Nelson Blake to John Bidwell, October 1851, JBSCML.
131 Ibid.; E. Nelson Blake to John Bidwell, "Tuesday morning," October, 19 November 1851. While Indians regularly plunged into the creeks, they did not recognize the value of hygiene in their garments, handling of items or in their quarters. Miners, of course, had no reputation for fastidious personal care either.
132 Conway; Stilson, Diaries, passim.
133 Bidwell, deposition, question 17; Oliver Wozencraft to Luke Lea: "It is expected that he [*Bidwell*] *will bring in* additional tribes from the mountains...." [emphasis

Endnotes

added]; Oliver Wozencraft to John Bidwell, 4 September 1851, JBSCML. It is clear at several points that, contrary to Bidwell's deposition version, in 1851, he did not give Wozencraft the impression those Indians had simply wandered on to his ranch in desire for a treaty, but inferred they had responded to his inducements.
134 Gerald Thompson, *Edward F. Beale and the American West* (Albuquerque: University of New Mexico Press, 1983), 46.
135 Oliver Wozencraft to John Bidwell, 3 September 1851, SCML. In 1865, Bidwell had a federal cattle contract which he cancelled for reasons not pursued in this research. However, the government held him to its terms. U.S. District Attorney Delas Lake to Maj. Gen. McDowell, U.S. Army, Pacific Division, 31 January 1865, U.S. Army, NAM.
136 McCorkle to Bidwell, 4 October 1851, JBSCML. While Bidwell's letter is missing, McCorkle's to him infers prior discussion.
137 Currie, 315; Bidwell, deposition, question 38.
138 Ibid.
139 Gwynne, 275.
140 Stephen Blake to John Bidwell, 19 November 1851, JBSCML.
141 John Bidwell to George McKinstry, 30 September 1848, JBSCML.
142 Bidwell, deposition, questions 35, 38.
143 Ibid.
144 Hurtado, 138–39. Other writers who addressed the Rancho Chico treaty negotiations include Annie H. Currie, "The Bidwell Rancheria," *California Historical Society Quarterly* 36 (December 1957); Dorothy Hill, *The Indians of Chico Rancheria* (Sacramento: State of California Department of Parks, 1980); Michele Shover, "John Bidwell and the Rancho Chico Indian Treaty of 1852," [Dogtown] *California Territorial Quarterly* (August 2000) is an earlier, less developed version; Michael J. Gillis and Michael F. Magliari, *John Bidwell and California: The Life and Writings of a Pioneer, 1841–1900* (Spokane: Arthur H. Clark, 2003).
145 U.S. Congress, "Schedule of Indian Land Cessions," *Annual Report of the Bureau of Indian Ethnology to the Secretary of the Smithsonian Institution*, vol. 18, Part 2, 1896–1897 (Washington, D.C., Government Printing Office, 1899), 784.
146 "Receipts for delivery of cattle to Chico, and affidavit of Patrick O'Brien," *Samuel Norris v. U.S.*, 30; Bidwell, deposition, questions 20–22.
147 Ibid.
148 California, Legislature, *Journal of the Third Session of the Legislature of the State of California* (San Francisco: G. K. Fitch, 1852), 44.

Chapter Two

149 Ibid. A later chapter addresses their relationship during the Civil War period.
150 Ellison, "Rejection of Treaties."
151 Ibid.
152 Joseph McCorkle to Luke Lea, in Gillis and Magliari, 294.
153 Bidwell to McCorkle, 20 December 1851, letters received by the Office of Indian Affairs, 1824–1881, California Superintendency, 1849–1880, Washington, D.C., Roll 32, NAM. All of Bidwell's quotes in this section are from this letter. See Appendix B.
154 Ibid.
155 Speech, Senator John C. Calhoun, 7 February 1837, *TeachingAmericanHistory.org*.
156 Bidwell, quoted in Gillis and Magliari, 206.
157 Quoted in Hurtado, 8; Madge R. Walsh, ed., *The Journal of Pierson B. Reading* (Chico: Association of Northern California Historical Research, 2008), vii.

158 Thomas Kerr, "An Irishman in the Gold Rush, the Journal of Thomas Kerr," *California State Historical Society Quarterly* 8, nos. 1 and 3 (1929). Kerr did not know that, in New Orleans, the Irish built levees instead of Blacks because Irish labor was as good and cheaper. This, at least, is common knowledge in New Orleans, where the author lived, but it has not been verified for mention here. For an even more tragic description of such observations, see John Marsh, "Unpublished Letters," *Overland Monthly* (February, 1890): 216.
159 Quoted in Robert Chandler, "The Failure of Reform: White Attitudes and Indian Response in California During the Civil War Era," *The Pacific Historian* 24, no. 1 (Spring 1980): 284–85.
160 Stuart, 54–55.
161 F. S. Clough, *The House at 5th and Salem* (Chico: Stansbury House Preservation Association, 1978), 44. The *Chico Enterprise*, 6 August 1875, asserted Bidwell treated Indians relatively well in 1855. Chapter Three enlarges on Bidwell's model, which was not based on the American South, but reflected his interpretation of moderate Mexican rancho operations and deed stipulations.
162 Ibid. As a man who treasured land, according to the memoir drafted in his old age, Bidwell said, "I had for [the Indians] a regard, a sympathy—knowing that their lands have always been taken from them without any compensation."
163 Ibid.
164 Ibid.
165 Bidwell to McCorkle, 20 December 1851.
166 Ibid.
167 Redick McKee to Governor John Bigler, 5 April 1852, NAM; *Official Correspondence between the Governor of California, the U.S. Indian Agents for California, and the Commander of U.S. Troops for California in Relation to Indian Difficulties in the Northern Part of the State* (Sacramento: E. Casserly, 1852), 715; Chad R. Hoopes, "Redick McKee and the Humboldt Bay Region, 1851–1852," *California Historical Quarterly* 49, no. 3 (September 1970): 213.
168 As mentioned in the Introduction, miners working on their own along the Feather River resented Bidwell's use of a large Indian labor force. In the 1880s, he and other big ranchers would incur the same kind of resentment for their reliance on Chinese workers who also worked hard for low pay.
169 California Legislature, *Journal of the Third Legislative Session*, 604.
170 Quoted in Hurtado, 140, from "Report of the Special Committee of the California State Senate to Inquire into the Treaties Made by the U.S. Commissioners in California," *California State Senate Journal*, 1852, 302–5; Bidwell to McCorkle, 20 December 1851, JBSCML. Anthropologist Robert Heizer published a stinging condemnation of the treaties in *The Eighteen Unratified Treaties of 1851–1852 Between the California Indians and the United States Government* (Berkeley: Archaeological Research Facility, Department of Anthropology, University of California, 1972). This author agrees with most of Heizer's criticisms. However, he overlooked that, in 1851, most Indians' sole chance for a modicum of security and decent conditions rested on the federal government's responsibility for them. The federal and California offices of Indian Affairs staff correspondence and reports which apply to northern Butte County in the treaty debate period were clearly supportive of the Indians' interests then. Even though the treaties presented the terms of appropriation, they offered the Indians a better condition than most—certainly the Mountain Indians—would have had without it. The present account and that of William Strobridge agree that federal officials, both executive and military, were notably more attentive to the Indians' plight than were state and local officials. An important consideration, as well, is that the treaty commissioners worked in

Endnotes

an impossible political environment. The ultimate problem with the treaties was that settlers recognized their terms left the Indians with substantial assets and opportunities, while they were determined to provide only for those Indians they deemed suited for work in the private sector. The anguish of the commissioners, which is unmistakable in their letters and reports to their federal supervisors, was not that they secured too little for Whites but that white opposition had obstructed decent conditions and security for the Indians. William Strobridge, *Regulars in the Redwoods: The U.S. Army in Northern California, 1852–1861* (Spokane: Arthur H. Clark, 1994).

171 California Senate, Report into Treaties, 598.
172 United States Congress, *Congressional Globe*, 32^d Cong., 1st sess., March 1852, 890. Wozencraft to Bidwell, 20 October 1851, JBSCML; cf. Bidwell deposition, question 16.
173 Wozencraft to Lea, 31 May 1851, NAM, 234.
174 McKee to Lea, 30 July 1852, NAM; McKee to Bigler, 5 April 1852, NAM; McKee to Bigler, 5 April 1852, NAM; *Barbour Report*; Michele Shover, "The Doctor, the Lawyer and the Political Chief," *The University Journal*, spec. ed. (California State University, Chico, 1982).
175 McKee to Bigler, 5 April 1852, McKee to Lea, 30 July 1852, *Barbour Report*.
176 *Butte Record*, 15 June 1852; *Red Bluff Beacon*, 26 January 1859; *Red Bluff Tri-Weekly Independent*, 3, 17 August 1861.
177 United States Congress, *Samuel Norris v. U.S.*
178 Beale to Lea, 11 May 1852, *Barbour Report*.
179 Ibid.
180 Ibid.
181 U.S. *Congressional Globe*, 36th Cong., 1st sess., 2365–2369, Senate debate, 26 May 1860.
182 Charles Howard Shinn, "The Story of a Great California Estate: Rancho Arroyo Chico, the Home of the Late General John Bidwell," *Country Life in America* 1, no. 3 (January 1902): 84; Guinn, *History of California*, 285–86; John Blythe, "Every Map Tells a Story," North Carolina Miscellany, ww.lib.unc.edu/blogs/nem/index.php/2010/07/30/every-map-tells-a-story/.
183 William Conway to Secretary of the Interior, 27 February, 23, 29 May 1914, file no. 33841-14, Roseburg, OR, record group CAG775, NAM, 310; Quoted in Margaret D. Jacobs, "Resistance to Rescue: The Indians of Bahapki and Mrs. Annie E. K. Bidwell," *Writing on the Range: Race, Class and Culture in the Women's West*, ed. Elizabeth Jameson and Susan Armitage (Norman: University of Oklahoma Press, 1997), 240.
184 Robert Chandler to author, summer 2007.
185 Kenny, 18. Kenny was the state's former attorney general in 1944 when the U.S. Court of Claims ordered financial compensation to Indian tribes. Of the $17 million settlement, the Indians had to return $12 million to the government for services to the Indians to date. Kenny's report was reissued by Cox Publishing in 1944, but the copy used here was produced by the State Printer without a publication date. That copy's references inferred it was written in the late 1910s or about sixty years after these events.
186 Quoted in Currie, 317.
187 Leo P. Kibby, "California, the Civil War, and the Indian Problem: An Account of California's Participation in the Great Conflict, Part II," *The Journal of the West* 4, no. 3 (1913): 387. A similar pattern of abuse took place in the Deep South where blacks were long arrested for impressments into private industrial labor.
188 Kenny, chapter one. Correspondence with Wozencraft in JBSCML.
189 Recorder's Office, Oroville, Butte County, California.

Chapter Three

190 Cook, *Conflict*, 566–67.
191 Bidwell, *In California Before the Gold Rush* (Los Angeles: Ritchie Press, 1948), 47, 50, 56.
192 Bidwell, "Dictation," 19–20, 75. This generalization is further discussed in chapters that address the 1860s.
193 Ibid., 17–18; Mansfield, 424; "Address of Bidwell," 9–29; Bill Anderson, "Settlement of Northern California, Part 3," [Dogtown] *California Territorial Quarterly* 12 (Winter 1992): 10.
194 Bidwell's notes, JBCSL. This was also what Indian agent Redick McKee was told by a northern California headman who, however, qualified his praise for Americans: while he preferred them to Mexicans, he regretted that Americans had taught his people to steal and lie. McKee to Edward Beale, 22 November 1852, NAM. Sherburne Cook discounted Mexican influence as unimportant on interior Indians in Northern California.
195 D. R. Seeper to John Bidwell, 29 July 1897, JBSCML.
196 Hurtado, *Indian Survival*, 102–4.
197 Ibid., 11.
198 Bidwell, "Dictation," 17.
199 According to Julian Dana, *The Sacramento River of Gold* (New York: Farrar and Rhinehart, 1939), 19, there were fifty Indian dialects in the Sacramento Valley. Bidwell rarely spoke of Rafael's role and never as special to him in a personal sense. When his wife asked him who his friends were, he did not name any. Bidwell, "Dictation."
200 Bidwell, "Dictation"; Cook, *Conflict*, 258.
201 Bidwell, "Dictation," 21. Author's discussion with professor of anthropology Frank Bayham, California State University, Chico, September 1997; Bidwell to McKinstry, 30 September 1848, JBSCML. The Maidu tribelets living in the foothills, whose culture and language were closer to the Mountain Maidu tribelets than to the Valley tribelets, sometimes collaborated as mentioned earlier.
202 Quoted in Hurtado, *Indian Survival*, 103. Presumably his motive in the co-pay was to see that they were not starved. Bidwell to McKinstry, 30 September 1848, JBSCML. Bidwell and McKinstry's other partner was William Dickey. According to James J. Rawls, employment of Indians as miners became increasingly uncommon after 1849 because Whites resented miners who copied the Spanish and Mexicans in their tight control of Indians as laborers. White miners became anxious that Indians in California would compete for their jobs and considered miners' command of such mine workers as closely resembling slavery. Rawls noted no abuses by Bidwell in his use of Indian workers. However, Bidwell's correspondence suggests Indians who mined for him were not always contented under his employment. With regard to the Indian labor-for-hire practice, Bidwell made such an arrangement as late as 1852 and with Robert Durham in 1863. Such practices continued to be used by later Chico employers who hired Chinese from labor contractors. Rawls, 38.
203 Bidwell, "Dictation," 56; Bidwell to McKinstry, 30 September 1848, JBSCML; Stout to Bidwell, 9 April, 19 March 1852, JBSCML; Hill, 32–33; Crowder, *Chico Enterprise*, 2 January 1918; Hurtado, *Indian Survival*, 103.
204 Bidwell to McKinstry, 30 September 1848, JBSCML.
205 Alex H. Barber to Bidwell, January 19, 1852, JBSCML.
206 The Stilson daily diaries, over six years, mentioned no Indians in the John Bidwell & Co., in Wood and Chapman or in his own later store. Bidwell had an early trading post for Valley Maidu on Little Chico Creek, according to Conway and

Emma Wilson. (This was probably the building Bidwell later rented to a Chinese butcher until an anti-Chinese mob burned it down in 1877.) Emma Wilson, "John Bidwell," *Here is My Land* (Chico: National League of American Penwomen, Butte County Branch, 1940), 85. Its location was where the ford crossed the creek. This section of the Oroville-Shasta Trail, in the nineteenth century, was called Old Chico Way. From the point where the trail crossed the southern bank of Big Chico Creek near Bidwell's store, this "pre-Chico Village" road immediately detoured east along the creek, which was the northern border of Potter's Half League. Old Chico Way then took the Trail on a sharp turn south and continued along Potter's eastern border. (In the mid-1870s, well after Bidwell purchased the Potter place, this north-south section of the Old Chico Way was renamed Olive Street.) While still the part of the Trail known as Old Chico Way, it continued across the Little Chico Creek ford. The Oroville-Shasta Trail, no longer Old Chico Way, continued southwest toward Little Butte Creek about half a mile west of the Compton Ranch. Where the new Potter's Half League map reveals Old Chico Way turning east, it also shows modern locations, including that of the present Rio Chico Way. This suggests that the present road was an equivalent one extending west from where the trail crossed Big Chico Creek. Annie Bidwell named Rio Chico Way in her new subdivision; her choice perhaps a gesture toward the road's early days as the east–west, creek-side farm road, Old Chico Way. The present account, therefore, concludes that when, after Bidwell bought the Potter ranch, he moved the Mechoopdas close to his headquarters, he also moved the Little Chico Creek trading post to that complex. The Indians knew John Bidwell & Co. served Whites, so it makes sense they distinguished that from their own "trading store." Conway mentioned Bidwell stayed above the store—either the Indians' trading store or in the Masonic Lodge which occupied the second floor of the older Bidwell store located on his ranch—for a time after Mountain Maidu burned down his new hotel and his attached residence in 1854. He likely moved to his new adobe hotel when it was completed and stayed there until his clapboard-sided federal farm house was built in 1857. Credit to David Nopel for collaboration in reconstructing this map. The map of Potter's Half League by W. H. Hutchinson shows the Trail's turn onto Old Chico Way. John Nopel Collection, SCML. Butte County Assessor's Map, City of Chico/Olive Street, refers to Olive Street as formerly Old Chico Way. An 1868 photo of headquarters across Big Chico Creek shows the Trail's turn onto the east–west farm road. SCML; Lois Halliday McDonald, *Annie Kennedy Bidwell: An Intimate History of Chico* (Chico: Stansbury Publishing, 2004), 316–17.

207 Records Office, Files of Butte County Auditor, license issued to A. H. Barber, 1 November 1851; Rancho Chico Account Book: Office Blotter, 7 June, 31 October 1860, JBCSL. Appreciation to Robert Chandler for additional information about beads.

208 Bidwell, "Dictation," 15 ff.

209 Ibid., 19. Bidwell's 1890s account of his earliest relations with Indians was written when strained relations between him and Chico residents led him to believe he was misunderstood and little appreciated by his community. Bidwell's memoirs also included examples of his equanimity in his later handling of Confederate rebels and actions by Whites against the Chinese.

210 D. F. Crowder, "The Eventful Yesterdays: The Story of Early Chico," *Chico Enterprise*, 28 December 1917 to 28 January 1918; Robert Anderson, *Fighting the Mill Creeks, Being a Personal Account of Campaigns Against the Indians of the Northern Sierras* (Chico: Chico Record Press, 1909).

211 Although late in life Bidwell remarked that his shrewdness with problematic people allowed him to avoid lawsuits, his correspondence with attorneys

documents numerous legal actions they took on his behalf. Vandorn to Bidwell, 10 December 1856, JBSCML; Lott to Bidwell, 14 October 1858, JBSCML; and others to him from George Adams Smith, JBSCML.
212 The cattle later reappeared from where they had wandered off. Parker, "Notes by the Bay"; Richard C. Harrison, Diary and Receipt Book, 1850–1853, courtesy of Peter Blodgett, Henry E. Huntington Library, San Marino; *Alta California*, 27 October 1850; Mansfield, 185–86. Bidwell led another aggressive pursuit party against Indians in 1853, according to Mansfield's source. Also see *Butte Record*, 1 March 1854.
213 Bidwell, "Dictation," 17.
214 Annie Bidwell to John Bidwell, in Chad Hoopes, *What Makes a Man* (Fresno, CA: Fresno Valley Publishers, 1973), 59: "I have attended the Methodist Church a few times but the unrestrained rejoinders so excite me that I believe I should lose my reason were I regularly to attend that Church"; Robert Chandler to author, fall 2007.
215 Marie Potts, *The Northern Maidu*, 43–45.
216 Bidwell, "Dictation," 18.
217 *San Francisco Alta*, 27 October 1850, copying *Marysville Herald*; Mansfield, 185. The writer Mansfield cited, who apparently had access to a fuller but flawed source, reported it was Nye who died. However, Nye later wrote letters to Bidwell. The above account introduces other information that reconciles the conflicting newspaper accounts. Thanks to Paul Bowman for his identification of the conflict site on an old Indian trail near Neal Road.
218 Wozencraft to Lea, 31 May 1852, NAM; Don M. Chase, *People of the Valley: The Concow Maidu* (Sebastopol, CA: Don M. Chase, 1973), 17–18; George Pettit, *Primitive Education in North America*, vol. 43, *University of California Publication in American Archaeology and Ethnology, 1946–1956* (Berkeley: University of California, 1956), 6; *Red Bluff Beacon*, 12 November 1959; *Butte Record*, 12 November 1859.
219 James Callen to Bidwell, 15 June 1852, JBSCML.
220 Ibid., 14 June 1852.
221 Chandler to author, November 2007.
222 *Alta California*, 7 July 1852.
223 Sherburne Cook, "The Method and Extent of Dietary Adaptation Among California and Nevada Indians," *Ibero-Americana* 35 (1945): 28; Anderson, 7.
224 *Chico Enterprise*, 2, 5, 10 January 1918. See Gillis and Magliari, *Bidwell and California*, regarding Bidwell's efforts to move issues that concerned Indians within the established justice system. Without that, private conflict resolution would continue to rely on force.
225 Ibid.
226 *Alta California*, 7 July 1852. This account treated Bidwell's "arrest" group as a pursuit party.
227 Bidwell, "Dictation," 20.
228 Ibid.
229 Ibid. Information on the tribelets is from Bidwell's notes, JBCSL.
230 The eleven Indians who died appear to have been ranch Indians because the newspaper account said that the dead were "well armed and died bravely." *Alta California*, 7 July 1852. Under those circumstances, a news account at the time would have included the names of the other dead and injured Whites, not just Frye and Soule, and they would not have described armed Whites in patronizing terms. Additionally, had eleven whites been killed, an alarm would have spread throughout the county and generated retaliatory strikes against the Indian perpetrators. Cf. Annie Bidwell, *Rancho Chico Indians*, 53; Bidwell, "Dictation," 21.

In an email to the author, Robert Chandler noted the imbalance in the proportion of Indians killed to whites killed in Bidwell's pursuit party. Relative to the size of the whole party, Chandler called the battlefield losses of Whites or Indians comparable to the proportion of Northern vs. Southern soldiers killed in Civil War clashes. Cf. Bidwell, "Dictation," 20–21.

231 Bidwell, "Dictation," 20. Forty years later he referred to the 1852 pursuit. It was not unusual for Indians on high ground, out of range of arrows or bullets, to taunt those below.

232 Frye's burial was the first in the Chico Cemetery. According to the late Larry V. Richardson, a member of the cemetery staff, the original marker and a later one disappeared. Richardson was the last person to know its exact location on a rise, since leveled, in the Pioneer section. Appreciation to David M. Brown for this information. R. B. Murford to Bidwell, 17 October 1852: "I'm sorry that Mr. Frye lost his life although I did not like him." Nelson Blake's sentimental references to deceased ranch friends omitted Frye. JBSCML. Simeon Moak, *The Last of the Mill Creeks and Early Life in Northern California* (Chico: privately published, 1923), 11; Butte County Census, *State Senate Journal and Appendices, 1852*. Note: in his dictation, Bidwell talked about Frye's death without mention of his name and with disapproval about the fuss made over the death of one white man. He said settlers showed no regret about the great number of Indians killed in clashes. He made this statement in such general terms that it had no obvious link to his subject, his party's clash with the Chico Creeks.

233 Ibid., 19–21; Blake to Bidwell, 19 June 1853; Bean to Bidwell, 17, 20 July 1853, JBSCML; *Butte Record*, 7 July 1852; *Alta California*, 7 July 1852. Bidwell wrote Blake in 1853 that, in 1852, he had considered riding out "once more" against the Mountain Indians, 13 May 1853, JBSCML; Johnston to Brown, 16 September 1850, NAM.

234 Butte Mills is probably the location mentioned. It became Dogtown, and, later, Paradise. Jim McDowell, "Magalia: A Town Nearly Forgotten," [Butte County Historical Society] *Diggins* 56, no. 3 (Fall, 2012): 46.

235 Charles Ferguson, *The Experiences of a Forty-Niner During Thirty-Four Years' Residence in California and Australia* (Cleveland: Williams, 1888), 81.

236 Bidwell Deposition.

237 D. M. Bean to Bidwell, 17, 20, 30 July 1852. No changes to the original wording. See also Callen's letter to Bidwell, 14 June 1852, JBSCML; Reed, 202. She spoke of a Mountain Maidu clash between tribelets in which one side decimated the other tribelet, except for one boy reared by her family as "Charlie." Miners referred to similarly aggressive Picas and Tigus as "Tigers." Because the reference here is to neighboring tribelets, the "Tigers" are thought to be Tigus. While men from these tribelets stole food and women from one another and warred with one another, they sometimes collaborated against outsiders. According to a miner in the early 1850s, the "Tigers" were "very much hated and feared by neighboring tribelets."

238 Others writing about that conflict might give more credit to the Anderson-Good party's 1859 claim (discussed later) of Yahi collaboration with Mountain Maidu and those Indians' ties to miners at a time when both tribes were desperately in need of allies and when both, despite rivalries, had intermittent cross-tribal relations.

239 Bidwell, "Dictation," 18. For analyses of conflicts in the early 1850s, see Mansfield and Hill. Annie Bidwell, *Rancho Chico Indians*, 71; Cook, *Conflict*, 23, 67. The Indians' descendants, who later related these events, mixed them arbitrarily with events in the early to mid-1860s, but that was such a thoroughly documented period that this event surely would have appeared in print somewhere. It is used here because its

makeup fits the 1852-1856 campaign by Butte Creeks; Annie Bidwell, *Rancho Chico Indians*, 72, where the name appears as Duka. In Hill's *Indians of Chico Rancheria*, Duka appears as Dupah, as it appears on the 1860 federal census.

240 E. Nelson Blake to Bidwell, 1853, JBSCML. Quoted by Nancy Leek in "John Bidwell and E. Nelson Blank: A Fifty Year Friendship," [Butte County Historical Society] *Diggins* (Winter, 2015). To this reader and in light of later information, her article suggests that Blake was a young man whom Bidwell would have mentored had he stayed in Chico.

241 Barber to Bidwell, 5 July 1853, JBSCML.

242 Bidwell, "Dictation," 17–18; Blake to Bidwell, 17 June, 16 October 1853; Blake to Annie Bidwell, ABCSL. Located back from the new adobe hotel, on the west side of the Oroville-Shasta Trail, was Bidwell's substantial frame farmhouse. It is unlikely that Bidwell remained living in his log cabin and built a substantial house for someone else. Michele Shover, "Bidwell's Earlier Mansion in the First Chico Village," [Butte County Historical Society] *Diggins* (Winter, 2012).

243 Bidwell, "Dictation," 18–19; Blake to Bidwell, JBSCML.

244 Ibid.; *San Francisco Alta*, 7 July 1852; Blake to Bidwell, 16 October 1853, JBCSL; United States Senate Resolution, March 3, 1859, "Depredations Committed upon Citizens of Butte County by Indians, 1852. Petition by Bidwell." The estimate of Bidwell employee Jacob Updegraff, in his deposition, placed the hotel's value at $6,000, indicating a very substantial building. *Butte Democrat*, 19 November 1859.

245 Bidwell, "Dictation," 18.

246 Barber to Bidwell, 5 July 1853, JBCSL.

247 During this period Bidwell apparently leased land across Chico Creek and on both sides of the Oroville-Shasta trail from the John Potter estate. The Mechoopdas' camp is variously cited as spread out back from the east side of the trail and from the creek south to present Third or Fourth streets.

248 Thomas Wright to Bidwell, 13 May 1853, JBCSL.

249 Robert Eccleston, *Diary*, 29 July 1853, at Bidwell's ranch, Bancroft Library, courtesy of Susan Snyder, head of Public Services. Mansfield, 120, gave the date as July 1, but the handwritten date in Eccleston's diary on the day of the race is July 29. The supply lists come from examples in his ledgers and correspondence with his Sacramento distributor about miners' preferences.

250 Ibid. The source does not mention the identity of the mare's owner. In 1867, Bidwell would condemn horse races as a waste of money and an abuse of horses. Quoted in Gillis and Magliari, 172. An error in the fall 2015 issue of *Diggins* [Butte County Historical Society] misidentified "Coon" as the "moniker" of Squire Clyde Garner. According to General Kibbe's pay records and others, Coon Garner was Conrad W. Garner. The two men, likely brothers, lived next to one another on Rock Creek.

251 *Butte Record*, 11 March, 8 July 1854; *Shasta Courier*, 9 December 1854.

252 Ibid., 8 July 1854.

253 Conway. Bidwell moved to his large "plain board house"—later known architecturally as a federal farmhouse—in 1857. See note 53. This description refines the analysis this author provided in "Bidwell's Earlier Mansion in the First 'Chico Village,'" [Butte County Historical Society] *Diggins* (Winter 2012).

254 *San Francisco Daily Express*, 31 December 1855; Bidwell to Seeper, 29 July 1897, JBCSL; cf. James T. Davis, *Trade Routes and Economic Exchange Among the Indians of California* (Ramona, CA: Ballena Press, 1974); Hurtado, 234–35.

255 Ibid.; Annie Bidwell, *Rancho Chico Indians*, 70–71; *Butte Record*, 12 January 1856. Conway gives a different number.

256 Bidwell, "Dictation," 18.

257 Ibid. 21; *Butte Record*, 12 January 1856; Annie Bidwell, *Rancho Chico Indians*, 70.

258 Conway.
259 *Butte Record,* 23 August 1856.
260 In other contests, Maidu fought with "very rude spears, clubs and stones." Powers, 301.
261 Charles W. Bush to Mr. and Mrs. Bush, 20 August 1850, Bancroft Library; Powers, 301.
262 Powers, 301.
263 *Butte Record,* 23 August 1856; Crowder, *Chico Enterprise,* 22 January 1918; Mansfield, 188. He described a similar battle that August below Oroville on the Feather River. Cf. *Oroville Record,* 16 August 1856.
264 Anderson, *Fighting the Mill Creeks; Red Bluff Beacon,* 29 July 1859; *Chico Enterprise,* 12, 14, 15, 22 January 1918. In his *Enterprise* memoir, Frank Crowder erroneously inferred from an Indian elder's remark that the split between the "two groups" — Mountain and Valley Maidu — began in 1859. He also noted he heard about a Valley Indian's remark that the Maidu had been enemies "once before." Crowder, "The Eventful Yesterdays."

Chapter Four

265 *Red Bluff Beacon,* 25 March to mid-June, 4 August 1859. Indians, horses and mules were the easiest livestock for Indians to move and they preferred their meat to that of cows. Farm animals filled the gap as their traditional foods became less available. Long accustomed to wild herds that grazed in the valley, Indians considered livestock theirs for the taking. By contrast, settlers captured wild cattle and horses, declared them their own and confined them within unmarked territory Indians considered theirs by right.
266 Schoonover, *Before Ishi.* In this web-published book, the author cites a truce also noted by Goldsborough Bruff in which valley farmers and the Yahi, after a brutal incident, kept a kind of peace until 1856 or 1857.
267 *Red Bluff Beacon,* 12 May 1858, citing the *Butte Record.*
268 Copied in *San Francisco Bulletin,* 31 May 1858.
269 Mansfield, 187.
270 *Oroville Record,* 29 November 1856; Claude Speegle, "The Thirteen Pages," 1997 transcription by Richard Burrill of notes by Homer Speegle's son, c. 1969. http://www.ishifacts.com/higood.asp.
271 Anderson, 20, 28; *Red Bluff Beacon,* 19 May 1858; Raphael and House; Schoonover, *Before Ishi,* 12, 15; *Shasta Herald,* 5 September 1859.
272 Capt. Henry Judah to Maj. W. W. MacKall, 28 August 1856, U.S. Army, NAM.
273 Bob Katz, "General George Crook," www.desertusa.com/mag99/may1/paper/ctc. [Website suspended]
274 Ibid., 30 May 1857. Capt. George Crook would become the Civil War general on the Union side. *Butte Record,* 23 May 1857; Katz. Sources on the conflicts ranging from Lassen Peak to the north are the Army officers' letters in the National Archives, Army, Letters Received. Abstracts of many appear in Bleyhl.
275 For example, drunken Indians in towns were regularly arrested, while enforcement officials ignored more serious offenses by settlers and Indians in remote areas. Cf. *Sacramento Union,* 1 September 1857.
276 There may be a historical link between Dr. E. W. Inskeep and the town of Inskip, originally a stage coach stop near the Feather River in the Sierra Nevadas.
277 *Red Bluff Beacon,* 21, 28 April, 12, 19 May, 2 June 1858; David D. Alt and Donald W. Hyndman, *Maps in Roadside Geology of Northern California* (Missoula, MT: Mountain Press Publishing Co., 1975), 88. The map shows the Inskeep location in

the outermost Sierra Nevada, but in close range to Lassen-based camps.
278 Ibid., 9 June 1859; Riddell, "Maidu and Koncow;" Schoonover, *Before Ishi*, chapter three.
279 Current thinking about the Yahi asserts their peaceful culture was maligned by Theodora Kroeber and others who attributed all the 1859 attacks on the valley to them. In place of that, the new vogue is to attribute those raids to renegades of every other tribe but them. This approach reduces Yahi to victims. The understanding of the historical and anthropological record relied on in the present account recognizes that, through history, Yahi were aggressive warriors on the valley and rivals of tribes around their canyon or mountain meadow villages. For example, the historical record demonstrates valley settlers, in the late 1840s, were terrified of their warriors, Mill Creeks, and anthropological accounts described all the Mountain Indian tribes as deadly rivals to one another. The change modern writers now emphasize, the close relationships that Mill Creeks and Deer Creeks developed with Valley Indians in Butte County, should be acknowledged. However, the present chapter, as well as five and six, clarify the Yahi's loss of control over their canyon to Mountain Maidu and others. It is likely some Yahi joined with the others, but no evidence clarifies their role. The chapters also address the process in summer 1862, when this "modern" moment of closeness crystallized. They describe the intimate contact between Mountain Maidu, some of whom raided out of Deer Creek Canyon, and peaceful Indians on Bidwell Ranch where the former awaited removal to Nome Cult Reservation in Round Valley. Some Mountain Maidu, who returned from the reservation to make homes in Deer Creek Canyon, maintained enduring ties with the Valley Indians they had come to know at Rancho Chico and on the reservation. In the removal period and after, the Yahi became so overwhelmed by the demands of Mountain Maidu and renegade Indians, as well as white pursuers, that two or three groups sought removal for protection. See chapter eleven.
280 *Red Bluff Beacon*, 9 June 1858.
281 Ibid.
282 Jerald Jay Johnson, "Ishi's Ancestors," 104.
283 *Red Bluff Beacon*, 31 August 1859. The reference to poison speaks to an Indian source since this was a distinctive Maidu weapon. For security, Old Doctor would have negotiated the meeting in advance with Sulemshews interested in his plan or willing to listen. Those willing to collaborate with the Yahi would have applied the poisons. This meeting may be what alerted the Mountain Maidu to the Yahi's weakness. (As an aside, the split within this tribelet on a key security issue is a telling example of strains between peaceful and warring members of the tribelets. It also illustrates why, even though peaceful Mountain Maidu relied on their Butte Creek warriors for defense, they also feared them. Like settlers, Mountain Maidu tribelets sometimes were divided among themselves.)
284 Schoonover, *Before Ishi*.
285 Johnson, "Ishi's Ancestors," 23; Jerald Jay Johnson, "The Yahi and the Southern Yana: An Example of Conservation, Genetic Isolation and an Impoverished Resource Base," *Proceedings of the Society for California Archaeology* 16 (2002): 95ff; Kroeber, *Handbook of Indians*, 636. Because he and Theodora Kroeber did not recognize the canyon-based collaborations, they mistakenly asserted the Mill Creek attacks were solely by the Yahi.
286 Johnson, "Ishi's Ancestors," 111; Orin Starn, *Ishi's Brain: In Search of American's Last "Wild" Indian* (New York: W.W. Norton, 2004); *Butte Record*, 10 January 1857. The population estimate from Steve Schoonover in *Before Ishi* agrees with other sources.
287 Orin Starn, email to author, 23 October 2007; Schoonover, *Before Ishi*.

Endnotes

288 "Ishi May Not Have Been All Yahi, UC Expert Says Tribe's Legendary Last Survivor of Mixed Ancestry," SFGate.com/Article Collections. Shackley observed that Ishi's arrows were "almost identical" to Wintu or Nomlaki styles. Richard Burrill has speculated that Ishi must have been part Mountain Maidu and that he fled toward Oroville accompanied by Maidu. Interview with Nancy Weigman on KCHO Radio, August 2011.
289 *Red Bluff Beacon*, 30 September 1857.
290 Schoonover, *Before Ishi*. Schoonover has an extended, close working knowledge of these areas that supports his research on the Yahi. He proposes that "the Yahis regarded the high meadows as their heartland.... The canyons were places the Yahi were forced into by winter ... a time of isolation and hardship," 15. Jerald Johnson made similar observations in his 1994 paper that is less developed on this point. Ishi grew up a Yahi who emerged into Oroville, California, in 1911 and became a University of California study subject for the rest of his life. *Shasta Herald*, 3 December 1859.
291 Capt. Henry Judah to Capt. D. R. Jones, 8 March 1856.
292 *Red Bluff Beacon*, 10 January 1857, 19 May 1858, 17 August 1859, U.S. Army, NAM.

Chapter Five

293 *Red Bluff Beacon*, 25 May, 21, 28 April 1858.
294 Stephen Powers may be the first observer to apply that name.
295 *Red Bluff Beacon*, 21, 28 April 1858.
296 Ibid., 9 June, 1858.
297 Ibid., 6 April 1859.
298 Bidwell, "Dictation," 19.
299 R. Anderson, 28.
300 *Red Bluff Beacon*, 3 August 1859.
301 *Butte Record*, 5 August 1854. Daugherty later went to prison for the murder of his Indian spouse.
302 M. Milleson to Brig. Gen. Neuman Clarke, 1 December 1857, U.S. Army, Pacific Division, NAM.
303 Lt. Michael Morgan to Headquarters, 1 July 1857, U.S. Army, Pacific Division, NAM. Cf. Morgan's September 15 letter: " Worthless whites ... are always found in some way connected with Indians in ... our center and towns."
304 *Red Bluff Beacon*, 6 April 1859; *Shasta Courier*, 9 December 1854; *Butte Record*, 13 December 1856.
305 Henry Judah to Maj. W.W. MacKall, 8 May 1858, U.S. Army, NAM.
306 *Red Bluff Beacon*, 23 April 1859. Anderson identified Spalding. John Breckenridge was the likely captain of the other party because he went on to be the men's next pick in June.
307 *Chico Enterprise*, 22 January 1859; *Red Bluff Beacon*, 6, 23 April 1859; *Butte Record*, 30 August 1856, 10 January 1857. "Doctor" was his formal first name. For remarks on Texas, see Gwynne, *Empire of the Summer Moon*.
308 *Red Bluff Beacon*, 23 April 1859.
309 Ibid., April 23, 1859; R. Anderson, 7; James Callen to John Bidwell, 20 July 1852, JBCSL; cf. Cook, *Conflict*, 227; R. Anderson, 7–10, describes what seem to be earlier "practice" sorties in which the detail differs from their mid-April 1859 attempt.
310 For example, ten puffs of smoke might mean ten pursuers with a big puff as the period on the message. *Red Bluff Beacon*, 24 July 1859; Speegle, "Thirteen Pages"; Richard Burrill, "Hi Good's Cabin Report," chapter two, http://www.ishifacts.com/higood.asp. Claude Speegle spoke of having seen a "stick ... jammed in a hole in

the rock in such a way that only a person could have done." That rock's location was a high point over the valley entrance to the canyon with space to crouch behind it. Apparently in this "signaling spot," a deerskin would have been used to manipulate smoke to send messages or to signal enemies' approach.

311 R. Anderson, 7-10.
312 *Red Bluff Beacon*, 23 April 1859.
313 Ibid., 27 April 1959.
314 Ibid., 18 May, 6 April, 23 March 1859. Other articles on similar raids appeared through March. An 1857 massacre in that area saw settlers kill forty Indians, including nineteen women and children. Those who survived in Yreka were sold for $24 to $75. A year later, Lt. Crook's unit killed eighteen Indians, wounded others, many of those, according to Crook, fatally. Capt. Henry Judah to Maj. W. W. MacKall, 9 September 1856, U.S. Army, Pacific Division, NAM; see also 11 July 1857. The Lassen killing may also have been Mountain Indian retribution for his assistance to Valley Indians in a dispute with them. Asa Fairfield Merrill, *Fairfield's Pioneer History of Lassen County to 1870* (San Francisco: H. S. Crocker Co., 1916), 177.
315 Tehama Petition to Governor Weller, May, 1859, California Indian Wars Files, CSA. Theodora Kroeber, who explained their dismissive attitude as the product of 1960s John Birch Society-type free-floating resentment against government, overlooked the local populace's reality-based assertion that the institutional constraints on Army regulars meant soldiers could not find, let alone defeat, Mill Creeks in their rugged canyon havens. T. Kroeber, *Ishi in Two Worlds*, 62.
316 Wozencraft to Luke Lea, U.S. Senate Misc. Documents, no. 688, 33rd Cong., spec. sess., Reports and Executive Data, 203-9.
317 Hubert Howe Bancroft, *The Works of Hubert Howe Bancroft*, vol. 24, 1860-1890 (The History Company: San Francisco, 1890), 55; Obituary, William C. Kibbe, *New York Times*, 26 January 1904.
318 Ibid.; cf. Osborne, *A. J. Granville Doll and the Formative Years of Red Bluff* (Chico: Association for Northern California Historical Research, 1985); *Red Bluff Beacon*, 1 June 1859; Petition, Tehama County Citizens, May 29 1859; Gov. Weller to Petitioners, 2 June 1859, Indian War Files, California Archives.
319 Sherburne Cook, "The American Invasion, 1848-1870," *Ibero-America* 25 (1945): 40-46.
320 *Red Bluff Beacon*, 18, 23, 25 May, 1 June 1859. Late twentieth-century interpretations of the McElroy killings and others with Indian and white victims in the headwaters region often appear ideological: Indians were good, therefore, their violence was acceptable and whites were bad, therefore, their violence was unacceptable and their killings by Indians justifiable. The object of the present account is to present each people in its complexity. Each people was made up of individuals with personal mixtures of good and bad influenced by situational conditions.
321 Ibid., 14 June 1859; Cook, "American Invasion," 40-46; cf. Gwynne, 173; Osborne. This reviews other Doll contributions to economic and civic life.
322 Maj. W. W. McKall to Capt. Franklin Flint, 3 June 1859, U.S. Army, Pacific Division, U.S. Army, NAM. A letter the same day from McKall to Flint demanded active advances against dangerous Indians in order to protect civilians. However, Flint only shared the less aggressive letter with residents and the restraint in his unit's actions satisfied neither instruction. He would later report the area problems were exaggerated. After malaria rapidly downed his unit and himself upon their arrival in Red Bluff, Flint became the next officer determined to secure assignments elsewhere.
323 Ibid., 20, 25 May, 1, 15 June 1859. The residents had reached a panic point, as the *Beacon* reflected in its call for control by the troops, even if they had to "exterminate"

Endnotes

the Mill Creeks. R. Anderson, 4, chapter three.
324 Appreciation to Mr. William F. Strobridge for his advice. *Red Bluff Beacon*, 25 May, 1 June 1859; Report, Dr. Robert Murray to Capt. Hannibal Day, 14 May 1850, Bleyhl.
325 *Red Bluff Beacon*, 15 June 1859.
326 Ibid., 20 March, 1, 3, 23 May, 6, 23 April, 1 June 1859; Carl E. Wheat, ed., "California's Bantam Cock: The Journals of Charles DeLong, 1854–1863," *California Historical Society Quarterly* IX (Winter, 1930): note 76; Tehama County Petition to Governor Weller, 11, 16 May 1859, California Indian Wars Files, CSA; Raphael and House, 164; T. Kroeber, *Ishi in Two Worlds*, 62. Weller, who had run for governor of Ohio, was a Mexican War veteran and had been a U.S. Senator from California and was no political novice.
327 *Red Bluff Beacon*, 14 June 1859; Cook, "American Invasion"; cf. Gwynne, 173; Osborne. From Sacramento later that summer, Flint accused the Tehama County residents of seeking a military campaign, not because Indians presented a serious threat, but because they wanted the state expenditures to pad their cashboxes.
328 J. C. Bradley to Governor John Weller, 16 May 1859, California State Indian Wars Files, CSA; R. Anderson, 7; *Red Bluff Beacon*, 1 June 1859.
329 Governor Weller to J. Granville Doll, 2 June 1859, Indian War Papers, CSA; *Red Bluff Beacon*, 1, 8 June 1859.
330 *Red Bluff Beacon*, 1 June 1859.
331 Ibid., 10 March, 6 April 1859. Mayhew's Crossing, according to Richard Burrill, was across the Oroville-Shasta Road from present-day Vina and near Deer Creek. Tehama still stands northwest of there by the Sacramento River and Red Bluff lies ten miles or so north, also along that river.
332 R. Anderson, 7–10; *Red Bluff Beacon*, 27 May, 1 June 1859; J. C. Bradley to Governor John Weller, 16 May 1859, California Indian Wars Files, CSA.
333 Ibid., 4. He believed that Indian violence began when his upstream neighbors, the Carters, killed Indians who had stolen livestock. *Butte Democrat*, 6 August 1859. Burrill's research notes in "Hi Good's Cabin Report" state that, until Anderson became of age, he could not become a full owner with his partner in the ranch. Their Texas counterparts were Jack Hays and, later, Sul Ross, who trained themselves in the Comanches' war methods. Both men rejected the Army's insistence on fighting on foot, as well as other tactics and improper equipment for the mounted Comanches' challenge. Gwynne, 138–50, 174–77.
334 R. Anderson, 4.
335 Reference to Breckenridge is a speculation based on his prominence among pursuers, who made him their captain through the 1859 campaigns. Anderson mentioned the presence of "leaders" in his early outings with Good and Spaulding. Inclusion of Obe Field follows Richard Burrill's identification of him as twenty-six years older than Good. If so, as Burrill suggests, he was a much senior and experienced woodsman. As such he was likely influential in the younger men's training. Burrill, www.ishifacts.com/higood.asp.
336 Moak, 11, 31.
337 Ibid., 20 May, 1, 9, 19, 22 June 1859.
338 "Kibbe's Report," in Heizer and Kroeber, 16.
339 Capt. Michael Morgan to Maj. W. W. MacKall, 15 April 1858, Bleyhl.
340 Ibid.; Bidwell, "Dictation," 19–20; *Red Bluff Beacon*, 3 August 1859.
341 Ibid., 22 June 1859; cf. R. Anderson, 19.
342 *Red Bluff Beacon*, 22 May, 22, 29 June 1859.
343 Ibid., 23 June 1859.
344 "Kibbe's Report," 16.
345 *Red Bluff Beacon*, 22 June, 1, 15, 22 October 1859; R. Anderson, 7. Later canyon

Indians would claim cross-tribal families of whom Ishi was a likely example. Anthropologist Jerald Jay Johnston hazarded that his facial shape resembled that of the valley Wintus. Johnson, "Ishi's Ancestors."

346 Lt. Col. Silas Casey to Lt. Col. Hasker, 25, 27 August, 1848, U.S. Army, NAM. While at Lassen's ranch he sent back to base thirty-six sick men and more in October. Capt. Warner described his company, en route from the valley to Benicia, as "a perfect moving hospital." Of eighty-five who had headed there from Sacramento, only two escaped the "sickness."

347 *Red Bluff Beacon*, 1, 15, 31 August 1859.

348 Stuart, 85; D. L. Spencer, "Notes on the Maidu Indians of Butte County," *Reprints of Various Papers on California Archaeology, Ethnology and Indian History*, ed. Robert F. Heizer (Berkeley: Archaeological Research Facility, Department of Anthropology, University of California, 1973), 52; "Kibbe's Report," 15.

349 Ibid. and elsewhere in this memoir.

350 R. Anderson, 40. Because the memoir focuses on Anderson's and Good's experiences, histories relying on it may have understated Breckenridge's performance.

351 *Red Bluff Beacon*, 15, 20 June 1859; R. Anderson, chapter two. Burns would serve under General Kibbe once his campaign began in August 1859.

352 R. Anderson, 7; *Red Bluff Beacon* 22, 27, 29 June 1859.

353 R. Anderson, 16–20. Some trails became named for them: the Moak and Sutherland trails, for example.

354 *Red Bluff Beacon*, 20 May, 1, 9, 19 June 1859.

355 R. Anderson, 17.

356 Ibid.

357 *Sacramento Daily Union*, 1 July 1859.

358 Anderson, 21.

359 Red *Bluff Beacon*, 29 June 1859.

360 Adj. Gen. William Kibbe to Capt. Francis Flint, Comd. of "A" Co, 6th Infantry, 11 July 1859, U.S. Army, NAM.

361 U.S. Senate, 34th Cong., 1st sess., Miscellaneous Document 67, vol. 1, 19 June 1856; William C. Kibbe, *The Volunteer: Containing Exercises and Movements of Infantry, Light Infantry, Rifle Men and Cavalry, as a Drill Manual for the Californian Militia* (Sacramento: B. B. Redding State Printer, 1855).

362 Ibid.; cf. Strobridge's helpful analysis of the Army's experience and perspective.

363 Dottie Smith, *The History of the Indians of Shasta County* (Redding, CA: CT Publishing Co., 1995), 23.

364 Adj. Gen. Kibbe to Capt. Flint, July 11, 1859, Military Dept. of Adjutant General and Indian War Papers, CSA; *Sacramento Daily Union*, 11, 15 July 1859.

365 Lt. Francis Flint to Governor John Weller, 30 July 1859, California Indian Wars Files, CSA; *Red Bluff Beacon*, 13, 15, 20 July 1859; See coverage by the *Shasta Herald* on various northern fronts; Thompson, chapter four.

366 General Kibbe to Governor John Weller, 9 November 1859, California Indian Wars Files, CSA.

367 Ibid.

368 General Kibbe to Governor Weller, 25 July 1859, California Indian Wars Files, CSA; *Red Bluff Beacon*, 13, 15, 20 July 1859; See coverage by the *Shasta Herald* on the northern fronts; cf. Strobridge treats the Mendocino situation; Thompson, chapter four.

369 *Sacramento Daily Union*, 11, 15 July 1859.

370 Theodora Kroeber also asserts, with no record to support her statement, that when Breckenridge's party turned to the Mountain Maidu territory in Butte County, they

were not so much tracking the Indians as the Indians were leading them away from their people. T. Kroeber, 66–68; T. T. Waterman, 43.
371 R. Anderson, 20.
372 *Red Bluff Beacon*, 3 August 1859.
373 The area around the present hamlet of Cohasset was known as North Point. In February 1877, when the Post Office demanded a single word name, a teenage girl submitted Cohasset from a poem she read. Cohasset is used here for modern specificity.
374 On Crowder, see Mansfield, 196.
375 *Chico Enterprise*, 17 January 1918.
376 Bidwell, "Dictation," 19–20; *Red Bluff Beacon*, 3 August 1859.
377 R. Anderson, 20.
378 Oliver Wozencraft to Luke Lea, 4 September 1851, NAM.
379 Kroeber, 63.
380 R. Anderson, 22; *Red Bluff Beacon*, 20 August 1859.
381 *Red Bluff Beacon*, 31 August, 14 December 1859; R. Anderson, 48; *Shasta Herald*, 10 September 1859; Federal Census of 1860, Chico Township, Butte County, California.
382 Ibid.
383 *Red Bluff Beacon*, 3 August, 7 September 1859. The term also applied to Indians accustomed to white life. Robert Anderson did not mention this scalping incident, 18–26. *San Francisco Daily Evening Bulletin*, 8 August 1859, copying *Shasta Herald*; *Red Bluff Beacon*, 17 August 1859.
384 R. Anderson, 22, 25; Voters Roll from 1852, Chico Township, Butte County, California, George McKinstry Collection, CSL; *The Great Register*, Mill Precinct, Butte County, California, CSUC Special Collections. Garner also acquired a ranch on Rock Creek.
385 Mansfield, *History of Butte County*, 536; R. Anderson, 27; *Chico Courant*, 24 February 1866. Members of this twenty-man party also included Bates, Adm. Williams and Daniel Sutherland.
386 R. Anderson, 25–26.
387 Ibid., 26.
388 Ibid., 37ff; Mansfield, 188; *Red Bluff Beacon*, 3, 17 August, 7 September 1859. The latter links a later Forks of Butte attack that summer to the Cold Springs/Deer Creek conflict just described. The 1859 Grand Jury report is missing. Pursuers, not uncommonly, recognized guns lost in battlefields as belonging to people they knew.
389 *Red Bluff Beacon*, 3 August 1859. It had been alerted to the Cold Springs plan, but not about the detour to Forks of Butte, which delayed it. The article does not name Cold Springs, but says after Forest Ranch they were headed to the head of Deer Creek to attack Indians there. Cold Springs is at the head of Deer Creek and apparently where they had been waiting out the Butte Creeks' return to Butte County.
390 *Shasta Herald*, 6 August 1859. Capt. Morgan's letters suggest his own chief desire was a transfer. It appears he wanted to suggest to his superiors that, beyond Nome Lackee Reservation, there was cause for troops in the valley—perhaps out of concern he might be ordered to the mountains.
391 R. Anderson, 27–29. Chief clerks supervised sales staff in small establishments.
392 In 1863, Wallace married an Indian woman he called "Nancy." Federal Census of 1860; Butte County Marriage Records, appreciation to the late Larry V. Richardson for this information.
393 Mansfield, 188.

Standoff

394 R. Anderson, 28.
395 Ibid., 34. See also Anderson's chapters six and seven.
396 *Butte Democrat*, 29 August 1859.
397 R. Anderson, 38.
398 *Butte Record*, 16 August 1859.
399 R. Anderson, 39–42; *Red Bluff Beacon*, 1 August 1859.
400 Ibid.
401 Ibid.; Stuart, 85; Spencer, "Notes on Maidu Indians," 52.
402 C. Hart Meriam, Papers Relating to Work with California Indians, 1850–1974, Indian Stocks and Tribes, BNEC 1556: 118, Bancroft Library.
403 *San Francisco Daily Evening Bulletin*, 8 August 1859, copying *Butte Herald*, 29 July 1859.
404 *Butte Democrat*, 29 August 1850. Although Wallace's name does not appear in the letter, the editor did not dispute Breckenridge's identification of him as Wallace.
405 *Red Bluff Beacon*, 10, 17 August 1859.
406 This remark references work through the mid-twentieth century. The sole focus on the Yahi has changed with evidence in publications by Steve Schoonover and this author in the late 1990s and early 2000s. Prolific Ishi specialist Richard Burrill has adopted their findings, but the compelling history of the Yahi has remained his principal interest.
407 *Butte Record*, 6 August 1859, quoted in Mansfield, 188.
408 *Red Bluff Beacon*, 17 August 1859.
409 Mansfield, 193. Guerilla fighters and modern special services fighters blacken their faces for night work.
410 *Red Bluff Beacon*, 7 September 1859.
411 *Butte Record*, 26 January 1853. They did not carry through on this threat.
412 Mark, note 26. Mark represents Breckenridge's view as this author's "claim." As the above quote from Breckenridge's letter demonstrates, he stated it and others in the area supported it (see above).
413 *Red Bluff Beacon*, 7 September 1859.
414 R. Anderson, 28.
415 Homer Mead Speegle, "The Eight Pages," 1997, in Richard Burrill's "Hi Good's Cabin Report."

Chapter Six

416 *Shasta Herald*, 20 August 1859.
417 Ibid., 20 August 1859. The other officers were 1st Lt. Robert Baily, Brevet 2nd Lt. Van Shell and 2nd Lt. McCarthy. "Burns" sometimes appears as "Byrnes."
418 Gwynne, 254–259, and passim. Later mentions here that compare or contrast Cheyenne experience rely on this splendid account.
419 *Shasta Herald*, 20 August, 14 September 1859; *Red Bluff Beacon*, 21, 24 August 1859.
420 *Butte Democrat*, 20 August 1859; *Red Bluff Beacon*, 24 August, 10 September 1859; *Shasta Herald*, 9 September 1859. See Steve Schoonover, "Kibbe's Campaign," *California* [Dogtown] *Territorial Quarterly* 20 (Winter 1994). The Army would later pay Garner $60 for his services in the California Volunteers' Pit River Expedition. While Daniel Sutherland served and Sandy Young, a figure in chapter twelve, did not receive pay on record, they would win California Indian Wars status with benefits. R. Anderson, 43; California Indian Wars, Ledger, Pit River Expedition, CSA; Other members were G. H. Stratton of Rock Creek and J.C. Morrill, a gold miner turned lumberman.
421 Ibid., 24 December 1859.

Endnotes

422 *Red Bluff Beacon*, 7 December 1859.
423 Ibid., 21 September 1859, and subsequent issues.
424 *Chico Enterprise*, 22 January 1918. The valley party used muzzle loaders.
425 R. Anderson, 9; Powers, "California Indian Characteristics," 308.
426 *Red Bluff Beacon*, 27 July, 31 August 1859; Adj. Gen. William Kibbe to Gov. Weller, 25, 30 July 1859, California Indian Wars Collection, CSA; According to the *Sacramento Union*, 12 December 1859, during that year in the mining area north of Butte Creek the Indians killed James Freeman, – Bowles, – McElroy, – Callaghan, William Patrick, Barney McMacken, Peter Lassen, – Clapper and thirteen other unnamed men.
427 Adj. Gen. William Kibbe to Gov. Weller, 30 July 1859, California Indian Wars Files, Camp Cass Returns, CSA; Strobridge, 219; *Red Bluff Beacon*, 14 September 1859.
428 Ibid., 14, 24 December, 26 October 1859; Adj. Gen. Kibbe to Gov. Weller, 30 July 1859, California Indian Wars Files, CSA.
429 *Red Bluff Beacon*, July 1859.
430 Ibid., 24 December 1859.
431 Ibid., 10 September 1859; cf. Gillis and Magliari, 268; *Red Bluff Beacon*, 14 December 1859.
432 *San Francisco Daily Evening Bulletin*, copying *Butte Herald*, 8 August 1859; *Butte Record*, 6 August 1859; *Butte Democrat*, 27 August 1859.
433 *Butte Democrat*, 18 August 1859; *Red Bluff Beacon*, 24 August, 26 October 1859.
434 *Red Bluff Beacon*, 7 September 1859. The newspaper names M. Armesby, who probably was Myron Ormesby, a Rock Creek farmer whose name appears above. Thanks to the late Larry V. Richardson who sorted this out.
435 Ibid.; *Butte Democrat*, 16 June 1860, on Cheesman in politics. According to Robert Chandler, he became a "typical, cautious bureaucrat" who would become Assistant U.S. Treasurer. This may be the "Cheeseman," p. 21 in the Butte County Census of 1850, if the transcriber misread his first initial.
436 Breckenridge, Sadorus, Ormesby and Stratton were held. The murder charges were linked to the Breckenridge party's actions at Forest Ranch.
437 Nothing about these Cox's Flat events reached the *Red Bluff Beacon*'s pages which reported on August 31 that, on the 24th, "a unit commanded by Captain Burns and, under the immediate direction of Kibbe himself, succeeded in surrounding the same rancheria attacked a few weeks ago by Breckenridge and took every Indian in it prisoner."
438 Bidwell, "Dictation," 19.
439 *Red Bluff Beacon*, 22, 24 August 1859; Marriage Records, Recorder's Office, Butte County, CA, September 1859. Appreciation to Larry V. Richardson for his assistance on marriage records.
440 Petition to James W. McDuffie, Superintendent of Indian Affairs for California from Citizens of Butte County, 17 September 1859.
441 Eric Josephson of Butte County's Maidu tribe in communication with author, 17 July 2011; *Red Bluff Beacon*, 15, 21 September, 5 October 1859.
442 *Butte Democrat*, 27 August 1859.
443 *Red Bluff Beacon*, 7 September 1859. This letter's wording built on ideas in the interview John Breckenridge gave, which the *San Francisco Evening Bulletin* printed August 20, 1859, in response to the questions about the Forest Ranch attack.
444 Adj. Gen. Kibbe to Gov. Weller, 29 November 1859, California Indian Wars Files, CSA; cf. *Red Bluff Beacon*, 31 August, 9 November 1859; *Shasta Herald*, 3 December 1859.
445 *Red Bluff Beacon*, 21 September, 5, 12 October 1859; *Shasta Herald*, 8 October, 3 December 1859. Most of the Indians sent to the Mendocino Reservation must have

Standoff

been transferred to Nome Cult Reservation by 1862, when about four hundred resided there. Cf. chapter seven. Researchers on Nome Lackee Reservation will find invaluable data in, Army Letters Received through the 1850s, National Archives. See Bleyhl, "Indian-White Relationships."

446 *Alta California*, 6, 15, 16 December 1859; *Red Bluff Beacon*, 14 October, December 1859.
447 *Butte Democrat*, 12 October 1859, 16 June 1860; *Red Bluff Beacon*, 31 August, 7 September, 5, 19 October 1859; *Sacramento Union*, 2 September 1859; Pit River Expedition Record of 1859, CSA.
448 *Shasta Herald*, 7 September 1859.
449 Adj. Gen. Kibbe to Gov. Weller, November 29, 1859, California Indian Wars Collection, CSA; *Alta California*, 15, 16 December 1959; *San Francisco Bulletin*, 14 January 1859; *Red Bluff Beacon*, 12 October 1859.
450 *Sacramento Daily Union*, 7 November 1859.
451 *Red Bluff Beacon*, 7 December 1859.
452 Ibid., 24 December 1859. "Tigers [Maidu Picas], Concows, Kimshews and other rancherias as far south as the Feather River.... [who], having the confidences of whites [miners], ... by doing so evaded detection."
453 The exception is Steve Schoonover's article on this in the *California Territorial Quarterly*.
454 Theodore H. Hittel, *History of California*, vol. 4 (San Francisco: N. J. Stone Co., 1898), 264; *Red Bluff Beacon* 7 September, 21 September 1859; R. Anderson, 38; *Chico Enterprise*, January 1918; *California, Report of Adjutant General William C. Kibbe*, 15 December 1862, CSA, 17.
455 *California, Report of Kibbe*, 17.
456 *Butte Democrat*, 12 November 1859, 28 January 1860; *Butte Record*, 17 August 1859; R. Anderson, 46.
457 Crowder, quoted in Mansfield, 196; R. Anderson, 44; Larry V. Richardson to Michele Shover, February 1999. Richardson recalled old timers in his youth who used the term "Mill Creeks" for any Mountain Indians associated with violence. This was the practice of Sim Moak, who arrived in 1863, well after Mountain Maidu began to raid out of Deer Creek Canyon. When he wrote his memoir, Moak referred to Mill Creeks as the general term for all hostile Indians. *New York Times*, 26 January 1904. After the Civil War, William Chauncy Kibbe returned to Brooklyn, the home of his youth, where he worked in the Hall of Records and died in 1904. Magliari, "Free State Slavery."
458 R. Anderson, chapter four; *Red Bluff Beacon*, June 1858. While Good usually placed orphans and women on reservations, he probably placed some with farmers, a common practice then.
459 Schoonover, *Before Ishi*, chapter ten.
460 Ibid.
461 *Marysville Appeal*, 3 July 1860.
462 The land south of Chico Creek was not "empty" when Bidwell bought it because it still sited Potter's rotting buildings and the Mechoopda rancheria.

Chapter Seven

463 Alvin Josephy, *The Civil War in the American West* (New York: Alfred Knopf, 1992), 237.
464 Bidwell, "Dictation," 26.
465 Josephy, 235.
466 *Alta California*, 9 August, 23 December 1861. Daniel is presumed to be the proper

Endnotes

Gibson because, as a Missourian, he was the only Southerner by that name in the federal census of 1860. Chico Township, Butte Co., California.
467 Mansfield, 231.
468 Cf. Shover, "The Doctor, the Lawyer," 1–38; McCorkle is a subject of that article. Winfield J. Davis, *History of Political Conventions in California, 1849–1862* (Sacramento: California State Library, 1892), 171–78. The fullest accounts of McCorkle's political adventures appear in Christopher Burchfeld's "The Golden State's First Senator and the Perils of Patronage," [Dogtown] *California Territorial Quarterly* (Spring 2911). This Stephen Field became the U.S. Supreme Court judge.
469 *Butte Record*, 13 July 1861.
470 Bidwell, "Dictation," 26. McCorkle did not win the election.
471 Ibid., 26–28.
472 Federal Census of 1860, Butte County, Chico Township, California. All of the nineteenth-century Butte County histories skirted the question of Chicoans' alliances in the Civil War. Until the early twentieth century, northern and southern state allegiances continued to divide the senior residents who, with their families, were an important component of potential volume buyers for these commercially produced histories. The proportion of Southern males given relies on listings from the United States Census, Chico Township, Butte County California, 1860. These percentages are based on 777 white males who were United States born. Not counted were 3 Chinese, 156 Native Americans, 2 African Americans, or 76 foreign residents. Northerners were 422; Southerners and Border State immigrants were 265. For further information, see Michele Shover, *Blacks in Chico, 1860–1865: Climbing the Slippery Slope* (Chico: Association for Northern California Records and Research, 1991), 2–4. Information on the woman who arrived in Chico Township as a slave appears in papers collected by this author, with additional research by descendent Carolyn Payne in the "Blacks in Chico" Collection of SCML.
473 Bidwell, "Dictation," 27.
474 *Butte Record*, 1 February 1862, 12 April 1862.
475 Ibid., 12 April, 21 June 1862; 21 June 1862; Josephy, 246.
476 Mansfield, 198–99 (1918 ed.).
477 *Butte Record*, 28 June 1862.
478 Moak (p. 11) said the Indians were attacking the Hickok children when Thomas Allen and Tom came on them. This seems unlikely because of the sequence set out below from other sources in footnotes 15 and 17. An oral interview with Helen Sommer Gage was reviewed.
479 *Chico Enterprise*, 11, 12 January 1918; Moak, 11; Mansfield, 218, 279; *Chico Enterprise*, 1 January 1918; R. Anderson, chapter ten; *Red Bluff Independent*, 1 July 1862; *Red Bluff Beacon*, 17 July 1862; *Butte Record*, 5 July 1862. The *Chico Enterprise* account best fits contemporary accounts in the timing of these events as they unfolded. The Hickok couple died in Butte County: Franklin S., in 1873, and Elvira, in 1875. They are buried in the Chico Cemetery where their family gravestones were destroyed by vandals. There are descendants, according to the late Larry V. Richardson.
480 There is no evidence that the bodies went to the family's home before going to Chico. However, because in their coffins they were clean and well-presented, it seems likely in those days that was the work of their mother and her friends at the Hickoks' home.
481 Moak, 11; Burrill, "Good's Cabin Report.
482 Erasmus D. Keyes, *From West Point to California* (Oakland: Biobooks, 1950), 62.
483 *Red Bluff Beacon*, 17 July 1862; Governor Leland Stanford to General George Wright, 27 June 1863, United States, Department of War, *The War of the Rebellion: A Compilation of the Official Records of the Union and Confederate Armies*, series 1,

Standoff

vol. 50 (Washington, D.C.: Government Printing Office, 1897), 28 (hereafter *Official Records*).
484 *Chico Morning Chronicle*, 17 July 1886. Crouter and Rolle (p. 108) reported that "The United States Army stood on call behind the whites ... Indian outbreaks were usually dealt with sternly." In the Sacramento Valley, sternness describes the Whites' response, but the "stern" actors were local volunteers in every case after the Cook unit's clashes with Hat Creeks or Pit Rivers in the late 1850s.
485 Guynn, 22, said they found the remains covered by stones along a bank of Mill Creek. Burrill, "Good's Cabin Report." Initial searchers for the Hickok children included Frank Crowder, Sylvester Eastman and Keefer mill employee James Clayton. Mansfield, (1918 ed.), 969, 1162–63; Mansfield, (1973 ed.), 537; www.ishifacts.com/higood.asp; A. L. Kroeber, 35–36.
486 R. Anderson, 55–56; Moak.
487 In his note by hand next to an article on this meeting pasted in his scrapbook (CSU Special Collections, Meriam Library), Bidwell said the most outspoken men were drunk at mid-day. Frank Crowder was at the meeting. *Chico Enterprise*, 17 January 1918.
488 Mansfield, 691; *Chico Morning Chronicle*, 16 July 1886; *Chico Record*, 24 July 1886. The two articles reflect differences between Guill and Bidwell on events of 1862 and 1863. The analysis here and later sorts out events and accusations between those two years. *Chico Enterprise*, 18–19 January 1918.
489 Crowder, *Chico Enterprise*, 11, 12 January 1918.
490 Henrietta Packer Compton, *Mary Murdoch Compton* (Chico: privately published, 1953), 85.
491 McDonald, *Annie Bidwell*, 86. She wrote about his problems with the Presbyterian Church. Bidwell's "Dictation" mentioned disappointment in the treatment of him by the Masonic chapter. Michele Shover, "John Bidwell: A Reconsideration," *Ripples Along Chico Creek* (Chico: Penwomen, 1992): 114.
492 Moak, 9.
493 *Butte Record*, 24 July 1886; Federal Census, 1860, Chico Township, Butte County. For further information on Washington Henshaw, see Michele Shover and Thomas Fleming, *Black Life in the Sacramento Valley, 1850–1934* (San Francisco: Max Millard, 1998), 2–3.
494 Frank Crowder in the *Chico Enterprise*, 11, 12 January 1918.
495 *Sacramento Union*, 2 July 1862; *Red Bluff Beacon*, 17 July 1862.
496 *Red Bluff Beacon*, 11 July 1862; *Sacramento Union* ,2 July 1862.
497 See references in chapters one and three.
498 Annie Bidwell, 54.
499 *Butte Record* (27 August 1864) provides an example of this usage. It appears that James Keefer and Robert Durham never attracted this level of antagonism.
500 Quoted in Robert Chandler, "The Failure of Reform: White Attitudes and Indian Response in California During the Civil War Era," *The Pacific Historian* 24 (Spring 1980): 288; Clough, *House at 5th and Salem*, 44. In response to the questions from his newly-arrived wife, Dr. Oscar Stansbury compared Bidwell's treatment of his Indians to the better masters of slaves in their home state of Maryland.
501 Cook, 304–5.
502 *Chico Enterprise*, 25 January 1918.
503 Stilson, Diary, 8 November 1863.
504 *Chico Enterprise*, 25 January 1918.
505 Bancroft, *History of California*, vol. 7, 309.
506 Behind Bidwell's generosity in that project was the influence of his new wife, Annie Kennedy Bidwell, who had arrived from Washington, D.C. with black servants,

whose attendance at the Methodist Church North likely made some of the white congregants uncomfortable.
507 *Chico Morning Chronicle*, 17 July 1886. This account on some points confuses events in 1862 and 1863. The present one extracts the descriptions that could only apply to the Chico meeting in 1862. *Chico Enterprise*, 11 January 1918.
508 *Butte Record*, 13 July 1861, 27 June 1863; Rockwell Hunt, *John Bidwell: Prince of California Pioneers* (Caldwell, ID: Caxton Printers, 1942), 183; Harry L. Wells and W. L. Chambers, *History of Butte County, California* (Berkeley: Howell-North Books, 1873), 174; *Chico Morning Chronicle*, 17 July 1886.
509 Bidwell's handwritten note on his copy of the *Chico Morning Chronicle*, 17 July 1886; cf. the speeches of U.S. Senator John C. Calhoun.
510 Bidwell, "Dictation," 40; Frank L. Klement, *Dark Lanterns: Secret Political Societies, Conspiracies and Treason in the Civil War* (Baton Rouge: Louisiana State University Press, 1984).
511 Josephy, 240.
512 Moak, 4; Bidwell, "Dictation," 27; *Oroville Union*, 9, 23 May 1863. While mentioned in the Butte County press in 1863, according to Robert J. Chandler, the Chico group did not appear in an 1864 circular.
513 *Butte Record*, 9 August 1862; *Sacramento Daily Union*, 2 July 1862; *Chico Enterprise*, 19 January 1918.
514 California, Petition to Leland Stanford from Butte County, 1862, Indian War Files, Military Collection, CSA; Wm. Kibbe to John Bidwell, 21 January 1863, JBSCML; *Official Records* 1162–63; *Butte Democrat*, 23 June 1862; *Sacramento Daily Union*, 26 June 1862; List of Ordinances Issued to Organized Militia, *Annual Report of The Adjutant-General of California in 1862* (Sacramento: State Printer, 1863), 146. This notes thirty-two rifles delivered to the "Citizens of Butte County" on July 2. Thanks to Robert Chandler for this document. General George Wright to State Adjutant General George Wright, 28 June 1863, Military Records, CSA. Thanks to George Stammerjohann for information on muskets versus rifles.
515 Petition, Citizens of Butte and Tehama Counties to the Governor, July 1863, Military Records, CSA.
516 *Butte Record*, 8 August 1862.
517 The author appreciates the advice of historian Robert Chandler regarding the responsibilities of the various authorities for response to Indian problems.
518 John Bidwell to Governor Leland Stanford, 17 July 1862, Military Records, CSA.
519 Ibid.; *Butte Record*, 9 August 1862.
520 *Official Records*, 27–28.
521 *Butte Record*, 9 August 1862; *Sacramento Daily Union*, 2 July 1862; *Chico Enterprise*, 19 January 1918.
522 *Red Bluff Beacon*, 22 July 1862. Most citizens probably could not distinguish by sight between California Volunteers and Army "regulars." The troops Wright sent up were California Volunteers.
523 *Butte Record*, 9 August 1863.
524 Ibid., 8 August 1862.
525 Ibid.
526 Burrill, "Good's Cabin Report." Burrill quoted an 1872 source, however, the present interpretation relies on Hi Good's contemporary Frank Crowder, who described such colorful dress as popular among men around Chico in the 1850s. *Chico Enterprise*, 17 January 1862.
527 Harmon Good to Governor Leland Stanford, 8 August, 13 July 1862, Military Records, CSA.
528 Adj. General Wm. Kibbe to Governor Leland Stanford, 15 August 1862, Military

Records, CSA; *Red Bluff Beacon*, 7 August 1862; *Red Bluff Independent*, 19 August 1862.
529 Ibid; *Official Records*, 550; *Red Bluff Independent*, 19 August 1862; *Chico Enterprise*, 15, 26 January 1918. Federal Indian agents or commissioners referred to Bidwell as a subagent in the early 1850s and as late as 1863 when Agent George Hanson called on the Chico rancher for help with Mountain Indian problems.
530 See Appendix D.
531 This became the site of the Children's Playground, on the corner of the Esplanade and Broadway. From that spot it would again move, this time to an area in back of Bidwell's home. Annie Bidwell mentioned in Annie Currie's article that, from her rooms, she could hear Indian children play in the creek. While before 1860 Mountain Maidu posed the threat to Mechoopdas, the significant threat to the tribelet after 1860 was from settlers who resented Bidwell. J. D. Powell mentioned the new rancheria's previous location as at the creek end of later named Flume Street in the late 1840s. J. W. Powell, "Indian Linguistic Families North of Mexico," *Seventh Annual Report of the Bureau of Ethnology to the Secretary of the Smithsonian Institution, 1885–1886* (Washington, D.C.: Government Printing Office, 1891). Moak, 9.

Chapter Eight

532 *Butte Record*, 15 October 1863; Stilson, passim.
533 Ibid., 15 August, 3, 4 September 1863.
534 Stilson, 3 September 1863. His Missouri experience appears in his 1861 and 1862 diaries.
535 Bidwell, "Dictation," 27. This example also appeared in the memoir of Frank Crowder, *Chico Enterprise*, 15 January 1918.
536 *Official Records*, 550, 572. Bidwell carried the brevet title of major from his contributions to the Bear Flag revolt against Mexico.
537 Camp Bidwell Post Returns, August, 1864, Chico, Butte County, California, 1800–1916, Microfilm 617, National Archives.
538 Bancroft, 289; Camp Bidwell Post Returns, December 1863.
539 Ibid., 24 January 1864.
540 Ibid., 25 March, 11 April 1864.
541 *Marysville Appeal*, 29 March 1864; Boyle, 192–203.
542 Stilson, 26 March 1864; Bidwell, "Dictation," 26; *Chico Enterprise*, 15 January 1915, Arabella Barham, Barham File, Butte County Historical Society Archive. Thanks to Liz Stewart for referring this file and the Butte County Historical Society's Nancy Brower for copying it. Bidwell, Stilson and Barham recalled how troops saddled Rebs with bricks or sand, then had them march until told to stop.
543 Mary Silsby to Mrs. H. H. Webb, 3 April 1864, SCML; Bancroft, 309.
544 Stilson, 18, 23 July 1864.
545 Irvin Ayres to John Bidwell, 24 August 1863, JBSCML. According to military field historian George Stammerjohann, Bidwell had previously enjoyed the courtesy rank of major as a U.S. Navy title which, according to state historian George Stammerjohann, approximated to paymaster and was not an equivalent to the rank of major in the U.S. Army. In being named Brigadier General, therefore, his elevation was the equivalent of an honorary for a civilian with no command authority. Bidwell encouraged California Volunteers officers to harass Rebs, referring to the soldiers on his ranch and himself as "we" in their actions. A recent Bidwell account asserts that Bidwell was the main force behind the soldiers' actions against local Rebs. While he encouraged such actions, he could not order

the Army-led State Militia to do so and there is no evidence the Chico militia, over which he did have authority, acted on any issue at all. According to Stilson's diary, they had no responsibilities beyond parades and the like.
546 "Chico Light Infantry," State Militias, Military Records, CSA; Stilson, 1863–1864, passim.
547 Stilson, 20 March 1865.
548 Mansfield, 228.
549 Stilson, 20 February 1864; Mansfield, 228–29; Robert J. Chandler, "Success to Civil War Tragedy: the Greathouse Brothers and Slicer's Express," *Western Express*, 46 (March 1996): 10–11; Leonard I. Richards, *The California Gold Rush and the Coming of the Civil War* (New York: Knopf, 2007), 232–33.
550 Stilson, 9 April 1864; Chandler, "Success," 4–58.
551 J. P. Steele to Hon. Wm. Dole, 25 April 1864, JBSCML; Bidwell, "Dictation," 27–29.
552 Bidwell, "Dictation," 28–29. In appreciation, Bidwell sent Grant a box of "Superior cigars" for which the commander took time from the war to send him a thank-you note. On 3 October 1864, from City Point, Virginia, Grant recalled the rancher's visit in camp on the Chickahominy River. Cf. Hunt. Generals Sherman and Grant would both attend Bidwell's wedding to Annie E. Kennedy in Washington where her father was prominent. ABCSL.
553 Ibid., 23 July 1864.
554 *Chico Enterprise*, 12 January 1918.
555 Camp Bidwell Post Returns, August 1864; *Oroville Union Record*, 27 August 1864. See above for a discussion of the term "black abolitionist."
556 Stilson, 22, 25 August 1864; Camp Bidwell Post Returns, August 1864; *Oroville Union Record*, 27 August 1864; Norris Bleyhl, *Three Military Posts in Northeastern California, 1849–1863* (Chico: Association for Northern California Records and Research, 1984), 10.
557 Mansfield, 228–29; Stilson, 5 October 1864; *Marysville Appeal*, 7 October 1864; *Santa Rosa Democrat*, 23 October 1863.
558 *Oroville Union Record*, 8 October, 3 December 1864; Stilson, 3 September, 30 December 1864. According to Robert Chandler, the local claim that the Gridley flour had been grown in Butte County and ground at the Bidwell mill could not have been the case as the project began in Gridley's Austin, Nevada, store. Historian Robert Chandler to author, 27 April 2001; Mansfield, 237.
559 *Oroville Union Record*, 1 October 1864.
560 Ibid., 2 October 1864.
561 Stilson, 18, 14 October 1864.
562 Ibid, 24 October 1864. Bidwell, the former Democrat, knew and respected Temple.
563 Mansfield quotes the *Oroville Union Record*, 5 November 1864; cf. Stilson, 5 November 1864.
564 Stilson, 15 December 1864.
565 Ibid., passim, 10, 16 December 1864, 7 February 1865; *Butte Record*, 11 April 1863.
566 Ibid., January, 3 October 1863, passim. For example, the County paid him $750 for a year's rent of Bidwell Hall to serve as the armory for the Chico Light Infantry. *Oroville Union Record*, 6 May 1865.
567 *Oroville Union Record*, 8 October 1864; Chico Light Infantry, Military Archive, CSA; Camp Bidwell Post Returns, October 1864; *Chico Courant*, 7 July 1866; cf. *Butte Record*, 11 August 1883.
568 Stilson, 10 April, 16 May 1865.
569 Ibid., 15 April 1865; Amanda Foreman, *A World on Fire: Britain's Crucial Role in the American Civil War* (New York: Random House, 2010), 780.
570 Ibid.

571 Ibid, 27, 19 April 1865; Moak, 15; *Official Records*, 1218; *Chico Enterprise*, 15 January 1918; Camp Bidwell Post Returns, November 1864–March 1865. Pvt. Hudson was convicted of murder and hanged in Sacramento.
572 *Oroville* Union *Record*, 20, 27 May 1865; Bleyhl, *Three Military Posts*, 13–15. Robert Chandler provided the information on Long Primer Hall. In 2012, [Butte County Historical Society] *Diggins* published an article with other information about Long Primer Hall. Printers used the term "long primer" for a 12-point font.
573 Ibid., 27 May 1865; Bleyhl, *Three Military Posts*, 13.
574 *Oroville Union Record*, 6 May 1865; Stilson, 13 May 1865; *Amador Ledger Dispatch*, 13 February 2011.
575 Stilson, 23 May 1865; General Wright to the Governor, 21 May 1865, California Military Collection, CSA.
576 Stilson, 1 June 1865.
577 *Chico Courant*, 16 December 1865.
578 Clough, 54, 57. See Bidwell Diaries.

Chapter Nine

579 Bidwell put up $2,000 for a surety bond the legislature required. This road was mentioned as completed in chapter eight, which, because it treats the entire Civil War period, leaps ahead in chronology.
580 George Hanson to Wm. Dole, 17 June 1863, NAM; *Red Bluff Beacon*, 5 October 1850; *Shasta Herald*, 2 June 1860, The reservations were the Mendocino and Round Valley.
581 Laney. The exact number of non-Bidwell rancheria Indians varied from three hundred to five hundred, according to different sources. James Short, Superintendent of Round Valley Reservation, to G. M. Hanson, 8 November 1862, NAM; George Hanson to John Bidwell, 28 October 1862, JBSCML; *Official Records*, 169. *Red Bluff Beacon*, 9 October 1862; A. G. Tassin, "The Chronicles of Fort Wright: The Concows," *Overland Monthly* 1–2 (July–August 1887): 170; *Sacramento Union*, 30 September 1862.
582 G. Wright to George Hanson, 13 October 1862; Bleyhl, "Indian-White Relationships"; Frank H. Baumgardner III, *Killing for Land in Early California: Indian Blood at Round Valley, 1856–1862* (New York: Algora Publishing, 2006), 233–41.
583 *Marysville Appeal*, 24 June 1859; George Hanson, Supplemental Estimate for Indian Service, Fiscal Year Ending 1864, NAM; cf. Coyote Man [Robert Rathbun], *Coyote Man, The Destruction of the People* (Berkeley: Brother William Press, 1973); *Red Bluff Beacon*, 5 October, 14 December 1859; *Shasta Herald*, 5 October 1859, 2 June 1860. While Kibbe had sent the Pit Rivers to the Mendocino and Nome Cult reservations, he moved most of them to the Klamath reservation in 1860; Hanson and others often used the term "Concows" for all the Kibbe captives at Round Valley (formerly Nome Cult). While Concows were the largest Maidu tribelet there, the reservation records and Hanson's correspondence also mentioned there were Nimshews, Kimshews and Picas with the Maidu. He had some sent to Tejon. No public records or reports identified Yahi among these captive Indians.
584 *San Francisco Bulletin*, 6 November 1862; *Red Bluff Beacon*, 9 October 1862.
585 George Hanson to John Bidwell, 28 October 1862, JBSCML; *Red Bluff Beacon*, 5 November 1859, 24 October 1859, 24 October 1862; Pamela A. Conners, *The Chico to Round Valley Trail of Tears* (Willows, CA: Mendocino National Forest Service), 7; *Official Records*, 169.
586 George Hanson to John Bidwell, 28 October 1862, JBSCML; Col. Francis Lippitt to Lt. Col. R. C. Drum, *Official Records*, 169–71; *Red Bluff Beacon*, 6, 9, 23 October 1862.
587 G. M. Hanson to Wm. Dole, 1, 8 November 1862, NAM.

Endnotes

588 Attachment. G. M. Hanson to Wm. Dole, 8 November 1862, NAM. Bidwell's Landing had come to be called Chico Landing.
589 Town Records of Dudley, MA; *The Eddys in America: A Genealogy* (Boston: privately published, 1930).
590 Research on James Eddy's death and his origins was the product of Ben Hughes' work in Tehama County after he found the Coroner's report and other records. For the present account, Gene Serr followed up with the probate report. He and Mary Lee Grimes traced Eddy's time in Tehama County prior to his Indian service employment.
591 A historical biography in the county mentioned Knotts as familiar with the reservation, perhaps having worked there.
592 Coroner's Investigation, James Eddy, deceased, 2 May 1864, California, Tehama County; Probate File, James Eddy; *Red Bluff Independent*, 5 May 1865.
593 *San Francisco Evening Bulletin*, 6 November 1862.
594 John Bidwell to Secretary of the Interior John Upham, 4 December 1863, NAM; James Eddy to John Bidwell, 20 January 1863, JBSCML; George Hanson to Wm. Dole, 17 June 1863, NAM.
595 R. L. Solomon to John Bidwell, 31 March 1862, JBSCML; J. S. Norris to John Bidwell, 20 May 1863, JBSCML; Henry Landt to John Bidwell, 22 May 1863, JBSCML. Rancho Chico residents were counted on the Federal Census of 1860, Chico Twp, Butte County, CA. Cf. Hill, 33.
596 Henry Landt to John Bidwell, 20 January 1863, JBSCML; Butte Record, 11 May and 24 June 1863; R. L. Solomon to John Bidwell, 20 May 1863, JBSCML; *Marysville Express*, 20 October 1863; Hill, *Indians of Chico Rancheria*, 66; Stuart, 65.
597 *Chico Enterprise*, 25 January 1918; James Eddy to John Bidwell, 21 May 1863, JBSCML; cf. Tassin, 179–80. Tassin, an Army officer who worked with the Butte County contingent, also made this point.
598 Ibid.
599 Oliver Wozencraft to Indian Affairs Office, 7 August 1851, NAM. This collaboration also occurred among Plains Indian tribes when they experienced pressure from settlers' raids or found themselves mixed together in reservations.
600 Kroeber Papers, Reel 161, frame 475, Bancroft Library. Thanks to Orin Starn, professor of cultural anthropology, Duke University, for a copy of this interview. Hurtado, 204. By this time, Mountain Maidu were among descendants of other tribes who had made homes along Deer Creek. Beverly Benner Ogle, *Spirits of Black Rock* (Paynes Creek, CA: privately published, 2003), 338.
601 Interview with Darwin B. Lyons, Reel 169, Frame 627, Ethnological Documents Collection, Bancroft Library. Thanks to Orin Starn for a copy of this. Cf. "Indian Youth Speak," [California State University, Chico] *Inside Chico State* 42, no. 8 (25 November 2012). This refers to tribal intermarriages characterized as "Yahi Maidu" from the Deer Creek area,
602 *Butte Record*, 9 May 1887; *Oroville Union*, 14 March 1863.
603 Ibid., 7 March 1863.
604 Mansfield, 200–1; *Butte Record*, 7 March 1863; *Oroville Union*, 14 March 1863; J. Bidwell to A. Hayward, 18 March 1863, JBSCML.
605 *Marysville Appeal*, 26 October 1859.
606 *Red Bluff Beacon*, 21 September 1859. This speaks of one hundred killed, 24 October 1862. *Marysville Appeal*, 26 October 1861. Tome-ya-nem's account appears in Tassin, "The Concow Indians," *Overland Monthly* (July 1887): 179–82. Thanks to Eric Josephson of the Butte County Maidu Tribal Council for his explanation that "Tome-ya-nem" was a term the Concows used for their leader, Yumyan, whose family also knew him as Bercha.

607 *Shasta Herald*, 5 November 1859; *Alta California*, 15 December 1859.
608 Ibid.
609 Smith, 136–37; *Red Bluff Beacon*, 2 November 1859, speaks to his 1859 capture. Beulah Johnson, "Old Station," *The Covered Wagon* (Riverdale, CA: Riverdale Press, 1974), 48–52.
610 Wm. Kibbe to Gov. John Weller, 30 September, 1859, NAM. This refers to the deaths of Callahan, McElroy and others. He says "there is no doubt that every civilized citizen, excepting perhaps one man who was attempting to avenge a Brother's murder, is barbarous. Kibbe believed the Indians' murder of the men above was their response after "an attack on the Indians." The reason for the men's entry into the camp is not on the record.
611 J. S. F. Eddy to John Bidwell, 21 May 1863, JBSCML; *Butte Democrat*, 7 July 1860; Schoonover, "Kibbe's Campaign," 45–49; Charles Martin, "The Battle of Eagle Peak: 1862," [Colusi Historical Society] *Wagon Wheels* 50, no. 2 (Fall 2000), reports from old timers that Hat Creek Liz was killed in the Battle of Eagle Creek in 1862 in Colusa County in a band of Indians stealing horses. She may have participated in that battle, but only if she had made a brief escape from Round Valley. However, Eddy and her brother were both qualified to make a valid identification of her as still alive in the Round Valley reservation party at Rancho Chico in 1863.
612 *Butte Record*, 15 September 1866.
613 Letter, Abraham Lincoln to M. Morris, 26 March 1843, mrlincolnfriends.org.
614 George Hanson to President Abraham Lincoln, 4 June 1863; Hanson to Wm. Dole, 17 June 1863, NAM; *Chico Index*, 24 June 1863; cf. Annie Bidwell, *Rancho Chico Indians*, 71; Laney.
615 *Sacramento Daily Union*, 11 June 1863.
616 Irene L. Sharp, *Sorensen Hill* (Paradise, CA: privately published, 1972), 1–22, 33; *Oroville Union*, 13 June 1863.
617 Ibid., *Butte Record*, 25 July 1859.
618 *Sacramento Daily Union*, 11 June 1863; *Oroville Union*, 14 March, 13 June 1863; R. Anderson, chapter twelve.
619 In May 1863, Isaac Allen was himself the object of a murder attempt by H. Stevens, who was captured, but Stevens disappeared after he left jail on $3,000 bail; Mansfield, 253. Allen did not die until 1870 in San Francisco. Bidwell, *Diaries*, SCML.
620 *Oroville Mercury*, 14 August 1951. The author is Mrs. Blum's daughter-in-law, who gives the wrong date of the crime.
621 Ibid., 25 July, 1 August 1863, in Mansfield, 200; *Butte Record*, 25 July 1863; *Oroville Mercury*, 14 August 1863.
622 Stilson, *Diaries*, 22 July 1863, SCML. According to Larry V. Richardson, Stilson was known as Charlie in his early Chico years and by Lewis in his later life as a lawyer. The above reconstruction of dates refines that of the *Oroville Union* in light of the journal entry by Stilson, in combination with the account of Thankful Lewis, which gives data on the incident.
623 Thankful Lewis Carson, in Mansfield, 202ff; *Oroville Union*, 1 August 1863.
624 Carson, "They talked together in their own tongue for awhile and I knew they were plotting to do us harm," 6.
625 Ibid.
626 George Crosette, in the *Chico Enterprise*, 25 January 1918.
627 Albert Hurtado, 7–8.
628 Tassin, 178; cf. Sim Moak in Mansfield, 203.
629 Mansfield, 210; *Chico Record*, 26 July 1904; Katie Josephson, "Katie Josephson's Mining Story," *Our History*, ed. Eric Josephson," www.maidu.com. Katie was

the granddaughter of the Maidu headman Tome-ya-nem or Bercha. Her mother Yohema married miner A. B. Clark. Mrs. Clark's 1904 version did not acknowledge Wells' role in permitting a chance for escape. The Indians' alternative explanation of what happened with Mike Wells appears in chapter ten.

630 Bidwell, "Dictation," 15.
631 Bidwell, "Dictation," 14–15. His federal farmhouse had a landing but no porch.
632 Stilson, 24 July 1863; Bidwell, "Dictation," 14.
633 R. W. Durham to John Bidwell, 26 August 1863, JBSCML. Quotes from Durham employ modern usage. *Oroville Union*, 4 July 1863.
634 Ibid.
635 Ibid.
636 Ibid.
637 Ibid.
638 George Hanson to Wm. Dole, 10 August 1863, NAM.
639 Stilson, 25 July 1863; cf. Carson in Mansfield; cf. George Hanson to Wm. Dole, 17 June 1863, NAM, 37.
640 George Hanson to General George Wright, *Official Records*, 543–44; George Hanson to Wm. Dole, 8 August 1863, NAM.
641 W. C. to John Bidwell, 26 July 1863, JBSCML.
642 Sources conflict on whether the meeting date was the 27th or the 28th. The 27th is used here because Hanson noted that date in his August 4 letter to Dole. See next footnote.
643 George Hanson to Wm. Dole, 4 August 1863, JBSCML; *Morning Chronicle*, 16 July 1886.
644 Ibid. Probably not a tree, but an extension from a hydraulic flume.
645 Ibid.
646 Bidwell, "Dictation," 17–19; George Hanson to Gen. Wright, *Official Records*, 543–44; Hanson to Wm. Dole, 8 August 1863, NAM; *Oroville Union*, 1 August 1863.
647 *Oroville Union*, 1 August 1863.
648 *Butte Record*, 1 August, 1863.
649 George Hanson to Wm. Dole, 4 August 1863, JBSCML; Mansfield, 211.
650 James Eddy to George Hanson, 28 July 1863, NAM 37; Stilson, 30 July 1863. In May 1863, Isaac Allen was himself the object of a murder attempt by H. Stevens, who was captured, but Stevens disappeared after he left jail on $3,000 bail; Mansfield, 253. Allen did not die until 1870 in San Francisco. Bidwell, *Diaries*, SCML.
651 Ibid.
652 *Chico Morning Chronicle*, 16 July 1886; Bidwell's later acquaintance with John Muir suggests real friendship. Michael J. Gillis, "John Bidwell and John Muir: The Forgotten Friendship," [Dogtown] *California Territorial Quarterly*, no. 21 (Spring 1995).
653 Lt. Col. A. E. Hooker to R. C. Drumm, 1 October 1863. *Official Records*, 632–33; *Chico Morning Chronicle*, 17 July 1886. cf. a note on the copy in the Bidwell Scrapbooks, SCML.
654 Annie Bidwell, *Rancho Chico Indians*, 24.
655 Hill, 69.
656 Hunt, 140.
657 *Butte Record*, 1, 8 August, 25 July 1863; *Sacramento Union*, 27 July 1863; Mansfield, 210–11. The Hupp Mill was located near present day Skyway above the Desabla Reservoir; Rathbun, 35. *Outline History of the California National Guard* (vol. 2, 558, Military Collection, CSA) attributes the Chico Guards' formation as linked to the Indian problems, however, the governor never assigned it to address Indian disputes with settlers in Butte County.

Standoff

658 General George Wright to Captain Augustus Starr, 27 July 1863, *Official Records*, 544; Augustus W. Starr, "Abraham Dubois Starr," *California Historical Quarterly* 27 (September 1948): 193–202. The author thanks Robert Chandler for this source. Scot R. Christensen, *Sagwitch: Shoshone Chieftain, Mormon Elder, 1822–1887* (Logan: Utah State University Press, 1999); cf. Rathbun.

659 Aurora Hunt, *The Army of the Pacific: Its Operations in California, 1860–1866* (Glendale, CA: Arthur C. Clark Co., 1951), 281–300.

660 Henry Landt to John Bidwell, 4 August 1863, JBSCML. Such requests, for example, regularly arrived from head cowboy Sandy Young at the Big Meadow camp.

661 Capt. A. Starr to Lt. Col. R.C. Drum, 10 August 1863, NAM.

662 Annie Bidwell, 71; *Butte Record*, 8 August 1863; Stilson, 30, 31 July 1863. These were probably the sixty-five Indians collected by R. C. Rose of Johnson's Ranch. Conners, 26. She says twenty-three soldiers arrived in Company F. Observers on hand counted forty. There were twenty-three of the company who went on the removal. Those who were not active in the removal were likely in Camp Bidwell's sick bay, a common destiny for soldiers on summer duty in the mid-Sacramento Valley.

663 Tassin, 13–14.

664 Henrietta Catherine Furnell, *From the Prairie to the Pacific*, ed. Mae Luman Hill (Chico: Association of Northern California Records and Research, 2005), 67–68.

665 Ibid. The family persuaded Mona's spouse to leave her with them with assurances that Kate's mother's marksmanship could handle any problem. Compton, 16–17, SCML; *Chico Morning Chronicle*, 17 July 1886; *Oroville Union*, 13 June 1863; *Butte Record*, 21 June 1863; Hill, 30.

666 *Dogtown Nugget*, 20, 23 April 1995, 8–11. The date on the reprinted letter says 1862, but this was an editorial error as the letter describes events linked to the Lewis incident a year later. Obituary of O. L. Clark, no date; Bertha Lee scrapbook, courtesy of Mary Hanson, Chico, California.

667 B. B. Brown to John Bidwell, 27 July 1863, JBSCML. This B. B. Brown died suddenly and another B. B. Brown settled his family in Chico in the mid-1860s.

668 *Oroville Union*, 1 August 1863; Moak, 19; Mansfield, 417.

669 Harold Farnsworth Gray and Russell E. Fontaine, "A History of Malaria in California," proceedings and papers of the 25th annual conference of the California Mosquito Control Association, 30 June 1957, 8. In 1849, Lt. Col. Silas Casey wrote Lt. Col. Joseph Hooker about the condition of his men camped at Lassen's Ranch. He had sent forty-nine men to Benicia who were too sick to work. He described his unit en route there as having the appearance of "a perfect moving hospital." Of eighty-five officers and men, only two did not become sick. They attributed the sickness to service spent in the valley before executing missions in the mountains.

670 *Red Bluff Beacon*, 1 June 1859; cf. Appendix B.

671 Bidwell to John Usher, Secretary of the Interior, 4 December 1863. Quoted in Gillis and Magliari, 303. Bidwell's remark in 1863 underlines that Mountain Maidu of the Sierra Nevada, who had been known as Butte Creeks in the 1850s, had "crossed over" and, since their operations base went into operation on Deer Creek, become known as Mill Creeks—or sometimes as "Deer Creeks."

Chapter Ten

672 *Butte Record*, week of August 17, 1863.
673 *Official Records*, 550; Stilson, 31 July 1863; *Butte Record*, 8, 27 August, 1863.
674 Ibid.
675 Stilson, 17, 12 August 1863.

676 Ibid., 26, 24 August 1863; Annie Bidwell, 71.
677 Capt. Morton to Lt. Col. R.C. Drum, *Official Records*, 562–63.
678 Ibid.
679 Ibid.
680 G. M. Hanson to Wm. Dole, 22 August 1863, NAM; Baumgardner, 220.
681 Stilson, 22 August 1863.
682 Hill, 41.
683 *Red Bluff Beacon*, 1 June 1859.
684 Henry Lyman, *The Practical Home Physician: History, Cause, Means of Prevention and Symptoms of All Diseases* (Chicago: George Cline, 1889), 67–68. The author is grateful for the loan of this from David York, R.N.; James Camy, Butte County Mosquito Abatement District, in telephone discussion with the author, June 18, 2004.
685 Gray and Fontaine, 8–9. For example, the communications among removal planners agreed about problems of Indian transport that point to sickness. Because they knew the Indians' problem was malaria, they did not need to name the disease. However, we can discover what they were talking about through other contemporary sources. *Indian Affairs Annual Report*, 1867, 40th Cong., 2[d] sess., House Executive Document I, 15 November 1867, 1–397, serial set 1326, 3.
686 Stilson, 17 September, 20, 28 November 1863.
687 Lee Pharmacy invoice to John Bidwell & Co., September 29, 1863. Enclosure, George Hanson to Wm. Dole, January 11, 1864, NAM; John Copeland, M.D., to author, 14 November 1996. Having reviewed the pharmaceuticals list, Copeland observed, "There was much medicine for malaria." Lyman, 66–68; Richard L. Johnson, M.D., to author, April 5, 2003, after he reviewed an earlier draft of this chapter: "I feel sure that some of the Indians were infected with Plasmodium vivax, others with P. falciparum, and still others with both. This would account for the very high morbidity and fatality rates. I know both varieties were present here in the Valley."
688 Michael Laris, "London Mosquitoes Show Malaria," *Washington Post*, 28 September 2002; Chris Matthews, "You've Got Malaria," *San Francisco Chronicle*, 18 August 2002; Dr. S. M. Sproul to John Bidwell, September 3, 1863, JBSCML.
689 A. G. Tassin, 12. Note: Roland Dixon, a principal anthropologist, cited the accounts of military cartographer Tassin (misspelled Fassin) as a primary source in his bibliography for "The Northern Maidu."
690 Mansfield, 211. Round Valley was embroiled with Indian v. Indian and Indian v. settler clashes. Cf. William J. Bauer, "Agricultural Labor, Race, and Indian Policy on the Round Valley Reservation, 1850–1941," PhD diss., University of Oklahoma, 2003.
691 George Hanson to President Abraham Lincoln, 4 June 1863, NAM.
692 George Hanson to Wm. Dole, 21 August 1863, NAM.
693 *Oroville Union*, 28 August 1863. A surviving reel containing this item is on microfilm in the State Library.
694 Mansfield, 211.
695 Ibid. Michael Wells was a likely collaborator with Rose in this.
696 *Official Records*, 573.
697 Michael Wells, like James Eddy, earned a place in a future catalogue of Butte County's heroes.
698 *Oroville Union*, 8 August 1863; D. M. Bean to John Bidwell, 17, 20, 1852, JBSCML.
699 Quote in Hill, 37; The Federal Census of northern Butte County townships in 1860. A few other ranches counted one or two Indian individuals in their households.
700 *Official Records*, 635–36; *Marysville Appeal*, 30 August 1863. The newspaper reported

that about 600 Indians were then at Pence's. The number was erroneous and, if some were at Pence's at any moment, they soon went on to Rancho Chico. The number 600 only approached correctness when it included the Bidwell Indians, but they were never at Pence's. The present analysis here reflects a reconsideration of the analysis in this author's *California Territorial Quarterly* article on the removal.

701 *Marysville Appeal*, 30 August 1863; *Butte Record*, 8, 15 August, 5 September 1863.
702 *Butte Record*, 5 August 1863; Stilson, 27 July 1863; cf. Conners.
703 *Marysville Appeal*, 30 August, 4 December 1863; *Chico Enterprise*, 25 January 1918; John Bidwell to Secretary of the Interior, NAM; Bidwell Store Ledger; Invoice, W. Lee and Co., 29 September 1863, NAM; Norris A. Bleyhl, *Three Military Posts in Northeastern California, 1849–1863* (Chico: Association for Northern California Records and Research, 1984), 3; George Hanson to John Bidwell, 29 August 1863, NAM; Hill, 72–73; Sonia Shah, *The Fever: How Malaria Has Ruled Mankind for 500,000 Years* (New York: Farrar, Strauss and Giroux, 2011), 89; George Hanson to John Bidwell, 29 August, 3, 9 September 1863; Lewis Downing to John Bidwell, 27 August 1863; John Bidwell to John Upshaw, 4 December 1863, NAM; John Bidwell, Tax Inventory Record, 1863, Records Office, Butte County, CA, JBSCML.
704 Ibid., 29 August 1863, JBSCML; Lt. Col. R. C. Drum to Lt. Col. Ambrose Hooker at Chico, *Official Records*, 562–63; cf. Annie Bidwell, 24. Her count seems inflated.
705 Butte County Tax Assessor A. G. Simpson to John Bidwell, July 29, 1863, JBSCML.
706 Hanson's words were: "The lives of your Indians are not only at risk, but also the life & property of yourself." Hanson to John Bidwell, 29 August 1863, JBSCML; *Official Records*, 634; *Oroville Union Record*, 5 September 1863.
707 George Hanson to John Bidwell, 29 August 1863, NAM.
708 Stilson, 24 August 1863.
709 Camp Bidwell Post Returns, September, 1863.
710 Lt. Col. A. E. Hooker to J. Bidwell, 30 August 1863, JBSCML; *Chico Enterprise*, 16 January 1918.
711 Camp Bidwell Post Returns, September, 1863. By use of old maps and Google, as well as old timer opinion and published mentions, Dave Freeman identifies this location of the military camp. He asserts the camp extended to Chico Creek, necessary to water the horses.
712 *Marysville Appeal*, 30 August 1863. The same article misidentifies the location of the Indians waiting removal.
713 John Bidwell to Secretary of the Interior, 4 December 1863, NAM; *Marysville Appeal*, 24 June 1863.

Chapter Eleven

714 Ibid.
715 George Hanson to John Bidwell, 11 September 1863, JBSCML.
716 Wikipedia. Nome Cult Trail, https://en.wikipedia.org/wiki/Nome_Cult_Trail.
717 Samuel Sproul to John Bidwell, 3 September 1863, JBSCML; *Marysville Appeal*, 30 August 1863. Sproul was on retainer to Bidwell as evidenced by Bidwell's later statement that he paid for all the Indians' care attendant to the removal.
718 Thanks to 1850s map specialist Dave Freeman of Artois, who reconstructed Company F's route by overlaying period maps on Google maps.
719 *Official Records*, 635–36.
720 Information on Sgt. Baldwin came from research by Brian Frontella of Oroville, a California Volunteers, Company F re-enactor who plays Sgt. Baldwin.
721 Freeman was told this by descendants of residents living along the removal route at the time.

Endnotes

722 *Marysville Appeal*, 30 August 1863; Hill, 32; John Bidwell to Secretary of the Interior James Upshaw, Dec. 4, 1863, NAM.
723 *Official Records*, 635.
724 Post Returns, Fort Wright, NAM; Pamela Conners, 33. Starr's journal indicated the lieutenant and his civilian aide arrived before the pack train. Starr's move ahead of the pack train is speculative, but fits subsequent events.
725 *Official Records*, 635. According to modern speculation, Starr's men had to find the lost freight wagon drivers, but this researcher found no verification for that on the record. Note: The apparently edited version of Starr's journal entry says the supply pack train arrived from *Round Valley* and all its wagons returned there. The original diary must instead have referred to Fort Wright wagons because the understanding was the military there, not the Indian Department at the reservation, had responsibility for transportation. It is also unlikely that the lieutenant who arrived just happened on the scene independent of the pack train, for which he was more likely the escort, riding ahead of the slower train. This journal entry is also suspect because it appears to obscure the role of Fort Wright's Capt. Douglas in the removal's failure. And, if the reservation was supposed to send wagons and refused, the military mission report would have blamed reservation management, but it did not because it could not. A later section of this chapter explores the evident doctoring of Eddy's journal to divert attention from the military's failures.
726 Ibid., 633–35.
727 Stilson, 4 September 1863; *Marysville Appeal*, 30 August 1863; Interview with Thelma Wilson, "A Mechoopda Descendant Relates Her Family's History," Association for Northern California Records and Research Oral History Program, 1972, SCML; George Hanson to Wm. Dole, 16 August 1863. Hanson states here that Wright agreed to send a detachment to deliver the Indians to the reservation. He did not infer or state that the reservation would take over their transport at Mountain House. *Official Records*, 634–36.
728 George Hanson to John Bidwell, 9 September 1863, JBSCML; Indian Department Invoice, 28 August 1863, NAM. Hill misread this as "I hope [sic] your Indians are not gone are they?"
729 John Bidwell to Secretary of the Interior James Upshaw, 4 December, 1863, NAM.
730 John Bidwell & Co. Ledger, 1853, CSL; George Hanson to John Bidwell, 11 September 1863, JBSCML; other correspondence between Bidwell and Indian Affairs in this period.
731 George Hanson to John Bidwell, 11, 19, 28 September 1863, JBSCML; Quoted in Hill, 78. Bidwell may have followed Hanson's advice on his legal relations with his Indian workers, but this researcher found no evidence to confirm that. *Oroville Union Record*, 28 September 1863, 6 May 1865; *Yreka Union*, 22 September 1864.
732 *Oroville Mercury*, 14 August 1951; *Butte Record*, 3 October 1863; *Union Record*, 5 March 1864; Mansfield, 215; Lt. Col. Ambrose Hooker to Col. R. C. Drum, 1 October, 1863, *Official Records*, 633–35; Camp Bidwell Post Returns, October 1863.
733 *Butte Record Union*, 8 August 1863.
734 Mansfield, 255; *Butte Record*, 8 August 1863; Lt. Col. Ambrose Hooker to Lt. Col. R. C. Drum, *Official Records*, 634. No effort was made to identify a link between Thomas Wells and Michael Wells.
735 *Butte Record*, 19 September 1863; George Hanson to John Bidwell, 29 August, 19 September 1864, JBSCML; Conners, 31.
736 Ibid.; *Butte Record*, 19 September 1863.
737 *Butte Record*, 19 September 1863; *Marysville Daily Appeal*, 8 September 1863.
738 *Official Records*, 634.
739 Freeman learned about the Indian shots from the descendants of a rancher where

377

removal Indians camped. T. Wilson, "Mechoopda Descendant."
740 A fuller portion of the letter is in Tassin, "Chronicles of Fort Wright," 12. The present account relies on Short's contemporary report which contradicts the statement omitted here that Douglas's efforts extended to Chico. Short stated that collection of sick and dead Indians extended to Mountain House near Eddy's camp. James Short to Indian Commissioner Charles Mix, 13 October 1863, NAM. In addition, no valley observers, such as scandal-hungry and anti-military newspapers, mentioned abandoned removal Indians along the valley route.
741 Elijah Steele to Charles Mix, Acting Commissioner of Indian Affairs: "Mr. Hanson also informs me that he has purchased and delivered on the Round Valley Reservation a large band of cattle, but under instructions of August 26th I shall not deem it my duty to receive them."
742 A. G. Tassin, "Chronicles of Fort Wright," 13. Note: At the same time California's Indian Commissioner William Dole was being replaced by Charles E. Mix. Elijah Steele to Charles Mix, 27 September 1863; James Short to Charles Mix, 13 October 1863, NAM.
743 Quoted by Edward D. Castillo, "The Impact of Euro-American Exploration and Settlement," in Heizer, 111.
744 Ibid.
745 Quoted in Conners, 39. Without Short's correspondence at hand to clarify her data, Conners apparently concluded that the reference to scattered Indians referred to the two small deliveries of Butte County Indians to Round Valley later in 1863.
746 Tome-ya-nem later said Douglas's men went to work to help the Indians along the trails all the way back to Chico. This was incorrect: they made no more than a start along the trail between Nome Cult and Mountain House.
747 While there were linguistic differences, many Maidu in the removal already had been kept at Round Valley Reservation between 1859 and 1863.
748 General George Wright to the Secretary of the Interior, 31 January 1863, NAM.
749 Enclosure in George Wright to Brigadier General L. Thomas, Adj. General, U.S. Army, Washington, D.C., 31 January 1863, NAM; James Short to Charles Mix, 13 October 1863, NAM; Captain C. D. Douglas to President Abraham Lincoln, 11 May 1864, Abraham Lincoln Papers, Washington, Library of Congress, 1959; United States Department of War, Office of the Adjutant General, *Martial Law in Round Valley, Mendocino, California, the Causes which Led to that Measure, the Evidence, as Brought Out by a Court of Investigation Ordered by Brig. Gen. G. Wright, Commanding U.S. Forces on the Pacific*, 1863, passim.
750 James Short to Abraham Lincoln, Abraham Lincoln Papers at the Library of Congress, www.mrlincolnandfriends.org/content-aside.asp?pageID=37&subjectID=2.
751 George Hanson to Abraham Lincoln, 4 June 1863, NAM.
752 Charles Douglas to R. C. Drum, 19 January 1863, *Official Records*. Douglas identified one reservation employee as "the only man on the reservation that does anything or seems to know they have a duty to perform."
753 Charles Douglas to Abraham Lincoln, Abraham Lincoln Papers at the Library of Congress, www.mrlincolnandfriends.org/content-inside.asp?pageID=37&subjectID=2.
754 Ibid.; A. G. Tassin, "Chronicles of Fort Wright," *Overland Monthly* 10 (August 1887): 173. While Tassin dates the Douglas letter as December, this is erroneous. Every aspect of the letter and subsequent events support that Douglas wrote to James Short in October.
755 James Short to Charles Mix, Commissioner of Indian Affairs, 13 October 1863, NAM. While, according to Bob Freeman, modern residents in the vicinity of the Mountain House have denied the presence of wild hogs in the area, they existed

Endnotes

then in the Sierra and there is no reason to doubt Indians' reports or Short's willingness to accept those reports. The author, an Iowa native, has heard about the dangers of domestic hogs gone wild and dangerous in Iowa forests during the nineteenth century, where they are no longer a threat.

756 Charles E. Pancoast, *A Quaker Forty-Niner: The Adventures of Charles Edward Pancoast on the American Frontier,*" ed. Anna Paschall Hannum (Philadelphia: University of Pennsylvania Press, 1930), 335; Vera Clark McKeen, with Michele Shover, *Vera Clark: A Concow Maidu Matron's Twentieth Century Life* (Chico: privately published, 1998), 5; James Short to A. P. [sic] Misker, 1864, NAM; Rathbun, 54; Wilson, op. cit.
757 James Short to Charles Mix, 13 October 1863, NAM; Pancoast, 170.
758 Ibid.
759 James Short to Abraham Lincoln, October, 1863, January 1864, Abraham Lincoln Papers at the Library of Congress, www.mrlincolnandfriends.org/content- insie.asp?pageID=37&subjectID=2.
760 James Eddy to Elijah Steele, 14 April 1864; Short to Charles Mix, 13 October 1863; Short to Wm. Dole, 15 May 1864, NAM.
761 John Bidwell & Co. Ledger, September 25, 1863, CSL; James Eddy to John Bidwell, 23 October 1863, NAM; W. Haven to John Bidwell, 2 October 1863, NAM; Affidavit of James Eddy, 18 April 1864, NAM; James Eddy, Deposition, 7 October 1864, in United States Department of War, *Martial Law*. Other evidence says the final movement of Indians from the trail took place in late November.
762 Appreciation to Donald Treco and Brian Frontella of the re-enactor group, Company F, Sacramento Rangers, who supplied information on Starr and Baldwin, whom they have researched in order to represent them.
763 One of the most troublesome entries appeared after Starr reached Chico. This is discussed below.
764 Hooker to Drum, 1 October 1863.
765 Ibid.
766 *Official Records*, 633.
767 Ibid.; cf. chapter six; Gottig Scherman to John Bidwell, 23 September 1863, cf. Hanson to Bidwell, 9 September 1863, John Bidwell Collection, CSUC Special Collections.
768 *Official Records*, 562, 633–34. For example, this interpretation entered Hill's account.
769 Ibid., 562.
770 The California Volunteers employed this tactic which was successful in discouraging Southern plots in Southern California, according to John W. Robinson, "Preserving the West for the Union, The California Volunteers, 1861–1866," *California Territorial Quarterly* (Spring 2013): 8.
771 Tassin, "Chronicles of Camp Wright," vol. 1, 124–32, vol. 2, 169–86; Also see correspondence of Fall 1863–Spring 1864, NAM; Lynwood Carranco and Estle Beard, *Genocide and Vendetta: The Round Valley Wars of Northern California* (Norman: University of Oklahoma Press, 1981), 102.
772 Col. Herbert M. Hart (Ret.), USMC, Historic Californian Posts: Fort Wright," http://www.militarymuseum.org/FtWright.html.
773 Carranco and Beard, 102.
774 Douglas to Drum, 19 January 1863, NAM; cf. Hanson to Dole, 25 April 1863, NAM; Wright to Dole, 24 October 1863, NAM; Steele to Dole, 2 November 1863, NAM; *Alta California*, 26 January 1863.
775 George Hanson to Wm. Dole, 22 August 1863.
776 George Hanson to Wm. Dole, 25 September, 14 November 1863, NAM, again express Hanson's dislike of Douglas.
777 E. Sparrow Purdy, Acting Assistant Attorney General, to Charles Douglas, 21

Standoff

November 1863; Charles Douglas to E. Sparrow Purdy, 24 November 1863, NAM.
778 W. L. Shafer to John Bidwell, 8 March 1863, JBSCML; Camp Chico Post Returns, 23 November 1863, 691.
779 Ibid.; See also deposition by James Eddy, fall 1863, NAM.
780 Ibid.
781 Hill, passim; Annie Bidwell, *The Rancho Chico Indians*, 65–72.
782 Edward S. Curtis, *The North American Indian: The Maidu*, vol. 14 (Seattle: E. S. Curtis, 1924), plate 492. Preacher helped the brick mason who worked on the Bidwell mansion in 1865. Annie Bidwell, 71–72; Wilson, 3.
783 Thelma Wilson, 3.
784 Gray and Fontaine, 4–14; Hill, 40–41.
785 Bain interview, Hill Collection; Dixon; *Red Bluff Beacon*, 31 August 1859; Interview with Leland Scott, summer 1966, Hill Collection; Rathbun, 55; cf. Riddell, in Heizer, 384. Note: Riddell and Sherburne Cook speculated about a malaria sweep through the Maidu in the early 1830s. This was likely small pox, according to Lewis, 43. Later Cook concluded it was an unidentified viral epidemic. A traveler through the area in about 1832 described the sickness as having the symptom of "great sloughing sores full of green matter," according to Edward Pancoast, 342. On another point, as mentioned in the Introduction, this author does not accept Riddell's distinction between Maidu and Concows. Her research supports the Maidu territorial boundaries described by Roland Dixon and used by Dorothy Hill, which placed Concows as a Mountain Maidu tribelet. White, *Frontier Army*, 10.
786 Bain interview, Hill Collection; cf. Leland Scott's similar views offered in Rathbun, chapter three; cf. Paul Bowman, *Maidu Indians on the Dogtown Ridge, California Territorial Quarterly* 17 (Spring 1994): 12; Annie Bidwell, 71–72.
787 Riddell, 379; Henry Azbill, "Some Aspects of Maidu Culture on John Bidwell's Rancho del Arroyo Chico," interview by Dorothy Hill, 1969, Hill Collection; Wilson, 3–4; Bain interview, Hill Collection; Rathbun, 55; Chase, *People of the Valley*, 17.
788 Dixon; Curtis, 109–10. The earliest source of this allegation in print was the comment by a Rancho Chico rancheria member who claimed that Bidwell had hidden his Indians to protect them from soldiers. However, other evidence establishes that Bidwell hid Indians from settlers and returned them to the ranch camp once Army-sent militia soldiers arrived to set up Indian protection. Cf. Currie, 319; cf. Rathbun, 53; Azbill interview, Hill Collection.
789 Potts, 43–45.
790 Bidwell, 71–72.
791 General George Wright to Asst. Adj. Gen. Richard Drum, 23 March 1865, *Official Records*, 1168, 9 February, 1865, 958: "As [a captain] is under orders for Chico, Camp Bidwell, I ... direct him to retain his Sharps carbines and ammunition until they can be replaced by Maynards"; Email, John Spangler to author, 17 June 2002, Military Collection, CSA; State Armorer John Schade, Inventory of Chico Light Infantry equipment, August 11, 1866. One source suggested the Sharps carbine was fitted for bayonets, but rarely for use out of conventional war except for ceremonial settings. Cf. John Adams Clark in Mansfield, 203.
792 Hill, 41; Communication to author from Kevin Hoffman, nineteenth-century military arms specialist, 17 June 2002; Communication from George Stammerjohann, 6 July 2004.
793 *Red Bluff Beacon*, 8 June 1859, 9 October 1862; Strobridge, passim. Telephone discussion between military historian William F. Strobridge and the author, March 2003.

Endnotes

794 Bidwell, 71–72.
795 Mansfield, 203; *Oroville Union*, 1 August 1863; Roy Scott, "A Maidu Descendent Relates His Family History," interview by Dorothy Hill, n.d., Hill Collection.
796 "California and the Civil War: 2nd Regiment of Cavalry, California Volunteers," http://www.militarymuseum.org/2dCavVC.html.
797 White, *Frontier Army*.
798 Cf. *Red Bluff Beacon*, 1 June 1859; Rathbun, 44.
799 Powers, *Tribes of California*, 302.
800 Hill, 41; Bain interview, Hill Collection.
801 Dixon; A. L. Kroeber, "Elements of Culture," 36–37. As previously mentioned, Alfred Kroeber's sources' memories reached to the 1840s and 1850s. Moak, 30; Rathbun, 60, 67–70, 96–98; cf. Powers, *Tribes of California*, 302.
802 *Plumas National Bulletin*, 6 April 1911; R. Anderson, 80–81.
803 Potts, 4; Riddell, 379; Azbill interview, Hill Collection.
804 Rathbun, 53–54, 113; Dixon; *Oroville Union*, 1 August 1863.
805 Richard C. Harrison, Diary and Receipt Book, 10 August 1850, Henry E. Huntington Library, San Marino,55; Anderson; Riddell, 380; *Oroville Union*, 1 August 1863.
806 *Oroville Union*, 1 August 1863.
807 *Butte Record*, 14 May 1870.
808 Powers, 301–2; Brewer, 339; Rathbun, 68; *Red Bluff Beacon*, 17 July 1862; *Butte Record*, 10 January 1857; cf. chapters six and eleven.
809 Starie Potts, interview by Dorothy Hill, 1 July 1965, Hill Collection; Dorothy Hill, "The Durham Oak," Hill Collection.
810 Affidavit of James Eddy, 18 April 1864, NAM.
811 Gray and Fontaine, 13–14; Camp Bidwell Post Returns, Chico, September 1863.
812 Bain interview, Hill Collection.
813 *Red Bluff Beacon*, 21 September 1859.
814 Riddell, 379.
815 Ibid., 15.
816 Tassin, 13. Note: During the time California's Indian Commissioner William Dole was temporarily replaced by Charles Mix, the bureaucracy was in disarray. Elijah Steele to Charles Mix, 27 September 1863; James Short to Charles Mix, 13 October 1863, NAM.
817 Scott interview, Hill Collection.
818 Ibid.; Rathbun, 55–56.
819 *Butte Record*, 25 July 1863; *Sacramento Union*, 27 July 1863; *Oroville Union*, 1 August 1863; Tassin, 13; Stilson, *Diaries*, 24 July 1863. The two Indians caught and killed had probably headed for refuge in Eddy's camp on Rancho Chico, but settlers intercepted them.
820 Mansfield, 209–10; See also Leland Scott in Rathbun, 53; Compare to the account by Yumyan, the Maidu Concow known as Tome-ya-nem in Tassin, 12–13, that supports the settler version.
821 Wilson, 2; *Official Records*, 634–36.
822 C. Hart Meriam, "Ethnographic Notes on Central California Indian Tribes," University of California Archaeological Survey, No. 68, Part III, completed by Robert F. Heizer, Dec. 1967, 315; John Bidwell to Annie Bidwell, 7 October 1884, refers to an interview finding from Jeremiah Curtin's research on Rancho Chico Indians, ABCSL.
823 Starie Potts.
824 This is speculative; the author's impression is based on the Bidwells' close control of the rancheria for the Indians' safety and to discourage their exposure to "loose" White conduct.

Standoff

825 The author thanks Charles Martin of the Colusi Historical Society and Richard Burrill for these anecdotes.
826 United States Army, *Statistical Report on the Sickness and Mortality of the Army of the United States, The Records of the Surgeon General's Office, 1839–1855* (Washington, D.C., A.O.P. Nicholson, Printer, 1856), courtesy of The Citadel: Military College of South Carolina.
827 Death record, County of Napa, 27 November 1907. This document is blurred. It may mean he lived in Solano County eleven years and had resided at Napa State Hospital for twenty-one months when he died.

Chapter Twelve

828 T. Phelps to John Bidwell, 12 May 1863, JBSCML.
829 Stilson, 27 February 1864.
830 Camp Bidwell Post Returns, 1 March 1864.
831 Ogle, 75.
832 Gwynne, 161.
833 Petition from Hi Good to the Governor, 19 July 1862, CSA; *Alta California*, 12 August 1862; Anderson, 63.
834 B. B. Brown to John Bidwell, 26–29 February 1864, 79, Hill Collection; Mansfield, 1008. B. B. Brown became unexpectedly ill and died on 19 March 1864, shortly after this event. Federal Census of 1860, Chico Township, Butte County.
835 Hurtado, *Indian Survival*, 212; *Red Bluff Beacon*, 12 October 1859.
836 *Butte Record*, 5 March 1864; Sandy Young to John Bidwell, 10 March 1864, JBSCML.
837 *Butte Record*, 8 March 1864; cf. Hittel, 264.
838 Ibid., 9 August 1862.
839 R. Anderson.
840 Union Army Maj. Gen. McDowell replaced George Wright as head of the Pacific Department.
841 R. Anderson, passim, also Crowder in *Chico Enterprise*, 21 January 1918; Stilson, 14 April 1864.
842 Stilson, 16 April 1864; *Butte Record* 5, 8 March 1864; *Official Records*, 823, 833; Mansfield, 215–17; P. A. McRae to John Bidwell, 30 April 1863, JBSCML.
843 Research at Red Bluff by Ben Hughes, Gene Serr and Mary Lee Grimes. Additional sources on Eddy for the remainder of this section are the deposition of Dr. William Hatch, Coroner's Investigation and *The Eddy Family in America*, with thanks to Mary Catherine Grobis of Fort Wayne, Indiana, certified genealogical researcher.
844 *The Eddy Family in America* (The Eddy Family Association, Inc., 1980).
845 Ibid. Eddy's method of suicide was more common in the nineteenth century than today. The eighteenth- and early nineteenth- century diary of Martha Ballard mentioned without evident surprise two such suicides by men in her New England neighborhood. Augustus Ulrich, *A Midwife's Tale* (New York: Vintage, 1991).
846 Stilson, 21–22, May 1864; James Eddy to John Bidwell, 25 October 1863, JBSCML; *Alta California*, 22 May 1864; United States Congress, "Estimate of Appropriation for Indian Service in California," *Congressional Globe*, 40th Cong., 2d sess., House Executive Document 200, vol. 15, 4 March 1868, serial set no. 1341.
847 *Official Records*, 876–77; *Butte Record*, 11 June 1864; Mansfield, 201, 216; Federal Census, Butte County, CA, 1860.
848 *Official Records*, 874–75; cf. Stilson, 16 June 1864.
849 Captain James Van Voast to Col. R. C. Drum, *Official Records*, 874–76; Chico Light Infantry Papers, Military Collection, CSA. Stilson, an officer, mentions no militia action against Indians between 1864 and the end of 1865. Passim.

850 *Official Records*, 880–81.
851 Ibid.
852 Ibid., 942–43; 889–81.
853 Capt. J. C. Doughty to Col. R. C. Drum, 10 August 1864; *Official Records*, 880–81, 1125, 1222; John Bidwell note in Bidwell Scrapbook on 1918, JBSCML; Stilson, 16 June 1864.
854 Stilson, 4, 9 September 1864; *Oroville Union Record*, 24 September 1864; *Official Records*, 137–38; Bidwell, "Dictation," 64–65.
855 *Official Records*, 942–43. Here, Captain Doughty used Good's title as elected head of Indian fighter companies.
856 Stilson, 27 February, 20–21 March, 16 June 1865. Simeon Moak's later account on p. 34 erred about the month, but his description and Stilson's are largely consistent. B. B. Brown to John Bidwell, 26 February 1864, JBSCML; Hill, 79; *Union Record*, 1 March, 11 June 1864; Mansfield, 215; *Chico Courant*, 24 March 1865; *Official Records*, 408, 1214.
857 *Official Records*, 408, 1214; General George Wright to the Governor, 21 May 1865; Capt. L. L. Patterson, C.V., April 5, 1865, Military Collection, California Archives.
858 Anderson, 9.
859 Brig. Gen. Wright also sent troops to Nevada to reinforce his men there. General George Wright to the Governor, 21 May 1865, Military Collection, California Archives.
860 *Chico Courant*, 18 November 1866; Moak, 24–26.
861 Stilson, 1, 2 August 1865. Stilson heard the ship had gone down off of Mendocino; Carl P. Schlicke, *General George Wright: Guardian of the Pacific Coast* (Norman: University of Oklahoma Press, 1988).
862 Were these Mill Creeks non-Maidu or principally or solely Mountain Maidu, by this time lumped together as Mill Creeks? There is no way to know who made up the party. Marie Potts remembered her kidnapped grandmother called the perpetrators Mill Creeks. She did not assign any role in her kidnapping to Mountain Maidu or other tribes who also camped in Deer and Mill creeks. A young person then might not have recognized distant Mountain Maidu tribelet members with different dialects. Maidu tribelet rivalry had not disappeared and traces linger even in modern times in such issues as casino development.
863 *Butte Record*, 21 July 1866; *Sacramento Union*, 9, 10 August 1865. A newspaper writer who reported Sutherland had killed twelve of the sixteen Indians who died at Three Knolls was not knowledgeable about weapons and confused. Anderson, Moak and others there made no such claim or inference.
864 Moak, *Last of Mill Creeks*, 18–19; *Sacramento Daily Union*, 9 August 1865. These two accounts conflict. This one relies on the *Union* for dates, but goes to Moak for detail because his is largely consistent with other accounts.
865 Moak, *Last of Mill Creeks*, 19. An 1865 article by one of the Concow men omits the circumstances that diverted them from Chico. Because the Moak and Anderson accounts were both firsthand and both gave compatible versions, this version leans toward theirs; Mansfield, 416; Jacob Moak to his parents, 21 November 1865, [*Paradise Post*] *Dogtown Nugget* (20–23 April 1995): 8–11.
866 Anderson, 72–73.
867 Ibid.; *Red Bluff Beacon*, 17 July 1862; *Oroville Union Record*, 1 August 1864; Simeon Moak quoted in Mansfield, 219; cf. Anderson, 71–73; Camp Bidwell Post Returns, August 1865.
868 *Butte Record*, 26 August 1863; Mansfield, 220. General *Butte Record* coverage dominates the logistics account above. It differs from Anderson's memory on the initial meeting place, but the account by Daniel Klauberg, one of the Concow

Valley men, was printed soon after he participated in the event.
869 *Official Records*, 942. While Doughty also reported another interpretation of the identifications from outlying settlers, one finds no support in other accounts.
870 The fifteen or so pursuers who entered the canyon included William Merathew, Simeon and Jacob Moak, two Gore brothers, Dan Sutherland, Jack Reed, Billy Boness, Tom Gore, Henry and/or Frank Curtis and Hardy Thomasson.
871 *Butte Record*, 26 August 1865.
872 The numbers killed vary in accounts. Ibid., 19, 26 August 1863; *Sacramento Union*, 16 August 1863; Stilson, 13 April 1864; R. Anderson, 75–80. On page 80, Anderson mentioned the killing of a "Billy" in an 1862 incident. As an aside, a year previous to the Three Knolls battle, soldiers had arrested a Dan Sills, Jr. when he appeared drunk at Camp Bidwell. In 1865, Anderson, who described the killing of Billy Sills given here, described him as having herded sheep "until a short time before this" and said he left the valley and joined the Mill Creeks. So it appears there were two Billies.
873 Petition to the Governor from H. Good, July 1862; R. Anderson, 48.
874 R. Anderson, 72–75; Moak, 20–21; *Butte Record*, 26 August 1863, 20 August 1865; Simeon and Jacob Moak, "Moaks Write Home," [*Paradise Post*] *Dogtown Nugget*, 20–23 April 1995, 1.
875 Moak, *Last of Mill Creeks*, 23.
876 Ibid., 24.
877 Mansfield, 223; *Chico Courant*, 24 March 1866.
878 Anderson, 47.
879 Richard Burrill, *Ishi Rediscovered* (Sacramento: Anthro, 2001).
880 Vera Clark McKeen, interview by Michele Shover, May 2002. See Michele Shover, *Vera Clark McKeen: A Maidu Matron's Twentieth Century Life* (Chico: privately published, 1998).
881 *Chico Courant*, 18 November 1859. The call for extinction in this came from Chico Township's G. P. Nance, who remained distraught after his return from Nevada, where a Dogtown teamster he was working with had been killed by arrow shots and his body mutilated by the Indian party. The victim left a wife and six children.
882 Velma Butler, "One Hundred Years on the Nimshew Ridge," *Tales of the Paradise Ridge* 6, no. 2 (1965): 3–21.
883 *Chico Enterprise Record*, 22 December 1963. This was copied from a later account in the early 1900s.

Appendix A

884 Copied from Hill, Indians of Chico Rancheria.

Appendix B

885 John Bidwell to Joseph McCorkle. NAM.

Appendix C

886 Bidwell, "Dictation," 14. The quote included examples of annoyances he mentioned. These are compressed in the quote here to economize space.
887 *Chico Morning Chronicle*, 17 July 1886.
888 *Chico Enterprise*, 15 January 1918. The same words appeared in Mansfield, 229:

"The troops were sent here on account of anti-union sentiment."

Appendix D

889 Robert F. Heizer and Theodora Kroeber, eds. *Ishi the Last Yahi: A Documentary History* (Berkeley: University of California Press, 1979); T. Kroeber, *Ishi in Two Worlds*.
890 Wikipedia. Ishi. https://en.wikipedia.org/wiki/Ishi.
891 Ishi was the Yahi who gave himself up and became the subject of anthropologists' study at UC Berkeley.
892 Dottie Smith, *The History of the Indians of Shasta County* (Redding, CA: CT Publishing Co., 1995).
893 Alfred L. Kroeber, "The Elusive Mill Creeks," *Ishi the Last Yahi: A Documentary History*. Edited by Robert F. Heizer and Theodora Kroeber (Berkeley: University of California Press, 1979).
894 Ibid.
895 In 1993 history writer Steve Schoonover was the first modern researcher to independently confirm Curtin's conclusion from his interviews with old county families that the Yahi did not act alone. Steve Schoonover, "The Three Knolls Massacre," [Dogtown] *California Territorial Quarterly* 15 (Fall 1993): 4–55. In pursuer Frank Crowder's 1918 memoir, he referred to the dangerous Indians in Butte County as "Mill Creeks." Mansfield, 1918 ed., 196.
896 In 1993, Steve Schoonover was the first modern researcher who confirmed Curtin's conclusion from his interviews with old county families that the Yahi did not act alone in valley or foothill raids.
897 Petition from the Citizens of Tehama County Petition to New Helvetia from Daniel Sill et al., 1847, courtesy of the Huntington Library; Col. R. B. Mason to Lt. John A. Anderson, "Message on California and New Mexico," 31st Cong., 1st sess., Senate Executive Document, 18, vol. 1, 24 January 1850, serial set no. 557, p.658.
898 T. Kroeber, *Ishi in Two Worlds*, 60.
899 Ibid., 60; John Bidwell, note, John Bidwell Collection, CSLS; T. T. Waterman," The Last Wild Tribe in California" in *Reprints of Various Papers on California Archaeology, Ethnology and Indian History*, ed. Robert F. Heizer. Berkeley: Archaeological Research Facility, Department of Anthropology, University of California, 1973. First published by *Popular Science Monthly*, March 1915. On p. 140 Waterman was uneasy about the extension to Butte Creek, however, which acknowledges that Butte Creek is "probably outside of the Yahi range." Even so, this did not lead him to exonerate the Yahi for the crime described.
900 A. Kroeber, "Elusive Mill Creeks," 80.
901 Jeremiah Curtin, *Creation Myths of Primitive America* in Heizer and Kroeger, 72; cf. T. Kroeber, *Ishi, Last of His Tribe*, 75.
902 Quoted in Richard Burrill, *Ishi Rediscovered* (Sacramento: Anthro, 2001), 99.
903 Quoted in Heizer and T. Kroeber, *Ishi the Last Yahi*, 125.
904 R. Anderson, 86; Crowder, "Eventful Yesterdays," January 1918.

Appendix E

905 Bruce E. Mahan, "The Scotch Grove Trail" [Iowa State Historical Society] *The Palimpsest* (November 1923): 385.
906 Josephine Sutherland, Esther Sinclair, and Mrs. Donald O. Sinclair, *Scotch Grove Pioneers* (Scotch Grove, IA: Monticello Express, 1937), 9.

907 Ibid., 2; J. W. Chalmers, *Red River Adventure* (Toronto: Macmillan, 1956), 141.
908 Sutherland, Sinclair, and Sinclair, 9.
909 Alexander Ross, *The Red River Settlement* (Minneapolis: Ross and Haines, 1957), 23.
910 Ibid. In 1970, I had a chance meeting with a fellow tourist, the Duke of Sutherland, at a hotel registration desk on the island of Mykonos in Greece. I took considerable surreptitious (I hoped) interest in his casual elegance and personal confidence as I listened to him negotiate for their last room, which the clerk had just promised me. I commiserated with him, suggesting that he might like to join my friends' camp on the beach. His response was cold. After half an hour, the clerk found lodging for each of us.
911 Lodge, R. C. *Manitoba Essays* (Toronto: Macmillan, 1937), 69–70.
912 Thomas Sutherland, *History of the Sutherland Family*. Private papers of Barbara Scot, n.d.," 3. Thomas Sutherland, 1873–1951, was a son of John Sutherland III, one of the brothers who joined the Gold Rush in Butte County. Having few other sources about the family in the nineteenth century, the author was unable to find independent verification for many of the family stories that follow. Cf. J. A. Gilfillan, "A Trip Through the Red River Valley," *North Dakota Historical Quarterly* 1, no. 4 (July 1927).
913 Information courtesy of family genealogist Judith Sutherland Pahnke.
914 T. Sutherland, 4. The Indians' visit was told to the author by her grandmother, Olive Moses Shover, the Sutherland boys' great-niece, who was the granddaughter of their sister, Catherine, known as Kate.
915 I can personally appreciate what a job it must have been to take those hogs across open country. I once saw farmhands moving a large herd from one field to another. The hogs took off on their own and spread across my Shover grandparents' five acres of manicured lawn not far from Scotch Grove. Everyone at Sunday dinner, including my mother and dignified aunts in their heels and fine dresses, flew out to the lawn where, with the hired men, they somehow restored order. For us, it was a lark!
916 T. Sutherland, 4; United States, Department of the Interior, Civil War Bounty Land Warrant Files, Daniel Sutherland, Land Warrant File 1348–133, document of naturalization.
917 T. Sutherland, 5, 8.
918 Ibid.
919 Ibid., 7; Louis J. Rasmussen, *California Wagon Lists*, vol. 1 (Colma, CA: San Francisco Historic Records, 1994), 66–67.
920 Lewis Dreibelbis to his wife, 11 May 1850, courtesy of Judith Sutherland Pahnke.
921 Sutherland, Lewis D. "Notes on the Sutherland Family," Portland, OR: Private papers of Eloise Sutherland Helgens, n.d., provided to the author by Barbara Scot. A son of Adam Sutherland, he was the nephew of Roderick and Daniel. Dreibelbis to his wife, 11 May 1850; T. Sutherland, 7–8.
922 Leila Sutherland Sturtevant, "Brief History of the John Sutherland Sr. Family," Aptos, CA: Property of Judith Sutherland Pahnke, 1925; T. Sutherland, 9.
923 Bidwell to McKinstry, 4 November 1848, JBCSL. Bidwell asked McKinstry to send fifty picks: "These should be of the medium size, not the largest—or smallest—these if sent soon will sell well."
924 "Statement Showing the Number and Names of Election Precincts in Butte County, State of California at the General Election ... Held September 3, 1851," Warren Sexton Collection, CSL; cf. chapter two.
925 United States, Federal Census, Butte County, 1852. Listed as John Southland, he was one of 530 people counted there. The age and nativity of the entry support that he was the individual identified.

Endnotes

926 T. Sutherland, 9; cf. Charles F. Lott, "As It Was in the Days of the 49'ers," [Butte County Historical Society] *Diggins* 43, no. 2 (Summer 1999): 34.
927 L. Sutherland, 6; Sutherland, Sinclair and Sinclair, passim.
928 Daniel Sutherland to David Sutherland, 21 December 1856, courtesy of Judith Sutherland Pahnke. Daniel had become a partner at that time in a gold operation at Somes Bar on the Klamath River.
929 United States, Federal Census, Butte County, CA, 1852.
930 T. Sutherland, op. cit.
931 P. H. Sheridan, The *Personal Memoirs of P. H. Sheridan* (New York: Charles L. Webster, 1888), 43.
932 T. Sutherland, 9–10.
933 Daniel Sutherland to David Sutherland, 21 December 1856.
934 Iowa, Jones County, Office of the County Clerk, Probate of Estate of Charles G. Moses.
935 Daniel Sutherland to David Sutherland, 21 December 1856; Howard Melendy, "Orleans Bar," *California Historical Society Quarterly* 39 (March 1960): 57.
936 Federal Census, Butte County, CA, 1860.
937 Ibid.; cf. chapter six.
938 Jill L. Cossley-Batt, *The Last of the California Rangers, The Capture of Joaquin Murieta* (New York: Funk & Wagnalls, 1928), chapter eight. In period press, his name appeared as Byrnes and Burns.
939 Ibid.
940 Ibid.
941 Ibid.
942 The name of the individual is written as D. Sunderland. A party member was H. L. Sunderlin, so the item may refer to him. However, the first initial is distinctly a D by comparison to the other Ds and Hs in the clerk's handwriting. The "Pit River Expedition of 1859 Claims Against Government Funds," MCSA; Sutherland Land Warrant. Note: Conrad Garner's separate pay item indicates that he did not continue as a volunteer after the Butte Creek incidents.
943 Simeon Moak to his family.
944 John Bidwell & Company Ledger, 1860, JBCSL; Federal Census, Butte County, CA, 1860.
945 Chico Cemetery, Mangrove Avenue, obituary of Roderick Sutherland, 1915 [unnamed newspaper] courtesy of Judith Sutherland Pahnke.
946 Petition to the governor, 1862, Indian Wars Files, CSA; Chapter eight.
947 T. Sutherland, 10; Federal Census, Butte County, CA, 1860; *Chico Enterprise*, 2 March 1883.
948 John Sutherland to David Sutherland from Camp New Hope, Georgia, 4 June 1864, Military Records, National Archives, Washington, D.C.
949 Chico Light Infantry Record, CSA. A William Sutherland who attended a drill with Daniel was likely William Sutherland of Tehama County, an Indiana native. The author appreciates the help of Frances Leinenger and Richard Burrill on this point.
950 *Butte Record*, 21 July 1863; See chapters on removal to Round Valley.
951 Quoted in Burrill, *Ishi Rediscovered*, 105. The rest of the statement, which says that Indians attacked no one else, does not stand up to contrary evidence.
952 *Chico Courant*, 26 April 1867. Indian pursuit party members whom Indians picked out for raids on their property included Sutherland, Simeon and Jake Moak, George Senedecker, Bolivar McGee, George Carter, Solomon and Tom Gore, Robert Anderson and Hi Good.
953 *Butte Record*, 21 July 1866; See chapter six.
954 Ibid., 26 August, 21 July 1865. This article was written by Daniel Klauberg, a

participant, within days of the events. In this interview with Dan Sutherland, he evidently stated that a dozen Mountain Indians had died in the 1865 Three Knolls attack on their Mill Creek camp, although this figure probably estimates those severely wounded and expected to expire.

955 For example, in one Indian confrontation, Robert Anderson carried on his person at least three weapons, permitting him to fire them in rapid succession. Schulz, 102.
956 *Butte Record*, 21 July 1866; Mansfield, 1918 ed., 223.
957 Ibid.
958 At this time, Mr. Woollen lived in the south Chico house that the author and her husband Barney Flynn purchased in 1976 and where she still resides. *Chico Courant*, 6 March, 17 April, 1, 22 May 1868.
959 Eva Marie Apperson, *We Knew Ishi* (Red Bluff, CA: Walker Lithograph, 1971), 57–58.
960 California, Butte County, Chico Township, Tax Records, 1868–1874; Author's brief conversation with Walter Rose, June 2003.
961 Bidwell Diaries, 3–4 March 1870 and others, SCML.
962 Sutherland Land Warrant.
963 S. Moak, 10. Please note: there is no record of Sandy Young as a captain in California Volunteers records. The real identity of Captain Young remains unresolved.
964 Bidwell had already brought in a butcher he backed, John Kempf. His partnership with Young seems to indicate strains between Bidwell and Kempf. Later, Kempf would become a key background figure in the anti-Chinese violence.
965 California, Butte County, Chico Township, Tax Records, 1871 and 1873; Bidwell Diaries, 28 September 1874; *Chico Enterprise*, 23 January 1918.
966 Apperson, 57–58.
967 *Chico Enterprise*, 18 August 1876.
968 Ibid., 20 April 1877. The author is grateful to Jerry Rohde of McKinleyville, who conducted primary research on Sutherland and Young in Humboldt, formerly Klamath County, for this article.
969 *Del Norte Record*, 19 July 1880; *Northern Advocate*, 10 November 1888; *Cascade Union*, 3 November 1888. In distant Butte County, the common understanding was Sandy Young's body had surfaced with a bullet in the head, which was attributed to Indians. Mansfield, 225; Richard Burrill to author in phone conversation.
970 Stilson, Campaign Ledger, SCML. The clerk noted his light complexion, fair hair and blue eyes.
971 In 1888, Sutherland probably read in the *Chico Chronicle Record* about the deathbed confession of Sandy Young's killer Hy Sewell, who made his way from Klamath back to Butte County where he held his secret for seven more years, only to reveal it to the friend who tended him. According to Klamath County sources, Young had been aware that Sewell presented a danger and instructed an Orleans Bar merchant never to reveal his whereabouts to a stranger. *Chico Chronicle Record*, 20 October 1888. Stories that Young was alive circulated years later, contributing to local mythology about Robert Anderson, Hi Good and their associates in Indian pursuits. Burrill, *Hi Good's Cabin*.
972 Frances Leinenger to Larry V. Richardson, 20 January 1980, courtesy of Larry Richardson; California, Butte County, Rock Creek Township, Tax Records, 1884–1892; Brief phone conversation with Warren Rose, son of Ruby Speegle Rose, 20 June 2003.
973 R. Anderson, 26–27; See chapter three; William B. Secrest, *When the Great Spirit Died: The Destruction of the California Indians, 1850–1860* (Sanger, CA: Quill Driver Press/Word Dancer Press, 2003); Chapter six, passim.

Index

Note: Common names, such as John Bidwell, Mechoopdas, Butte Creeks and Mill Creeks, and locations, such as Chico and Red Bluff, are not included in the index.

A

Akey, David 154
Allen, Isaac 186, 196
Allen, Thomas 140
Anderson, Robert 70, 84, 92, 98, 107, 109, 116, 119, 121, 131, 141, 142, 146, 153, 181, 185, 243, 256, 263, 264
Antelope 76, 96, 98, 104, 111
Azbill, Henry 238, 241, 242

B

Bain, Bud 239, 244
Baker, B. F. 170
Bald Rock Jim 246
Baldwin, William 218, 251
Bancroft, Hubert 55, 149, 160, 163
Banks, John 264
Barber, Alex 8, 53, 59, 63, 64, 68
Barham, Charles 161
Beale, Edward 43, 102
Bean, D. M. 62, 63
Bidwell, Annie 15, 45, 55, 56, 238
Bidwell, Annie 197
Bidwell-government treaty 17, 26, 35, 52
Bigler, John 38
Billie 123

Black Rock 131, 132
Blair, Charles 85
Blake, Nelson 24, 25, 27, 63
Blake, Stephen 27
Blum, Mr. 186
Boness, Billy 266
Bowman, Bully 93, 142, 151, 269
Bradley, J. C. 91
Breckenridge, John 86, 93, 97, 104, 108, 121, 124, 131, 137, 142, 245
Brewer, William 35, 148
Broderick, David 138
Brown, B. B. 201
Bryson, Ed 107
Bueno, John 268
Buffum, A. C. 255
Burns, William 98, 99, 121, 123, 124, 126
Burrill, Richard 270

C

Calhoun, John 34, 35, 37
Callen, James 58
Camp Bidwell 160, 169, 206, 214, 221, 225, 230, 233, 247, 254, 256, 260
Carson, Thankful 245
Carter, George 93

389

Cartin (possibly George Carter) 99
Chandler, Robert 46, 56
Chapman, Gus 168, 203, 205, 209
Chard, William G. 181
Cheesman, David 125
Chico Landing 176, 177, 182, 186, 195, 261
Chico Light Infantry 162, 165, 166, 168, 198
Chico Tom 238, 239
Clark, Alfred Burr 116
Clarke, Neuman 76, 90
Clark, John Adams 249
Clark, O. L. 189, 201
Clough, Frederick 172
Code Talkers 16
Conway, William 46, 180, 238, 241
Cook, Sherburne 19, 58, 89, 116, 148, 250
Cooper, Emma 15, 16, 17, 18, 28
Coxs Flat 125
Cronk, Catherine 88
Cronk, Mr. 88
Crook, George 76, 95
Crosette, George 159, 179, 188
Crowder, Frank 59, 70, 86, 106, 118, 122, 133, 141, 144, 146, 163, 165
Currie, Annie. 15

D

Daugherty, Pat 85
Davis, Jefferson 138, 160, 169
Davis, John W. 220
Day, Hannibal 4, 6
Dayton 159
Diamondville 125
Dodge, E. K. 69
Dogtown 186, 211, 221, 255
Dole, William P. 208

Doll, J. Granville 89
Doty, C. J. 205
Doughty, James 161, 165, 169, 170, 260, 261, 262
Douglas, Charles 174, 219, 224, 225, 227, 229, 235
Douglas, Stephen 137
Downey, John 130
Drum, R. C. 200, 206, 222, 234, 260
Dupah 63
Durham, Robert 147, 190, 192, 212, 260

E

Eddy, James 176, 195, 198, 205, 210, 218, 223, 234, 235, 246, 256
Eddy, Joseph 169
Edwards, Jack 250
Eel River Rangers 130
Ellison, W. H. 32
Evansville 161

F

Fabela, Casamiro 50, 59, 63
Farrelly, Phillip 165
Feilner, John 243
Field, Obe 93, 142, 269
Field, Stephen 31, 138
Fillmore, Millard 2, 37, 44
Fitzgerald, Edward 12
Flint, Franklin 90, 95
Forest Ranch 108, 118, 121, 133, 184
Forks of Butte 108, 118, 121, 126, 140, 186
Fort Wright 174, 224, 225, 226, 236, 250
Frango, Jack 238
Frye, Amos 59, 61
Furnell, Kate 200

G

Galland, Samuel 257
Garner, Conrad 65, 109, 110, 122, 124, 127
Gibson, Daniel 137
Girr, Jacob 138
Good, Harmon 70, 92, 98, 109, 114, 121, 131, 142, 151, 153, 155, 173, 180, 181, 185, 203, 246, 256, 260
Gore, James 265, 269
Gore, Solomon 185
Gore, Tom 141
Gramps, John 116
Gramps, Martin 116
Grant, Ulysses S. 163, 164
Gray, George 149
Greathouse, Ridgely 163
Gregory, Oliver 170
Guill, John 144, 149
Guynn, Pleasant 110, 143
Gwin, William 32, 34, 37, 40, 44, 137

H

Hall, Long Primer 170
Hanson, George 174, 184, 192, 197, 203, 206, 210, 217, 227, 234, 235, 247
Harper, Miles 137
Harrison, Archibald 96, 97, 103
Harrison, Richard 246
Hart, Herbert M. 236
Hatch, William 258
Hat Creek Liz 182
Hayes, George 181
Helltown 185
Henshaw, Matilda 146
Henshaw, Washington 146
Hickman, Mr. 91
Hickok, Elvira 140, 267
Hickok, Frank 140, 149, 153, 195, 201, 267
Hickok, Frankie 142, 243, 246
Hickok, Frederick 150
Hickok, Ida 141
Hickok, Minnie 141
Hill, Dorothy 15, 208, 238
Honcut 27, 74
Hooker, Ambrose 197, 215, 220, 222, 230, 231, 233, 234, 235, 246, 260
Hooker, Seth 91
Hudson,. Frank 169
Humboldt Road 161, 171, 173, 178, 199, 253, 256, 261, 262
Hunt, H. B. 198
Hurtado, Albert 3, 17, 28, 188

I

Idaho Stage 171
Indian Jim 139
Inskeep, E. K. 76, 95, 96, 97, 100, 104, 111
Iron Canyon 59
Ishi 78, 79, 117

J

Jack 66
Jarboe, Walter 130
Joe 53
Joe Shoe Fly 239
Johnson, Jerald 78
Johnston, Adam 2, 4, 6, 8, 10
Johnston, Albert 137
Joseph 139
Josephy, Alvin 137
Judah, Henry 75, 95
Judah, Henry 86
Judd 96

K

Keefer, James 70, 140, 142, 147, 212
Keefer, Rebecca 140
Kelley, George 156
Kenny, Robert 46
Kentucky Blood 69
Kibbe's Guards 89
Kibbe's Rangers 128
Kibbes Rangers 121, 123, 133, 152
Kibbe, William 89, 95, 111, 118, 121, 153, 173, 175, 256
Kibby, Leo 47
King, M. T. 105, 122
Knights of the Golden Circle 150
Knotts, S. Willis 177
Kroeber, Theodora 79, 89, 105, 108, 117, 118
Kulmeh 23

L

Lafonso 53
Landt, Henry 125, 179, 199
Lassen, Peter 85
Lassen Rangers 162
Latham, Milton 44, 137
Lea, Luke 24, 32, 41, 43
Lee, Robert E. 164, 169
Lee, Wesley 205, 221
Leggett, Horatio 116
Lewis, Jimmy 187, 211, 243, 248
Lewis, Johnny 187, 248
Lewis, Mary Ann 187, 189
Lewis, Sam 187, 192, 198, 259
Lewis, Thankful 187, 188, 191, 201
Lincoln, Abraham 167, 169, 170, 184, 228
Lincoln,Abraham 137
Lindsey, William 110, 114
Lippitt, Francis 174, 175
Livergood, D. W. 169, 170
Llano Seco Ranch 145
Loder, Richard 219
Lott, Charles 31
Luc-a-yan 12
Lusk, Frank 45
Lyon, D. B. 180

M

Malo Joe 109, 114
Martin, John 99
Mayhew, James 91
Mayhews Crossing 91, 92, 101, 111
McClellan, George 167
McCommon, William 258
McCord, John 99
McCorkle, Joseph 26, 29, 31, 38, 47, 138, 222, 297
McDaniel, Thomas 194
McDowell, Irvin 256
McIntosh, Perry 110
McKeen, Vera Clark 269
McKee, Redick 11, 15, 38, 41
McKinstry, George 28
Mechoopda cemetery 46
Melendy, William P. 224, 226, 228, 229, 232, 236, 237
Mellen, H. B. 154
Miller, Joaquin 17
Miller, Joseph 263
Moak, Jacob 201
Moak, Levi 201
Moak, Simeon 70, 94, 110, 146, 151, 264, 267
Mona 200
Moolah 126
Moore, J. G. 194
Moore, Mary 262
Morehead, James 139
Morgan, Michael 96

Morgan, Mrs. Thomas 259
Morgan, William 261
Morrison, Richard 186
Morton, Alfred 160, 207, 215, 219, 220, 223
Mountain House 139, 219, 223, 229
Murieta, Joaquin 318

N

Napanni 12, 17
Neal, Duncan 59
Ned 66, 84
Nimshew 221
Nord 137
Norris, Samuel 25, 29, 38, 40, 42
Nottingham, F. A. 257
Noyes, Lt. 232
Nye, Michael 57, 59

O

Oak Hill Cemetery 259
Odd Fellows 170
OFarrell, R. H. 145
Ogle, Beverly Benner 254
Old Captain 185
Old Doctor 78, 114, 123
Ona 53
Oregon Charlie 239, 242
Oroville Guard 162, 198
Oroville-Shasta trail/Road 10, 52, 84, 105, 133, 218

P

Pancoast, Charles 229
Patrick, James 76
Patrick, William 96
Pence Hotel 201
Pence Ranch 181, 259, 261
Peyti, Antonio 51, 52
Pinkston, William 116

Pit River Expedition 95, 119, 121, 128
Pond, Charles 205
Potter, John 4, 29, 133
Potters Half League 351
Potts, Marie 240
Potts, Starie 246, 250
Powers, Stephen 19, 21, 244
Prairie House Hotel 132
Pratt, Willard 142
Preacher, Billy 238

R

Rafael 12, 17, 24, 25, 52, 198
Rathbun, Robert 245
Reading, Pierson 24, 34, 148
Reavis, David 139
Red Bluff 101
Reservations
 Feather River 9, 28
 Mendocino 128, 174, 181
 Nome Cult 128
 Nome Lackee 42, 44, 75, 80, 85, 87, 96, 127, 128, 129, 131, 156, 174, 175
 Round Valley 104, 172, 173, 175, 176, 178, 181, 182, 183, 195, 205, 210, 216, 217, 223, 231, 232, 236, 244, 253, 255, 257, 259, 289
 Smith River Valley 210
 Tejon 128
 Yumalacca 114, 121
Rock Creek 69, 111, 121, 142, 146, 196, 201, 211
Rose, R. C. 211
Rose, Robert 212, 213
Rountree, Joseph 93, 111, 116
Royce, Charles 45
Rutledge, Ann 228

393

S

Sadorus, A. M. 77, 84, 111, 113, 143
Sadorus, Henry 122
Sandys Corral 161
Sanitary Commission 165
Schaeffer, James 67
Schoonover, Steve 78, 79, 131
Scott, Leland 229, 239, 240, 243, 245
Scott, Roy 243
Sexton, Warren 144
Shackley, Stephen 79
Shave Head 183
Short, James 174, 184, 211, 224, 226, 233, 247
Sills, Billy 266
Sills, Dan 266
Silsby, Mary 161
Simmons, William 99
Slim 99
Smith, John 47
Smith, John Barnett 201
Smith, Rosanna 263
Smith, W. N. 194
Snedecker 186, 201
Sorenson, Anna Campbell 185
Sorenson, Neil 185
Soule, Mr. 59
Spalding, Jack 86
Spangler, John 242
Spaulding, Jack 93
Speegle, Claude 118
Speegle, Homer 75, 118
Speegle, Mel 118
Sproul, Samuel 142, 202, 209, 259
Stanford, Leland 142, 152, 153, 156, 162
Stansbury, Libby 172
Stansbury, Oscar 35
Starn, Orin 78

Starr, Augustus 160, 168, 198, 205, 214, 217, 242, 246, 248, 250, 251, 261
Steele, Elijah 224, 229, 236, 237, 257
Stevenson, Edward 87, 177
Stevenson, Harriet 88
Stewart, Al 170
Stilson, Charles 25, 148, 151, 159, 160, 163, 165, 187, 190, 200, 203, 206, 213, 220, 225, 254, 256, 262
Stilson, Thomas 166
St. Johns, S. D. 126
Stoneman, George 12, 44
Strommer, John 186
Stuart, Granville 3, 35, 179
Stuart, R. 11
Sublet, William 142
Sumner, Edwin 151
Sunderland, Hank 122
Sunedecker, Mr. 145
Sutherland boys 333
Sutherland, Daniel 110, 122, 162, 166, 243, 263, 266, 269
Sutter, John 22, 34, 50, 51

T

Tassin 188
Tatham, John 139
Taylor 59
Tehama House 177
Tehama Village 177
Tehama Volunteers 92, 97, 98, 102, 104, 121, 129, 133, 142
Thomas, Lucius 170
Thomasson, Hardy 187, 266, 267
Thomasson, Margaret 187
Thomasson, Nate 187
Three Knolls 266, 267
Tippee 126
Tom 88

Tome-ya-nem 126, 174, 181, 200, 210, 224, 226, 242, 247
Tremont House 258
Tremont, John 132
Tribelets
Concow 11, 23, 62, 66, 124, 126, 189
Feather River 180
Hat Creek 83, 90, 95, 96, 103, 111, 123, 127, 129, 173, 180, 181, 182, 216
Honcut 27
Kimshew 5, 11, 23, 57, 62, 74, 77, 124, 126, 134, 185, 212, 259, 261, 270
Nimshew 61, 62, 66, 84, 185, 194
Odawi 15
Pica 5, 11, 23
Pit River 83, 85, 90, 95, 96, 103, 111, 123, 127, 129, 173, 180, 181, 216, 243
Sulemshew 59, 61, 77, 78
Tigu 15, 62
Tribes
Cherokee 45
Colusi 26
Paiute 74
Wintu 42, 79, 130
Wylacki 174, 181
Yahi 71, 75, 79, 90, 132

U

Updegraff, Jacob 59
Updegraff, Jake 63

V

Van Voast, James 260

W

Wagner, Fred 138
Wallace, Richard 111, 116, 118

Walsh, Michael 145
Warner, J. J. 39
Weatherbee, Ira 268
Weller
John 102
Weller, John 89, 91, 103, 124, 130
Wells, Michael 144, 189, 211, 222, 248, 257
Wells, Thomas 221, 234
Williamson, William 65
Wilson, Thelma 229, 238, 240, 249
Wintu 80
Wood, George 133, 167, 168, 220, 234, 255, 260
Woodman, James 166, 171
Workman, Robert 263, 267, 268
Wozencraft, Oliver 2, 5, 14, 17, 22, 23, 29, 31, 38, 41, 42, 44, 88, 108, 129, 180
Wright, George 143, 154, 155, 157, 160, 170, 174, 193, 206, 222, 227, 233, 255, 260, 263
Wright, Lt. Thomas 12
Wright, Thomas 58, 64, 65, 144, 165, 170

Y

Yohema 116
Young, Alexander 151, 179, 212, 263

About the Author

PHOTO BY DAVIDYORKDESIGN.COM

Michele Shover was professor of political science at California State University, Chico. Twenty years of her work on nineteenth-century history in Butte County appears in *Exploring Chico's Past*. Direct inquiries to her at mshover@csuchico.edu.

www.ingramcontent.com/pod-product-compliance
Lightning Source LLC
Chambersburg PA
CBHW021916180426
43199CB00031B/44